Trinity, Church, and the Human Person

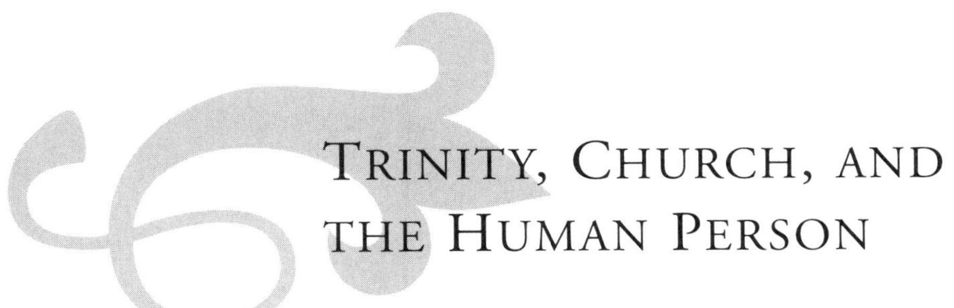

Trinity, Church, and the Human Person

Thomistic Essays

Gilles Emery, OP

Sapientia Press
of Ave Maria University

Sapientia Press
of Ave Maria University
1025 Commons Circle
Naples, FL 34119
888-343-8607

Cover Design: Eloise Anagnost

Cover Image: St. Thomas Aquinas Writing. Etching by Adrien Mastrangelo (Rome, private collection).

Printed in the United States of America.

Library of Congress Control Number: 2006939255

ISBN-10: 1-932589-34-1

ISBN-13: 978-1-932589-38-2

Deliver me, my God, from the much speaking which I suffer from inwardly in my soul, which is so wretched in your sight and flies to your mercy for refuge. . . . When we do attain to you, there will be an end to these many things which we say and do not attain, and you will remain one, yet all in all, and we shall say one thing praising you in unison, even ourselves being also made one in you.

St. Augustine, *De Trinitate* XV,28,51

CHAPTER 9

CHAPTER 10

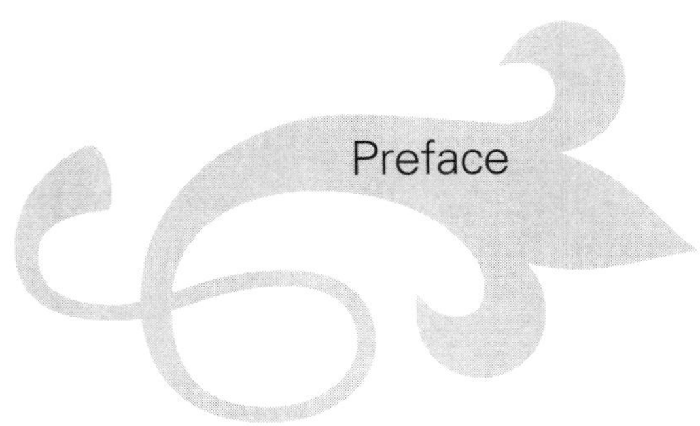

Preface

A COLLEAGUE, a professor of Old Testament, recently asked me what had led me to write books and articles on the Trinity: Had I been motivated by academic reasons or, rather, by a personal interest flowing from the experience of faith? This question took me by such surprise that at first I could not answer him but remained speechless. Then, after a moment of reflection, I formulated my response: I wished to study Trinitarian doctrine, and that of St. Thomas in particular, in order to explore in an academic manner the confession of faith that is at the heart of Christian experience. In the studies that I have written, it seems to me that I have never separated personal meditation on the faith of the Church and the dimension of academic research. It is faith that sustains the intellectual quest. Theology is an exercise that employs the resources of human culture in order to account for the faith.

The ten essays collected in this volume are the expression of one such search, personal and academic, intellectual and spiritual. These studies were carried out independently from one another. They would not have been brought together into a book without the initiative of my friend Matthew Levering, who conceived the project of this book and proposed it to Sapientia Press. I would like to say that this book has two authors: Matthew Levering, who had the idea of this collection, and myself, who wrote these essays.

The majority of these studies have already appeared, in French or in English, in journals or in books. I have updated them, with some modifications and additions, for the present volume. Each essay was written first in French, then translated into English by various translators, whom I cordially thank for their work. The essays can be grouped into three sections: First, the Trinitarian thought of St. Thomas Aquinas (chapters 1, 2, 3, and 4);

second, the sacraments, the Church, and the human person (chapters 5, 6, 7, and 8); and third, the reception of the teaching of St. Thomas on the mystery of God and God's relationship to human beings (chapters 9 and 10).

The first section, which is the most important, concerns the Trinitarian theology of St. Thomas Aquinas. Those who have read some pages of the treatise of St. Thomas on the Trinity know that his Trinitarian doctrine is difficult and that it engages in technical, sometimes very complex, discussions, for example about the concepts of relation and person, or about the analogy of the word and of love. Why has St. Thomas developed this body of teaching? What is the intention that animates his research? The first two essays attempt to respond to this question. In his Trinitarian theology, St. Thomas proposes to his readers a *spiritual exercise*, with an ecclesial purpose, that is to say, to the benefit of all believers. Thomist Trinitarian theology—it is necessary to emphasize strongly—is alien to rationalism: It is not separated from the spiritual quest. Furthermore, it does not constitute a solitary enterprise, but it is an ecclesial task at the service of truth. This theme of truth is the subject of the third essay. St. Thomas developed a profoundly Trinitarian account of truth and of our reception of truth—of *all* truth. This Trinitarian approach to truth is, even today, little known. It concerns not only the "immanent Trinity" but also the "economic Trinity": The Thomist theology of truth coincides with the theology of the economy of creation and salvation, which leads to the contemplation of God for himself. These considerations are directly linked to the fourth essay included in this book: How does St. Thomas exhibit the personal dimension of the creative and salvific act of the Trinity? It has often been assumed that, for St. Thomas, the Trinitarian economy is exclusively explained by the unity of action of the three Persons; but this is a reductive view. The reading of the texts shows that, for St. Thomas, each divine Person acts according to a proper and distinct mode. This teaching possesses great importance for understanding the coherence of the Thomist doctrine on the "immanent Trinity" and the "economic Trinity," and for perceiving the profound personalism that animates his account.

These first four chapters constitute, in a certain way, a complement to my book *Trinity in Aquinas* (Ypsilanti, MI: Sapientia Press, 2003). They are the continuation and the deepening of the research that I began when I wrote my dissertation on *La Trinité créatrice* (Paris: Vrin, 1995). Since that time, I have not ceased to study Trinitarian theology and the value of the thought of Thomas Aquinas. Often I have taken up again the same questions, and by completing them and developing them have sought to attain a better understanding of the faith and a better appreciation of the proper task of Christian theology of the Trinity.

The second group of studies concerns the sacraments, the Church, and the human person. One finds here, in the first place, two essays concerning the ecclesial dimension of the sacraments of the Eucharist and Penance according to St. Thomas. In these two cases, I attempted to show that, for St. Thomas, the personal dimension and the ecclesial dimension of our relationship with God are neither separated nor juxtaposed, but rather constitute the two aspects of one and the same reality. I have joined to these two essays a note on the reception of the Greek Fathers in St. Thomas, in order to highlight the ecumenical dimension of his theology. He proposes to develop neither a "Western" nor an "Eastern" theology, but a Catholic theology that benefits from the foundations laid by the patristic tradition recognized in its fullness. Lastly, this group of essays contains also a study in fundamental anthropology, on the unity of the human person. Very often, the understanding of the human person in terms of "soul" and "body" raises a suspicion of dualism. But anthropological dualism is foreign to St. Thomas. I therefore wanted to show how, in a coherent manner, St. Thomas brings together the unity of man (against every form of dualism) and the primacy of the soul, that is, man's spiritual dignity (against every form of materialism). This conception furnishes an essential anthropological foundation for the understanding of the sacraments of the Church.

The last group brings together two essays on the reception of St. Thomas in Charles Journet and George Lindbeck. Despite evident differences, these two authors found in St. Thomas a master. They are united in a very vivid perception of the transcendence of the mystery of God, which goes beyond our human understanding. Concerning Charles Journet, I propose to explore his reflection on the mystery of God as regards the question of evil. My approach to Lindbeck is more general: I attempted to show what Lindbeck retains from St. Thomas and how he interprets him. The two last essays of this book thus make an echo of the first section: They direct the attention of theology to what constitutes its center and its subject, that is to say, God himself in his transcendent being and in the relationships that he has with us.

This collection of essays certainly does not pretend to offer the last word on the subjects treated. It poses some questions and proposes certain limited responses, which raise in their turn many other questions. Behind these questions, there is not only the thought of St. Thomas, but also many discussions of contemporary theology. My profound conviction is that St. Thomas offers one of the best ways to assist our contemporary theology to attain the *ressourcement* that is indispensable for it. If this book serves to suggest to readers the interest and the value of the thought of St. Thomas for such renewal, then it will have attained its goal.

Fr. Gilles Emery

Abbreviations Used to Refer to Aquinas's Works

ST	*Summa theologiae* I = first part; I–II = first part of the second part; II–II = second part of the second part; III = third part
Sent.	Commentary *(Scriptum)* on Peter Lombard's *Sentences* I Sent = Commentary on the first book of the *Sentences*, and so on.
SCG	*Summa contra Gentiles* *SCG* I = first book of the *Summa contra Gentiles*, and so on.
In Ioannem	*Super Evangelium sancti Ioannis lectura*
In Matthaeum	*Super Evangelium sancti Matthaei lectura*
In Rom	Commentary on St. Paul's epistle to the Romans (and so on)
ch.	chapter
dist.	distinction
q.	question
a.	article
qla	*quaestiuncula* ("little question" within an article)
corp.	*corpus* (body of an article)
arg.	argument (objection)
ad	reply to an argument (to an objection)
lect.	*lectio* ("lesson")
#	numeration used in the Marietti edition of Aquinas's works

CHAPTER 1

The Purpose of Trinitarian Theology in St. Thomas Aquinas

IN OUR DAY an important renewal of Trinitarian theology has come to the fore.[1] Studies on the Trinity proliferate, leaving their mark on the entire body of theological reflection. This burgeoning renewal poses a question as to the purpose of Trinitarian doctrine: What is the role of a treatise on the Trinity? There are several aspects to this question. It is linked, in the first place, to a general understanding of the nature of theology, notably its speculative character and practical dimensions, and also to theology's particular status in relation to philosophical reflection on God. In the second place, the question of the purpose of Trinitarian theology has a bearing on its relation to other points of doctrine. Should Trinitarian doctrine be understood, as Karl Barth would have it, as a determination of the doctrine of revelation, or rather, according to Hegel's view, as the expression of the conditions of God's self-communication? Is Trinitarian theology at the service of anthropology or of other branches of thought?

Without going into these questions here in depth, which would require a detailed discussion, I propose to look at a third aspect of the question, which, though closely connected with the two mentioned above, deals more directly with the content of Trinitarian doctrine. What is the goal of the classic Trinitarian theology that develops the notions of "processions," "relations," "persons," and "properties"? In other words, what is the purpose of a specifically *speculative* Trinitarian theology such as that of St. Thomas Aquinas? After outlining the general scope of this question, I

[1] Translation by Sr. Mary Thomas Noble, OP, of "Le propos de la théologie trinitaire spéculative chez saint Thomas d'Aquin," *Nova et Vetera* (French) 79/2 (2004): 13–43.

propose to examine the explanations given by St. Thomas in the course of his Trinitarian treatises, so as to clarify the purpose underlying the elaboration of a speculative theological treatise on the Trinity.

1. Trinitarian Faith and Theology

For Christian theologians, the Trinity is not simply one subject of study among others. When Christians proclaim their faith they are confessing their belief in the Holy Trinity, as they bear witness to it in the Nicene Creed or the Apostles' Creed. The content of these Creeds is faith in the Trinity, within which the Church places the confession of the mysteries of Christ. Trinitarian theology therefore constitutes the heart of the doctrinal reflection whose goal is to give an account of the faith of the Church. St. Thomas Aquinas indicated this very clearly at the beginning of several of his theological treatises:

> The Christian faith principally consists in acknowledging the Holy Trinity, and it specially glories in the cross of our Lord Jesus Christ.[2]
>
> The Lord taught that the knowledge that gives happiness consists in knowing two things: the divinity of the Trinity and the humanity of Christ [. . .]. This is why all the knowledge of faith is related to these two things: the divinity of the Trinity and the humanity of Christ.[3]

Since the subject matter of theology is the mystery of God in himself and in his relationship to creatures,[4] the task of teaching about the Triune God will be to manifest the three persons in their unique divine being and in their hypostatic distinction, while considering these persons in their eternal immanence and in the economy of creation and grace. This is how St. Thomas, in the *Summa theologiae*, studies the three divine Persons in the unity of their essence (*Prima Pars,* questions 2–26), and then in their mutual distinction (questions 27–43), thus preparing the way for the study of creation and the economy of grace (the remainder of the *Summa theologiae*).

Although several aspects of these explanations give rise to important controversies among theologians,[5] the central position accorded to Trini-

---

[2] St. Thomas, *De rationibus fidei,* ch. 1; translation by Joseph Kenny, OP, "Saint Thomas Aquinas, Reasons for the Faith," *Islamochristiana* 22 (1996): 31–52, at 32.

[3] *Compendium of theology* I, ch. 2. St. Thomas also expresses the same reality in Christological terms: "All Christian faith relates to the divinity and humanity of Christ" *(De articulis fidei et Ecclesiae sacramentis I, prol.).*

[4] *Summa theologiae* I, q. 1, a. 7.

[5] Among controversial questions, the following should be noted in particular: the subject matter of theology, the link between the unity of the divine being and personal

tarian faith is largely granted today. The doctrine of the Trinity does not treat only one sector of the faith, nor is it an isolated chapter in Christian theology, but in setting forth the mystery of God it also lays open to us the foundation and goal of all the other affirmations of the faith.[6] We should note that the contemporary renewal of studies of the mystery of the Trinity is characterized in particular by the attention given to the repercussions of Trinitarian faith, that is, to the relationships of Trinitarian faith to other affirmations of faith, and to the practice of the Christian life.[7] But in this area a difficulty often crops up, or rather a malaise in regard to the Thomist doctrine of the Trinity: With the best will in the world, many readers become discouraged by such notions as "processions," "relations," and "properties." Doesn't this body of doctrine make of Trinitarian theology an enterprise for specialists only? Doesn't it render Trinitarian theology foreign to spiritual experience, something beyond the life and thought of believers?

We find examples of this difficulty in some of the observations of Karl Rahner. In his judgment, Western Trinitarian theology, originating with St. Augustine, "must produce the impression that it can make only purely formal statements about the three divine Persons, with the help of concepts about the two processions and about the relations. Even these statements, however, refer only to a Trinity which is absolutely locked within itself—one which is not, in its reality, open to anything distinct from it; one, further, from which we are excluded, of which we happen to know something only through a strange paradox."[8] The result of this, according to Rahner, is that "the treatise on the Trinity locks itself in even more splendid isolation, with the ensuing danger that the religious mind finds it devoid of interest."[9]

Only a profound misunderstanding could have led Karl Rahner to associate the name of St. Thomas with such a formalistic decline of Trinitarian

plurality (divine essence and distinction of persons), and the relationships between the eternal immanence of the Trinity and the economy in time.

6 Cf. Walter Kasper, *The God of Jesus Christ,* trans. Matthew J. O'Connell (New York: Crossroad, 1984), 313: "The formal object or point of view from which the doctrine of the Trinity deals with the whole of the Christian faith is God as ground and goal of all these confessional statements."

7 This objective is systematically explored in the insightful essay of David S. Cunningham, *These Three Are One: The Practice of Trinitarian Theology* (Malden and Oxford: Blackwell, 1998, reprinted 1999); see my account in *Revue Thomiste* 100 (2000): 615–17. In spite of the tendency observable in certain authors to reduce Trinitarian teaching to the plane of mere function, such research does not in itself exclude the primacy of the contemplative or speculative dimension of theology.

8 Karl Rahner, *The Trinity,* trans. Joseph Donceel (New York: Crossroads, 1998 [1970]), 18.

9 Ibid., 17.

doctrine.[10] In fact, according to St. Thomas the revelation of the Trinity was "necessary" (a relative necessity in view of the end willed by God for men), in order that we might better grasp God's creative action and, above all, might receive knowledge of the salvation he accomplished through the mission of the Son and the Holy Spirit:

> The knowledge of the divine persons was necessary to us on two grounds. The first is to enable us to think rightly on the subject of the creation of things. For by maintaining that God made everything through his Word we avoid the error of those who held that God's nature necessarily compelled him to create things. By affirming that there is in him the procession of Love, we show that he made creatures, not because he needed them nor because of any reason outside him, but from Love of his own goodness [. . .]. The second reason, and the principal one, is to give us a true notion of the salvation of mankind, a salvation accomplished by the Son who became flesh and by the gift of the Holy Spirit.[11]

In the *Summa theologiae*, the study of the properties of the persons seeks to show these persons in their divinity and their distinction, throwing light on their eternal existence and on their action in our favor. We can see this economic purpose in the study of the property of the Father, and especially in the study of the property of the Word (the Father spoke and made all things through his Word) and of the Holy Spirit (the Spirit is the Love through whom the Father and the Son love each other and us).[12] Moreover, the Trinitarian treatise reaches its climax in the study of the divine missions, that is, in the Trinitarian foundation of the economy of grace (question 43). Whereas at first one might perhaps have suspected the speculative reflection to be deprived of interest for the economy of creation and salvation, one discovers in reality a doctrine that accounts for the foundations of God's action and for the depth of the relations that the world and men hold with God.

Nonetheless, we still have to ask: Why did St. Thomas take such pains to develop a speculative theology of the Trinity by means of the notions of procession, relation, person, property, and so on? What was the intention that gave rise to this theological enterprise? What purpose did the theologian have in mind as he worked out a speculative doctrine of the Trinity? Was it really necessary or wise? These questions do not touch merely on

---

10 See Gilles Emery, *Trinity in Aquinas* (Ypsilanti: Sapientia Press, 2003 [Naples, FL, 2006]) 166–75.

11 St. Thomas, *ST* I, q. 32, a. 1, ad 3.

12 See notably ibid., q. 33, a. 3; q. 34, a. 3; q. 37, a. 2, corp. and ad 3.

the sound exegesis of St. Thomas. They also involve his integration in our contemporary Trinitarian debate. Actually, a fruitful reading of the Trinitarian theology of St. Thomas can be made only by taking into account the intention that motivated him. If we ignore this intention, we risk making an irrelevant judgment about his Trinitarian doctrine or attributing to him a purpose he never had.

2. Biblical Exegesis and Trinitarian Theology

Let us clarify first of all what Trinitarian theology is about. We might be tempted to make a division between the biblical exegesis done by St. Thomas in his commentaries on Scripture and the speculative doctrine that he formulated in the *Summa theologiae* (*Prima Pars,* questions 27–43) or in other systematic works. However, in both cases we find the same Trinitarian theology. A detailed study[13] reveals that between the Trinitarian doctrine in the commentary on the Gospel of St. John and that in the *Summa theologiae*, there is no significant difference regarding the sources, the end in view (that is, to render an account of revelation), or the content of each. The biblical commentary gives an ample presentation of the notion of procession, the mode of the immanent procession of the Son and of the Holy Spirit (mode of intellect and of will or love), the doctrine of the real relations according to origin, relative opposition, personal properties, personal subsistence, the doctrine of the Word, the eternal origin of the Spirit, the unity of Father and Son as one principle of the Holy Spirit, the relation of the persons to essence and to properties, the equality of the persons, and the relationship between the divine Persons and creatures, as well as several problems about Trinitarian language. At the risk of startling the reader, one must even add that on certain speculative themes (the doctrine of the Word) the teaching in the biblical commentary goes further than the teaching in the *Summa theologiae.*

Basically, the commentary on St. John clearly shows that St. Thomas did not separate biblical Trinitarian theology from speculative Trinitarian theology: It is the same theology, that is, the same teaching of Scripture, reflected upon and explained, that we find in both works. However, the biblical commentary gives fuller development to certain themes that, without being absent from the Trinitarian treatise in the *Summa*, are given less space there: the unity of the knowledge and will of the Father and the Son, and

---

13 See G. Emery, *Trinity in Aquinas,* 271–319 ("Biblical Exegesis and the Speculative Doctrine of the Trinity in St. Thomas Aquinas's Commentary on St. John"), where textual references can be found for the research, some of the results of which are reproduced here.

also the action of the divine Persons in the world. As to properly speculative themes (personal properties, the origin and distinction of the persons, and so on), the biblical commentary presents these either in the explanation following the biblical pericope (this is most often the case), or in the questions, objections, or *excursus* occasioned by the reading of the text (more rarely). In all these instances, speculative exegesis is neither superimposed nor juxtaposed to the biblical exegesis, but it is integrated into the biblical reading: Its object is to show the doctrinal content of the words of the Gospel.

Comparison of the commentary on St. John and the *Summa theologiae* enables us to see the unity that *Sacra doctrina* has for Thomas. The aim that he pursues in explaining Scripture is identical to the goal of Scripture itself and to that of Christian theology: to teach revealed truth and to distance it from error, so as to grasp that which we hope to contemplate one day in full light. In the John commentary and in the *Summa*, speculative reflection is engaged in disclosing the truth taught by revelation (that is to say, in *making it more articulate* for us). The most speculative consideration of the Trinitarian relations and properties falls within the scope of the biblical exegesis, for the purpose of the latter is to draw forth the deep meaning of the scriptural text with the help of reason, in faith.

The main difference between the *Summa theologiae* and St. Thomas's biblical commentaries lies in the order of exposition, that is, in the organization of the material. While his biblical exegesis sets forth the Trinitarian doctrine according to the text being commented upon (bringing out also the scriptural roots of certain points of doctrine, or their relationship, for example the eternal procession and the mission of the persons), the *Summa theologiae* arranges its questions according to their mutual implications and internal coherence (*ordo disciplinae*: the order of exposition). When we speak of the Trinitarian theology of St. Thomas, we are talking therefore about his speculative theology as it is formulated in his commentaries on Scripture and in his systematic works.

3. The Prerogatives of Faith and the Rejection of Rationalism

St. Thomas rules out with great determination those "necessary reasons" by which certain theologians attempted to show the necessity of the Trinity for the believer exercising reason. He not only excludes the possibility of natural reason attaining to knowledge of the Trinity, but equally removes all elements of necessity from the reasons that theologians from the time of St. Anselm and Richard of St. Victor had propounded to establish Trinitarian faith. St. Bonaventure, for example, combined the tradition of Pseudo-Dionysius and those of Anselm and Richard. Before him, the earliest Franciscan masters had already explained that the goodness of God provides the reason for the plurality of divine Persons: It is the nature of the good to communicate itself *(bonum diffusivum sui)*; since the divine goodness is perfect, its communication must therefore be perfect, and this requires that there be a plurality of persons: The perfect goodness of God thus implies the communication of the entire divine substance in God himself by the generation of the Son and the spiration of the Holy Spirit.[14] St. Bonaventure made use of this teaching in elaborating his "necessary reasons" based on the following motives: the diffusion of the Good (if God did not communicate himself by a perfect diffusion of his entire substance, he would not be the sovereign and perfect Good); the beatitude, charity, liberality and joy of God (these attributes demand a plurality of persons in God, since their perfection cannot exist in a solitary mode); the perfection, primacy, and perfect actuality of God. The conclusion necessarily follows: "It is therefore necessary to affirm a plurality of persons."[15]

Thus, according to St. Bonaventure, the sound consideration of the unity of God leads necessarily to the affirmation of the Trinity: The recognition of the Trinity is "included" in the affirmation of the divine unity, and the reasons invoked allow one to explain this inclusion in a manner that carries the force of necessity. For Bonaventure, the believing mind can thus rise to the contemplation of the Trinity on the basis of the perfection that reason must necessarily recognize in God.

St. Thomas was vigorously opposed to this kind of apologetic project in Trinitarian theology. Neither the goodness of God, nor his happiness, nor his knowledge, nor his liberality are arguments capable of proving that the plurality of the divine Persons is a matter to be accepted out of necessity by our reason.[16] Only "the truth of faith" *(veritas fidei)*, to the exclusion of all other reasons, leads to the knowledge of the three divine Persons.[17] This position implies a clear distinction between the domains of faith and reason. This straightforward distinction is one of Thomas's most outstanding features as contrasted, in particular, with St. Bonaventure. The reasons used by theology to exhibit the mystery of the Trinity will never be arguments of philosophical necessity, but they either will be taken from Holy Scripture (in this case, they derive their cogency from the principles of faith) or will be plausible arguments ("adaptations" or "prob-

---

14 Alexander of Hales, *Summa theologica,* Book I, #317 (Quaracchi: Editiones Collegii S. Bonaventurae, 1924), 465–66.

15 St. Bonaventure, I *Sent.*, dist. 2, a. un., q. 2; I *Sent.*, dist. 27, pars 1, a. un., q. 2, ad 3; *Quaestiones disputatae de Mysterio Trinitatis,* qq. 1–8; *Hexaemeron* XI,11; *Itinerarium mentis in Deum,* ch. 6.

16 St. Thomas, *ST* I, q. 32, a. 1, ad 2.

17 I *Sent.*, dist. 2, q. un., a. 4; cf. *ST* I, q. 32, a. 1.

able arguments"),[18] that is, "arguments that show that what faith proposes is not impossible."[19]

Thomistic epistemology in Trinitarian matter is thus marked by two fundamental connected theses: (1) the strict exclusion of the idea that Trinitarian faith can be established by necessary reasons;[20] (2) the impossibility of conceiving of the Trinity by a process of deduction from the divine unity, that is, the impossibility of thinking of the Trinitarian plurality of persons as derived from the essential attributes.[21] This second thesis, too often neglected, is one of the fundamental characteristics of St. Thomas's Trinitarian theology. With more rigor than most of his contemporaries, he does away with the epistemological confusion between our knowledge of the divine essence and our knowledge of the personal plurality in God; with the utmost firmness he refuses to conceive of the personal plurality in God as the fruit of an essential fecundity of the divine being. Hence it is necessary to clarify the role of human reason in Trinitarian theology.

We have now reached a point where we can better grasp the problem facing Trinitarian theology: If, on the one hand, man's natural reason cannot have access to the Trinity (faith alone provides this knowledge) and if, on the other hand, the speculative reasons advanced by Christian theology to account for God being Trinity are not necessary demonstrations, then what could be the value of a speculative discussion that makes use of "reasons," and what is the discussion for? What end is the theologian pursuing in this type of research?

4. "To Grasp Something of the Truth That Suffices for Excluding the Errors"

In his Trinitarian theology, St. Thomas develops several themes that he applies to God according to the rules of analogy (person, relation, order, origin, procession, and so on). The properties of the persons are likewise set forth by means of analogies drawn from anthropology (word, love). The use of these analogies enables St. Thomas to clarify the purpose of his Trinitarian doctrine. The most enlightening example is doubtless provided by the three pillars of Trinitarian doctrine, which are procession, relation, and person. These three points of doctrine form the subject matter of the first

[18] Ibid., dist. 3, q. 1, a. 4, ad 3 *(adaptationes quaedam)*; *SCG* I, ch. 8–9.

[19] *ST* II–II, q. 1, a. 5, ad 2: "[. . .] persuasiones quaedam manifestantes non esse impossibile quod in fide proponitur."

[20] See Robert L. Richard, *The Problem of an Apologetical Perspective in the Trinitarian Theology of St. Thomas Aquinas* (Rome: Gregorian University Press, 1963).

[21] See G. Emery, *Trinity in Aquinas,* 165–208. Cf. Hans Christian Schmidbaur, *Personarum Trinitas: Die trinitarische Gotteslehre des heiligen Thomas von Aquin* (St. Ottilien: EOS Verlag, 1995).

three articles of the treatise on the Trinity in the *Summa theologiae* (*Prima Pars,* questions 27, 28, and 29), on which the entire treatise rests. Before providing a synthesis in the *Summa,* St. Thomas had given a detailed analysis of it in his disputed questions, *De potentia* (questions 8, 9, and 10).

Procession

When St. Thomas treats of the procession of the Son and the Holy Spirit, he explains that the notion of "procession" stems historically from the necessity of showing, in opposition to "Arianism," the *possibility* of an immanent origin in God, an origin whose term is co-essential with its principle:

> The early doctors of the faith were compelled to discuss matters of faith on account of the insistence of heretics. Thus Arius thought that existence from another is incompatible with the divine nature, wherefore he maintained that the Son and the Holy Spirit, whom Scripture describes as being from another, are creatures. In order to refute this error the holy Fathers had to show that *it is not impossible* for someone to proceed from the Father and yet be consubstantial with him, inasmuch as he receives from him the same nature the Father has.[22]

According to these explanations, the doctrine of procession took its origin from the Homoian controversy (and from the controversy against Anomoeanism, the more radical form of opposition to Nicaea).[23] On the one hand, this debate led Catholic thought to show that the divine consubstantiality of the Father, Son, and Holy Spirit "is not impossible."[24] Research on the *immanent* processions, that is, the processions accounting for the real distinction and divine interiority of the Son and Holy Spirit, expressed this concern. On the other hand, the affirmation of *two Trinitarian processions* stemmed historically from the necessity of showing, in opposition to Pneumatomachians (the "fighters against the Spirit"), the divinity of the Holy Spirit. Although he is not *engendered* like the Son, the Holy Spirit must nevertheless be recognized as God:

> Now the Son, in that he receives from the Father the nature of the Father, is said to be *born* or *begotten.* But in the Scriptures the Holy

22 *De potentia,* q. 10, a. 2. Translations of the *De potentia* are taken (with slight modifications) from St. Thomas Aquinas, *On the Power of God,* Literally translated by the English Dominican Fathers, 3 vols. (London: Burns Oates and Washbourne, 1934).

23 St. Thomas is aware of some features of the radical Anomoian position of Eunomius of Cyzicus. While Arius denied the *equality* of the Father and Son, Eunomius maintained the *dissimilarity* of Father and Son (*ST* I, q. 42, a. 1, ad 2).

24 *De potentia,* q. 10, a. 2.

> Spirit is called neither *born* nor *begotten*, but is said to be *from God (est a Deo)*. This is why Macedonius thought that the Holy Spirit is not consubstantial with the Father, but his creature: For Macedonius did not believe it possible for anyone to receive from another the latter's nature unless he were born of him and were his son. He therefore judged that if the Holy Spirit receives from the Father the latter's nature and essence it must infallibly follow that he is begotten and a Son. In order to refute this error, it was therefore necessary for our doctors *(doctores nostri)* to show that the divine nature can be communicated by a twofold procession, one being generation or birth *(generatio vel nativitas)* and the other not: *And this is the same as to seek the distinction between the divine processions.*[25]

The study of the distinction between the two processions aims therefore to account for the divinity of the Holy Spirit and his hypostatic subsistence. Whatever might have been the historical role played by Macedonius in this controversy, St. Thomas here formulates a question that was actually at the origin of speculative pneumatology. Origen had been among the first to ask this question, though rather in a way of trial: Just like the Son, the Holy Spirit is associated with the Father in glory and in dignity (it is the Trinitarian rule of *homotimia*, or "equal honor" rendered to the three persons). But how to grasp that the Holy Spirit, although he is not the Son, still comes forth from the Father, and is therefore God?[26] The denial of the divinity of the Holy Spirit in the fourth century by certain heterodox groups called for a deepening of this point of doctrine. St. Athanasius of Alexandria brings up the following argument raised against the divinity of the Holy Spirit by the *Tropikoi* of Thmuis:

> Again, they say: If the Holy Spirit is neither a creature nor an angel, but proceeds from the Father, then he too is a Son, and he and the Word are two brothers. If he is a brother [of the Word], how is the Word the only Son, or how is the one named after the Father and the other after the Son? Again, how, if he comes from the Father, is he too not said to be begotten, or to be a son, but is simply said to be the Holy Spirit?[27]

---

25 Ibid., q. 10, a. 2: "Et hoc est quaerere processionum distinctionem in divinis."

26 Origen, *On Principles,* Preface 4 (cf. *Sources Chrétiennes* 252, 82–83): "The Apostles handed down to us that the Holy Spirit is associated in honour and dignity with the Father [and the Son]. But in His case it is not clear whether He is to be regarded as born, or not born, and whether or not we should consider Him to be a Son of God. For these are points which have to be inquired into out of Sacred Scriptures according to the best of our ability."

27 St. Athanasius of Alexandria, *Letter to Serapion* I,15.

The same objection of the "fighters against the Spirit" was brought to the fore by St. Gregory Nazianzen, who, going a step further, offered a speculative solution. Here, taken from among several texts, is the argument of the Pneumatomachians reported by St. Gregory:

> The Holy Spirit, you say, is either unbegotten or begotten. If he is unbegotten, there are two Unoriginates. If he is begotten, you make a further subdivision: He comes either from the Father or from the Son. If he comes from the Father, there are two Sons, and they are Brothers! [. . .] But, he adds, if he comes from the Son, then we get a glimpse of a divine Grandson![28]

These objections may surprise the modern reader, but they tell us about a real difficulty. The personal origin in God was understood at first, in the first stages of patristic controversies touching the divinity of the Son, in terms of "generation" or "birth." Now the notion of generation enables one to grasp the origin (or property) of the Son, but not of the Holy Spirit. To account for the divine hypostasis of the Holy Spirit, one must be able to show an origin different from generation. In order to respond to these questions, St. Gregory of Nazianzus emphasizes the ineffable character of the generation of the Son and of the procession of the Spirit, then highlights the doctrine of relation and hypostatic properties.[29] In his explanations, St. Gregory introduces the notion of a divine coming forth "by procession" to designate the origin or property of the Holy Spirit, distinct from that of the Son:

> The Holy Spirit is truly the Spirit coming forth from the Father, not in the manner of the Son, for it is not through generation, but *by procession (ekporeutos)*, since I must coin a word for the sake of clarity.[30]

It is this *ekporeusis*, translated in St. Thomas's Latin as *processio*, that constitutes the origin and personal property of the Holy Spirit.[31] The same

[28] St. Gregory of Nazianzus, *Oration* 31, 7 (cf. *Sources Chrétiennes* 250, 287–89).

[29] Ibid. 31,8–9 (cf. *Sources Chrétiennes* 250, 290–93).

[30] Ibid. 39,12 (cf. *Sources Chrétiennes* 358, 174–75).

[31] St. Thomas, *ST* I, q. 32, a. 3. In Latin Trinitarian theology, the word *"processio"* (which we translate in English as "procession") will thus have two senses: a general sense which applies to the two origins (the origin of the Son and that of the Holy Spirit), and a more restricted sense according to which this word designates exclusively the personal origin of the Holy Spirit. It is again by reason of a deficiency of vocabulary, St. Thomas explains, that the Latin language uses the same word to designate the *origin* and the personal *relation* of the Holy Spirit (namely, "procession"), while it uses different words to signify the origin of the Son *("generatio")* and the relative property of the Son *("filiatio")*; cf. *ST* I, q. 28, a. 4.

question also occupied a central position in Augustine's *De Trinitate*: "It is a difficulty, too, in what manner *(quomodo)* the Holy Spirit is in the Trinity, whom neither the Father nor the Son, nor both, have begotten, although he is the Spirit both of the Father and of the Son."[32] St. Augustine is well aware of the problem: "Why is the Holy Spirit neither believed nor understood to be begotten by God the Father, so that he also may be called a Son?"[33] It is precisely in order to find an answer to this question that St. Augustine moves to the consideration of the image of the Trinity in the human soul: Love does not come forth from our mind by being engendered or begotten like the word, but it proceeds in another way.[34] In St. Augustine (and then in St. Thomas), the doctrine of the Holy Spirit as Love thus intends to manifest the origin and property of the Holy Spirit, in order to account for Catholic faith in the divinity and personal distinction of the Holy Spirit.[35]

In the *De potentia*, St. Thomas explains that the understanding of the generation of the Son as an immanent procession and the distinction between the two processions within the Trinity are an attempt on the part of Christian reason to show the *possibility* of the divinity of the Son and the Holy Spirit in their personal distinction, in opposition to the heresies that dominated the theological controversies of the fourth century. This is the way in which the *Summa theologiae* proceeds. The point of departure of the reflection on the Trinity, in the first article (question 27, article 1), which sets the tone for the entire treatise on the Trinity, offers a speculative interpretation of the difficulties of "Arianism" and "Sabellianism":

> Some have taken this procession to be like the coming of effect from cause. And so Arius said that the Son comes from the Father as the first of his creatures, and that the Holy Spirit comes from the Father and the Son as a creature of both. According to this view neither the Son nor the Holy Spirit would be true God. [. . .] Others have taken this procession to be like the going of cause into effect, by setting it in motion or impressing its likeness on it. Sabellius took it in this sense, maintaining that God the Father himself is called Son inasmuch as he had taken to himself flesh from the Virgin; also that he, too, is called Holy Spirit inasmuch as he sanctifies and vivifies rational creatures. [. . .] A careful study of these opinions shows that both Arius and Sabellius took procession to be going forth to something outside *(ad aliquid extra)*. This is why neither posited procession within God himself *(in ipso Deo)*.[36]

32 St. Augustine, *De Trinitate* I,5,8; cf. II,3,5.

33 Ibid. IX,12,17.

34 Cf. ibid. IX,12,17–18.

35 Cf. ibid. XV,25,45; XV,26,47; XV,27,48; XV,27,50.

36 St. Thomas, *ST* I, q. 27, a. 1.

The theologian is seeking a way to show, in all appropriateness, a true *procession* in God. The analogy should enable one to grasp an "immanent procession" capable of accounting for real relations, that is, to show that the persons are distinguished not by their substance but by relations based on an action leading to a procession. This doctrine of the "immanent procession" constitutes the point of departure for the treatise on the Trinity. In order to show its necessity, St. Thomas's reflection is based on an interpretation of the difficulties of "Arianism" and "Sabellianism": These heterodox doctrines could not understand the existence of a true Son in God, because they conceived the generation of the Son in the manner of an action of God in the world. Thus, although diametrically opposed, these two heresies were united in a common error. We notice here that St. Thomas is not content with describing the errors, but proposes an interpretation that seeks their speculative root.

St. Thomas takes from Aristotle the distinction between two kinds of actions: "immanent" action, which remains within the acting subject (to know, to will, to feel), and "transitive" action, which moves on *(transit)* to an exterior reality (to heat, to build, to make).[37] In both cases the action leads to a procession: procession of an interior reality in the case of immanent action; procession of an exterior reality in the case of transitive action. By analogy, one must recognize these two types of action in God: the Trinitarian processions in one case, and the action of creation and the divine economy in the other.[38] The example repeatedly given by St. Thomas is that of an architect: The architect conceives in his mind the plan of the building he is going to construct and wills this construction (immanent action); then the architect realizes his plan concretely by constructing the building (transitive action). Now, "what comes forth as the result of a procession *ad extra* must be diverse from that which is the source."[39] If the concept of transitive action were applied to the procession of the divine Persons, then "the persons who proceed would be outside of the divine nature *(extra naturam divinam),*" just as the nature of the house that is built is other than the nature of the architect's mind who conceived and willed it.[40] "Arianism," in conceiving the generation of the Son as a transitive action, a priori precludes any chance of grasping the true divinity of the Son and the Holy Spirit. At the opposite extreme, Sabellian modalism

37 See notably *SCG* II, ch. 1 (#853); *De potentia,* q. 9, a. 9; q. 10, a. 1; *ST* I, q. 27, a. 1. (The numbers given in parentheses refer to the numeration used in the Marietti edition of Aquinas's works.)

38 *De potentia,* q. 10, a. 1; *SCG* II, ch. 1 (#854).

39 *ST* I, q. 27, a. 1, ad 2.

40 *De potentia,* q. 9, a. 9. This article, which treats of the "number" of persons in God, presents the doctrinal impasses of Arianism, pneumatomachian semi-Arianism, and Sabellianism.

presents a mode of thought that, basically, agrees with later "Arianism" in a way: It allows one to maintain the divinity of the Son and the Holy Spirit but confuses them with the Father, as modes adopted by the Father *when he acts in the world.* The association of Arius and Sabellius in connection with the one same error is not surprising. In wishing to avoid Sabellianism, Arius falls into the contrary error, but the contraries meet at one point: Both attribute the generation of the Son to "an external nature," that is, to the production of a creature (Arius) or to the incarnation (Sabellius).[41] Thus, "If we reflect on this carefully, both Arius and Sabellius took procession as bringing about an external reality."[42]

This is why, in order to avoid the "Arian" and "Sabellian" error, a Catholic treatise on the Trinity should start off not by considering the action of God in the world (transitive action), but by considering an immanent action whose term remains within God himself *(in ipso Deo)*:

> Every procession corresponds to some sort of action; and as corresponding to action directed towards something external there is an outward procession *(processio ad extra)*, so with action that remains within the agent we observe an inward procession *(processio quaedam ad intra).* The best example of this appears *(et hoc maxime patet)* in the intellect where the action of understanding remains in him who understands.[43]

St. Thomas mentions here the procession of the word in the intellect of the knower, and he will develop his teaching on love from the same perspective (the procession of an "impression" or "affection of love" in the will of the lover).[44] In both cases, it is the purpose of defending the faith that leads to the elaboration of a Catholic teaching on the Trinitarian processions. Continuing the patristic tradition, St. Thomas views his own reflection as a manifestation of the truth of the faith, when confronted with the pitfalls of heresies. Now the heresies were partly connected with a thesis in the speculative order: The "Arians" did not want to believe that the Son possesses the same divinity as the Father and "they could not understand it," their position being motivated by a deliberate refusal but also by an intellectual difficulty.[45] St. Thomas does not present here in detail the various aspects of "Arian" subordinatianism and of "Sabellianism,"[46] but pro-

---

41 *SCG* IV, ch. 7 (#3425).

42 *ST* I, q. 27, a. 1.

43 Ibid.

44 *ST* I, q. 27, a. 3 and a. 4; q. 37.

45 *SCG* IV, ch. 6 (#3387). This remark echoes St. Augustine, *De Trinitate* XV,20,38.

46 He did so elsewhere, particularly in *SCG* IV, chs. 5–6. On St. Thomas's knowledge of "Arianism," see Peter Worrall, "St. Thomas and Arianism," *Recherches de Théologie Ancienne et Médiévale* 23 (1956): 208–59; 24 (1957): 45–100.

poses a doctrinal interpretation of their common error, with the object of finding the speculative way that, while enabling one to avoid the error, will lead to the contemplation of the truth.

To sum up, St. Thomas seeks to discover the internal logic of heresies and their roots, so as to find the way that, by contrast, will empower one to manifest the Catholic faith. To avoid error, one would therefore have to take another point of departure than that of "Arianism" (Homoian or Anomoian doctrines) and of Sabellian modalism. This other point of departure, as we have seen, consists in the doctrine of immanent procession. It is the necessity of conceiving an immanent procession that leads to exploiting the doctrine of the Word and of Love. Actually, the activity of the intellect (formation of the word) and the activity of the will ("spiration" of love) constitute the sole operations capable of leading to the procession of an immanent term in a purely spiritual being.[47] If one took another point of departure, according to St. Thomas, one would not succeed in escaping the difficulties of subordinatianism and modalism. And if one refused to have recourse to the analogy of the Word and of Love, one would deprive oneself of every means of sustaining the possibility of conceiving (without contradiction) the common divinity and personal distinction of Father, Son, and Holy Spirit. One could certainly *affirm* the divinity and personal distinction of the Son and Holy Spirit, but one could no longer *show* how it is intelligible to our minds. This is why St. Thomas explains:

> In God there cannot be any origin but what is immaterial and consistent with an intellectual nature, such as the origin of word and love. This is why, if the procession of the Word and Love does not suffice for inserting the personal distinction *(ad distinctionem personalem insinuandam)*, there could not be any personal distinction in God.[48]

Relation

When St. Thomas comes to the doctrine of Trinitarian relation, he begins by noting that "for all Catholics, it is certain that there are relations in God."[49] In fact, "the truth of faith *(veritas fidei)* implies that the only distinction in God is taken from opposed relations."[50] And when he explains that these relations are indeed real, he begins his exposition with a similar observation. This question, like the preceding one, arises from problems created by the heresies of the patristic period:

---

47 *ST* I, q. 27, a. 5.

48 *De potentia*, q. 9, a. 9, ad 7.

49 I *Sent.*, dist. 26, q. 2, a. 1.

50 *Quodlibet* XII, q. 1, a. 1.

> Those who follow the teaching of the Catholic faith must hold that there are real relations in God. The Catholic faith teaches that there are in God three persons of one essence. Now every number results from some kind of distinction. Therefore, in God there must be some distinction not only in respect to creatures, who differ from him in nature, but also in respect to someone subsisting in the divine nature. But this distinction cannot regard anything absolute, since whatever is predicated of God absolutely denotes the divine essence, so that it would follow that the divine persons differ essentially: This is the heresy of Arius. This distinction cannot be purely conceptual either, for [. . .] it would follow that the Father is the Son and the Son is the Father [. . .] and then the divine persons would differ in name only: This is the Sabellian heresy. It remains to be said, therefore, that the relations in God are real. *And so, in following the teaching of the saints [the Fathers], we must try to find out how this may be, although our reason is not able to grasp it fully.*[51]

In these explanations we find again the motives already advanced in the study of the processions. Theological research on the relation stems from the confrontation of the Catholic faith with "Arianism" and "Sabellianism." St. Thomas intends to continue the reflection begun by the Fathers of the Church, who, faced with heresies, made use of relation to express an authentic Trinitarian monotheism. St. Thomas is not very explicit, however, as to the patristic sources of his teaching on relation. He does indicate St. Augustine and Boethius, but his references to the Greek Fathers are fewer, although he did know them at least indirectly.[52]

Today we are in a better position to appreciate the historic sources of the doctrine of relation. Relation made its entrance into Trinitarian theology from the very first moment of the Arian crisis. In his *Profession of Faith to Alexander of Alexandria*, before the Council of Nicaea, Arius maintained that the Son is not co-eternal with the Father, and he added: "Nor did he have being at the same time as the Father, as some say in speaking of 'rel-

[51] *De potentia*, q. 8, a. 1: "Quod qualiter sit, sequendo sanctorum dicta, investigari oportet, licet ad plenum ad hoc ratio pervenire non possit" (emphasis mine).

[52] For example, the *Libellus de fide Trinitatis* (a compilation of Eastern patristic texts with glosses, which St. Thomas examined at the request of Pope Urban IV) presented the thought of St. Gregory Nazianzen as follows: "The Father is called 'unbegotten' and 'Father' not by reason of his essence but in a relative way by reason of his property of paternity; and the Son, likewise, since he draws his origin from the Principle, is not so called because of his nature but by reason of his relation to another" (§23; Leonine edition, vol. 40 A, 127); cf. St. Gregory of Nazianzus, *Oration* 29,16 (cf. *Sources Chrétiennes* 250, 210–11); *Oration* 31,7 and 31,9 (cf. *Sources Chrétiennes* 250, 286–89 and 290–93); *Oration* 42,15 (cf. *Sources Chrétiennes* 384, 80–83).

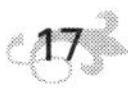

atives' *(ta pros ti)*."[53] This remark of Arius indeed suggests that already at the beginning of the fourth century Alexandrian Catholics (whose identity remains a tricky question)[54] were using the Aristotelian category of relation to show the co-eternity of the Father and the Son: Relative beings are simultaneous;[55] if *Father* and *Son* are indeed mutually related names, then whenever there was a Father, there must have been a Son. But it was left to the Cappadocian Fathers to explore this doctrine in a more systematic way; the first of them to do so was St. Basil of Caesarea. In his *Contra Eunomius*, St. Basil made relation a central feature of his argument against Anomoianism.

> Among names, some are connected to the thing itself, as an absolute, and when they are pronounced they signify the substrate of the realities in question; others are said in connection with beings other than themselves, and are only made known through their relation *(schesis)* with the others in connection with which they are spoken. For example, *man, horse, cow,* express each of the named entities; but *son, slave* or *friend* just indicate a connection with the term to which it is joined. This is why what is expressed by the word "offspring" *(gennema)* does not lead one to think of a substance *(ousia)*, but to conceive the entity in question as connected to another. For "offspring" is called "offspring" as springing *from someone.* In fact, since what it puts before us is not the notion of a subject but an indication of relation *(schesis)* to another thing, isn't it the height of insanity to decide that it means the substance *(ousia)*?[56]
>
> It is clear from the examination of these names, that is, *father* and *son*, that they are not of such a kind as primarily to evoke the idea of corporeal passion; but spoken through themselves, they just express the relation *(schesis)* of the one to the other. *Father* is the one who supplies for another the principle of his being in a nature like his own, *son* is the one who receives from another through generation the principle of his being.[57]

---

53 *Athanasius Werke,* vol. 3/1: *Urkunden zur Geschichte des arianischen Streites 318–328*, ed. Hans-Georg Opitz (Berlin/Leipzig: De Gruyter, 1935), 13. It is the vocabulary of Aristotle *(ta pros ti)* that one finds from the beginning of the history of Trinitarian relation.

54 See Marie-Odile Boulnois, *Le paradoxe trinitaire chez Cyrille d'Alexandrie* (Paris: Institut d'Études Augustiniennes, 1994), 391–93.

55 Aristotle, *Categories* 7 (7 b15).

56 St. Basil, *Against Eunomius* II,9 (cf. *Sources Chrétiennes* 305, 36–37).

57 Ibid. II,22 (cf. *Sources Chrétiennes* 305, 92–93). On this elaboration of St. Basil, see Bernard Sesboüé, *Saint Basile et la Trinité: Un acte théologique au IVe siècle* (Paris: Desclée, 1998).

There are therefore two kinds of names, substantial and relative. Correspondingly there will be two levels in our knowledge of God the Trinity: that of *substance* and that of the relative *properties* of hypostases. Language about God must be effected through the "combination" of these two elements.[58] This use of relation aims principally at showing that the Son, although he is neither the Father nor "unbegotten," is yet fully God: "Not to be the Father" does not strip the Son of his divinity, since the names *Father* and *Son* do not express the substance of divinity but the mutual *relation* (or "manner of being in relation") of Father and Son. The category of relation likewise enables one to show the eternal coexistence of the Son: "For as soon as the Father existed, the Son also existed, and the Son immediately enters into the notion of the Father."[59] Relation also enables us to disclose the consubstantiality of the persons and to show that generation in God does not indicate any imperfection connected with corporality or change: It is not a question of a "passion" but of "a relation of one to another." Because of the challenge posed by Eunomius of Cyzicus, the notion of relation would be used from then on to account for Trinitarian monotheism. This is what we encounter in St. Gregory Nazianzen, for example, when he gives us his synthesis of the properties of the persons.[60] In the West, St. Augustine was heir to this teaching and transmitted it to the Latin Middle Ages.[61]

This venture is not an attempt to "comprehend" the Trinity, for our reason cannot fully grasp the mystery of the relations in God. When St. Thomas seeks to perceive the divine relations, he wishes to show believers that faith in the Trinity is able to resist objections raised against it on rational grounds. The Trinitarian relation, based on procession (our mind sees relation as resulting from an action) aims to show the real distinction of persons while affirming their divine consubstantiality. The real relations (paternity, filiation, spiration, procession) account for the personal otherness of the Father, of the Son, and of the Holy Spirit, but in a way that respects their common divinity: The persons are not distinguished by reason of their substance, since this is identical, but by reason of the relations that constitute them within the divine nature. According to St. Thomas, the doctrine of person as a "subsistent relation" is an immediate prolongation or extension of this teaching. By enabling us to rule out errors, theological research thus offers believers a path to contemplation of the mystery.

58 St. Basil, *Against Eunomius* II,28 (cf. *Sources Chrétiennes* 305, 117–23).

59 Ibid., II,12 (p. 47).

60 St. Gregory of Nazianzus, *Oration* 31,9 (cf. *Sources Chrétiennes* 250, 290–93).

61 See notably Irénée Chevalier, *Saint Augustin et la pensée grecque: Les relations trinitaires* (Fribourg: Librairie de l'Université, 1940); this ancient study remains one of the best works on the subject. Cf. also Irénée Chevalier, *La théorie augustinienne des relations trinitaires* (Fribourg: Librairie de l'Université, 1940).

The Person

In connection with the notion of "person" (the third pillar of Trinitarian theology), St. Thomas formulates his most complete explanations of the goal sought by the speculative doctrine of the Trinity:

> The plurality of persons in God belongs to those realities that are held by faith and that natural human reason can neither investigate nor grasp in an adequate manner; but one hopes to grasp it in Heaven, since God will be seen by his essence, when faith will have given way to vision. However, the holy Fathers have been obliged to treat it in a manner developed because of objections raised by those who have contradicted the faith in this matter and in others that pertain also to the faith; they have done it, however, in a modest manner and with respect, without pretending to comprehend. And such a search is not useless, since by it our spirit is elevated to get some glimpse of the truth that suffices for excluding the errors *(nec talis inquisitio est inutilis, cum per eam elevetur animus ad aliquid veritatis capiendum quod sufficiat ad excludendos errores)*. This is why St. Hilary explains: *Believing in this, namely the plurality of persons in God, set out, advance, persevere. And though I may know that you will not attain the end, still I shall praise you for your progress. He who pursues the infinite with reverent devotion, even though he never attains it, will profit from advancing forward.*[62]

These explanations summarize the purpose of speculative knowledge of the mystery of the Trinity. This is the project that St. Thomas puts to work in all of his writings: Trinitarian theology is directed toward a contemplative end that will also supply Christians with ways to defend their faith.[63] This helps us to understand better the more discreet observations of the *Summa theologiae* where St. Thomas links his own research to the Fathers of the Church who, faced with heresies (Unitarian monarchianism in particular), put forward the notion of *person*:

> The word *person* cannot be found in the Scripture of the Old and New Testaments as referring to God. Nevertheless that which is meant by this word occurs many times in holy Scripture, namely that God is supremely self-subsisting and most perfect in knowledge. Were we bound to speak of God only in the very terms themselves of Scripture, it would follow that no one could ever speak of God in any language

---

62 *De potentia*, q. 9, a. 5; cf. St. Hilary, *De Trinitate* II,10 (ed. Pieter Smulders [Brepols: Turnhout, 1979], 48).

63 Trinitarian theology is thus woven into an extension of the ancient Creeds that developed and clarified the ecclesial expression of faith in the Father, Son, and Holy Spirit, when confronted with errors asserted by heretics (*ST* II–II, q. 1, a. 8, ad 3).

> other than that in which the Old and the New Testaments were delivered. The urgency of arguing with heretics made it necessary to find new words to express the ancient faith about God. Nor need we avoid such innovation as profane (the Apostle warns us to avoid profane verbal innovations [1 Tm 6:20]), since it is not profane, for it does not lead us astray from the sense of Scripture.[64]

These explanations are in strict conformity with the purpose of speculative theology presented above in connection with the notion of "procession." The use of the word *person* should follow the patristic rule handed down by Pseudo-Dionysius: We should neither think nor say anything about God "beyond what has been divinely revealed to us in the Sacred Scriptures."[65] Our reflection on *person* should have no other aim, therefore, than to help us to understand what revelation tells us of God the Father, Son, and Holy Spirit. As to the conditions for engaging in such reflection, they were supplied by the need to respond to the heresies. Without pretending to "comprehend" God, the theologian was thus led to grasp something of the truth by having recourse to the intellectual resources at his disposal, in order to render an account of revelation in opposition to the heresies that defaced it. It must be clear that, in Aquinas's theological project, priority does not go to the rejection of errors, but to the manifestation of the truth: The "principal end" of Trinitarian theology is the grasp of divine Truth.[66] In this exercise, which is contemplative by nature, the Christian theologian experiences a foretaste of the Truth that all believers hope to contemplate in the beatific vision.

Truth and Error

In order to clarify the "function" of the concepts used in Trinitarian theology, a comparison of the treatise on the Trinity in the *Summa theologiae* with that in the *Summa contra Gentiles* will be found most useful. Actually, the Trinitarian treatise in the *Summa contra Gentiles* has its own tripartite structure: Firstly, St. Thomas sets out the fundamentals given in Scripture; secondly, he sets out the interpretation of Scripture in accordance with the Catholic faith as opposed to heresies; thirdly, he discusses and refutes rational objections against the Catholic faith in the Son and the Holy Spirit. In this third part, he recalls several times that theology offers a limited understanding of the truth taught by revelation, as far as is possible.

---

64 *ST* I, q. 29, a. 3, ad 1.

65 Ibid., arg. 1; cf. *SCG* IV, ch. 24 (#3621); *De potentia*, q. 10, a. 4, arg. 12.

66 *Super Boetium de Trinitate, Expositio Prohemii* (Leonine edition, vol. 50, 78): "Et subiungit finem debitum, insinuans quidem finem principalem, qui est interior, scilicet perceptio diuine ueritatis, et explicans finem secundarium, scilicet iudicium sapientis."

In the *Summa contra Gentiles* this project of the believing mind is often characterized by Augustinian formulae, such as *utcumque mente capere, utcumque concipere,* or *utcumque accipi* (to grasp as much as the mind is capable of, to conceive in some fashion, to understand as well as possible).[67] These formulae suggest the imperfection of our knowledge of the Trinity and point us to the similitudes by which we have access to a certain knowledge of the Trinitarian mystery. Now it is precisely at this third stage, which refutes the objections raised against the Catholic faith, that St. Thomas makes use of his teaching on the Word and Love, as well as the other major speculative themes (teaching on relation and person)[68] to which he will give the first place in his *Summa theologiae.* The pillars of speculative thought of the *Summa theologiae* are the doctrinal elements that in the *Summa contra Gentiles* are advanced to respond to the rational arguments formulated against Trinitarian faith. In brief, the *Summa theologiae* does not take up again the biblical and patristic material of the *Summa contra Gentiles,* but it organizes and deepens the speculative themes that serve to grasp something of the truth in order to avoid errors and respond to rational objections: procession, relation, person, and the doctrine of the Word and Love.

The manifestation of truth and the criticism of errors constitute two aspects of one theological enterprise. To avoid errors, it is not enough to produce scriptural texts; one must show the conformity of the Catholic faith and Scripture, and one must again respond to the arguments that are opposed to the Church's faith. For its part, the truth will not be fully disclosed until we have refuted the errors opposing it. Now the most interesting errors are those that attack the truth most profoundly. In regard to the Trinity, those errors are Sabellian modalism, Arianism, and pneumatomachian semi-Arianism (in the sense that classical heresiology gave to these words), in their ancient forms. It is to them that St. Thomas gives his fullest attention (rather than to the errors of medieval heterodox theologians and movements). To manifest the truth and to avoid error, this is the

67 *SCG* IV, ch. 1 (#3348); ch. 11 (#3468); and ch. 13 (#3496): The entire doctrine of the Word is found between these expressions, by a sort of inclusion; see ch. 19 (#3557). These formulae refer to the incomprehensibility of the mystery and are linked with the plan to defend the faith against errors. The term *utcumque* appears elsewhere, often in the context of the knowledge of God, to avoid all presumption of perfect knowledge and to indicate the function of analogies; see, for example, *SCG* II, ch. 2 (#859); *SCG* III, ch. 49 (#2270) and ch. 113 (#2873); *SCG* IV, ch. 21 (#3575). For the influence of St. Augustine (*De Trinitate* and *Sermons on John*), see for instance St. Thomas's *Catena in Matthaeum* 3:17 (Marietti edition, vol. 1, 55) or the *Catena in Ioannem* 14:26 (vol. 2, 524).

68 For the method and plan of the Trinitarian treatise in the *Summa contra Gentiles,* see G. Emery, *Trinity in Aquinas,* 73–89.

twofold task of the Sage, formulated and worked out in the *Summa contra Gentiles*.[69] This task is well fulfilled in the Trinitarian treatise in the *Summa theologiae*, beginning with its very first article, as has been mentioned above.

In reality, St. Thomas formulates this project in the first question of the *Summa theologiae*, when he explains that theology is an *argumentative* science. When the Christian theologian is debating with heretics, he can use Sacred Scripture as well as the articles of faith that his opponent accepts. And when his opponent will concede nothing of revelation, it remains for the theologian to refute the arguments raised against the faith, for "arguments brought against the faith are not demonstrations but arguments which can be solved *(solubilia argumenta)*."[70]

The elaboration of a speculative reflection on the Trinity, using analogies and philosophical resources, has therefore a twofold purpose: the contemplation of revealed truth, which in turn enables one to defend the faith against errors. The goal of Trinitarian theology is to show that faith in the Trinity is reasonably conceivable (we can reasonably contemplate the Trinity in faith), and that therefore arguments against Trinitarian faith cannot stand. Since the principles of human reason come from God, they cannot be contrary to the faith that is given by God.[71] For this reason arguments opposed to Trinitarian faith "do not have demonstrative force, but are either probable reasons *(rationes probabiles)* or sophisms *(rationes sophisticae)*."[72] Actually, in some cases one can refute arguments against Trinitarian faith by establishing that they are erroneous: Then it is a matter of sophisms. But in other cases one cannot establish directly the intrinsic falsity of the argument:

> Realities belonging to faith cannot be proved in a demonstrative way; for this reason, the falsity of certain [statements] contrary to the faith eludes the possibility of demonstration, but one can show that they are not necessary proofs.[73]

In this last case, one can merely show that the arguments contrary to the faith are just "probable reasons," that is, arguments that, in spite of a certain plausibility from the viewpoint of the philosophical reason, do not

---

69 Cf. *SCG* I, ch. 1; on this subject, one might refer to the enlightening study of René-Antoine Gauthier, *Saint Thomas d'Aquin, Somme contre les Gentils: Introduction* (Paris: Éditions Universitaires, 1993), 143–63: "The task of the Sage."

70 *ST* I, q. 1, a. 8.

71 *SCG* I, ch. 7 (#44 and 47); cf. *Super Boetium de Trinitate*, q. 2, a. 3; *ST* I, q. 1, a. 8.

72 *SCG* I, ch. 7 (#47).

73 *Super Boetium de Trinitate*, q. 2, a. 3.

necessarily stand. And in order to show this, it would be necessary to establish an alternative by proposing other "plausible reasons."

In fact, when one shows the intelligibility of Trinitarian faith by "persuasive arguments," one shows—without proving the faith—that the arguments of the heretics and the rational objections to Trinitarian faith do not have the force of necessity, since in suggesting another viewpoint one establishes a cogent alternative, capable of showing the truth of the faith. It is not exactly a matter of showing the strict and complete convergence of faith and reason, but rather their non-divergence, or better still, the fittingness of the truth. Hence, if there is an apologetic dimension of Trinitarian theology, it would be a rather indirect one.[74] Such is the function of "similitudes" *(similitudines, verisimilitudines)* or of "plausible reasons" *(rationes verisimiles)*, that is, analogies that allow one to account for faith in three divine Persons, principally the Augustinian analogy of word and love.[75] From a rational standpoint, they constitute fitting arguments,[76] or "likely arguments which show that what faith proposes *is not impossible*."[77] Their object is neither to prove the faith nor to convince those who do not share the Christian belief in the Trinity,[78] but they enable believers to see the intelligibility of their faith.

If one refuses to use speculative reason in this way, one can indeed *assert* the Trinity, but one will not be able to *manifest* (that is, to render more manifest to our minds) the truth of Trinitarian faith. This task, which is proper to speculative theology, is very clearly expressed in a celebrated *Quodlibet* in which St. Thomas explains that if the master or professor is content merely to rest his case on "authorities" (authoritative texts in Christian doctrine), the hearers will doubtless know what is true and what is false, but they will have no idea of the meaning of the truth being proposed to them:

> So it is necessary to rest one's case on reasons which seek out the roots of the truth and enable people to understand how what is proposed is true *(quo modo sit verum)*. Unless one does this, if the master bases his answer solely on authorities, the listener will indeed

---

74 On the apologetics proposed by St. Thomas, see my short exposition in *Thomas d'Aquin, Traités: Les raisons de la foi, Les articles de la foi et les sacrements de l'Église*, Introduction, traduction du Latin et notes par Gilles Emery (Paris: Cerf, 1999), 24–30.

75 *Super Boetium de Trinitate*, q. 2, a. 3: "It is thus that Augustine, in his book on the Trinity, makes use of numerous similitudes drawn from philosophical teachings to manifest the Trinity." Cf. *SCG* I, chs. 7–9.

76 *ST* I, q. 32, a. 1, ad 2.

77 Ibid. II–II, q. 1, a. 5, ad 2.

78 *SCG* I, ch. 9 (#54); cf. *De rationibus fidei*, ch. 2.

know that things are so, but he will have acquired neither knowledge nor understanding, and will go off with an empty head.[79]

This is what speculative Trinitarian theology aims to do: to manifest the truth, that is, to show *how* one can understand the truth of revelation and of the faith of the Church. The teaching on the Trinitarian processions, on relations, persons, and properties, lies within the scope of this purpose. In making some understanding of the truth possible, Trinitarian theology gives believers a foretaste of what they hope to contemplate in the blessed vision of God: Such is the essentially contemplative dimension of Trinitarian theology.

In describing this purpose, it is perhaps not enough to say that heresies were the "occasion" of St. Thomas's speculative Trinitarian theology. It may be equally insufficient to explain that the defense of the faith is a function "in some way accidental"[80] of Trinitarian doctrine. In fact, the heresies that give rise to the controversy determine in part the question that is asked, and in determining this question, they also contribute, obliquely, to the response that the theologian will give. They provide the setting, so to speak, for the inquiry. To put it still more precisely, the manifestation of truth and the refutation of errors are closely connected, in such a way that the one cannot be accomplished without the other. If we add that with St. Thomas these heresies are principally those of antiquity (of which he gives a speculative interpretation on the basis of positive documentation), we must take into account, perhaps more than it is usually done, the *historical* character of his speculative reflection on Trinitarian matters. This attention paid to history does not imply that one should relativize dogmatic tradition regarding the Trinity. It allows us, rather, to enter the better into a properly speculative understanding of this tradition and to take the measure of its depth.

5. Why Investigate Personal Properties and Notions?

The treatise on the Trinity seeks to clarify the *personal relations*, that is to say, the *properties* that, in distinguishing the persons, account for their plurality and enable us to perceive the features proper to each one. Relations, properties, notions: Why was this research conducted with such care by St. Thomas? Is it really necessary, or even wise? At first glance, one might

79 *Quodlibet* IV, q. 9, a. 3 (Leonine edition, vol. 25/2, 340). See Jean-Pierre Torrell, "Le savoir théologique chez saint Thomas," *Revue Thomiste* 96 (1996): 355–96.

80 Hyacinthe Dondaine, in *Saint Thomas d'Aquin: Somme théologique, La Trinité*, vol. 1 (Paris/Tournai/Rome: Éditions de la Revue des Jeunes, 1950; repr. Paris: Cerf, 1997), 257.

perhaps be tempted to consider this body of doctrine as a superb exercise in logic, a sort of theological Glass-Bead Game.

This difficulty is not entirely new. St. Thomas met it, although in another form, and gave a detailed response. The occasion was provided by the ideas of Praepositinus of Cremona. Chancellor of the University of Paris at the beginning of the thirteenth century, Praepositinus had stirred up a tremendous debate concerning the "notions" *(notiones)* in God. This technical term used in Trinitarian theology designates the proper personal characteristics that enable us to know each person distinctly. Since the three divine Persons are distinct, it is necessary to recognize something proper to each one, that is, something by which they are distinguished and by which we can know them. For Peter Lombard, whom the masters, beginning with William of Auxerre,[81] ordinarily followed, there are five notions: the paternity and innascibility of the Father, the filiation of the Son, the procession of the Spirit, and the common spiration (notion of the Father and Son who "spirate" or breathe forth the Holy Spirit).[82] During the twelfth century and throughout the beginning of the thirteenth, the debate was lively: Some theologians thought these "notions" were infinite in number, some counted six, others three, and still others thought there were none.[83]

Praepositinus of Cremona aligned himself with the last solution: He saw no grounds for recognizing such notions. As for him, when we say that the Father is characterized by *paternity* (the Father is distinguished from the Son by his "paternity"), this affirmation simply means that "the Father is the Father." The relative properties (paternity, filiation, procession) are only "manners of speaking" *(modi loquendi)*. In properly speaking of God, we are reduced to the common *essence* of the three persons and the three *persons* themselves: We can properly say only that the three persons are distinct and that they are one God. The rest can be discarded: There are no "properties" in God himself, and we do not have to recognize "notions."[84]

81 William of Auxerre, *Summa aurea,* Liber I, tract. 7, ch. 1–2 (ed. Jean Ribaillier [Paris: Vrin; Grottaferrata: Editiones Collegii S. Bonaventurae, 1980], 110–18). Cf. Johannes Schneider, *Die Lehre vom dreieinigen Gott in der Schule des Petrus Lombardus* (Munich: Max Hueber, 1961), 172–80.

82 This was the common teaching of the masters at the time of St. Thomas (cf. *ST* I, q. 32, a. 3).

83 Praepositinus of Cremona, *Summa "Qui producit ventos,"* Book I, ch. 12,2 (ed. Giuseppe Angelini, *L'ortodossia e la grammatica: Analisi di struttura e deduzione storica della Teologia Trinitaria de Prepositino* [Rome: Gregorian University Press, 1972], 277). Praepositinus took his inspiration from previous authors; cf. Johannes Schneider, *Die Lehre vom dreieinigen Gott,* 172–80.

84 Praepositinus of Cremona, *Summa* I, ch. 12 (ibid., 275–80); see the explanations of G. Angelini, who detects here a certain "nominalist orientation" in Praepositinus (ibid., 181–85).

Confronted with this question, St. Thomas begins by recalling the *simplicity* of God. God is not composed of this and that: In God, the person is really identical with the divine essence and is not composed of a property. "Our natural reason cannot know the divine simplicity as it is in itself: this is why our mind apprehends and names God according to its own mode, that is, from the milieu of sensible beings, from which it receives its knowledge."[85] In our world, we use concrete words to designate concrete realities (a flower, a bird), and abstract words to signify the principles or "forms" of these realities (the whiteness of the flower, the animality of the bird). This language parallels our knowledge of things: Our minds pick up the composition or complexity of the corporeal realities of our world. We cannot do otherwise when we speak of God, since we speak of him in our human language: We speak of the *wisdom* of God (an abstract name), as well as of *God* himself (a concrete name), and in the same way we speak of the *Father* (a concrete name) and of his *paternity* (an abstract name). In doing this, we are not affirming that the *relative property* of paternity is really something different from *the person of the Father himself*, but our grasp of the mystery is affected by this twofold mode of our knowledge and our language. Why is it necessary to take this into account when one reflects on the Trinitarian mystery?

> We are obliged to do so for two reasons. The first is the pressure of heretics. For since we confess the Father, the Son, and the Holy Spirit to be one God, they demand to know: *How are they one God, and how are they three persons?* And to the first question, we answer that they are one by their essence or deity; so there must also be some abstract terms by which we may show that the persons are distinct: these are the properties or notions, that is, abstract terms like *paternity* or *filiation*. Therefore, the divine essence is signified as *what* ("quid"), the person as *who* ("quis"); and the property as *whereby* ("quo")."[86]

These explanations are very instructive. They take us back to the question encountered by the Cappadocian Fathers in their debate with Modalist, Homoian, and Anomoian doctrines. Our faith confesses three hypostases or three persons in God: the Father, the Son, the Holy Spirit. But how to show that the Three, whilst being the same God, are not mixed up with each other? How to grasp and show that the Father is neither the Son nor the Holy Spirit? In order to demonstrate the true divinity of the three persons, it was necessary to draw on the concept of "essence" *(ousia)*, by which each one of the three persons is truly God. In the same way, to

85 St. Thomas, *ST* I, q. 32, a. 2.
86 Ibid.

show the true plurality and the distinction of persons, it was necessary to pick out the characteristics through which the Father is Father, the Son is Son, and the Spirit is Spirit. The doctrine of properties, as we find it in its first full development in St. Gregory Nazianzen,[87] was born of this question: In seeking the characteristics of the persons, one could show their distinction in unity, in opposition to modalism and to subordinatianism, which denied either the true divinity or the true plurality of these persons. The investigation of relations and properties, in St. Thomas, has the same goal. If we reject such a study, then theology will remain silent in face of the challenge of heterodox doctrines, and we will no longer be able to give an account of our faith in the Trinity. Here again we see the concern that associates speculative Trinitarian theology with the need to account for our faith when it is challenged by teachings that break away from it.

Moreover, to be able to show that the Father is distinct from the Son and the Holy Spirit, it is necessary to recognize that the Father possesses one relation to the Son and another to the Holy Spirit. Therefore it is necessary to distinguish clearly between the relation of paternity (relation of Father to Son) and the relation of spiration (relation to the Holy Spirit). Without this, one might well offer a fine affirmation of the Trinity of persons, but one would not have shown their distinction. Now, in the Father, paternity is not a different reality from spiration (these two "notions" of *paternity* and *spiration* do not divide the person of the Father: The Father is one). To account for Trinitarian faith it is necessary therefore to use the "abstract" language of notions and properties, in order to show "that through which" the Father is distinct from the Son and from the Holy Spirit, they themselves being mutually distinct.[88]

In seeking to clarify Trinitarian relations and "notions," Trinitarian theology will therefore examine "that through which" the persons are distinct, "that through which" they are constituted as such (for example, that through which the Son is Son and distinct from the Father). In this field more than in any other, the theologian knows that his research is bound to our human mode of knowing God. The doctrine of "notions" as abstract names is less a matter of the persons in themselves than of our human knowledge of the mystery.[89] In truth, the person of the Father is simple: In the Father, there is no real difference between *what* he is (God), *who* he

[87] See, for example, St. Gregory Nazianzen, *Oration* 39,12 (cf. *Sources Chrétiennes* 358, 172–77).

[88] *ST* I, q. 32, a. 2; it is the second reason that "compels" us to recognize notions or properties.

[89] This was strongly emphasized by Cajetan, who notes, in connection with the abstract names or *notions*: "This question does not concern the reality [the divine reality: the three persons] considered absolutely, but the reality *insofar as it is signified and apprehended by us.*" Cajetan, *In Primam,* q. 32, a. 2; Leonine edition, vol. 4, 352.

is (the Father), and *that through which* he is the Father (paternity). But our grasp of the mystery requires that we perceive that through which he is Father, and therefore that we clarify "notions," for it is only thus that we can manifest his personal distinction and give an account of our faith in three persons who are one God.

6. Trinitarian Theology Is a Spiritual Exercise

The motive animating such research is formulated very suggestively in the *Summa contra Gentiles*, in connection with the truths that faith alone makes known to us through our acceptance of revelation. The following explanations apply above all to the mystery of the Trinity.

> In order to manifest this kind of truth, one must provide likely, probable reasons *(rationes aliquae verisimiles)* for the exercise and encouragement of the faithful *(ad fidelium quidem exercitium et solatium)* and not in order to convince opponents; for the insufficiency of these reasons would rather confirm them in their error if they thought that we adhered to the faith for such weak reasons.[90]

The prologue of Book IV of the *Summa contra Gentiles*, where we find the treatise on the Trinity, formulates the same purpose in similar words. Human knowledge of the mystery of God obtained through revelation is compared here to a little drop *(parva stilla)*. The revealed mysteries are presented to us in Sacred Scripture in the form of similitudes and words that are at times obscure, "in such a way that only studious men can succeed in understanding a little, while others revere these mysteries as hidden, and unbelievers cannot tear them off."[91] Envisaged in this way, Trinitarian theology is a form of study practiced like an exercise and destined for believers. In this context, the word "exercise" indicates a lengthy, in-depth study, in the course of which the mind becomes capable of extracting from Scripture the teaching of the faith contained therein,[92]

90 *SCG* I, ch. 9 (#54). It is not easy to give an accurate translation of the word *solatium*, which means: support, assistance, succor, consolation, domestic help, and sometimes even entertainment (see, for instance, *ST* I, q. 51, a. 1, arg. 1; *ST* II–II, q. 168, a. 3, ad 3). In the Latin text of the Letter to the Hebrews 6:18 according to the Vulgate, *solatium* translates the Greek *paraklesis* (strengthening, encouragement, exhortation).

91 *SCG* IV, ch. 1 (#3345): "ut ad ea quomodocumque capienda soli studiosi perveniant, alii vero quasi occulta venerentur, et increduli lacerare non possint."

92 *ST* II–II, q. 1, a. 9, ad 1: "The truth of faith is contained in sacred Scripture, but diffusely, in diverse ways and, sometimes, darkly *(obscure)*. The result is that to draw out the truth of faith from Scripture requires a prolonged study and an exercise *(longum studium et exercitium)*."

and succeeds in grasping the depth of the truth.[93] This kind of study is a *spirituale exercitium*.[94] In the formula "spiritual exercise," the adjective "spiritual" carries a religious sense (seeking knowledge of God in faith) without for all that losing its anthropological significance (*spiritual* as distinguished from *manual* or *corporeal*).[95]

Although it is not a question of an explicit quotation, we should note that the vocabulary and the theme of "exercise" are an echo of St. Augustine's *De Trinitate*, which St. Thomas meditated upon. The end pursued by St. Augustine in his *De Trinitate* is to "render an account *(reddere rationem)* of this: The Trinity is the one and true God."[96] This purpose is supported by the desire to manifest the truth of Trinitarian faith in opposition to those who reject or deform it. In having recourse to Scripture and then to reason,[97] the Bishop of Hippo invites the reader to a search after the truth about God, which requires a "purification of our mind *(purgatio mentis)*."[98] In the second part of his work, St. Augustine proposes a climbing exercise, a rising from degree to degree *(per corporalia ad incorporalia)*, in order to discover in creatures, as in a mirror, some similitude of the divine Trinity: in the corporeal works of God, in the "exterior man," in the "interior man," in his spiritual faculties, and above all in his spiritual acts of union with God.[99] Doubtless we should see in the theme of the "spiritual exercise" a Christian deepening of ancient views (Stoicism and Epicureanism,

---

93 Cf. *SCG* I, ch. 4, (#24); *SCG* II, ch. 60 (#1370); *ST* II–II, q. 10, a. 7.

94 In *SCG* III, ch. 132 (#3047), in connection with the activities of mendicant religious, St. Thomas explains that the accomplishment of certain activities takes a long time: "This is the case with the study of wisdom, teaching, and other spiritual exercises *(spiritualia exercitia)* of this sort." Cf. also *ST* II–II, q. 122, a. 4, ad 3.

95 The expression "spiritual exercise" occurs several times in the works of St. Thomas. It is applied to study and teaching (*SCG* III, ch. 132 [#3047]), to the religious state, and to activities proper to this state (*ST* II–II, q. 189, a. 1; *Contra Impugnantes,* ch. 5, ad 8 [Leonine edition, vol. 41 A, 92]) and, more generally, to the practice of virtues (*In Eph* 3:14 [#166]; *ST* III, q. 69, a. 3). For the nuances of the vocabulary of "spirituality," see Jean-Pierre Torrell, "*Spiritualitas* chez saint Thomas d'Aquin," *Revue des Sciences Philosophiques et Théologiques* 73 (1989): 575–84.

96 St. Augustine, *De Trinitate* I,2,4.

97 Ibid.

98 Ibid. I,I,3.

99 Augustine gives a summary of this complex exercise at the beginning of Book XV of his *De Trinitate.* The vocabulary of "exercise" appears notably in *De Trinitate* XIII,20,26; XV,1,1; XV,6,10. On the Augustinian concept of Trinitarian theology as a spiritual exercise, see Basil Studer, *Mysterium caritatis: Studien zur Exegese und zur Trinitätslehre in der Alten Kirche* (Rome: Pontificio Ateneo S. Anselmo, 1999), 291–310: "La teologia trinitaria in Agostino d'Ippona" (the author is wrong, however, in opposing St. Thomas to St. Augustine on this point, cf. 308–9).

but also neo-Platonism) according to which philosophy was a spiritual exercise.[100] In spite of obvious differences, the elevation of the spirit proposed by St. Augustine presents certain likenesses to the spiritual exercises required by Plotinus to lift oneself up to a grasp of the One.[101] In a Christian setting, however, the spiritual exercise takes on a different aspect.[102] It is performed on the foundation of revelation, through divine grace, in the adherence of faith to the Triune God. In this context, the mention of heresies comes as no surprise. Rather, it is a common characteristic of patristic Trinitarian thought. St. Augustine explained moreover that God permits heresies for the exercise *(exercitatio)* and strengthening of believers in the faith *(probatio)*.[103]

In a manner comparable to St. Augustine's teaching on the Trinity, in spite of differences in sources and method, St. Thomas presents his theology of the Trinity to the faithful as a spiritual exercise *(ad fidelium exercitium)*, by means of which they may contemplate, with ongoing study and research, the Trinity who is one God. The soteriological dimension of speculative Trinitarian theology clearly lies within the scope of this project. As we have noted above, St. Thomas explains that the revelation of the Trinity was "necessary" in order that we might understand creation, and above all the salvation accomplished by the mission of the divine Persons.[104] Knowledge of the divine Persons enables believers to acknowledge the gift made to them in the divine economy: Knowledge of creation and salvation requires knowledge of the divine Persons. This is the knowledge that revelation offers. It is likewise this knowledge that, in accord with its purpose and proper resources, speculative Trinitarian theology will seek to manifest.

Even when St. Thomas is studying the mission of the divine Persons, in that question in the treatise on the Trinity that offers the clearest soteriolog-

---

100 See Pierre Hadot's basic study: *Exercices spirituels et philosophie antique* (Paris: Études Augustiniennes, 1981); idem, *Qu'est-ce que la philosophie antique?* (Paris: Gallimard, 1995), 276–333: "Les exercices spirituels." On the theme of *exercitatio mentis* in the Fathers of the Church, see Basil Studer, *Schola christiana: Die Theologie zwischen Nizäa (325) und Chalzedon (451)* (Paderborn: Schöningh, 1998), 16–19.

101 Concerning Plotinus, see Pierre Hadot's explanations in: Plotin, *Traité 9 (VI, 9)*, Introduction, Traduction, Commentaire et notes par Pierre Hadot (Paris: Cerf, 1994), 45 and 139–42.

102 See Henri-Irénée Marrou, *Saint Augustin et la fin de la culture antique* (Paris: De Boccard, 1958; repr. 1983), 299–327: "Exercitatio animi." This *exercitatio* is a training that disposes the believers' mind to the contemplation of God's truth.

103 St. Augustine, *Sermo Morin Guelferbytanus 33*, in *Patrologiae cursus completus, Series Latina, Supplementum,* Volumen II**, ed. Adalbert Hamman (Paris: Garnier, 1960), 650–51.

104 St. Thomas, *ST* I, q. 32, a. 1, ad 3.

ical developments (*Prima Pars,* question 43), he is faithful to the basic intention that motivates the entire treatise. In fact, the teaching on the mission of the Son and the Holy Spirit comes after the study of the equality of the persons, in a section treating of "the mutual comparison of the persons" (questions 42–43).[105] The study of the mission compares the persons by showing their unity and their distinction. To study the missions is to show once more the consubstantiality of distinct persons, that is, to show the persons in their divine essence and their properties. In considering the sanctifying action of the Trinity, the theologian does not cease to fix his attention on the immanent mystery of the Trinity, and inversely, the study of the immanent Trinity is achieved within the study of the Trinitarian economy. In this context, the equality of the three persons receives special attention. St. Thomas insistently emphasizes the fact that, from the vantage point of the divine Persons, mission implies neither inferiority nor separation, but only the "procession of origin" of the Son and the Holy Spirit, consubstantial with the Father.[106] We should also note that the sanctifying action of the divine Persons is shown by means of the doctrinal themes brought out in the preceding questions: procession, relation, person, and essence, the presence of the known within the knower (through the word), and the presence of the loved within the lover (through the "impression" of love). In studying the sending and the gift of the divine Persons in grace, St. Thomas does not relinquish his fundamental object, which is to manifest the common divinity and real distinction of Father, Son, and Holy Spirit.

The purpose of Trinitarian theology, for St. Thomas, is therefore at one and the same time ambitious and modest. It is ambitious, for Trinitarian theology sets out to show (that is, to make more manifest to our minds) the distinction of the persons in unity, not only in their economic action but also, more profoundly, in their eternal immanence. And yet his purpose remains modest: It is a matter of studying in order to grasp but a little, in an imperfect and incomplete manner, of the truth of God that the believer hopes to contemplate in the full light of the beatific vision; the knowledge thus gained makes for the exclusion of errors. St. Thomas has expressed this purpose, using the words of St. Hilary already quoted above in the reading of his *De potentia.* In the *Summa contra Gentiles,* he recalled the same words of St. Hilary, introduced by an allusion to the "exercise" carried out by means of research into speculative reasons accounting for faith in the Trinity:

105 *ST* I, q. 42, prol.; cf. q. 39, prol.

106 Ibid., q. 43, a. 1 and 2; a. 7, ad 1. The unity of action of the Trinity is clearly recalled: a. 4, ad 2; a. 7, ad 3.

> It is useful for the human mind to exercise itself with such reasons, however weak they are, provided there be not presumptuous attempt to comprehend or demonstrate. For the ability to perceive something of the highest realities, if only with feeble, limited understanding, gives the greatest joy [. . .]. In accord with this thought, St. Hilary declares in his book *On the Trinity*, speaking of this sort of truth: In faith, *set out, go forward, persevere. And though I may know that you will not attain the end, still I shall praise you for your progress. He who pursues the infinite with reverent devotion, even though he never attains it, always profits nonetheless from advancing forward. But in penetrating this secret, in plunging into the hidden depth of this Birth unlimited* [the generation of the one God begotten by the one unbegotten God], *beware of presumptuously thinking you have attained a full understanding. Know, rather, that this is incomprehensible.*[107]

The theologian who practices this kind of Trinitarian theology sees himself as a believer carrying on a *contemplative exercise* so as to better grasp the "little drop"[108] of divine knowledge that is communicated to us through revelation. In presenting "likely reasons" for refuting objections raised against the faith, this theologian enters into an understanding of a transcendent mystery that is the source of a profound and intense spiritual joy.[109] The purpose of Trinitarian theology, as St. Thomas understands it, finds an exceedingly clear expression in the words he uses to show the fruitfulness of the research inaugurated by the Fathers of the Church: By the speculative search into the mystery of the Trinity, carried on "for the exercise and the strengthening of believers" as a foretaste of the beatific vision, "the mind is lifted up to lay hold of something of the truth that suffices for excluding the errors."

---

107 *SCG* I, ch. 8 (#49–50). Cf. St. Hilary of Poitiers, *De Trinitate* II,10–11 (ed. Pieter Smulders [Brepols: Turnhout, 1979], 48–49).

108 *SCG* IV, ch. 1 (#3345).

109 The words used by St. Thomas to signify this spiritual fruit are very suggestive: "a vehement joy" (*vehemens gaudium*: *SCG* I, ch. 5 [#32]), "the highest joy" (*iucundissimum*: *SCG* I, ch. 8 [#49]).

CHAPTER 2

Trinitarian Theology as Spiritual Exercise in Augustine and Aquinas

ST. THOMAS presents his speculative Trinitarian doctrine as an extension or personal development of the teaching of the Fathers and of St. Augustine in particular.[1] Thus, for example, when he introduces his teaching on Trinitarian relations, St. Thomas explains that he is going to unfold it "by following the statements of the holy [Fathers]";[2] and when he shows the plurality of the persons, he announces that he is going to do it "especially in accordance with the way by which Augustine manifested it,"[3] in other words, by means of the analogy of the word and of love. In Thomas's Trinitarian theology, recourse to "similitudes" drawn from creatures (the use of the notion of substance and relation, the observation of Trinitarian vestiges, the exploitation of anthropological analogies) is presented expressly as a reflection extending the path traced out by Augustine in his *De Trinitate*.[4]

---

1 English translation by John Baptist Ku, OP. The second part of this essay appeared in French: "La théologie trinitaire spéculative comme 'exercice spirituel' suivant saint Thomas d'Aquin," *Annales theologici* 19 (2005): 99–133.

2 *De potentia*, q. 8, a. 1: "Qualiter sit, sequendo sanctorum dicta, investigari oportet." The references on particular points of doctrine are numerous; see for instance *De potentia*, q. 10, a. 2: "doctores nostri."

3 Ibid., q. 9, a. 5: "Ad manifestationem ergo aliqualem huius quaestionis, et praecipue secundum quod Augustinus eam manifestat." Let us recall that in this context, the doctrine of the word and love makes it possible to show the unity of persons and their distinction by relations.

4 See, for example, *Super Boetium de Trinitate*, q. 2, a. 3: "Sicut Augustinus in libro *De Trinitate* utitur multis similitudinibus ex doctrinis philosophicis sumptis ad manifestandum Trinitatem."

But is St. Thomas faithful to the spirit that motivated the inquiry of the Bishop of Hippo? Does he grasp St. Augustine's objective, and does he respect it? Numerous studies call into question the authenticity of St. Thomas's Augustinian heritage. And it is not rare that the spiritual inquiry of St. Augustine is juxtaposed over against the speculative exposition of the Trinitarian faith of Aquinas. Thus, according to Basil Studer, St. Thomas was trying to explain the mystery of the divine processions by means of analogies drawn from the interior life of man, while St. Augustine was instead aiming at a spiritual exercise *(exercitatio mentis)*.[5] While St. Augustine was proposing a sapiential contemplation, St. Thomas "limited himself in his questions on the Trinity (Ia, q. 27–32) to a purely intellectual dialectic."[6] Certain authors, juxtaposing the spiritual objective of St. Augustine to the speculative thought of St. Thomas, reproach the latter for having weakened the Augustinian sense of Trinitarian paradox by seeking to represent the mystery with a conceptual objectification.[7] Even the finest experts on St. Thomas sometimes allow themselves to be led to such juxtapositions: "living dialectic of union with God" in St. Augustine, doctrine "more purely intellectual" in St. Thomas.[8] It is certain that writing eight and a half centuries after St. Augustine and in profoundly different circumstances, St. Thomas did not limit himself to repeating his master. But does his objective differ radically from Augustine's? This is the question that I propose to consider here in examining these two authors' explanations of the objective or intention of their Trinitarian theology.

1. St. Augustine: *Exercitatio Mentis*

Scripture and Reason

The purpose of St. Augustine's *De Trinitate* is "to account for the Trinity being the one and only and true God."[9] St. Augustine seeks in particular

5 Basil Studer, *Mysterium caritatis: Studien zur Exegese und zur Trinitätslehre in der Alten Kirche* (Rome: Pontificio Ateneo S. Anselmo, 1999), 308–9.

6 Fulbert Cayré, "Théologie, sagesse et contemplation dans le *De Trinitate*," in *Œuvres de saint Augustin*, vol. 16: *La Trinité* (Books VIII–XV), trans. P. Agaësse and J. Moingt (Paris: Desclée de Brouwer, 1955), 639.

7 See the critique of Michel Corbin, *La Trinité ou l'excès de Dieu* (Paris: Cerf, 1997), 21–86. To the Thomistic objective, which in his opinion seeks the "control" of human understanding over the Trinity, the author juxtaposes a "patristic proposition" that deliberately rejects every reference to the thought of St. Thomas.

8 Hyacinthe Dondaine, in: St. Thomas d'Aquin, *Somme théologique: La Trinité*, vol. 1 (Paris: Cerf, 1997), 7.

9 *De Trinitate* I,2,4: "reddere rationem, quod Trinitas sit unus et solus et verus Deus." Our translation is taken, with some modifications, from St. Augustine, *The Trinity*, Introduction, translation and notes by Edmund Hill, OP, ed. John E.

to show the unity, equality, and inseparability of the Father, Son, and Holy Spirit.[10] To give account of this *(reddere rationem)*, his inquiry includes two sections. The first part shows the unity of the three persons "by the authority of the Holy Scriptures"; the second proposes to manifest the dogma of the Church (the teaching of Scripture) by speculation.[11] St. Augustine submits his whole reflection to a double criterion: Holy Scripture and, at another level (under the guidance of Scripture), reason.[12] This distinction, which is not a separation, is founded on the very action of God, who is the source of Scripture, and who is also the source of the creatures that offer the similitudes from which human understanding can be lifted toward God. Thus, if one searches for the substance of God "either through his Scriptures *(per Scripturam)* or his creatures *(per creaturam)*," it is because "both are offered us for our observation and scrutiny in order that in them he may be sought, he may be loved, who inspired the one and created the other."[13] The explanations given at the beginning of Book XV are very clear: "Whether [the nature of God] is Trinity, we ought to demonstrate, not merely to believers by the authority of divine Scripture, but also to the ones who understand, if we can, by some reason."[14] That is why, having spelled out the teaching of Scripture (which suffices for faith), Augustine responds to "those who demand the reason concerning such things," "by making use of the creatures which God has made [. . .],

---

Rotelle (New York: New City Press, 1996). For the Latin text and its numbering, I have followed the edition of the Bibliothèque Augustinienne (Paris: Desclée de Brouwer, 1955) and the edition by W. J. Mountain: Sancti Aurelii Augustini, *De Trinitate libri XV,* 2 vols. (Turnhout: Brepols, 1968).

10 *De Trinitate* XV,3,5. This does not mean that Augustine starts with unity in order to consider the three persons subsequently. Unity is rather what St. Augustine seeks to show by considering the teaching of revelation concerning the Father, the Son, and the Spirit (ibid.); see the numerous texts pointed out by Marie-François Berrouard in St. Augustin, *Homélies sur l'évangile de saint Jean XXXIV–XLIII* (Paris: Institut d'Études Augustiniennes, 1988), 278. Cf. Marie-François Berrouard, "La Trinité est le seul Dieu," in St. Augustin, *Homélies sur l'évangile de saint Jean CIV–CXXIV* (Paris: Institut d'Études Augustiniennes, 2003), 475–78; see idem, "La Trinité qui est Dieu," in *Augustin: Le message de la foi,* ed. Goulven Madec (Paris: Desclée de Brouwer, 1987), 99–117.

11 *De Trinitate* I,2,4; cf. XV,3,5. For the complex structure of the *De Trinitate,* see Edmund Hill in St. Augustine, *The Trinity,* 21–27.

12 *De Trinitate* III, prooemium 2. This reference to Scripture and reason is recalled in numerous reprises; see, for example, *De Trinitate* IV,6,10; XV,20,39.

13 Ibid. II, prooemium; cf. XV,20,39.

14 Ibid. XV,1,1: "Quae utrum sit Trinitas, non solum credentibus, divinae Scripturae auctoritate; verum etiam intelligentibus, aliqua, si possumus, ratione jam demonstrare debemus." Cf. *De Trinitate* XV,27,49: "videatur mente quod tenetur fide."

especially through that rational or intellectual creature which was made to the image of God."[15]

The purpose of reason is formulated thus: to give account of that which one holds by faith for the sake of understanding. The study of the Trinitarian mystery therefore entails two *modes*: Having spelled out the Trinitarian faith according to Scripture and the Tradition of the Church (Books I–VII), Augustine treats this *same* Trinitarian faith "in a more inward manner" *(modo interiore)* in order to grasp to some extent, by means of images, what the faith confesses (Books VIII–XV).[16] Augustine's main purpose is to show the conformity of Catholic faith with the teaching of Holy Scriptures.

This purpose implies a very clear priority of faith with respect to the inquiry of reason, formulated in numerous reprises: "We must believe before we can understand."[17] The order of inquiry thus consists in a path that takes its direction from biblical faith: "Let us first adhere through faith, that there may be that which may be quickened by understanding."[18] Understanding is the reward of faith.[19] St. Augustine's objective therefore eschews all rationalism. The analysis of the image of God takes place precisely in order to aid the believer in grasping to some extent what he holds by faith. The question posed by Augustine in the study of the image of God is not "How are we going to believe ?" but "If there is some way in which we can see by our understanding what we believe, what might this way be ?"[20] This purpose is strictly that of faith's understanding: "I desired to see with my understanding that which I believed."[21] The

---

15 Ibid. XV,20,49: "Admonuimus eos qui rationem de rebus talibus poscunt, ut invisibilia ejus per ea quae facta sunt, sicut possent, intellecta conspicerent, et maxime per rationalem vel intellectualem creaturam quae facta est ad imaginem Dei."

16 Ibid. VIII,1,1. In the summary given at the beginning of Book XV, Augustine states clearly that it was in Book VIII that he began "to raise the intention of the mind [. . .] in order to understand" (XV,6,10). Book VIII can also be considered as a transition between Books I–VII and Books IX–XV.

17 Ibid. VIII,5,8.

18 *Tractatus in Iohannis Evangelium* XXVII,7: "Prius haereamus per fidem, ut sit quod vivificetur per intellectum." *Tractatus in Iohannis Evangelium* XXIX,6: "Intellectus enim est merces fidei. Ergo noli quaerere intelligere ut credas, sed crede ut intelligas." Cf. also *Tractatus in Iohannis Evangelium* XXXIX,3; *Sermo* 122,1; and so on. The references to the Latin text of St. Augustine's *Homilies on St. John* are taken from Sancti Aurelii Augustini, *In Iohannis Evangelium Tractatus CXXIV*, ed. Radbodus Willems (Turnhout: Brepols, 1954).

19 *Tractatus in Iohannis Evangelium* XXIX,6: "Intellectus enim merces est fidei." Cf. XLVIII,1.

20 *De Trinitate* XV,6,9: "Sed si aliquo modo per intelligentiam possumus videre quod credimus, quis iste erit modus ?"

21 Ibid. XV,28,51: "Desideravi intellectu videre quod credidi."

inquiry of understanding exits the act of faith. Faith unleashes intellectual inquiry, judges it, nourishes it, makes it fruitful, and completes it.

The Similitude of the Image of God

The Augustinian usage of similitudes in order to manifest the Trinitarian mystery has given rise to an immense philosophical and theological body of literature. I do not intend to take up this vast debate here, but only to outline a few hints provided by Augustine himself. One must note first that the study of the image of God does not occupy first place in St. Augustine's thought. First place goes rather to *the unity of action* of the Father, the Son, and the Holy Spirit, that is, to their common operation. Augustine's understanding of the inseparability of Father, Son, and Holy Spirit implies a solid teaching on *God's simplicity* (the Triune God is non-composite), *immutability* (the divine Persons are not submitted to change), and *incomprehensibility* (the Triune God is beyond human understanding). The analysis of the image of God occurs in a second step in order to manifest to our understanding how we can conceive this common action of the three persons, within the frame of God's simplicity, immutability, and incomprehensibility.

Beginning with Book VIII, having shown according to Scripture and the Tradition of the Church that the Trinity is the only one God, Augustine sets out to give a rational account of it (this reflection has already been prepared in the preceding books),[22] in particular "through charity": "Here at last our minds began to perceive in some fashion the Trinity, like lover and what is loved and love."[23] Having reached this point, Augustine pursues his reflection *(disputatio)* in Book IX, by turning to the image of God *(ad imaginem Dei quod est homo secundum mentem)* in considering the triad of *mens, notitia* (by which *mens* knows itself), and *amor* (by which it loves itself and its knowledge), in order to manifest their essential unity and equality. Aware of the difficulty of his explanation, Augustine pursues his exposition in Book X with the examination of a "clearer" *(evidentius)* trinity of *mens*: memory, understanding, and will *(memoria, intelligentia, voluntas)*. At this point, still aware of the difficulty of his plan, Augustine digresses from his discussion of the mind as an image of the Trinity in order to find a trinity in the perception of corporeal things, in which the distinction will appear more clearly to readers (albeit the expression of unity is weaker here). Thus Book XI considers the "trinity of the exterior man."[24] From there, Augustine takes up again

22 See the summary given in ibid. XV,3,5: "ratione etiam reddita intelligentibus."

23 Ibid.: "Et per charitatem [. . .] per quam coepit utcumque etiam Trinitas intelligentibus apparere, sicut sunt amans, et quod amatur, et amor." Cf. ibid. VIII,8,12: "Imo vero vides Trinitatem, si charitatem vides."

24 Book XI considers two "trinities" successively: the trinity of perception (the body that is seen, the form that is impressed from it, and the intention of the will that

the inquiry into the interior man, in a movement of development that goes from the exterior to the interior *(introrsus tendere)*. Distinguishing "science" (which concerns temporal realities) and "wisdom" (the contemplation of eternal realities), Book XII offers a sort of transition that shows that not every Trinitarian similitude is an "image of God." Following this movement of interior ascension *(introrsum ascendere)*, Book XIII presents an exercise of the purification of the heart through faith that leads to wisdom. On this basis, Book XIV returns to the image of God in the soul (that of Book X), by showing that the image is in the soul when this soul is turned toward God, by virtue of the *reformatio* that procures true wisdom for the soul. Finally, Book XV offers a paradoxical crowning of the whole of this inquiry. On the one hand, Augustine rises from the trinity of man to that of God, by showing the unity and distinction of the divine Persons (the Son as Word and the Holy Spirit as Charity). On the other hand, he ends his work with a confession of ignorance; it is impossible to grasp the Trinitarian mystery, the Trinity cannot be explained: "We say many things and do not attain (Sir 43:27)."[25] The inquiry of understanding *(disputatio)* therefore gives way to prayer *(precatio)*.[26]

Readers of Augustine will notice without effort that his approach is complex—carried away by detours, repetitions, and digressions. Each solution seems only to make the problem bounce back. It must be added that the analysis of *mens*, in a Trinitarian context, does not constitute an inquiry of a purely philosophical order. It is guided, nourished, and completed by faith. It is in reflecting the light that comes to it from God that the *mens* becomes somehow enlightening, by reflection. Augustine's inquiry shows that the soul discovers its Trinitarian structure by analyzing the conditions of its faith in God (that is the sense of Book VIII). If the mystery of God the Trinity can somehow be enlightened by the image of God, it is because it throws its own light upon this image. The mystery of God the Trinity is not enlightened from outside; rather it is the source of the light.[27] That is why the analysis of the relationship of the soul to itself does not suffice: "The trinity of the mind is not really the image of God because the mind remembers and understands and loves itself, but because it is also able to remember and understand and love him by whom it was made."[28] The soul is the image of God because it is called to see God.[29] This intellectual

couples the two together) and the trinity of memory (the image of the body that is in the memory, the form derived from it when the thinking attention turns to it, and the intention of the will joining the two together).

25 *De Trinitate* XV,28,51.

26 Ibid.

27 Cf. ibid. XV,23–24,44.

28 Ibid. XIV,12,15. Augustine insists often on this aspect which, like many others, will be repeated by St. Thomas: *De Veritate,* q. 10, a. 7; *ST* I, q. 93, a. 8.

29 *De Trinitate* XIV,8,11.

inquiry is not separated from an affective approach; rather it is enlivened by a love that leads the mind toward an effort to understand ("We are carried away by love to track down the truth"),[30] and it is accomplished in love ("Let me love you").[31] Augustine thus requires of his readers or listeners not only attention but also devotion.[32] He recalls constantly that the Trinitarian image must be grasped according to a contemplative wisdom, with love. The more one loves God, the more one sees him.[33] Let us yet add that the analysis of *mens* is not first of all "psychological" in the modern sense of the term, but rather ontological. In turning toward God, whose image it is, the soul attains what it is, its proper nature.[34]

The Function of the Similitude of Image

The analysis of the image of God in man emerges as the fulfillment of the program that St. Augustine had traced out at Cassiciacum, shortly after his conversion: "God and the soul, that is what I desire to know.—Nothing more?—Nothing whatever."[35] In the *De Trinitate*, an aspect of this vast program that reunites the study of God and that of man in a continual back-and-forth appears in the foreground. The analysis of this image intends to reveal to the mind "something" of the mystery of God the Trinity. This "something" is before all else the substantial unity and equality of the Father, the Son, and the Holy Spirit in their distinction. The similitudes and traditional comparisons borrowed from the material world (the sun, a ray, the root, the branch, the fruit, and so on) that one finds among numerous Fathers before St. Augustine (Hippolytus, Tertullian, and many others) occur infrequently in St. Augustine. Clearly, he wanted better than that! The created similitudes that he retains, in particular that of the image of God, are adduced in order to aid in grasping the *unity of action* of the divine Trinity, the *inseparability* of the Three,[36] their *mutual immanence*[37] and *equality*,[38] *their unity of essence or substance*,[39] in a distinction that

---

30 Ibid. I,5,8.

31 Ibid. XV,28,51.

32 See, for example, *Sermo* 52,15 (PL 38, 359).

33 *De Trinitate* VIII,8,12-VIII,9,13.

34 Cf. Étienne Gilson, *Introduction à l'étude de saint Augustin* (Paris: Vrin, 1943), 294.

35 *Soliloquia* I,2,7: "Deum et animam scire cupio.—Nihil de plus?—Nihil omnino." Cf. E. Hendrickx, in St. Augustin, *La Trinité*, vol. 1 (Paris: Desclée de Brouwer, 1955), 9–10.

36 See, for example, *De Trinitate* IX,4,6.

37 See, for example, ibid. IX,5,8; IX,10,15.

38 See, for example, ibid. IX,4,4; IX,11,16; X,11,18.

39 See, for example, ibid. IX,4,4–7; IX,5,8; IX,12,18; X,11,18; XI,3,6–7; XV,3,5; and so on.

excludes confusion.[40] The similitudes aim in particular at giving some idea of the relations of origin. Through these St. Augustine wants to manifest to the mind what constitutes the object itself of his treatise: The Trinity is only one God, God is Trinity.

The distinction between the *generation of the Son* and the *procession of the Holy Spirit,* which the image of God (in particular the similitude of the word and charity) attempts to manifest, also occupies a central place in St. Augustine's inquiry. Far from being marginal, this question (the Holy Spirit is not generated) appears from the very beginning of the *De Trinitate.*[41] Augustine judges it to be "extremely difficult" *(difficillimum).*[42] This question is born of the Pneumatomachian controversy and aims to manifest the full divinity of the Holy Spirit by giving account of his distinction with respect to the Son. The similitude of love or the will makes it possible to show in some way how we can grasp that the Holy Spirit is not generated (he is not the Son): Love is not generated.[43] It is proper to the will not to be produced as an "offspring" *(proles)* from a "parent" *(parens),* but rather to unite *(copulare)* the one generating and the one generated.[44]

Thus the study of this image is designed to suggest the unity and distinction in God the Trinity, to give believers some grasp of understanding, to glimpse by reason what they hold by faith. Such an objective is addressed to believers. However, in one passage of the *De Trinitate,* St. Augustine seems to suggest that he is addressing an audience broader than just believing Catholics. In Book XV, when he tries to show that the procession of the Holy Spirit is distinguished from the generation of the Son, having observed that this concerns an extremely difficult question, he writes out an excerpt of a sermon for the benefit of the less sophisticated minds, stating, "I have transcribed these words from that sermon into the present book, but there I was speaking to the faithful, not to unbelievers."[45] This observation seems to indicate that St. Augustine had the ambition of being read by unbelievers or by heretical Christians in order to show that the mystery of the Trinity is not unreasonable, since the human mind offers an image of it. One can discern that he has not ruled out leading them to the faith at the same time that he advances the faith-

---

40 See, for example, ibid. IX,4,7–IX,5,8; IX,12,17; cf. VIII,4,6.

41 Ibid. I,5,8; II,3,5. The question is taken up again in full measure in Book XV (XV,25,45; XV,26,47; XV,27,48; XV,27,50).

42 Ibid. XV,27,48.

43 Ibid. IX,12,17–18.

44 Ibid. XIV,6,8; XIV,7,10; XIV,10,13; XV,27,50. Cf. also XI,7,12; XI,8,15-XI,9,16; XI,11,18.

45 Ibid. XV,27,48: "Haec de illo sermone in hunc librum transtuli, sed fidelibus, non infidelibus loquens."

ful already cultivated in understanding this faith. Besides, this is the way Augustine conceives "knowledge of the faith."[46]

This function of the image is well expressed in the *Contra Sermonem Arrianorum.* There St. Augustine explains first that the Trinity is not three gods but only one God: The Father acts inseparably with the Son and the Holy Spirit in one single operation. Then he adds that there is in man "something similar *(simile quiddam),*" even though in no way comparable to God the Trinity, something where one can in a certain way grasp the *unity of action* that Catholic faith recognizes in God the Trinity: It is the image of God that consists of memory, understanding, and will. Recalling once more the dissimilarity between the created image and God the Trinity, St. Augustine concludes by explaining that he wanted to employ the image of the creature,

> so that they [the "Arian" heretics], if they can do it, might understand that what we say about the Father, the Son and the Holy Spirit *is not absurd,* namely that they accomplish their works inseparably.[47]

Recourse to the similitude of this image thus aims at a double end (at least). On the one hand, it seeks to nourish the *understanding of the faith* for Christians who can grasp such explanations. On the other hand, it makes it possible to manifest the *plausibility of the faith* to unbelievers: The Trinitarian faith does not appear impossible to reason; it is not absurd. This second point is certainly not central in the *De Trinitate.* Heretical teachings are often mentioned, but St. Augustine wants to lead his inquiry "in the peace of the Catholic faith, with peaceful study."[48] This aspect is often developed in other works. He explains, for example, in connection with the heretics, in his *Homilies on St. John*:

> For inasmuch as they have not understood how the divinity of Christ is set forth to our acceptance, they have concluded according to their will. And by not discerning aright, they have brought in most troublesome questions *(quaestiones molestissimas)* upon Catholic believers;

---

46 Cf. ibid. XIV,1,3: "It is one thing merely to know what a man must believe in order to gain the happy life which is nothing if it is not eternal, but another thing to know how this may help the godly, and be defended against the godless, which the Apostle seems to call by the proper name of knowledge (scientia)."

47 *Contra sermonem Arrianorum* 16, (*Corpus Scriptorum Ecclesiasticorum Latinorum* 92, 78): "Sed ideo tantum hoc commemorandum putavi, ut etiam de ipsa creatura aliquid adhiberem, *unde isti, si possunt, intellegant, quam non sit absurdum, quod de Patre et Filio et Spiritu Sancto dicimus, inseparabilia fieri ab omnibus opera non solum ad omnes, verum etiam ad singulos pertinentia.*"

48 *De Trinitate* II,9,16: "in pace catholica pacifico studio requiramus."

> and the hearts of believers began to be disturbed and to waver *(exagitari et fluctuare)*. Then immediately it became a necessity for spiritual men, who had not only read in the Gospel anything respecting the divinity of our Lord Jesus Christ, but had also understood it *(etiam intellexerant)*, to [. . .] fight in most open conflict for the divinity of Christ against false and deceitful teachers; lest, while they were silent, others might perish.[49]

The problem posed by the heretics is not only voluntary (refusal of the faith) but also intellectual. In the *De Trinitate*, Augustine explains for instance that Eunomius of Cyzicus (whom heresiology labeled as an Anomoian) *could not grasp* and *did not want to believe*,[50] since his heresy was tied to a difficulty of an intellectual order. Thus to defend the faith against heresies, one must have an *understanding* of this faith. Such a task is demanded of spiritual men in order to protect the faith of those who are weaker and to show the plausibility of the Catholic faith to those who do not share it.

Knowing "a Little Bit"

St. Augustine constantly recalls that the mystery of God is incomprehensible. The famous formulas of his sermons are well-known: "If you have grasped, it is not God; if you were able to understand, then you have understood something else in God's place."[51] The *De Trinitate* is no exception. God the Trinity cannot be "understood,"[52] he cannot be spoken (he is ineffable),[53] he cannot be explained,[54] his mystery is not "grasped,"[55] we do not know him.[56] In this domain more than in any other, one must exclude all presumption *(praesumptio)*.[57]

---

49 *Tractatus in Iohannis Evangelium* XXXVI,6. Here it is a matter of the unity of substance of Christ with his Father.

50 *De Trinitate* XV,20,38: "Qui cum non potuisset intelligere, nec credere voluisset."

51 *Sermo* 52,6,16 (PL 38, 360): "Si cepisti, non est Deus: si comprehendere potuisti, aliud pro Deo comprehendisti." Here Augustine makes this affirmation before presenting the image of God in man. Cf. *Sermo* 117,3,5 (PL 38, 663), in connection with the divine Word: "Et Deus erat Verbum. De Deo loquimur, quid mirum si non comprehendis ? Si enim comprehendis, non est Deus. Sit pia confessio ignorantiae magis quam temeraria professio scientiae."

52 See, for example, *De Trinitate* XV,7,13.

53 See, for example, ibid. VII,4,7; XV,23,43.

54 See, for example, ibid. XV,27,50. Cf. *Sermo* 52,9,21 (PL 38, 363–64): "Non possum dicere, non possum explicare."

55 Ibid. XV,27,49: "non capitur"; cf. ibid. VIII,1,2: "non potest intueri."

56 See, for example, ibid. VIII,5,8.

57 See, for example, ibid. II,1, Prooemium; X,1,1.

When St. Augustine evokes the light that the study of the image of God can offer, and when he treats our human knowledge of the mystery, he speaks of a very limited knowledge: knowing "inasmuch as we can *(quantum possumus)*,"[58] "as far as human weakness is able,"[59] "after our limited manner,"[60] "as much as God the Trinity allows,"[61] "in some way."[62] Among the words that Augustine uses to qualify the knowledge that we can have of the Trinitarian mystery, in particular to signify the imperfection of the knowledge offered by an image, one of the most characteristic is the adverb *utcumque* (in whatever manner, in some fashion, to some extent).[63] This vocabulary will be abundantly repeated by St. Thomas. Speculative reflection does not give comprehension of God the Trinity, but it makes it possible to *insinuate* his mystery (*insinuare*: to make manifest, often with the meaning of inserting by indirect or subtle means, teaching in a skillful way, giving an idea of something).[64] This indirect knowledge of the Trinity through similitudes and this image, which insinuates in some way the mystery of God the Trinity for our understanding, constitutes a knowledge "through a mirror in an enigma" *(per speculum in aenigmate)*, according to the words of St. Paul (1 Cor 13:12).[65]

In every case (and not only at the end of Book XV of the *De Trinitate*), Augustine emphasizes the radical *dissimilitude* of this created image with respect to the uncreated Trinity. In the resemblance, one must also see the great dissimilarity.[66] Therefore it is never a matter of "comparing"

58 See, for example, ibid. I,2,4; cf. VIII,5,8: "quantum datur."

59 See, for example, ibid. II,1, Prooemium: "pro captu infirmitatis humanae"; VII,4,9; IX,1,1; IX,2,2; XIII,20,26; XV,1,1; XV,20,39.

60 See, for example, ibid. III,11,21: "pro modulo nostro"; XIII,20,26: "pro nostro modulo"; and so on.

61 See, for example, ibid. VIII,2,3.

62 See, for example, ibid. XV,6,9: "aliquo modo"; XV,9,16: "quomodocumque"; XV,21,40: "quantulumcumque." Cf. XV,21,40; XV,22,44; and so on.

63 See, for example, ibid. IX,1,1; IX,12,17 ("in mente humana utcumque investigare conamur"); XI,7,11; XV,3,5 ("cernebamus utcumque"); XV,11,20 ("hominis verbum, per cujus similitudinem sicut in aenigmate videatur utcumque Dei Verbum"); XV,14,24 ("verbum nostrum [. . .] utcumque simile est [. . .], utcumque illi simile"); XV,24,44; XV,27,49 ("per intelligentiam utcumque cernandam"); and so on. This vocabulary occurs as well in other works of St. Augustine. See, for example, *Contra Faustum* 22,14: "Eligit doctrina sapientiae per quaslibet corporeas imagines et similitudines utcumque cogitanda insinuare divina."

64 See, for example, *De Trinitate* XI,5,9 ("personam Spiritus insinuare"); XI,7,11; XIV,6,8; XV,17,27; XV,27,50 ("nativitatis et processionis insinuari distantiam"). Cf. VI,10,11 ("insinuare propria"); cf. II,11,20; VII,3,5; VIII,4,7; XI,1,1.

65 See, for example, ibid. XIII,20,26; XIV,17,23; XV,8,14; XV,9,15–16; XV,11,20; XV,20,39; XV,22,44; and so on.

66 See, for example, ibid. XV,20,39: "magnam dissimilitudinem"; XV,23,43: "magna disparitas."

the creature with God.[67] Augustine takes care to note in detail the dissimilarities of the image with respect to God the Trinity.[68] He rules out the possibility of identifying the Father with one's memory, the Son with one's understanding, and the Spirit with one's love.[69] The image allows a glimpse of the relations and the unity of the Trinity, by analogy, but without identification of one element of this image with a certain divine Person (the same goes for St. Thomas). These elements of criticism are integrated into the knowledge that we can have of God: "For it is not a small part of knowledge [. . .] to able to know what he is not *(quid non sit)*."[70]

Exercitatio

The use of Trinitarian similitudes, in their function of understanding the faith (and of the defense of the faith against errors), is presented in St. Augustine as an "exercise of the mind." This theme belongs to the pedagogical culture *(paideia)* of antiquity. It is present in many philosophical currents (Stoicism and Epicureanism, neo-Platonism) that conceive philosophy as a "spiritual exercise."[71] In spite of obvious differences, the elevation of the spirit proposed by St. Augustine presents certain likenesses to the spiritual exercises required by Plotinus to lift oneself up to a grasp of the One.[72] For Augustine, the musical, literary, and philosophical disciplines have as their end to lift the spirit from corporeal things toward incorporeal realities; they "prepare" the soul for the contemplation of eternal truth. In his *De quantitate animae*, for example, Augustine explains that the study of the liberal arts not only supplies reason with arguments but also "exercises the spirit to render it capable of perceiving subtler realities" *(nam et exercet animum ad subtiliora cernenda)*. Such study prevents the spirit from being dazzled by their light and slipping back into darkness, finding itself incapable of contemplating them face to face.[73] H.-I. Marrou has

67 Sermo 52,19 (PL 38, 362): "dissimilem rem dico. Nemo dicat: Ecce quod comparavit Deo." *Contra sermonem Arrianorum* 16 (*Corpus Scriptorum Ecclesiasticorum Latinorum* 92, 76): "Est in homine simile quiddam, quamvis nequaquam illius trinitatis, quae Deus est, excellentiae comparandum."

68 See, for example, *De Trinitate* XV,13,22-XV,16,26; XV,22,42-XV,23,43. Cf. *De civitate Dei* XI,26.

69 *De Trinitate* XV,7,12; cf. XV,17,28.

70 Ibid. VIII,2,3; cf. *De ordine* II,16,44: "[. . .] De summo illo Deo, qui scitur melius nesciendo."

71 See Pierre Hadot's basic study: *Exercices spirituels et philosophie antique* (Paris: Études Augustiniennes, 1981); idem, *Qu'est-ce que la philosophie antique?* (Paris: Gallimard, 1995), 276–333: "Les exercices spirituels."

72 Concerning Plotinus, see Pierre Hadot's explanations in Plotin, *Traité* 9 (VI,9), Introduction, Traduction, Commentaire et notes par Pierre Hadot (Paris: Cerf, 1994), 45 and 139–42.

73 *De quantitate animae* 15,25 (PL 32, 1049).

demonstrated the central place this exercise has in the thought and practice of St. Augustine. Before being able to contemplate the truth, the soul must become accustomed to its light through a preparatory training, a sort of spiritual gymnastics. The *exercitatio* introduces the soul to the climate of supra-sensible realities and causes it to blossom there little by little. This aspect is omnipresent in St. Augustine. To be able to contemplate the truth, the soul needs an *exercitatio*, a conditioning of the spirit that renders it capable of looking at the light.[74]

So one discovers that the interminable detours, repetitions, and digressions of the *De Trinitate* are on purpose and are part of Augustine's deliberate intention:[75] to exercise the spirit of his reader, to lead it to the ascension toward God the Trinity by sharpening the tip of his soul *(acies mentis)*. This objective is recalled each time Augustine glances retrospectively at the preceding books.[76] It is formulated very clearly, for instance, at the beginning of Book XV: "We wanted to train the reader *(exercere lectorem)* in the things that were made, so that he might know Him by whom they were made."[77] In this Christian setting, the spiritual exercise takes on a specific aspect.[78] It is performed on the foundation of revelation, through divine grace, in the adherence of faith to the Triune God.

St. Augustine recalls constantly that God cannot be measured by visible and mortal things. Therefore in order to grasp God to some extent, man needs a "purification of mind,"[79] *both moral and intellectual,* because only purified minds *(purgatissimae mentes)* can glimpse God.[80] The source of this purification that renders the human spirit capable of contemplating

---

74 Henri-Irénée Marrou, *Saint Augustin et la fin de la culture antique* (Paris: De Boccard, 1983), 299–327: "Exercitatio animi." This exercitatio is a training that disposes the believer's mind to the contemplation of God's truth. One finds a great number of references here to the works of Augustine as well as enlightening explanations. See Basil Studer, *Augustins De Trinitate: Eine Einführung* (Paderborn: Schöhningh, 2005), 59–84; cf. my review in *Freiburger Zeitschrift für Philosophie und Theologie* 52 (2005): 782–85.

75 H.-I. Marrou, *Saint Augustin,* 319–20. On the Augustinian concept of Trinitarian theology as a spiritual exercise, see Basil Studer, *Mysterium caritatis,* 291–310. The author is wrong, however, in opposing St. Thomas to St. Augustine on this point, cf. 308–9.

76 See, in particular, *De Trinitate* XIII,20,26; XV,1,1; XV,3,5; XV,6,10. Cf. XV,27,49.

77 Ibid. XV,1,1.

78 On this theme of *exercitatio* in the Fathers of the Church, see Basil Studer, *Schola Christiana: Die Theologie zwischen Nizäa (325) und Chalzedon (451)* (Paderborn: Schöningh, 1998), 16–19.

79 *De Trinitate* I,1,3; IV,18,24.

80 Ibid. I,2,4.

eternal realities is *faith*[81] and charity that faith enlivens.[82] Along with faith, Augustine also notes the purificatory role of prayer (purification of desire), virtuous action, and abstention from sin, which is necessary in order to grasp the mystery of God.[83]

Augustine emphasizes in particular that in order to glimpse God, the spirit must purify itself of corporeal representations and "phantasmata."[84] The spirit must not stop at created images but must rise to what the created realities "insinuate."[85] This is precisely the usefulness of the study of creatures, and the goal of the exercise. The *exercitatio* proposed by Augustine is an *ascension (ascendere, erigere mentis intentionem, superius)* toward God from the image that is inferior and unequal to him,[86] and it is at the same time a gradual movement *toward the interior (introrsus tendere).*[87] From these corporeal realities and sensible perception, Augustine invites his reader to turn toward the spiritual nature of man, toward the soul itself and its grasp of incorporeal realities, in a manner ever more interior *(modo interiore),* in order to rise toward the divine Trinity.[88] The exercise of the spirit is "a gradual ascension toward the interior,"[89] in other words an *elevation* from inferior realities toward superior realities and a *penetration* from exterior realities toward interior realities.[90] One enters and one rises in a gradual manner by degrees *(gradatim).*[91] Such is the way characteristic of Augustine: "Pull back into yourself *(in teipsum redi)* [. . .] and transcend yourself."[92]

The pedagogical intention of this exercise is manifest: By considering the image inferior to God, knowledge starts with what is "more familiar"

---

81 Ibid. IV,18,24; IV,19,25; XV,24,44.

82 Ibid. VIII,4,6: "Nisi per fidem [Deus] diligatur, non poterit cor mundari."

83 Ibid. IV,21,31.

84 Ibid. VII,6,11–12.

85 Ibid. VIII,4,7.

86 Ibid. VIII,10,14; X,12,19 (conclusion of Book X); XI,7,11; XV,6,10.

87 Ibid. XI,11,18.

88 Ibid. VIII,1,1; XI,1,1; XIII,20,26.

89 Ibid. XII,8,13: "Ascendentibus itaque introrsus quibusdam gradibus." On the gradual (gradatim) aspect, see ibid. XIII,20,26 (conclusion of Book XIII); cf. XV,2,3.

90 Ibid. XIV,3,5: "Nempe ab inferioribus ad superiora ascendentes, vel ab exterioribus ad interiora ingredientes." This is the way of Books XI to XIV: exterior man, trinity of perception and memory, interior man, knowledge of temporal realities, then wisdom and contemplation of eternal realities.

91 The gradation of beings created by God is detailed elsewhere, for example, in *De civitate Dei* XI,16: living creatures, sensate, intellectual, immortal.

92 *De vera religione* XXXIX,72; cf. *De civitate Dei* XI,28 (about the image of God): "Ad nosmetipsos reversi surgamus ad illum"; *Tractatus in Iohannis Evangelium* XX,11: "Transcende et corpus, et sape animum; transcende et animum, et sape Deum."

(familiarius) and easier *(facilius)* for us, in order to direct *utcumque* the spirit's gaze toward what is above us and more difficult to grasp.[93] This movement is not linear; rather Augustine works a constant back-and-forth meant to render the spirit's tip gradually "better exercised" *(exercitatius)* in order to grasp the Trinitarian mystery.[94]

This *exercitatio* concerns not only the similitude of the image. It is applied, in a more general manner, to the reading of Holy Scripture concerning God the Trinity and Christ. Augustine notes, for example, that by showing us that the Holy Spirit is the Spirit common to the Father and the Son, Scripture suggests *(insinuat)* to us the Charity by which the Father and the Son love each other mutually: "In order to exercise us *(ut nos exerceret sermo divinus)*, the divine Word has caused us to inquire with greater zeal, not into those things that lie openly at hand, but into those that are to be searched out in the depths, and brought to light from the depths."[95] Augustine often proposes the same method of *exercitatio*, of purification and elevation of spirit, in his homilies and in his reading of Scripture.[96] With his clear words, Christ has nourished the small and the great; with his more difficult words, he has "exercised" the spirit of those who are capable of it, in order to raise their understanding toward the contemplation of truth.[97]

Augustine clearly rejects all esotericism: Scripture gives everyone the necessary nourishment. Nevertheless he calls "spiritual" Christians to exercise, in order to understand the words of Christ more profoundly, in order to receive not only "milk" but also the "solid food" of doctrine (cf. 1 Cor 3:1–3). Believers thus progress in understanding their faith.[98] This progress fulfills the very will of God, who calls men to see him: God does not want us to be nourished by milk only; rather he wants us to be able to take solid food also, by understanding.[99] This is an exigency inherent in faith, the characteristic of an "adult" faith that strives to know. And for this reason,

93 *De Trinitate* IX,2,1; IX,12,17 (love is not generated); XI,1,1 (study of the exterior man); XI,7,11; XIII,20,26 (conclusion of Book XIII); XV,6,10. Cf. *Sermo* 52,5,15.

94 See, for example, *De Trinitate* IX,12,17; XV,3,5; XI,7,11.

95 Ibid. XV,17,27.

96 See, for example, *Tractatus in Iohannis Evangelium* XVIII,11.

97 See, for example, ibid. XVIII,1.

98 See the numerous texts of St. Augustine indicated by Marie-François Berrouard in St. Augustin, *Homélies sur l'évangile de saint Jean LXXX–CIII* (Paris: Institut d'Études Augustiniennes, 1998), 470–74. The author notes that the qualifier "carnal" in Augustine designates not only practical behavior but also a defect in the inquiry of faith's understanding (p. 473).

99 See the explanations and numerous texts of Augustine indicated by Marie-François Berrouard in St. Augustin, *Homélies sur l'évangile de saint Jean XLIV–LIV* (Paris: Institut d'Études Augustiniennes, 1989), 454–59.

God has permitted heresies.[100] An understanding of the faith protects believers from the false doctrines of the heretics. In fact, those who have a weak and "unexercised" spirit *(inexercitata mente)* are supported by the "milk of faith," but they risk being seduced by the corporeal images of God that the heretics propose. But other believers, accustomed to solid food, have understanding as well, thanks to their "exercised" soul, and they are better able to resist heretical doctrines.[101] In a word, God permits heresies for the exercise *(exercitatio)* and strengthening *(probatio)* of believers in their faith.[102] The Augustinian objective of *exercitatio* thus constitutes the soul of his Trinitarian meditation, carried by the desire to rise toward God with a pure heart, to see God:

> *We see now through a mirror in an enigma, but then it will be face to face* (1 Cor 13:12). So what we have been trying to do is somehow to see Him by whom we were made by means of this image which we ourselves are, as through a mirror. [. . .] *Looking at the glory of the Lord in a mirror, we are being transformed into the same image from glory to glory as by the Spirit of the Lord* (2 Cor 3:18). [. . .] So, we are being changed from form to form, and are passing from a blurred form to a clear one. But even the blurred one is the image of God, and if image then of course glory, in which men were created surpassing the other animals. [. . .] From the glory of faith to the glory by which we shall be like him, because *we shall see him as he is* (1 John 3:2).[103]

In summary, the *exercitatio* refers to the reading of Scripture and to the understanding of the faith, and is tied directly to three principal themes. The first is the *inseparable operation* of the three persons, with a stress on the *incomprehensibility* of the Triune God. Orthodox Trinitarian faith appears especially in the affirmation of the inseparable operation of the Trinity.[104] The analysis of the image of God serves to show how we can grasp the inseparable activity of the Father, the Son, and the Holy Spirit, that is, the unity without confusion of the Trinity. The second theme is that of the *simplicity* and *immateriality* of the divine Trinity. Attributing to the divine Trinity what belongs to creatures but not to God would constitute a

---

100 *Tractatus in Iohannis Evangelium* XXXVI,6. See the texts indicated by Marie-François Berrouard in St. Augustin, *Homélies sur l'évangile de saint Jean XXXIV–XLIII* (Paris: Institut d'Études Augustiniennes, 1988), 465–67.

101 *Tractatus in Iohannis Evangelium* XCVIII,4.

102 St. Augustine, *Sermon Morin Guelferbytanus 33*, in *Patrologiae cursus completus, Series Latina, Supplementum*, Volumen II**, ed. Adalbert Hamman (Paris: Garnier, 1960), 650–51.

103 *De Trinitate* XV,8,14.

104 Cf. ibid. I,5,8. This theme is omnipresent in Augustine's Trinitarian thought.

"sacrilegious error."[105] Thirdly, the exercise is tied directly to a process of *purification* of the mind that is indispensable to grasping the truth of God. In every case, *exercitatio* is based on faith; moreover, it is not limited to an intellectual purification, but it implies a moral purification as well.

2. St. Thomas Aquinas: *Ad Fidelium Exercitium et Solatium*

In the explanations that follow, the expression "speculative theology" will designate the doctrine, ordered conceptually, by which the theologian seeks to manifest the faith (in other words, to *render it more manifest*) to the understanding of believers by proposing "reasons." The meaning of such reasons and the task of speculative theology are very well expressed in a celebrated *Quodlibet* in which Thomas explains that if the master or professor is content to rest his case on "authorities" (the texts that are authoritative within theology), his audience will doubtless know what is true and what is false, but they will not have any idea what the truth proposed to them means:

> So it is necessary to rest one's case on reasons which seek out the roots of the truth and which enable people to see how what one proposes is true *(oportet rationibus inniti investigantibus veritatis radicem, et facientibus scire quo modo sit verum quod dicitur)*. Unless one does this, if the master's response is based purely on authorities, the listener will know that things are so, but he will have achieved neither knowledge nor understanding and will go away with an empty head.[106]

The objective here is an understanding of the faith. It is not a matter of proving the faith, but of grasping to some extent what one believes—in other words, to help believers to enter into a better understanding of what they believe by showing *how (quo modo)* what the faith proposes is true.[107] Let us add that this objective does not belong exclusively to synthetic works like the *Summa theologiae*; one finds it in St. Thomas's biblical commentaries as well. Since the end of a Thomistic reading of Scripture is to manifest the truth of revelation to the minds of believers, speculative doctrine fully takes part in biblical exegesis.[108]

---

105 Ibid. IX,1,1.

106 St. Thomas, *Quodlibet* IV, q. 9, a. 3. See Jean-Pierre Torrell, "Le savoir théologique chez S. Thomas," *Revue Thomiste* 96 (1996): 355–96.

107 Ibid.: "Ad instruendum auditores ut inducantur ad intellectum veritatis quam credunt."

108 See G. Emery, *Trinity in Aquinas,* 271–319: "Biblical Exegesis and the Speculative Doctrine of the Trinity in St. Thomas Aquinas's Commentary on Saint John." The terms "contemplative" and "speculative" mean practically the same thing and

Speculative Trinitarian Theology: Understanding the Faith

St. Thomas's Trinitarian theology is characterized by a very clear rejection of all rationalism. St. Thomas rules out with great determination those "necessary reasons" by which theologians of his time attempted to show the necessity of the Trinity for the believer exercising reason.[109] In the domain of truths belonging exclusively to the faith, the speculative reasons advanced by theologians do not have philosophical demonstrative force; rather they are "approximations," "adaptations," or "probable arguments" *(rationes verisimiles, verisimilitudines).*[110] St. Thomas explains that the reasons advanced in Trinitarian theology (procession by mode of intellect and will, analogy of the word and love) are "fitting arguments" seeking to show the coherence and intelligibility of the faith, and also to eschew errors contrary to the faith.[111] When St. Thomas discloses the intelligibility of the faith through "likely arguments," he shows—without *demonstrating* the faith—that the arguments of the heretics (Arianism, Sabellianism), and the arguments of those who reject the Trinity, do not have the force of necessity: He does this by indicating a different approach that establishes an alternative. This is the function of the "comparisons" *(similitudines, verisimilitudines)* or of "likely reasons" *(rationes verisimiles)*, that is, the analogies that allow one to give an account of faith in three divine Persons—chiefly, the Augustinian analogy of the word and love. We will return to this topic further on. For the moment, let us keep in mind that in the domain of Trinitarian faith, some assertions are drawn from the principles of the faith, that is, from Holy Scripture, while others constitute fitting arguments, "persuasions or probable arguments which show that *what the faith proposes is not impossible.*"[112] We encounter here the explanations of St. Augustine.[113]

---

designate the same reality (*speculativus* is used more often in the treatises that are inspired by Aristotelianism, whereas the word *contemplativus* appears more frequently in the treatises drawing on Christian sources); cf. Servais Pinckaers, "Recherche de la signification véritable du terme *spéculatif*," *Nouvelle Revue Théologique* 81 (1959): 673–95.

109 See Gilles Emery, *La théologie trinitaire de saint Thomas d'Aquin* (Paris: Cerf, 2004), 34–48. For a shorter account: G. Emery, *Trinity in Aquinas,* 23–25.

110 I *Sent.*, dist. 3, q. 1, a. 4, ad 3 *(adaptationes quaedam)*; *SCG* I, chs. 8–9.

111 *ST* I, q. 32, a. 1, ad 2: "Inducitur ratio quae non sufficienter probat radicem, sed quae radici iam positae ostendat congruere consequens effectus; [. . .] non tamen ratio haec est sufficienter probans [. . .]. Secundo modo se habet ratio quae inducitur ad manifestationem Trinitatis: quia scilicet, Trinitate posita, congruunt huiusmodi rationes."

112 Ibid. II–II, q. 1, a. 5, ad 2: "Rationes quae inducuntur ad probandum ea quae sunt fidei non sunt demonstrativae, sed persuasiones quaedam manifestantes non esse impossibile quod in fide proponitur."

113 See footnote 47 above: "quam non sit absurdum."

The Incomprehensibility of the Trinity and the Insufficiency of Reasons

St. Thomas constantly rules out the idea that the mystery of God can be "understood" *(comprehendere)* by a created intellect: No creature can know God in all his profundity as far as he is knowable.[114] If a created intellect were to "comprehend" God, this would signify that God does not exceed the limits of the created intellect:[115] This is "impossible," St. Thomas adds, in terms that directly evoke St. Augustine.[116] The mystery of the Father and of the Son remains incomprehensible for us.[117] The generation of the Word is incomprehensible, as is the mode of this generation;[118] so is the procession of the Holy Spirit.[119] As for the distinction of the generation of the Word from the procession of the Holy Spirit, which occupies a central place in St. Thomas's Trinitarian reflection as in St. Augustine's, it also remains incomprehensible: St. Thomas says this with the words of St. Augustine, handed on by Peter Lombard.[120] Even the works of the Trinity (the vestige and image of the Trinity) that lead us to a certain knowledge of the mystery remain incomprehensible for us.[121] The result of this is that every approach to the mystery of the Trinity will have to be carried out with humility, with neither the intention nor the pretension of comprehending *(modeste et reverenter absque comprehendi praesumptione)*.[122] The theological inquiry of understanding God the Trinity must therefore rule out every "presumption" *(praesumptio)*.[123] St. Thomas explains this approach of the believer in St. Augustine's terms: "To reach God in some way with the mind is a great happiness; but to comprehend him is impossible."[124]

---

114 *ST* I, q. 12, a. 7.

115 *SCG* III, ch. 55 (#232).

116 See footnote 51 above.

117 *In Ioannem* 1:18 (#218); *In Ioannem* 10:15 (#1414); and so on.

118 *In Ioannem* 1:1 (#31); *SCG* IV, ch. 13 (#3495); *In Matthaeum* 1:1 (#15): "Quia etsi aliquo modo dicimus Filium genitum, modum tamen quo gignitur, nec homo, nec angelus potest comprehendere."

119 I *Sent.*, dist. 13, divisio textus.

120 Ibid.; cf. Peter Lombard, *Sententiae*, Book I, dist. 13, ch. 3 (Petrus Lombardus, *Sententiae in IV libris distinctae*, vol. I/2 [Grottaferratta: Editiones Collegii S. Bonaventurae, 1971], 123); Augustine, *Contra Maximinum* II, ch. 14,1 (PL 42, 770).

121 I *Sent.*, dist. 3, q. 2, a. 1, arg. 1 and ad 1.

122 *De potentia*, q. 9, a. 5; cf. *SCG* IV, ch. 1 (#3348); *Super Boetium de Trinitate*, q. 2, a. 1.

123 *Super Boetium de Trinitate*, q. 2, a. 1. Thomas notes three forms of presumption: pretending to comprehend, placing reason before faith (wanting to know in order to believe), and wanting to surpass the limited mode of human knowledge.

124 *In Ioannem* 1:5 (#102); St. Augustine, *Sermo* 117,3,5 (PL 38, 663). See St. Thomas, *ST* I, q. 12, a. 7; *ST* I–II, q. 4, a. 3, arg. 1; *De potentia*, q. 7, a. 1, arg. 2.

In addition, Thomas constantly recalls the "deficiencies" of all our human representations of God. Since God is incomprehensible and transcendent, he cannot be represented by any adequate similitude.[125]

> The realities of the faith are proposed to the understanding of believers not in themselves, but through certain words which *do not suffice* to express them, and through certain similitudes which *do not suffice* to represent them; that is why it is said that one knows them *through a mirror in an enigma.*[126]

The reasons adduced by the theologian, like the similitudes that Scripture uses to signify the Trinitarian mystery, will be deficient because no creature can adequately represent the transcendent perfection of God. Following Augustine, Thomas adds that the image of God *(imago Dei)* does not escape this deficiency: "Similitudo Trinitatis relucens in anima est omnino imperfecta et deficiens."[127] Therefore there is no *ratio sufficiens*—not even the image of the Trinity—for disclosing the Trinitarian faith.[128] St. Thomas explains this with the greatest clarity: "Of the unity of the divine essence and the distinction of the divine persons, one finds no sufficient similitude in created things."[129] The similitudes are fitting only *secundum aliquid*, by a sort of "conjecture," in the measure to which they participate in God, in a deficient manner.[130] The intimate mystery of God remains hidden.[131] It follows that our knowledge of God, in faith, is a knowledge *per speculum*, a knowledge through a mirror in an enigma (1 Cor 13:12), which St. Thomas explains with the words of St. Augustine.[132]

Again following Augustine, Thomas often uses the adverb *utcumque* to signify the limits of our knowledge of the mystery of God the Trinity: *utcumque mente capere, utcumque concipere, or utcumque accipi* (to grasp as

125 *ST* I–II, q. 102, a. 4, ad 6.

126 III *Sent.*, dist. 24, q. 1, a. 2, qla 3, corp.

127 I *Sent.*, dist. 3, q. 1, a. 4, ad 2; cf. *ST* I, q. 56, a. 3: "Nulla similitudo creata est sufficiens ad repraesentandum divinam essentiam. Unde magis ista cognitio tenet se cum speculari." See, for example, specification of the differences between the divine Word and a created word in *De rationibus fidei* (ch. 3), where one encounters Augustine's explanations.

128 *ST* I, q. 32, a. 1, ad 2; I *Sent.*, dist. 10, q. 1, a. 1; *De potentia*, q. 8, a. 1, ad 12. Cf. *SCG* I, ch. 3 (#18); *De potentia*, q. 8, a. 1: "[. . .] ad plenum ad hoc ratio pervenire non possit."

129 *In Dionysii de divinis nominibus,* Prooemium: "Ea de Deo tradidit quae ad unitatem divinae essentiae et distinctionem personarum pertinent. Cuius unitatis et distinctionis sufficiens similitudo in rebus creatis non invenitur."

130 Ibid.

131 *In 1 Cor* 12:13 (#800–1).

132 *ST* I, q. 12, a. 2, sed contra; St. Augustine, *De Trinitate* XV,9,16.

much as the mind can, to conceive in some fashion, to understand as well as possible).[133] The term *utcumque* appears often in the context of the knowledge of God, to avoid all presumption of perfect knowledge and to indicate the function of analogies.[134] In the *Summa contra Gentiles*, the entire doctrine of the Word is found between these expressions, in a sort of inclusion.[135]

Knowing How God the Trinity Is Not

Along with Augustine and Pseudo-Dionysius, St. Thomas maintains that one can know neither what God is *(quid)* nor how God is *(quomodo)*: One can grasp only that God is *(quia est)*, what God is not *(quid non est)*, and how he is not *(quomodo non est)*. These explanations, laid out from the very beginning of the *Summa*,[136] are at the heart of his doctrine of analogy and the divine names.[137] They apply not only to the natural knowledge of God, but also to the knowledge of God through revelation. Revelation lifts our mind to the knowledge of realities unknown to natural reason, but the *mode* of our knowledge remains the same: We know God "through a mirror" by means of creatures.[138] St. Thomas explains this in particular when he treats the generation of the Son or the "speaking" of the Word:

> It is not permitted to scrutinize the mysteries on high with the intention of comprehending them. This appears in what St. Ambrose writes: "One can know *that* he [the Son] is born, but one must not question *how* he is born." Because to question the mode of his birth is to seek to know what his birth is; now, on the subject of divine realities, we can know *that* they are but not *what* they are.[139]

---

133 *SCG* IV, ch. 1 (#3348); ch. 11 (#3468) and ch. 13 (#3496); see ch. 19 (#3557). These formulae refer to the incomprehensibility of the mystery and are linked with the plan to defend faith against errors. For the direct influence of St. Augustine (*De Trinitate* and *Sermons on John*), see St. Thomas's *Catena in Matthaeum* 3:17 (Marietti edition, vol. 1, 55) or the *Catena in Ioannem* 14:26 (vol. 2, 524). See footnote 63 above.

134 See, for example, *SCG* II, ch. 2 (#859); *SCG* III, ch. 49 (#2270) and ch. 113 (#2873); *SCG* IV, ch. 21 (#3575).

135 *SCG* IV, ch. 11 (#3468): "His consideratis, utcumque concipere possumus qualiter sit divina generatio accipienda"; and ch. 13 (#3496): "Haec ergo sunt quae de generatione divina, et de virtute Unigeniti Filii Dei, ex Sacris Scripturis edocti, utcumque concipere possumus."

136 *ST* I, q. 2, prol.

137 Cf. ibid. I, q. 12, a. 12–13.

138 *Super Boetium de Trinitate,* q. 6, a. 3; cf. *ST* I, q. 12, a. 13, ad 1.

139 Ibid., q. 2, a. 1, ad 4: "Non licet hoc modo scrutari superna misteria, ut ad eorum compreensionem intentio habeatur; quod patet ex hoc quod sequitur 'Licet scire quod natus sit, non licet discutere quomodo natus sit': Ille enim modum nativitatis

> Although natural reason is able to succeed in proving that God is intellect, it is not able to discover adequately his mode of understanding. Just as we are able to know *that* God is but not *what* he is, even so we are able to know *that* God understands, but not *how* he understands. Now to understand by conceiving a Word belongs to the mode of understanding: Wherefore reason cannot prove this adequately, but it can form a kind of conjecture by comparison with what takes place in us.[140]

An understanding of the faith can grasp neither what *(quid sit)* the Word in God is nor how *(quomodo)* the Father generates his Word. It can only form a certain conception by "conjecture" from a study of a created word, through a mirror (analogy). To know "what the Word is not" or "how he is not" does not constitute a total ignorance: It definitely concerns a certain knowledge, albeit "confused," founded on the affirmation that there is a Word in God according to the teaching of the faith.[141] We encounter here the explanations of Augustine: "The analogy from our intellect does not establish anything about God conclusively because it is not in the same sense that we speak of intellect in God and in us. And that is why Augustine says that it is by faith that one arrives at knowledge but not vice versa."[142] Thus Thomas refers explicitly to Augustine in order to mark out the limits of the study of the image of God in Trinitarian theology, and to signify the order of understanding the mystery: It is faith that seeks understanding, and not understanding that precedes faith. Placing reason before faith would be a sin: the sin of presumption.[143] These explanations raise a question: What can be the value of a speculative research that makes use of "reasons," and what is the point of the discussion?

---

discutit, qui querit scire quid sit illa nativitas, cum de divinis possimus scire quia sunt, non quid sunt."

140 *De potentia*, q. 8, a. 1, ad 12: "Licet ratio naturalis possit pervenire ad ostendendum quod Deus sit intellectus, modum tamen intelligendi non potest invenire sufficienter. Sicut enim de Deo scire possumus quod est, sed non quid est; ita de Deo scire possumus quod intelligit, sed non quo modo intelligit. Habere autem conceptionem verbi in intelligendo, pertinet ad modum intelligendi: Unde ratio haec sufficienter probare non potest; sed ex eo quod est in nobis aliqualiter per simile coniecturare." The term *conjecturare* is an echo of St. Augustine, *De Trinitate* XV,17,28 *(conjectare)*; XV,21,40 *(conjicere).*

141 Cf. *De potentia*, q. 7, a. 5. Cf. *ST* I, q. 13, a. 10, sed contra; *Super Boetium de Trinitate,* q. 6, a. 3: "De Deo et de aliis substantiis immaterialibus non possemus scire an est nisi sciremus quoquo modo de eis quid est sub quadam confusione."

142 *ST* I, q. 32, a. 1, ad 2. See footnote 18 above.

143 *Super Boetium de Trinitate,* q. 2, a. 1.

Manifesting the Truth of the Faith and Eschewing Errors

It is in exposing his doctrine of relation, person, the Word, and Love that St. Thomas explains the meaning of the analogies that the theologian examines in order to manifest the Trinitarian faith. One of the best explanations is found in the study of *personal plurality* in God:

> The plurality of persons in God belongs to those realities that are held by faith and that natural human reason can neither investigate nor grasp in an adequate manner; but one hopes to grasp it in Heaven, since God will be seen in his essence, when faith will have given way to vision. However, the holy Fathers have been obliged to treat it in a manner developed because of objections raised by those who have contradicted the faith in this matter and in others that pertain also to the faith; they have done it, however, in a modest manner and with respect, without pretending to comprehend. And such a search is not useless, since by it our spirit is elevated to get some glimpse of the truth that suffices for excluding the errors *(nec talis inquisitio est inutilis, cum per eam elevetur animus ad aliquid veritatis capiendum quod sufficiat ad excludendos errores).* This is why St. Hilary explains: *Believing in this,* namely the plurality of persons in God, *set out, advance, persevere. And though I may know that you will not attain the end, still I shall praise you for your progress. He who pursues the infinite with reverent devotion, even though he never attains it, will profit from advancing forward.*[144]

These explanations summarize the purpose of speculative knowledge of the mystery of the Trinity. This is the plan that St. Thomas puts to work in all of his writings: Trinitarian theology is directed toward a *contemplative* end that will also supply Christians with ways to *defend their faith.* The manifestation of truth and the criticism of errors constitute two aspects of one theological enterprise. To avoid errors, it is not enough to adduce scriptural texts; one must show the conformity of the Catholic faith and Scripture, and one must again respond to the arguments that are opposed to the Church's faith. For its part, truth will not be fully disclosed until we have refuted the errors opposing it. The elaboration of a speculative reflection on the Trinity, using analogies and philosophical resources, has therefore a twofold purpose: the contemplation of revealed truth, which in turn enables one to defend the faith against errors. The goal of Trinitarian theology is to show that faith in the Trinity is reasonably conceivable (we can reasonably contemplate the Trinity in faith), and that therefore arguments against Trinitarian faith cannot stand. It is not a matter of proving the faith,

[144] *De potentia,* q. 9, a. 5; St. Hilary of Poitiers, *De Trinitate* II,10 (ed. Pieter Smulders [Brepols: Turnhout, 1979], 48).

but of showing the intelligibility of the faith by using "plausible" or "likely reasons." By giving believers some grasp of the mystery, these "reasons" show that arguments against Trinitarian faith can be answered, and they provide believers with a foretaste of the truth that they hope to contemplate in the beatific vision. It must be clear that the contemplation of the truth is neither limited nor subordinated to the exclusion of errors. Rather, contemplation of the truth *for itself* is the very end (the primary end) of speculative theology, and such a theological purpose involves the critical discussion of errors.

St. Thomas adduces these same explanations when he presents the Trinitarian *relations*.[145] He repeats them when he explains the use of the word *person* in Trinitarian theology.[146] He brings them up again when he proposes his doctrine of immanent *processions*.[147] And he reiterates the same explanations when he seeks to show the *distinction* of the generation of the Son from the procession of the Holy Spirit. In order to avoid the error of Arius, "the holy Fathers had to show that *it is not impossible* for someone to proceed from the Father and yet be consubstantial with him, inasmuch as he receives from him the same nature the Father has."[148] And since Pneumatomachians could not accept that the divine nature was communicated otherwise than by generation (origin of the Son), "it was therefore necessary for our doctors *(doctores nostri)* to show that the divine nature can be communicated by a twofold procession, one being generation or birth *(generatio vel nativitas)* and the other not: *And this is the same as to seek the distinction between the divine processions*."[149] It is precisely in order to find an answer to this question that St. Thomas, following St. Augustine, moves to the consideration of the image of the Trinity in the human soul: Love does not come forth from our mind by being generated or begotten like the Word, but it proceeds in another way.[150] In St. Thomas, as in St. Augustine, the doctrine of the Holy Spirit as Love thus intends to manifest the origin and property of the Holy Spirit in order to account for the Church's faith in his divinity and in his personal distinction from the Son.

---

145 *De potentia*, q. 8, a. 1: "Reliquintur ergo quod oportet dicere, relationes in Deo quasdam res esse: Quod qualiter sit, sequendo sanctorum dicta, investigari oportet, licet ad plenum ad hoc ratio pervenire non possit."

146 *ST* I, q. 29, a. 3, ad 1; *De potentia*, q. 9, a. 4.

147 *ST* I, q. 27, a. 1.

148 *De potentia*, q. 10, a. 2: "Ad cuius erroris destructionem necessarium fuit sanctis patribus manifestare quod non est impossibile esse aliquid procedens a Deo Patre quod sit ei coessentiale, in quantum accipit ab eo eamdem naturam quam Pater habet."

149 Ibid., q. 10, a. 2: "Et hoc est quaerere processionum distinctionem in divinis."

150 Cf. St. Augustine, *De Trinitate* IX,12,17–18.

Along with Augustine, Thomas notes that heresies are partly connected with a thesis in the speculative order. He explains with Augustine, for instance, that the "Arians" (a label applying not only to supporters of Arius but also to later "Homoians" and "Heteroousians") did not want to believe that the Son possesses the same divinity as the Father and *they could not understand it*, their position being motivated not only by a deliberate refusal but also by an intellectual difficulty.[151] To respond to heresies, therefore, one must manifest the plausibility of the orthodox faith by showing that it does not propose anything impossible: Such is the goal of the "reasons" drawn from the analogy of intellect and love. They constitute a contemplation offering to believers the means to defend their faith.

We have already noted above that as far as the Trinity is concerned, Thomas dismisses necessary reasons invoked by other theologians. He does not look to prove the faith but rather to show its intelligibility with speculative reasons, the plausibility of which human thought can recognize (reasons of fittingness). Since the principles of human reason come from God, they cannot be contrary to the faith that is given by God. For this reason arguments opposed to Trinitarian faith "do not have demonstrative force, but are either probable reasons *(rationes probabiles)* or sophisms *(rationes sophisticae)*."[152] Actually, in some cases one can refute arguments against Trinitarian faith by establishing that they are erroneous: Then it is a matter of sophisms. But in other cases one cannot establish directly the intrinsic falsity of the argument:

> Realities pertaining to faith cannot be proved demonstratively; likewise, the falsity of certain statements contrary to faith cannot be demonstrated, but one can show that they are not necessary.[153]

In this last case, one can merely show that the arguments contrary to the faith are only "probable reasons," that is, arguments that, in spite of a certain plausibility from the viewpoint of the philosophical reason, do not necessarily stand. And in order to show this in a comprehensive manner, one must establish an alternative by proposing other "reasons": It is here, as we have already noted, that the Trinitarian analogies come into play. Faith, which surpasses human reason, fulfills our mind without doing it any violence. In these explanations, we will observe the three modes of

---

151 *SCG* IV, ch. 6 (#3387): "Non enim intelligere poterant, nec credere volebant, quod aliqui duo, secundum personam distincti, habeant unam essentiam et naturam." See footnote 50 above.

152 *SCG* I, ch. 7 (#47).

153 *Super Boetium de Trinitate,* q. 2, a. 3: "Sicut enim ea quae sunt fidei non possunt demonstrative probari, ita quaedam contraria eis non possunt demonstrative ostendi esse falsa, sed potest ostendi ea non esse necessaria."

reasoning indicated by St. Thomas: demonstrative, probable, and sophistic arguments. The distinction among these three types of reasoning comes from the first lines of Aristotle's *Topics*,[154] which provide a common element of Scholastic logic.[155] Although "probable reasons" receive a different sense in St. Thomas than in the "dialectical syllogism" of Aristotle, it is easy to notice that St. Thomas uses Aristotelian logical categories in order to clarify his plan as a theologian: The Aristotelian categories are put to use in service of the Augustinian project of understanding the faith.

The Exercise and the Consolation of Believers

The purpose of St. Thomas's Trinitarian theology is what he expresses, in a more general manner, concerning truths that the faith alone can make known to us and that one cannot demonstrate with reasons:

> In order to manifest this kind of truth, one must provide likely, probable reasons *(rationes aliquae verisimiles)* for the exercise and comfort of the faithful *(ad fidelium quidem exercitium et solatium)* and not in order to convince opponents; for the insufficiency of these reasons would rather confirm them in their error if they thought that we adhered to the faith for such weak reasons.[156]

St. Thomas expresses here the task of speculative theology concerning the mystery of the Trinity and of Christ. It is a matter of manifesting *(manifestare)*, in other words, *rendering more manifest to our minds,* the truth of the faith. The means is equally clear: These are probable or plausible reasons and not demonstrations. The addressees are also identified: It concerns believers *(fideles)*. And the end of such an undertaking is expressed by the words *exercitium* and *solatium*. It is not easy to translate *solatium* (or *solacium*) with a single term. This word can mean relief in sorrow or misfortune, solace, comfort, support, (domestic) help, service, consolation, compensation, or even entertainment.[157] In St. Thomas's Latin Bible, the word *solatium* translates the Greek term *paraklèsis* (exhortation, appeal, address, summons, encouragement, intercession, consolation).[158] In the

154 Aristotle, *Topics* I,1 (100a 25–101a 4). I thank Professor Luca Tuninetti who pointed this out to me.

155 See, for example, the division of syllogisms in William of Sherwood, *Introductiones in Logicam,* ed. Hartmut Brands and Christoph Kann (Hamburg: Felix Meiner Verlag, 1995), 78: "Syllogismus alius est demonstrativus, alius dialecticus, alius sophisticus. [. . .] dialecticus vero est ex probabilibus, faciens opinionem."

156 *SCG* I, ch. 9 (#54).

157 See, for instance, St. Thomas, *In Gal* 1:1 (#8); IV *Sent.*, dist. 48, q. 2, a. 1; *ST* I, q. 51, a. 1, arg. 1.

158 See, for instance, 1 Macc 12:9 or Heb 6:18. Cf. St. Thomas, *In Rom* 1:2 (#27) and 7:22 (#585).

natural domain, St. Thomas associates it in particular with the security procured through the possession of temporal goods or financial aid,[159] but also with the support that spouses or friends give each other,[160] or even the enjoyment that entertainment and the theater provide (the *solatium* that the virtue of *eutrapelia* procures).[161] In the domain of grace, he links it in particular to the virtue of hope (hope procures *solatium*),[162] peace, and contemplation,[163] in other words, to "spiritual consolation."[164] The study of the Holy Books is a special source of *solatium* by procuring "a remedy against tribulations."[165] At the beginning of his *Contra Impugnantes*, he notes that the adversaries of mendicant religious life want to deprive mendicants of *spiritualia solatia* by refusing them the right to study and to teach, "so that they can neither resist adversaries nor find the consolation of the Spirit in the Scriptures: That is the trick of the philistines."[166] This last passage suggests well the meaning that one must give to the word *solatium* in the *Summa contra Gentiles* I, ch. 9: The search for "reasons" in order to manifest the faith procures for believers support, remedy, defense, and spiritual consolation by giving them a grasp of the intelligibility of their faith and showing them that this faith resists the objections (heresies and rational arguments) that are posed to it.

As to the word "exercise" *(exercitium)*, it indicates the nature and purpose of the theologian's study. St. Thomas often applies this theme of exercise (*exercitatio* and *exercitium*) to study and teaching sustained by perseverance, training, and frequent practice.[167] The study and teaching of wisdom are counted among the "spiritual exercises" *(spiritualia exerci-*

---

159 IV *Sent.*, dist. 49, q. 4, a. 1, sed contra 2 and ad 3; *Contra Impugnantes*, ch. 6, §6, ad 17 (Leonine edition, vol. 41 A, 104).

160 *In Isaiam* 3:17 and 3:25 (Leonine edition, vol. 28, pp. 29 and 31).

161 *ST* II–II, q. 168, a. 2; a. 3, ad 3.

162 See *SCG* III, ch. 153 (#3252); *De veritate*, q. 17, a. 2, arg. 8; *In Heb* 6:18 (#324).

163 See, for instance, *In Isaiam* 7:14 and 48:22 (Leonine edition, vols. 28, 59, and 200).

164 *In Rom* 15:5 (#1149): "Deus autem patientiae, scilicet dator, Ps. LXX, v. 5: tu es patientia mea, et solatii, idest qui spiritualem consolationem largitur." On the tight link between *solatium* and *consolatio*, see *Contra Impugnantes*, Prol. (Leonine edition, vol. 41 A, 52); *In Isaiam* 1:7 and 6:8 (Leonine edition, vol. 28, pp. 12 and 51); *In Heb* 13:22 (#772).

165 *In 2 Tm* 4:13 (#158).

166 *Contra Impugnantes*, Prol. (Leonine edition, vol. 41 A, 52): "eis subtrahere nituntur spiritualia solatia, corporalia onera imponentes. Primo enim eis pro posse studium et doctrinam auferre conantur, ut sic adversariis resistere non possint nec in Scripturis consolationem Spiritus invenire. Et haec est astutia Philistinorum, I Reg. 13:19."

167 Cf. *ST* III, q. 86, a. 5, ad 3; *De veritate*, q. 24, a. 10; III *Sent.*, dist. 37, q. 1, a. 5, qla 1, arg. 2.

tia) that lead one to know God and to love him.[168] This exercise is comparable to a "school."[169] In the formula "spiritual exercise," the adjective "spiritual" carries a religious sense (seeking knowledge of God in faith)[170] without losing, for all that, its anthropological significance (*spiritual* as distinguished from *manual* or *corporeal*).[171] In various contexts, the theme of exercise is especially tied to difficulties, tribulations, and adversities: Difficulties and tribulations are the occasion of an *exercitium* or *exercitatio* that makes it possible to overcome them. Thus, for instance, Providence uses demons, evildoers, troubles in this life, dangers, and tribulations in general for the *exercitatio* of just men, that is, to make them stronger.[172]

As far as doctrine is concerned, St. Thomas presents exercise as an "elevation" of the spirit that takes place according to a progression. This elevation starts with the "easiest" things in order to reach the "most difficult" things:[173] It begins in the senses, with sensible representations and the imagination, in order to reach intelligible realities.[174] The exercise consists in passing from corporeal realities to spiritual realities, from light things to those that are more arduous, from a simple teaching to a more subtle teaching, from faith to a spiritual understanding of the faith.[175] The theme of exercise also implies (as with Augustine) an order of disciplines

---

168 *SCG* III, ch. 132 (#3047): "studium sapientiae, et doctrina, et alia huiusmodi spiritualia exercitia." Cf. *ST* II–II, q. 122, a. 4, ad 3.

169 St. Thomas explains this in connection with religious life which he considers an exercise for coming to the perfection of charity: "exercitium sive schola perfectionis" (*Quodlibet* IV, q. 12, a. 1, ad 7; cf. ad 9). Cf. *ST* II–II, q. 186, a. 3: "exercitium et disciplina."

170 The expression "spiritual exercise" is applied to study and teaching, to the religious state, and to activities proper to this state (*ST* II–II, q. 189, a. 1; *Contra Impugnantes,* ch. 5, ad 8; Leonine edition, vol. 41 A, 92) and, more generally, to the practice of virtue (*In Eph* 3:14 [#166]; *ST* III, q. 69, a. 3). Voluntary poverty constitutes an "exercise" as well (*ST* II–II, q. 186, a. 3, ad 4).

171 Cf. for example *Contra Impugnantes,* ch. 5, § 3 (Leonine edition, vol. 41 A, 89–90): The works of piety (among which Aquinas counts the study of Holy Scriptures, teaching, and preaching) are distinguished from *corporalis exercitatio, corporale exercitium,* and *labor manuum*; cf. ibid., ad 8: The *exercitia spiritualia* are distinguished from the *opera manualia* (p. 92); cf. *In 1 Tm* 4:8 (#153–62). For the nuances of the vocabulary of "spirituality," see Jean-Pierre Torrell, "*Spiritualitas* chez saint Thomas d'Aquin," *Revue des Sciences Philosophiques et Théologiques* 73 (1989): 575–84.

172 See, for example, *ST* I, q. 64, a. 4; q. 109, a. 4, ad 1 (demons); q. 114, a. 1, arg. 3 and ad 3; *ST* I–II, q. 87, a. 7; *In Matthaeum* 13:29 (#1149); *Catena in Lucam* 8:23 (Marietti edition, vol. 2, 114–15); IV *Sent.,* dist. 46, q. 1, a. 2, qla 3, ad 3 and ad 4. References to these themes are numerous.

173 *ST* II–II, q. 189, a. 1, ad 4: "a facilioribus ad difficiliora."

174 See, for example, ibid. I, q. 1, a. 9, ad 2.

175 Cf. *In Heb* 5:14 (#269–74).

of knowledge,[176] which prepares minds so that they become capable of grasping realities that transcend the senses and the imagination. Three aspects of this exercise of wisdom merit mention on this topic.

Errors and Heresies

In the context of the quest for an understanding of the faith, the theme of exercise appears first of all tightly linked to the challenge posed by heresies. "After the divine truth was manifested, certain errors arose on account of the weakness of human minds. But these errors have exercised *(exercuerunt)* the understanding of believers to search out and grasp the divine truths more attentively *(diligentius)*."[177] The most complete explanations are found in a *reportatio* on the first letter to the Corinthians, in connection with St. Paul's words: "Nam oportet haereses esse" (1 Cor 11:19).[178] Following St. Augustine, St. Thomas explains that heresies take on a double utility *(utilitas)*. First, because of heresies "the holy doctors were more exercised *(magis exercitati)* in order to bring the truth of the faith to light, and their minds were rendered more subtle *(subtiliata)*."[179] "After the heresies, the saints spoke more prudently *(cautius)* of the things of the faith, as Augustine on the subject of grace after the Pelagians, and as Pope Leo on the subject of the Incarnation after Nestorius and Eutyches."[180] The second benefit of heresies is to manifest the constancy of the faithful in the faith *(constantia fidei)* by making those who resist these heresies stronger and more proven *(probati)*.[181] The same goes for philosophical

---

176 *Sententia Ethic.* VI,7 (Leonine edition, vol. 47/2, 358–59): logic, mathematics, natural philosophy, ethics, then the study of wisdom and divine realities.

177 *SCG* IV, ch. 55 (#3939).

178 This text was published among the *Reportationes ineditae Leoninae* in the edition of the works of St. Thomas serving as a basis for the *Index Thomisticus*: S. Thomae Aquinatis, *Opera omnia ut sunt in indice thomistico,* ed. Roberto Busa, vol. 6 (Stuttgart: Frommann, 1980), 367. This text is from the manuscript Padova, Bibliotheca Antoniana 333. Undoubtedly one will have to await the Leonine edition of the Commentary on St. Paul to obtain more details concerning the double recension of the Commentary on 1 Cor.

179 *Reportationes ineditae Leoninae,* 367: "Una est quia sancti doctores ex hoc sunt magis exercitati ad veritatem fidei elucidandam, et eorum ingenia magis subtiliata."

180 Ibid. On this same theme, with the example of St. Augustine, see *Contra errores Graecorum,* prol. (Leonine edition, vol. 40 A, 71).

181 *Reportationes ineditae Leoninae,* 367. The other commentary given by the Marietti edition (#628) indicates St. Thomas's Augustinian sources: *Enchiridion* and *De civitate Dei.* St. Thomas, citing St. Augustine, notes a double utility of heresies here as well: "ad maiorem declarationem veritatis," and "ad manifestandam infirmitatem fidei in his qui recte credunt" (I wonder whether the word "infirmitas" given by the Marietti edition is correct).

errors: These errors are the occasion of an exercise *(exercitium)* that gives rise to a clearer *(limpidius)* grasp of the truth; regarding those who have spoken of the truth superficially, although we do not accept their opinion, they provide us with the occasion of an exercise *(exercitium)* of inquiry into the truth.[182] The same explanations are applied again to events. By exercising his disciples in grasping the parables according to their spiritual sense, Christ leads them to understand that the events *(res gestae)* of the First Covenant are figures *(figurae)* of the New Covenant.[183] This teaching comes in particular from St. Augustine.[184] It makes it possible to clarify the meaning of *exercitium* in the *Summa contra Gentiles* I, ch. 9: The "reasons" adduced by the theologian in order to manifest the faith do not prove the faith but exercise the mind of the believer to better grasp the truth of the faith with prudence and precision, by giving him the occasion to confirm the faith. And thanks to studious men capable of refuting errors, those who possess a simpler faith are confirmed in the faith.[185]

The Obscurities and Figurative Language of the Scriptures

This theme of exercise appears as well, in a great number of reprises, in connection with the difficulties, "obscurities," and figurative language of the Holy Scriptures. This obscure language is useful for two tightly linked reasons: (1) for the exercise of studious men *(ad exercitium studiosorum)*, and (2) to protect revelation from the derision of unbelievers *(contra irrisiones infidelium)*.[186] The divine truth is sometimes given in a "hidden" manner "so that unbelievers might not make a mockery of it and so that the simpler believers will not be lead into error."[187] As to the exercise invoked for the first reason, it concerns "studious" men, that is, readers formed by the doctrinal and spiritual reading of Scripture. This exercise consists in an "elevation of the mind" that leads from created similitudes and obscure

182 *Super Metaphysicam* II, lect. 1 (#287–88): "Inquantum priores errantes circa veritatem posterioribus exercitii occasionem dederunt, ut diligenti discussione habita, veritas limpidius appareret. [. . .] Etiam illis, qui superficialiter locuti sunt ad veritatem investigandam, licet eorum opiniones non sequamur, quia etiam aliquid conferunt nobis. Praestiterunt enim nobis quoddam exercitium circa inquisitionem veritatis."

183 *In Matthaeum* 13:52 (#1206). Here St. Thomas distinguishes the crowds, to which Jesus spoke in parables, and the disciples, "exercised" *(exercitati)* to grasp this teaching in its spiritual sense.

184 Ibid. See the Augustinian texts cited in the *Catena in Matthaeum* 13:52 (Marietti edition, vol. 1, 224).

185 *ST* II–II, q. 10, a. 7.

186 Ibid. I, q. 1, a. 9, ad 2; cf. I *Sent.*, dist. 34, q. 3, a. 2. See Vincent Serverat, "*L'irrisio fidei.* Encore sur Raymond Lulle et Thomas d'Aquin," *Revue Thomiste* 90 (1990): 436–48.

187 I *Sent.*, dist. 34, q. 3, a. 1.

expressions to the grasp of intelligible spiritual realities.[188] Here we are very close to the Augustinian *exercitatio.* The Augustinian inspiration appears explicitly in the *Commentary on St. John* 10:6, where St. Thomas takes up St. Augustine's explanation concerning the words of Christ: "He gives what is plain, for food; what is obscure, for exercise."[189] The ignorance revived by the "proverbs" (figures, parables) of Christ "was useful for the good and the just who tried to grasp them, as an exercise, for giving praise to God; for while they do not understand, they believe and praise the Lord and his wisdom which is so far above them."[190] Other authors are invoked as well to explain this pedagogy of revelation. In his *Catena in Lucam*, for example, St. Thomas reports the explanations of Theophylactus: Christ speaks first of all by means of "similitudes" in order to attract the attention of his listeners *(ut attentiores faceret auditores)* and to exercise them *(exercitare)*, and also so that those who are unworthy *(indigni)* will not be able to grasp the spiritual sense of the obscure words.[191] "The secrets of the faith should not be exposed to unbelievers."[192] Here again St. Thomas invokes a defense of the faith.[193]

The Wise and the Simple

As with St. Augustine, the theme of exercise brings to bear a distinction between the "wise" and the "simple" or the "small". By "wise", one must

---

188 *ST* I, q. 1, a. 9, ad 2: "Ut mentes quibus fit revelatio, non permittat in similitudinibus permanere, sed elevet eas ad cognitionem intelligibilium." Ibid. II–II, q. 1, a. 9, ad 1: "longum studium atque exercitium." This exercise is required in order to be capable of teaching (*In 1 Tm* 4:13 [#171]). Cf. *In Dionysii de divinis nominibus* I, lect. 2 (#65): "In Scripturis exprimuntur nobis intelligibilia per sensibilia, et supersubstantialia per existentia, et incorporalia per corporalia, et simplicia per composita et diversa."

189 St. Augustine, *Tractatus in Evangelium Iohannis* 45,6: "Pascit enim manifestis, exercet obscuris." See the indication of other texts of St. Augustine on the same theme in St. Augustin, *Homélies sur l'Evangile de saint Jean XLIV–LIV,* ed. M.-F. Berrouard (Paris: Études Augustiniennes, 1989), 54. Aquinas cites this text of St. Augustine in his *Catena in Ioannem* 10:6 (Marietti edition, vol. 2, 472); in his Commentary on St. John, he comments on this passage, clarifying that plain food is given to the crowds of believers and that exercise is addressed to the disciples: "Pascit Dominus manifestis, scilicet fideles turbas, exercet obscuris, scilicet discipulos" (*In Ioannem* 10:6 [#1379]).

190 St. Thomas, *In Ioannem* 10:6 (#1380): "Utilis et bonis et justis ad exercitium in Dei laudem quaerentibus: nam dum ea non intelligunt, credunt, glorificant Dominum, et eius sapientiam supra se existentem." Exercise produces a conscience more alive in the faith for the praise of God.

191 *Catena in Lucam* 8:4 (Marietti edition, vol. 2, 110).

192 *De rationibus fidei,* ch. 8.

193 *Super Boetium de Trinitate,* q. 2, a. 4. Cf. Augustine, *De doctrina christiana* IV, ch. 9 (PL 34, 99).

understand believers experienced in reading the Scriptures and in understanding the faith. As to the "simple" or "small," these are believers "still only slightly initiated in the perfect doctrine of the faith."[194] Against all elitism, Thomas explains that the *same reality* of faith must be handed on to the wise and the small, without any difference; nevertheless, the *mode* of this handing on is not identical. Drawing on St. Augustine, he explains that when one proposes the realities of the faith to the small *(parvuli)*, it is not fitting to treat the realities in their difficulties or to explore them to the very bottom.[195] This applies especially to the "mystery of the Trinity" and to the "sacrament of the Incarnation," subjects about which St. Paul hands on "very difficult" *(valde difficilia)* and "arduous" *(ardua)* teachings.[196] The example often developed by St. Thomas is that of the birth of the Word:

> It is easy enough to know by simple faith *(per simplicem fidem est satis facile)* that the *Word became flesh* [Jn 1:14], because this can come into the imagination and in a certain manner into the senses. But to know the *Word* that *was in the beginning with God* [Jn 1:1] surpasses all the senses and can only be grasped by reason, and with numerous difficulties—the greatest difficulties.[197]

Thus there is an order of teaching *(ordo doctrinae)* that corresponds to spiritual progress in the faith: It is the order by which one passes from "easier" things to "more difficult" things.[198] In this way, the believer must first be nourished by "milk"[199] in order to be able to obtain solid food later: One must first receive the nourishment of the "Word made flesh" in order to be able to grow and become capable of receiving the teaching concerning "the Word that was in the beginning with God."[200] The heretics committed the error of modifying this order, in yielding to the presumption of

194 *In 1 Cor* 3:1 (#124): "tamquam parvulis in Christo, id est, parum adhuc introductis in perfectam doctrinam fidei, quae spiritualibus debetur."

195 *In Heb* 5:13 (#270): "Eadem enim utrisque proponenda sunt, sed parvulis proponenda sunt, sed non exponenda nec pertractanda: quia intellectus eorum magis deficeret, quam elevaretur."

196 Ibid.

197 Ibid. (#271); see *Contra doctrinam retrahentium*, ch. 7 (Leonine edition, vol. 41 C, 50); *ST* II–II, q. 189, a. 1, arg. 4.

198 *ST* II–II, q. 189, a. 1, ad 4: "de ordine doctrinae, prout transeundum est a facilioribus ad difficiliora."

199 "Milk," in the symbolic sense, signifies the "teaching for the simple" *(simplicium doctrina)*: *In Isaiam* 60:16 (Leonine edition, vol. 28, 237).

200 *ST* II–II, q. 189, a. 1, ad 4; cf. arg. 4. This interpretation is taken from the Gloss; cf. Peter Lombard (PL 191, 1172). On this subject, one notes a pedagogical priority of the economy (the Word made flesh) with respect to theology (the eternal Word with his Father). See *Contra doctrinam retrahentium*, ch. 7 (Leonine edition, vol. 41 C, 50).

obtaining solid food before the opportune time.[201] Now, spiritual doctrine ("solid food")[202] must be given to each according to his ability and disposition.[203] The realities of the faith must therefore be handed on in a simple manner to the simple and "in a subtler manner for subtler men."[204]

One more clarification must be added. As far as knowledge of the faith is concerned, the "spiritual doctrine" proposed to the *maiores* is not a pure matter of understanding; rather it demands as well a right affectivity and inclination toward God. Under this aspect, sacred doctrine is distinguished from other domains of knowledge. In other sciences, intellectual perfection suffices. But the "doctrine of Sacred Scripture" requires a double perfection, intellectual and affective. It communicates realities that not only are the object of speculation *(speculanda)* but that must be received in charity *(approbanda per affectum)*.[205] St. Thomas clarifies: Theology is not geometry! Such is the condition of welcome to "solid doctrine." It requires that its addressees be accomplished, both in the intellectual order and in the affective order.[206] Thus conceived, Trinitarian theology demands the practice of *prayer* (as the example of Thomas himself shows) by which the soul is purified, elevated toward the spiritual reality of God, and ordered to God by devotion.[207] There is nothing more foreign to Thomas Aquinas than a rationalist conception of theology. These explanations are summarized in an excerpt from Letter 137 of St. Augustine (to Volusian), which St. Thomas cites in the preface of his *Catena in Matthaeum*: Sacred Scripture is accessible to all men *(omnibus accessibilis)*, but its deeper mysteries are penetrable to very few *(paucissimis penetrabilis)*. It invites all not only "to be fed with the truth which is plain," but also to be exercised by the truth that is concealed *(etiam secreta exerceat veritate)*: By these means wayward minds are corrected, weak minds are nourished, and strong minds are filled with joy.[208]

---

201 Ibid.

202 Cf. *In 1 Cor* 3:2 (#125–30).

203 *In Ioannem* 4:32 (#635).

204 *In Matthaeum* 25:15 (#2039): "Apostolus 1 Cor 3, 2: tamquam parvulis in Christo lac potum dedi vobis, non escam. Ideo magis subtilibus magis subtilia dedit."

205 *In Heb* 5:14 (#273). This does not call into question the priority of the speculative dimension of sacred doctrine (cf. *ST* I, q. 1, a. 4). Rather this teaching recalls that the study of sacred doctrine fits into the scheme of the integral organism of the life of faith in the Church.

206 Ibid. (#274). Solid food must be handed on to those, who through their training *(consuetudo)*, have exercised senses *(exercitatos sensus)*, in other words, to the exercised man *(exercitatus)* capable of right judgment.

207 *In Dionysii de divinis nominibus* III (#232–33).

208 *Catena in Matthaeum*, Praefatio (Marietti edition, vol. 1, 8): "Modus enim ipse quo sancta Scriptura contexitur, est omnibus accessibilis, paucissimis penetrabilis [. . .]. Sed invitat omnes humili sermone, quos non solum manifesta pascat, sed etiam

The Image of the Trinity

Thus in Trinitarian theology, the doctrine of image in Thomas has a function similar to that which it has in Augustine. It offers an "exercise" for contemplating the truth, in the manner of a foretaste of the beatific vision, by showing believers an understanding of their faith, making it possible for them to defend the faith against errors. In this context, the study of the Word and Love serves to manifest or "insinuate" the unity and the distinction of the Father, Son, and Holy Spirit, both in their eternal immanence and in the economy of grace.[209]

Like Augustine, Thomas searches out an analogy for grasping to some extent the unity of the divine Trinity, *per speculum,* starting from what is most known to us. Chapter 11 of the fourth Book of the *Summa contra Gentiles,* where Thomas presents his mature doctrine concerning the Word for the first time, shows perfectly well the direction of his approach. He uses the criterion of the intimacy of a procession. The believing mind looks for a mode of emanation in which the term that proceeds is interior to its principle (distinction in unity). Like Augustine, Thomas observes a "gradation" in beings, through which we progress to discover a procession ever "more interior."[210] In inanimate bodies, a procession takes place in an exterior manner; therefore it will not be a suitable aid for grasping the Trinitarian mystery. In the first degree of animate bodies (vegetative, first degree of life), one discovers an emanation that proceeds from the interior; but this procession takes place "toward the exterior," to the point where the term that proceeds (for example, the fruit that proceeds from the tree) is completely separated from its principle; furthermore, Thomas observes that the first principle of such an emanation remains exterior. Above this degree, bodies gifted with a sensate soul (animals) offer an example more suggestive of an interior emanation: This is the analogy of sensible perception, which recalls—with important differences—the first trinity of the exterior man in Augustine (the form of a perceived body is imprinted in the senses, and from there it proceeds into the imagination and the memory). But here again, the principle and the term of the procession are different. Therefore in order to find an example of an intimate procession, one must ascend again to consider the intellect, which constitutes the "highest degree of life." Since it is capable of *reflection,* the intellect (with will and love, which

secreta exerceat veritate, hoc tam in promptis quam in reconditis habens. Sed ne aperta fastidirentur, eadem rursum aperta desiderantur, desiderata quodammodo renovantur, renovata suaviter intimantur. His salubriter et prava corriguntur et parva nutriuntur et magna oblectantur ingenia." Cf. St. Augustine, *Epistola* 137,18 (PL 33, 524).

209 This objective is very clear from the very first question of the Trinitarian treatise of the *Summa theologiae* (*ST* I, q. 27).

210 See footnote 89 above.

are linked to it) will be able to suggest the intimacy between a principle and the term of a procession. But here again Thomas observes a gradation, by "degrees." In the case of the human intellect, the principle of knowledge comes from outside, by means of the senses; above man, the angels offer a better example of a knowledge coming "from inside," but their thought remains different from their being (there is not an identity of substance between the angels' intellectual conception and their being). Therefore it will be necessary to gradually leave behind the conditions proper to creatures in order to glimpse the conditions of a divine procession in which the intimacy is a perfect unity of nature. Thus Thomas observes that "the more elevated the nature, the more intimate to itself what emanates from it *(magis ei est intimum).*"[211] Beginning with an observation of the world, then in the study of the life of the mind and of love, he invites his reader to discover that the more elevated the degree of life, "the more the operation of that life will be contained in intimacy *(magis in intimis continetur).*"[212] The doctrine of the "immanent operation," which constitutes the point of departure of the Trinitarian treatise of the *Summa theologiae,* expresses precisely the *results* of this inquiry in which the mind raises its gaze toward the conditions of superior forms of life, up to God himself.[213]

Such is the function of the analogy of the word and love.[214] It expresses the result of the inquiry by which Thomas *appropriates and extends Augustine's reflection* in an original way. He retains the similitude of the word and love because it makes it possible to glimpse, to some extent, the distinction in unity (unity without confusion), in a manner "less foreign" to the spiritual nature of God: "God is not of a fleshly nature, requiring a woman to copulate with to generate offspring, but he is of a spiritual or intellectual nature, indeed beyond every intellectual nature. So generation should be understood *as it applies to an intellectual nature.*" This is the reason why, "even though our own intellect falls far short of the divine intellect," Aquinas turns the "similitude" of the image of God in the human mind.[215] In a similar context, when Augustine was seeking to show the distinctive property of the Holy Spirit, he explained: "With regard to

211 *SCG* IV, ch. 11 (#3461); cf. #3464: "magis ad intima devenitur."

212 Ibid. IV, ch. 11 (#3464).

213 *ST* I, q. 27, a. 1: "Secundum actionem quae manet in ipso agente, attenditur processio quaedam ad intra: et hoc maxime patet in intellectu, cuius actio, scilicet intelligere, manet in intelligente." Cf. ad 2 ("intima intelligenti"); ad 3: "procedere ut intimum et absque diversitate." See the enlightening explanations given in the *De potentia,* q. 10, a. 1. And the same applies to love; see *SCG* IV, ch. 19; *ST* I, q. 27, aa. 3–5; q. 37.

214 *SCG* IV, ch. 11 and ch. 19. Cf. *ST* I, q. 27, aa. 1–5; q. 37, aa. 1–2. Cf. G. Emery, *La théologie trinitaire de saint Thomas d'Aquin,* 217–31, 270–93, 399–424.

215 *De rationibus fidei,* ch. 3.

the Holy Spirit, I pointed out that nothing in this enigma would seem to be like Him, except our love, or will, or charity."[216] Confronted with the same problem, St. Thomas adds: "If the procession of the word and love does not suffice for inserting the personal distinction, then there could not be any personal distinction in God."[217] In other words, if one doubts that the analogy of the word and love suffices to give an idea of personal distinction in the unity of substance, if one rejects this speculative "reason," then one can well *assert* that God is a Trinity, but one cannot *disclose* the truth of Trinitarian faith, one cannot make the faith *more manifest* to the believer's mind in search of an understanding of the mystery.

Another important point concerning the Thomistic doctrine of image must be added. The analogy of knowledge and love *of the self* must not be opposed to the knowledge and love *of God* by grace. Both aspects come from Augustine. The theme of knowledge and love *of the self* is quite present in the *De Trinitate*,[218] although there it concerns an imperfect image because in this case it is not an "immutable" reality that the souls knows and loves.[219] But this theme possesses the advantage of suggesting the *identity of being* because what the soul knows and what the soul loves is the same reality as the soul itself.[220] This makes it possible to give a certain idea of the *consubstantiality* of the Trinity. And this is precisely the aspect that Thomas retains: When he adopts the analogy of the knowledge and love of the self, it is *under the aspect* that makes possible an account of an essential unity (by generating the Son and spirating the Spirit, the Father *communicates his own nature* to them).[221] But for St. Thomas, who follows St. Augustine expressly, the image of God in man resides *primo et principaliter* in the knowledge and love *of God*, that is, in the participation in the knowledge and love that God has of his own mystery.[222] Knowledge and love of the self constitutes a sec-

216 St. Augustine, *De Trinitate* XV,21,41.

217 St. Thomas, *De potentia*, q. 9, a. 9, ad 7: "Si processio verbi et amoris non sufficit ad distinctionem personalem insinuandam, nulla poterit esse personalis distinctio in divinis."

218 See, for example, *De Trinitate* IX,2,2; IX,5,8; and so on.

219 *De Trinitate* IX,6,9.

220 See, for example, *De Trinitate* IX,2,2: "Amans enim et quod amatur, hoc idem est, quando se ipse amat."

221 See, for example, *SCG* IV, ch. 11 (#3469); *ST* I, q. 37, a. 1: "When someone knows and loves himself, he is present to himself not simply by an entitative identity, but also as the 'object' known in the knower, and loved in the lover." Cf. *De rationibus fidei*, ch. 3: "The word of our intellect can be likened to a concept or offspring, especially when the intellect knows itself, and the concept is a likeness of the intellect coming from its intellectual power, just as a son has a likeness to his father, from whose generative power he comes forth."

222 *ST* I, q. 93, a. 8 (with a quotation of the *De Trinitate* XIV,12,15); cf. a. 4; *De veritate,* q. 10, a. 7.

ondary aspect of this image *(secundario), to the extent* that it prepares for and reflects knowledge and love of God himself, in other words, inasmuch as the mind that knows and loves itself is transported toward God: "Not because the mind reflects on itself absolutely, so as to come to a halt in itself, but so that it can ultimately go on to turn toward God."[223] The sinful man is the image of God in an inferior degree (he remains capable of knowing and loving God), but only the holy man (who knows and loves God according to the image of grace) "represents" God the Trinity to some extent, insofar as God dwells in him.[224] Thomas explains this at greater length in his *De veritate*, with a clear Augustinian accent:

> Within the knowledge through which the soul knows itself, there is an *analogous* representation *(secundum analogiam)* of the uncreated Trinity, in that, as the soul knows itself it engenders of itself a word, and love proceeds from both. Thus the Father, in speaking himself, begets his Word from all eternity, and the Holy Spirit proceeds from both. Whereas, in the knowledge through which the soul knows God, the soul itself is *conformed to God (Deo conformatur)* in the way that any knowing thing is, in some way, assimilated to the known object.[225]

Just as the economic dimension is present in Thomas as well as in Augustine (the Son is the Word by which the Father speaks himself and all things, the Spirit is the Love by which the Father and the Son love each other and communicate their love to creatures and to the Church),[226] so the eschatological dimension of this image is present in both authors. Commenting on 2 Corinthians 3:18 ("We all who with unveiled faces reflect as in a mirror the glory of the Lord, we are transformed into his likeness, from glory to glory, as by the Lord who is Spirit"), Thomas repeats Augustine's profound views verbatim:

> We know the glorious God by the mirror of reason, in which there is an image of God. We behold him when we rise from a consideration of ourselves to some knowledge of God, and we are transformed. For since all knowledge involves the knower's being assimilated to the thing known, it is necessary that those who see be in some way transformed

---

223 *ST* I, q. 93, a. 8.

224 I *Sent.*, dist. 1, q. 2, a. 1, ad 4.

225 *De veritate,* q. 10, a. 7: *secundum analogiam* is distinguished from *secundum conformationem,* the latter being an echo of the Augustinian theme of the mind's *reformatio.*

226 See G. Emery, *Trinity in Aquinas,* 171–75: The doctrine of the Word and Love is not limited to the "immanent Trinity" but accounts as well for the Trinitarian economy of creation and grace.

> into God. If they see perfectly, they are perfectly transformed, as the blessed in heaven by the union of fruition: *When he appears we shall be like him* (1 Jn 3:2); but if we see imperfectly, then we are transformed imperfectly, as here by faith: *Now we see in a mirror dimly* (1 Cor 13:12).[227]

The full knowledge of God through a mirror of an image takes place when the believer rises *(assurgit)* above himself in order to grasp something of the mystery of God *(cognitio aliqua)*. This elevation of faith procures for the believer a conformation to God *(transformatio)* that is a foretaste of the full deification in the beatific vision. This is the mystery that the theologian seeks to give account of. The study of this image is carried by the same desire of elevation, and it is completed by the same transforming knowledge of faith.

3. Conclusion

The purpose of Trinitarian theology for St. Thomas is therefore at one and the same time ambitious and modest. It is ambitious, for Trinitarian theology sets out to show (that is, to make more manifest to our minds) the distinction of the persons in unity. And yet this purpose remains modest: It is a matter of studying in order to grasp but a little. Knowledge of the mystery of God given by revelation is compared to a little drop *(parva stilla)*. And this "little drop" of God's mystery is presented to us in Sacred Scripture in the form of similitudes and words that are at times obscure, "in such a way that only studious men can succeed in understanding a little, while others revere these mysteries as hidden, and unbelievers cannot tear them off."[228] Envisaged in this way, Trinitarian theology is a form of study practiced as an exercise and addressed to believers, in order to elevate their minds to the contemplation of God and to make them search for God who is known by faith and loved by charity. St. Thomas expresses this purpose with the words of St. Hilary of Poitiers in his commentary on Boethius's *De Trinitate*, in the *Summa contra Gentiles*, and in the disputed questions *De potentia*. Here is the intention and the very nature of speculative Trinitarian theology (with a clear mention of the "exercise" carried out by means of inquiry into "reasons"):

---

227 St. Thomas, *In 2 Cor* 3:18 (#114). See footnote 103 above.

228 *SCG* IV, ch. 1 (#3345): "Haec etiam pauca quae nobis revelantur, sub quibusdam similitudinibus et obscuritatibus nobis proponuntur: ut ad ea quomodocumque capienda soli studiosi perveniant, alii vero quasi occulta venerentur, et increduli lacerare non possint." This prologue is placed at the beginning of the study of the mystery of the Trinity and of Christ.

> It is useful for the human mind to exercise itself with such reasons, however weak they are *(utile tamen est ut in huiusmodi rationibus, quantumcumque debilibus, se mens humana exerceat)*, provided there be not presumptuous attempt to comprehend or demonstrate. For the ability to perceive something of the highest realities, if only with feeble, limited understanding, gives the greatest joy [. . .]. In accord with this thought, St. Hilary declares in his book *On the Trinity*, speaking of this sort of truth: *In faith, set out, go forward, persevere. And though I may know that you will not attain the end, still I shall praise you for your progress. He who pursues the infinite with reverent devotion, even though he never attains it, always profits nonetheless from advancing forward. But in penetrating this secret, in plunging into the hidden depth of this birth unlimited* [the generation of the one God begotten by the one unbegotten God], *beware of presumptuously thinking you have attained a full understanding. Know, rather, that this is incomprehensible.*[229]

This exercise is an "elevation of the mind"[230] so as to be made more like God, in an inquiry that tends always "more and more" toward God.[231] We cannot know the essence of God the Trinity, but we can "tend" *(tendere)* toward the mystery above ourselves *(superius)*, through contemplation, in order to know and love him more.[232]

The speculative objective of Thomas Aquinas in Trinitarian theology must not be opposed to the spiritual objective of Augustine. Admittedly there are important differences. Thomas doesn't present the details of the complex developments of the inquiry as Augustine does; instead he observes another *ordo disciplinae.* Thomas exposes the results of his inquiry *(via expositionis)* rather than the path that led to these results *(via inventionis)*. In addition, Thomas's doctrinal resources are many and varied, and his Trinitarian theology is intended to be academic. It distinguishes (without separating!) infused wisdom given by God from the wisdom acquired through study. But despite these and other differences, Thomas remains faithful to the spiritual objective of Augustine. He has taken up in his own explanations, in an academic theology, the fundamental intuitions of the

---

229 Ibid. I, ch. 8 (#49–50). Cf. *De potentia*, q. 9, a. 5; *Super Boetium de Trinitate*, q. 2, a. 1, ad 7. St. Hilary of Poitiers, *De Trinitate* II,10–11 (ed. Pieter Smulders [Brepols: Turnhout, 1979], 48–49). It is a question here of the eternal generation of the Son.

230 *De potentia*, q. 9, a. 5: "Nec talis inquisitio est inutilis, cum per eam elevetur animus ad aliquid veritatis capiendum quod sufficiat ad excludendos errores. Unde Hilarius dicit."

231 *Super Boetium de Trinitate*, q. 2, a. 1, ad 7: "Humana mens semper debet moveri ad cognoscendum de Deo plus et plus secundum modum suum; unde dicit Hilarius."

232 Cf. *In Dionysii de divinis nominibus* I, lect. 1 (#15).

Bishop of Hippo. Both the nature and purpose of Trinitarian theology in these two doctors are similar in a way that would surprise readers accustomed to a rationalist reading of Thomas: Speculative Trinitarian theology constitutes an exercise, an elevation of the believing mind, a training in order to see the simple and incomprehensible Triune God, which procures a foretaste of the beatific vision and makes it possible to give an account of the Trinitarian faith.

CHAPTER 3

Trinity and Truth: The Son as Truth and the Spirit of Truth in St. Thomas Aquinas

RECENT RESEARCH, sparked by a renewed interest in the entire field of Christian mystery, has led to the rapid development of Trinitarian theology, and has given rise to various essays on the Trinitarian dimension of truth.[1] Without a doubt the most suggestive example of this renewal has been provided by Hans Urs von Balthasar. In his *Theologik*, Balthasar proposes a Trinitarian doctrine of truth with a rare wealth of content.[2] Taking his cue from Heidegger, Balthasar sees truth as the "non-hidden" character of being, the opening out and unveiling of being revealing itself. From this perspective, truth appears in the relation of the Son to his Father and to the Spirit. Manifested in Christ, truth reveals itself as a relation of person to person. For Balthasar, the Son is Truth insofar as he manifests the goodness, love, and grace of the Father, of whom he is the perfect expression. We have access to this truth in the Holy Spirit, that is, in the love with which the Father

1 Translation by Sr. Mary Thomas Noble, OP, of "Le Verbe-Vérité et l'Esprit de Vérité: la doctrine trinitaire de la vérité chez saint Thomas d'Aquin," *Revue Thomiste* 104 (2004): 167–204.

2 Hans Urs von Balthasar, *Theologik,* vol. 1: *Wahrheit der Welt* (Einsiedeln: Johannes Verlag, 1985); vol. 2: *Wahrheit Gottes* (Einsiedeln: Johannes Verlag, 1985); vol. 3: *Der Geist der Wahrheit* (Einsiedeln: Johannes Verlag, 1987). For a good account of Balthasar's trilogy on truth, see Gilbert Narcisse, *Le Christ en sa beauté: Hans Urs von Balthasar et saint Thomas d'Aquin,* vol. 2 (Magny-les-Hameaux: Socéval, 2005), 375–455. On the personal dimension of truth, see Jörg Disse, "Person und Wahrheit in der Theologie Hans Urs von Balthasars," in *Gott für die Welt: Henri de Lubac, Gustav Siewerth und Hans Urs von Balthasar in ihren Grundanliegen,* ed. Peter Reifenberg and Anton van Hooff (Mainz: Matthias Grünewald, 2001), 367–84.

and the Son encounter each other and cause us to exist. With a contribution of Rémi Brague, the French *Dictionnaire de Spiritualité* illustrates well the theological proposition resulting from such a reflection: Truth is found in the relationship of the Son to the Father, that is, in the very personal being of the Son. This is attested in a human mode in the life of Jesus, who relates everything to his Father and who, in his kenosis, gives place to the Spirit. Thus envisaged, truth is implicated in the "Trinitarian interplay," calling for a relation through freedom and interiority.[3] However, the Trinitarian theology implied by these views is so different from Scholastic doctrines on the Trinity that they can hardly be integrated into a consistent reading of the medieval masters.

The proposal of a Trinitarian relationship to truth may well find a number of stimulating elements in St. Bonaventure. On the one hand, the Franciscan master associates truth particularly with the person of the Son. He appropriates truth to the Son but also recognizes a *proper exemplarity* of the Son. For Bonaventure, the Son *properly* proceeds as the "exemplary reason" for other realities, that is, as the divine Model of all creatures.[4] On the other hand, in reuniting the notions of truth and certitude, St. Bonaventure enunciates the Trinitarian principle of our knowledge of the truth: "Only the Trinity as Trinity is the perfect reason for all knowledge of the true."[5] But how does truth relate to the Trinitarian mystery in the thought of St. Thomas? Does Aquinas propose a Trinitarian grasp of truth, and in what manner? In an attempt to answer this question, I propose to

3 Rémi Brague, "Verité. III. Problématique moderne et spiritualité," in *Dictionnaire de Spiritualité*, vol. 16 (Paris: Beauchesne, 1994), cols. 444–53, especially cols. 452–53. An analogical approach, with reference to Thomas Aquinas, has been proposed by Bruce D. Marshall, *Trinity and Truth* (Cambridge: Cambridge University Press, 2000); see my critical review in *Revue Thomiste* 101 (2001): 620–23.

4 On the appropriation of truth to the Son, see, for example, St. Bonaventure, *Breviloquium* I, ch. 6 (*Opera omnia,* vol. 5 [Quaracchi: Editiones Collegii S. Bonaventurae, 1892], 214–15). On the proper exemplarity of the Son, see St. Bonaventure, I *Sent.*, dist. 6, a. 1, q. 3, ad 4 (*Opera omnia,* vol. 1 [Quaracchi: Editiones Collegii S. Bonaventurae, 1882], 130). See Gilles Emery, *La Trinité créatrice* (Paris: Vrin, 1995), 193–96. For a fuller view of the teaching of Bonaventure, see Renato Russo, *La metodologia del sapere nel sermone di S. Bonaventura* "Unus est magister vester Christus" (Grottaferrata: Editiones Collegii S. Bonaventurae, 1982).

5 St. Bonaventure, *Quaestiones disputatae de Mysterio Trinitatis,* q. 7, a. 2, ad 7 (*Opera omnia,* vol. 5, 112): "Sola trinitas ut trinitas est plenissima ratio cognoscendi omne verum per quam fit, ut omne verum cognitum memoriter teneatur, retentum memoriter intelligatur clarius, et intellectum placeat ut ametur." This anthropological explanation (the image of the Triune God in man) is linked to the action of the divine Trinity: the Father reveals himself through the Son, the Father and the Son manifest themselves to us through the Holy Spirit (ibid.).

consider here St. Thomas's teaching on the Son as Truth and on the Spirit of Truth, that is, on the Trinitarian foundations of a theology of truth.

1. The Son, Truth

Like Albert the Great, Alexander of Hales, and Bonaventure, Thomas discusses several definitions of truth. In one of them, drawn from St. Augustine, the name *Truth* designates properly the person of the Son: Truth is "the supreme likeness of the primordial Principle, without any unlikeness."[6] In this passage of *De vera religione*, Augustine mentions two aspects of truth that occupy a central position in the reflection of Thomas Aquinas on the Trinitarian dimensions of truth. The first is that of manifestation. In fact, St. Augustine begins by establishing that "truth manifests that which is." He then shows that things are true insofar as they realize unity, that is, in the measure in which they resemble primordial unity. Now things resemble the unity of the primordial principle through the Truth that is the perfect image of this primordial principle. Here, then, we have the second aspect: It is through the Truth that is the Word and Image of the Father in person, that things are true; it is through this Truth that they participate in the primordial principle.[7] This Trinitarian grasp of truth rests on three fundamental elements: (1) the order of the transcendental *truth* in regard to the transcendental *one* (the true is defined by its resemblance to the one); (2) the unity of the principle of being and the principle of truth (things are true in the measure in which they are); (3) the constitution of the truth of things by the supreme Truth (the truth of things flows from the supreme Truth, which, in its turn, must be taken from its relationship to the One).

The Attribution of Truth to the Son

When St. Thomas examines this Augustinian approach to truth, in his *Commentary on the Sentences*, he finds there two definitions of truth. According to the first (truth manifests that which is), truth is identified with being, to which it adds the idea of *manifestation*; it is indeed a question of an intellectual manifestation.[8] St. Thomas accepts this without difficulty

6 Cf. St. Augustine, *De vera religione* XXXVI,66.

7 Ibid.

8 St. Thomas, I *Sent.*, dist. 19, q. 5, a. 1: "Quaedam enim veritatis definitio datur secundum hoc quod veritas completur in manifestatione intellectus; sicut dicit Augustinus, lib. De vera religione: *veritas est qua ostenditur id quod est.* [. . .] Patet etiam ex dictis, quod veritas addit supra essentiam secundum rationem, scilicet ordinem ad cognitionem vel demonstrationem alicujus." St. Thomas gives this quotation in terms identical with the *Summa fratris Alexandri* (Book I, vol. 1 [Quaracchi: Editiones Collegii S. Bonaventurae, 1924], #89, 141–42).

while clarifying the point that, when one considers the true as the manifestation of being, one envisages truth not in its formality (the *ratio veri*) but "according to an effect following upon it," that is, according to the consequences of the truth in the mind of the one who has discovered it.[9] On this basis, the attribution of Truth to the person of the Son is immediately considered as an appropriation. As to the second Augustinian definition, which considers Truth as "the supreme resemblance to the primordial principle without any unlikeness," it designates truth *insofar as it is appropriated to the Son,* just as knowledge is also appropriated to him.[10] The *Summa theologiae* gives these two definitions in the determination of the subject of truth: Is truth in the intellect or in the thing? According to the first Augustinian definition, truth is considered insofar as it is in the intellect; but according to the second, truth is recognized in the thing, although in relation to the intellect.[11] Here precisely is what will justify the appropriation of truth to the Son: Truth entails a relationship *(ordo)* to the intellect, and therefore bears an affinity with the intellectual process that characterizes the generation of the Son as the *Word* conceived by the Father.[12]

These brief observations call for several clarifications. In the first place, St. Thomas does not consider truth as an exclusive property of the Son. He frequently designates the Son by the name *Truth,* but without denying that the other divine Persons are equally the Truth (he often adds that it is a question here of appropriation). If the truth cannot be attributed in a proper and exclusive way to one divine Person, this is because of a fundamental principle of Trinitarian doctrine. The names that signify a divine Person in a proper and distinct way are names that, by their very notion, designate a real relation of origin.[13] Now the divine intellect involves only a distinction of reason in regard to the being or essence of God. By virtue of the divine simplicity, we must recognize that the intellect is really identical with the divine essence. When we affirm that God knows himself, we are not introducing any real difference between the divine intellect and the

---

9 St. Thomas, *De veritate,* q. 1, a. 1. This point is quite important. The definition of truth in terms of "conformity of thing and intellect" expresses that in which the intelligible determination of truth is formally completed, while the definition in terms of "manifestation of being" *(manifestativum esse)* expresses an effect, namely manifestation, following on what truth formally is.

10 I *Sent.,* dist. 19, q. 5, a. 1: "Quaedam autem datur secundum quod appropriatur Filio, cui etiam appropriatur cognitio, scilicet ab Augustino, lib. De vera religione: *veritas est summa similitudo principii quae sine ulla dissimilitudine est.*"

11 *ST* I, q. 16, a. 1.

12 Ibid.: "Ad veritatem autem rei secundum ordinem ad intellectum pertinet definitio Augustini in libro De vera religione: *veritas est summa similitudo principii, quae sine ulla dissimilitudine est.*"

13 Ibid., q. 34, a. 1; cf. q. 37, a. 1.

reality known. Now, the relation involved by the very notion of "truth" is a relation of the intellect to the reality known; such relation is expressed by the proper definition of truth as "the correspondence of the thing and the intellect" *(adaequatio rei et intellectus)*. Since, in God's self-knowledge, the divine intellect and the reality known by the divine intellect are not really distinct (they are the same one God), the divine truth, taken as such, does not include any "real relation of principle," any real order of origin. *Truth* is therefore an essential name, that is, one common to the three persons by virtue of their identical divinity.[14] In other words, the divine intellect and the divine *res* known by the intellect of God are essential realities. Since truth concerns precisely this relationship of intellect and *res*, it does not constitute a property of the Son but is attributed to him by appropriation: "Truth, since it concerns the intellect, is appropriated to the Son."[15]

In order to understand correctly the appropriation of truth to the Son, it is well to add a clarification that concerns, in a general way, every Trinitarian appropriation. Insofar as it is appropriated ("formally"), a divine attribute not only designates what the name of this attribute signifies, but also includes the property of the person since the appropriation of this attribute rests on the affinity it enjoys with the personal property. The concept of an "appropriated attribute," as such, thus includes the notion of this attribute and also the personal property.[16] The notion of "an essential appropriated attribute" as such, is therefore richer, to my mind, than the notion of "an essential attribute." In this way, "truth appropriated to the Son," joining the attribute of truth and the person of the Son, conveys more than "the divine truth." Thus, for example, we find unity "in the Father," equality "in the Son," connection "in the Holy Spirit."[17] Otherwise put, the appropriated attribute is the attribute considered *in the person to whom it is appropriated.*[18] In the case of truth, the truth appropriated to the Son is therefore the truth considered *in the Word.*

The Trinitarian dimension of truth, under the aspect of the relationship involved in this notion, is comparable to that of equality.[19] Augustine

---

14 *De veritate,* q. 1, a. 7.

15 *ST* I, q. 39, a. 8.

16 I *Sent.*, dist. 31, q. 1, a. 2, ad 3; *ST* I, q. 39, a. 7, ad 3. See I *Sent.*, dist. 9, expositio textus: "In appropriato autem, inquantum hujusmodi, intelligitur ratio proprii."

17 Cf. ibid., dist. 31, q. 3, a. 2.

18 St. Thomas explains this also in connection with St. Hilary's ternary issue: *aeternitas—species—usus* (ibid., dist. 31, q. 2, a. 1). The appropriated eternity is the eternity "which is in the Father as being appropriated to him"; beauty or splendor *(species)* is considered to be "in the Image, that is in the Son, who is properly Image."

19 The close link between truth and equality is brought out in a medieval definition of truth, which St. Thomas did not, however, retain: "The truth of a thing is none other than the equality of its existence *(aequalitas existentiae ejus)* which the intellect

emphasized the *resemblance* that is a part of the notion of truth. For Thomas as well, truth consists in a correspondence, an adequation, a congruence. One might envisage this correspondence under the aspect of a relationship between persons: From this standpoint we must say that the Son is "the Truth of the Father,"[20] or that the Word is "equal to the Father."[21] But this strictly personal aspect does not constitute the formal notion of divine truth, any more than it constitutes the notion of equality; these attributes (truth, equality) also pertain to the divine essence (this is how divine wisdom is equal to divine goodness). Formally speaking, divine Truth consists in the parity or equality of the divine intellect and essence.[22] The Son is Truth because he is God, and it is by appropriation that Truth will be especially associated with him. These explanations are fundamental. Yet they do not exhaust reflection on the relationships of the Son and of Truth.

The Word, Truth Engendered

In his study of the name *Word*, St. Thomas, in the *Summa contra Gentiles*, takes particular care to avoid any essentialist concept of the Word. When he explains that the Son proceeds as Word "by way of the intellect," he does not intend to restrict the divine understanding to the relationship that the Father has with his Son. There is not "more intellect" in the Son than in the Holy Spirit.[23] The act of understanding as such is common to the three divine Persons, and it is therefore incapable of distinguishing one of them from the others. What pertains to the Son is to be the *Word conceived*, *formed*, or *expressed* by the Father.[24] These explanations are based on the analysis of the word in human knowledge: The word is not that by means of which the intellect is formed, it is not that which prompts the intellect into the act of understanding (this function belongs to the *species intelligibilis*); nor is it the reality that we know. The word is rather the concept or *"intentio intellecta"* that the intellect, formed by the intelligible *species* of the reality, expresses interiorly about this known reality. The property of the word is *to proceed* from the intellect that forms it and to represent the thing known, in such a way that it is the immanent objective term *in which* the activity of knowing is accomplished. This makes of the word a relative term: The word is formed by the intellect and yet distinct

understands in grasping the thing such as it is." See Marie-Dominique Chenu, "Une définition pythagoricienne de la vérité au moyen âge," *Archives d'Histoire Doctrinale et Littéraire du Moyen Age* 36 (1961): 7–13.

20 *In 1 Cor* 2:10 (#100).

21 *In Ioannem* 1:1 (#29): The divine Word is "equal to the Father, since he is perfect and since he expresses the whole being of the Father."

22 *De veritate*, q. 1, a. 7, ad 2; cf. *ST* I, q. 39, a. 8.

23 *De potentia*, q. 10, a. 2.

24 *SCG* IV, ch. 11; *ST* I, q. 34, a. 1, ad 2 and ad 3.

from it (since it is the immanent term brought about by the intellect), while being related to the thing that is known within it.[25] For this reason, the notion of "word" implies a *real relationship* with the intellect that is its principle.[26] Let us remember that for St. Thomas this real relationship (real distinction) does not appear formally in the notion of truth: This is why Truth is not a proper or exclusive name for the Son. We discover here one of the fundamental differences between the notion of *word* and that of *truth*. The real relationship set up by the notion of *Word* is not the relationship of the intellect to the reality known (notion of truth), but is the relationship that the Word has to the principle that "utters" him.[27] In order to signify the Son under the aspect of truth, in a distinct way, it is therefore necessary to signify this real relationship to the principle. Just as one will say that the Son is personally "Wisdom begotten,"[28] one will properly say that the Son is personally *Truth begotten*, "the Truth who proceeds from the Father"[29] or "the Truth of the Father."[30]

These explanations could lead us to think that the attribution of Truth to the Son works by a kind of addition, as if we added a relationship of origin to what the name "truth" signifies. But the affinity of Word and Truth is more profound:

> Truth is the conformity of a thing to the intellect, and this results when the intellect conceives the thing as it is. Therefore, the truth of our intellect belongs to our word, which is its conception. Yet although our word is true, it is not truth itself, since it is not true of itself but because it is conformed to the thing conceived. And so the truth of the divine intellect belongs to the Word of God. But because the Word of God is true of itself [. . .], the Word of God is truth itself.[31]

---

25 See Yves Floucat, *L'intime fécondité de l'intelligence: Le verbe mental selon saint Thomas d'Aquin* (Paris: Téqui, 2001), 155–65.

26 *De veritate,* q. 4, a. 2, ad 1; *SCG* IV, ch. 11; *ST* I, q. 34, a. 1; *In Ioannem* 1:1 (#25).

27 *ST* I, q. 34, a. 1, ad 3.

28 *SCG* IV, ch. 12 (#3484): "The Son, who is the Word of God, is properly called *Wisdom begotten.*"

29 *ST* III, q. 59, a. 1: "The Son is Wisdom begotten (Sapientia genita), the Truth who proceeds from the Father and represents him perfectly."

30 *In 1 Cor* 2:10 (#100): "Veritas Patris."

31 *In Ioannem* 14:6 (#1869); cf. *In Ioannem* 18:38 (#2365). The English translation of passages from Aquinas's *Super Evangelium S. Ioannis lectura* are taken from St. Thomas Aquinas, *Commentary on the Gospel of John,* Part I, trans. James A. Weisheipl and Fabian R. Larcher (Albany, NY: Magi Books, 1980); Part II, trans. James A. Weisheipl and Fabian R. Larcher (Petersham, MA: St. Bede's Publications, 1999).

In human knowledge, the grasp of truth *presupposes* the conception of the word. The word therefore plays a decisive role in the process of knowing the truth. In order to attain truth in the strict sense, a correspondence of the intellectual concept with the known reality is necessary. Now by definition the word is the concept of the thing known. It is *in the word*, which is related to the known reality, that the intellect grasps this reality. Knowing the truth as such depends therefore on the word (and not only on the so-called intelligible *species*), since it is in the word that the intellect grasps the reality as it is. In order that there be truth, the presence of the word is required. This is why St. Thomas writes: "The truth of our intellect belongs to our word *(veritas ergo intellectus nostri pertinet ad verbum nostrum)*."[32] Applied to God with the necessary refinements (St. Thomas emphasizes here that the divine Word is true *of itself*, by virtue of its identity with the divine essence, while our human word is true by virtue of something else, namely its correspondence to reality), these explanations mean that Truth is applicable to the Word not only because he is God (by this title, the three persons are Truth). Truth is applicable per se to the Word as such because he is the Word and *insofar as he is the Word*.[33]

The explanation of the formal relationship between word and truth rests on the precise notion of word, which the analysis of the human process of knowing has enabled us to bring out. In the strict sense, the knowledge of truth consists in the judgment of conformity between the intellect and the thing known.[34] To know the truth is to know this conformity.[35] This is why truth lies in "the intellect composing and dividing."[36] St. Thomas does not write explicitly that this judgment is a word.[37] He adds the clarification, however, that the word has to do not only with grasping the essence of a thing, but also with forming complex enunciations:

> The intellect forms two things, according to its two operations. (1) According to its operation which is called "the understanding of indivisibles," it forms a definition. (2) While according to its operation by which it unites and separates, it forms an enunciation or something of

---

32 *In Ioannem* 14:6 (#1869).

33 Ibid.: "Veritas enim convenit ei per se quia ipse est Verbum. [. . .] Veritas ergo intellectus divini pertinet ad Verbum Dei."

34 Cf. *ST* I, q. 16, a. 2: "When the intellect judges that a thing corresponds to the form which it apprehends about that thing, then first it knows and speaks the truth."

35 Ibid.

36 Ibid.

37 Y. Floucat, extending St. Thomas, evokes in this connection "an interior word of judgment" (*L'intime fécondité de l'intelligence,* 140: "une parole intérieure du jugement").

> that sort. Hence, what is thus formed and expressed by the operation of the intellect, whether by defining or enunciating, is what the exterior vocal sound signifies. So Aristotle says that the notion *(ratio)* which a name signifies is a definition. Hence, what is thus expressed, that is, formed in the soul, is called an interior word. Consequently it is compared to the intellect, not as that by which the intellect understands, but as that in which it understands, because it is in what is thus expressed and formed that it sees the nature of the thing understood. Thus we have the meaning of the name *word*.[38]

The word intervenes not only in the simple apprehension of the nature of things, but also in reasoning directed to judgment (and to knowledge of truth). In its activity of composition and division, in the formation of statements, the intellect incorporates the simple or complex words that it has previously formed so as to arrive at the contemplation of truth, in which it rests. For this reason, the formation of a perfect word is achieved by the human mind only at the end of a process: "As long as the intellect, in so reasoning, casts about this way and that, the formation [of the word] is not yet complete."[39] St. Thomas distinguishes on the one hand the activity of searching (cogitation, investigation), and on the other the completion of the process of forming the word. This process is not fully completed until "a word is formed according to a perfect contemplation of the truth."[40] These explanations given in regard to a simple word may be applied to a complex word as well. It is in the word *(in quo)* that the intellect grasps the known thing. Likewise, it is in the "complex word" that the intellect, composing and dividing, grasps and contemplates truth. And in the discursive activity of the intellect, "one word proceeds from another word when the mind proceeds from the consideration of one truth to the consideration of another truth."[41] According to these explanations, the word intervenes at each stage of knowledge of truth: in the knowledge of the true thing, in the knowledge of the truth as such, and in the progress ending in the knowledge of a more profound truth.

In God himself, there is no longer any question of discursive reason. God knows himself immediately through himself in a pure and simple act of understanding.[42] St. Thomas explains in this connection that the divine Word, in contrast to human words, is not "in potency" before being "in

---

38 *In Ioannem* 1:1 (#25).

39 Ibid. (#26).

40 Ibid. Aquinas makes it very clear: It is only when the intellect has conceived the notion of the thing perfectly that for the first time it has the notion of the complete thing and a word *(ratio verbi)*.

41 *De potentia*, q. 9, a. 9, ad 1.

42 Cf. *ST* I, q. 14, a. 7.

act." It is eternal and one.[43] While the conception of the word is *necessarily* required for the human contemplation of the truth, St. Thomas does not write that the conception of the divine Word distinct from the Father necessarily appertains to the notion of divine truth or to the notion of divine knowledge as such (this would be to prejudice the prerogatives of faith, which alone causes us to know the divine Person of the Word).[44] But he shows that, when faith has caused us to know the divine Person of the Word, and "insofar as divine realities can be named by human words,"[45] the attribution of truth to the Word appears most fitting: "The uncreated truth of the divine intellect is appropriated to the Son who is the very concept of the divine intellect and the Word of God. For truth is a consequence of the intellect's concept."[46] In the *Summa theologiae*, St. Thomas explains that only the Father "speaks the Word." The verb "to speak" *(dicere)* designates precisely the personal "relation of principle" that the Father bears to his Word. But although only the Father "speaks" or "utters" the Word, the whole Trinity and all that is contained in the Father's knowledge is expressed or "is spoken" in the Word. Thus the act of speaking includes firstly a relation to the word thus brought forth (in God, it is a question of generation), but it also includes, through the word, a relation to the reality expressed and contained in this word:

> "To speak" *(dicere)* is nothing else than to utter a word. But, by means of this word *(mediante verbo)*, "to speak" involves or includes a relationship to the thing understood; it is in the uttered word that the thing understood is manifested to the one who understands.[47]

The divine Word is certainly not the means whereby the Father knows.[48] The Father, like the Son and the Holy Spirit, knows all things through himself, through his essence. But in a fruitful act, the Father begets his Word, who is so to speak the "fruit" of his wisdom (that is, the imma-

---

43 *In Ioannem* 1:1 (#26); *SCG* IV, ch. 11 (#3470).

44 Philosophical thought can discover the presence of a word within the divine mind (see *SCG* I, ch. 53), but it cannot reach the personal distinctiveness and hypostatic subsistence of this Word (see *ST* I, q. 32, a. 1, ad 2).

45 *De rationibus fidei,* ch. 3.

46 *In Ioannem* 18:38 (#2365): "Veritas increata intellectus divini appropriatur Filio, qui est ipsa conceptio divini intellectus et Dei Verbum. Veritas enim conceptionem intellectus consequitur." See footnote 33 above.

47 *ST* I, q. 34, a. 1, ad 3.

48 Cf. I *Sent.*, dist. 32, q. 2, a. 1: When one affirms that the Father is wise "through his begotten Wisdom," one does not mean to say that the Son is a principle (a cause) of the Father's wisdom, but one is signifying that the Father expresses all he knows in the Son or through the Son whom he begets.

nent term of the Father's personal act of speech). In the Word whom he begets, the Father expresses all that he knows. Now, "truth follows upon the intellect's conception." This is why truth appears in an eminent way in the Son himself who, being the Word, is personally "the conception of the divine intellect."[49] Far from being arbitrary, the appropriation of truth to the Son is strictly based on the notions of "word" and "truth," and thus provides us with a deep insight into the Word's personal mystery.

This is why St. Thomas, in his reading of the Gospel, appropriates *judgment* to the Son. The power to judge is common to the three persons by virtue of their identical divinity. But judgment, according to its formal notion (that is, by virtue of its definition), concerns the Word more specifically. As a matter of fact, "the reason or the rule of judgment *(ratio iudicii)* is the law of wisdom or of truth according to which the judgment is passed. Since the Son is Wisdom begotten, and Truth proceeding from the Father, who represents the Father perfectly, the power to judge is properly attributed to the Son of God."[50] The Word's proper mode of action, in judgment, comes from his personal relation to the Father: "The Father judges all things through his Son insofar as the Son is his wisdom and his truth."[51] We will return to this action of the Father *through the Word* later.

The Light and Truth of the Father: The Word Manifests the Father

St. Thomas constantly associates the theme of *manifestation* with the Word. We have already cited the notion of manifestation in one of the Augustinian definitions of truth. This manifestation leads to important developments in passages explaining that the Word is Light.

In his first works (his *Commentary on the Sentences* and his disputed questions *De veritate*), St. Thomas explains what a word is by direct reference to the notion of manifestation. "The name *word* is imposed because of some manifestation."[52] He makes it clear that the notion of manifestation is included in the meaning of the name of *word*.[53] Such a manifestation harks back of itself to the intellect, which is why this name *word* is reserved for the manifestation of the intellect.[54] The complete notion of *word*, according to the explanations found in *De veritate*, thus includes two elements: (1) the origin, the coming forth from another; (2) the manifestation

49 *In Ioannem* 18:38 (#2365).

50 *ST* III, q. 59, a. 1.

51 Ibid., q. 59, a. 1, ad 2.

52 *De veritate,* q. 4, a. 2, arg. 1: "Nomen verbi a manifestatione imponitur." See q. 4, a. 1, arg. 7 and ad 5.

53 Ibid., q. 4, a. 3: "Verbum enim manifestationem quandam importat"; cf. arg. 5: "Verbum de sui ratione manifestationem importat."

54 Ibid., q. 4, a. 3.

by way of the intellect.[55] This manifestation not only has to do with the external word, but goes back first of all to the interior word. Through its interior word, the intellect manifests to itself the reality that is known; the external word that signifies the interior word appears at the end of the process of signification.[56] Thus the begotten Word first manifests the Father to himself from all eternity (such eternal manifestation comes before any other manifestation in the economy of creation and grace). The Word also manifests his Father externally by his effects in the world, especially in the mysteries of his incarnation; this economic manifestation is rooted in the eternal manifestation:

> It is true that we manifest something to another only by means of a vocal word *(verbum vocale)*. Yet one manifests something to oneself by means of the word of the heart *(verbum cordis)*; and, since this manifestation takes place before the other manifestation, the name *word* first applies to the interior word *(verbum interius)*. Similarly, the Father has been manifested to all by means of the Word incarnate, but the Word begotten from all eternity has manifested the Father to himself. This is why the name *Word* does not belong to the Son merely insofar as he is incarnate.[57]

It goes with the very notion of "Word" to manifest the one who utters this Word.[58] Although St. Thomas's later works show a deepening of his teaching on the Word, the notion of manifestation is not abandoned. The word conceived by the mind is described as "the manifestation of the wisdom of the knower."[59] In the judgment of St. Thomas, echoing St. John Chrysostom, this is St. John's reason for choosing the name *Word* to designate the Son at the beginning of his Gospel: "Since the idea of manifesting

---

55 Ibid., q. 4, a. 4, ad 6: "The name 'word' implies not only the idea of origin and of imitation, but also that of manifestation." Ibid., q. 4, a. 5, sed contra 4: "The Son, because he is the *Son*, represents the Father perfectly in that which is intrinsic to the Father; but the name *Word* adds the note of manifestation." Cf. I *Sent.*, dist. 27, q. 2, a. 2, qla 1, arg. 2: "To the notion of 'intellect', the word adds only an order of manifestation"; *In Dionysii de divinis nominibus*, ch. 1, lect. 1 (#25): "The word has to do with a manifestation of knowledge"; *Quodlibet* 10, q. 4, a. 1, arg. 2: "Verum addit supra ens manifestationem."

56 *De veritate,* q. 4, a. 1, ad 7.

57 Ibid., q. 4, a. 1, ad 5. The English translation of this passage is taken (with modifications) from: St. Thomas Aquinas, *Truth,* vol. 1, trans. Robert W. Mulligan (Chicago: Henry Regnery Company, 1952), 174.

58 See I *Sent.*, dist. 15, q. 4, a. 1; III *Sent.*, dist. 1, q. 2, a. 2: "The Word manifests the One who speaks him."

59 *SCG* IV, ch. 12 (#3483): "Ipsum autem sapientiae verbum mente conceptum est quaedam manifestatio sapientiae intelligentis."

is implied better in the name *Word* than in the name *Son*, he preferred to use [here] the name *Word*."[60]

To signify this function of manifestation belonging to the Word, St. Thomas often has recourse to the theme of light. This theme is directly linked with that of truth, since "light is truth."[61] Light *(lux)* means "that which effects a manifestation in the sense of sight" and, by extension, it applies to the manifestation brought about by all knowledge.[62] Taken in its first sense, that is, according to what the term "light" is originally intended to mean, light will only be applied to spiritual realities metaphorically. But if we hold more precisely to the notion of *manifestation*, it is quite proper to attribute light to intellectual realities.[63] Light is the *medium* through which the vision takes place, that is "that which provides manifestation in any kind of knowledge."[64] Therefore, in the spiritual order, a being receives the attribute of light to the extent that it is intelligible. Now God is sovereignly manifest to himself; he is sovereignly intelligible. The divine essence, because it is pure act, is therefore light itself *(ipsa lux)*.[65] To be light is proper to God: God is light by essence.[66] Still more precisely, the light reflects the divine *wisdom*, for wisdom formally signifies the intellectual activity of God that consists in a pure act of knowledge.[67] And the same holds for *truth*, for truth is closely bound to light: "Truth is the illumination of the intellect."[68] The minds of men and angels share in the light insofar as such rational creatures are capable of grasping the truth itself, "which can be manifested and is manifestive to all."[69] As for God, as we have already noted, he is Light and Truth itself because in him intellect and essence coincide in absolute unity and in a sovereign intelligibility.[70]

---

60 *In Ioannem* 1:1 (#31). On the theology of the Word in Aquinas's commentary on St. John, see Graziano Perillo, *Teologia del Verbum: La Lectura super Ioannis Evangelium di Tommaso d'Aquino* (Naples: Luciano Editore, 2003).

61 *In Ioannem* 14:6 (#1868): "Lux autem veritas est."

62 *ST* I, q. 67, a. 1; *De potentia*, q. 4, a. 2, ad 3.

63 *ST* I, q. 67, a. 1. See II *Sent.*, dist. 13, a. 2. Through these explanations, St. Thomas seeks to offer a unified view of different philosophical traditions about light. For more details on this theme, see Joseph Kieninger, *Das Sein als Licht in den Schriften des hl. Thomas von Aquin* (Vatican City: Editrice Vaticana, 1992).

64 *ST* I, q. 67, a. 1: "Omne illud quod facit manifestationem secundum quamcumque cognitionem." See *ST* I, q. 74, a. 2; q. 111, a. 1.

65 *In 1 Tm* 6:16 (#268).

66 *In Ioannem* 12:46 (#1713).

67 *SCG* IV, ch. 12 (#3483).

68 *In Ioannem* 8:44 (#1250).

69 *In Ioannem* 1:4 (#97).

70 Cf. *In Ioannem* 8:44 (#1250): "Veritas est illuminatio intellectus; Deus autem est ipsum lumen." Cf. *In Matthaeum* 24:26 (#1949): "Veritas est lumen."

The divine Word is therefore Light as he is Truth. Because of his personal property, the Word "expresses the entire being of the Father,"[71] he "manifests the Father himself."[72] Expressing everything that is contained in the intellect of the Father, "he expresses everything that is in God, not only the persons, but also creatures."[73] To sum up: "In God, the *Word* conceived by the intellect of the Father is a person, and all things that are in the Father's knowledge, whether they refer to the essence or to the persons, or even to the works of God, are expressed by this Word."[74] This is how St. Thomas explains the name "light," which St. John's prologue attributes to the Son:

> Light is not only visible in itself and by itself, but through it all else can be seen. So the Word of God is not only light in himself, but he also manifests all that is manifested. [. . .] The Son is the Word of God in whom the Father speaks himself and speaks all creatures; so he is, properly speaking, the light of men.[75]

The hypostatic property of the Word stands out eloquently when St. Thomas clarifies the personal relationship of the Son to the Father by means of the theme of *splendor*, which, as contrasted with light, not only signifies the intelligibility of the divine being, but expresses more precisely the personal relationship of the Son to the Father:

> The very word of wisdom conceived by the mind is a manifestation of the wisdom of the one who understands, just as in our case all habits are manifested by their acts. Since, then, the divine wisdom is called *light*—for it consists in the pure act of cognition, and the manifestation of light is the *splendor* proceeding therefrom—, the Word of divine wisdom is rightly called *splendor of light*. Thus the Apostle says of the Son of God [Heb 1:3]: *He is the splendor of the glory [of God]*. Hence, also, the Son ascribes to himself the manifestation of the Father. He says in John [17:6]: *Father, I have manifested thy name to the men whom thou gavest me.*[76]

---

71 *In Ioannem* 1:1 (#29): "Totius esse Patris expressivum."

72 Ibid., 6:37 (#918): "Verbum est manifestativum ipsius Patris."

73 Ibid., 1:1 (#27).

74 *ST* I–II, q. 93, a. 1, ad 2; cf. *ST* I, q. 34, a. 3; I *Sent.*, dist. 27, q. 2, a. 3; *De veritate,* q. 4, a. 4 and a. 5; *SCG* IV, ch. 13.

75 *In Ioannem* 1:7 (#118); cf. ibid. 1:8 (#123): "The Son of God is Light by his very essence."

76 *SCG* IV, ch. 12 (#3483). English translation: St. Thomas Aquinas, *Summa contra Gentiles, Book Four: Salvation,* Translated, with an Introduction and Notes, by Charles J. O'Neil (Notre Dame, IN: University of Notre Dame Press, 1975), 91–92. On this subject, see Denise Bouthillier, "*Splendor gloriae Patris:* Deux collations du Super Isaiam de saint Thomas d'Aquin," in *Christ among the Medieval Dominicans:*

The theme of splendor emphasizes the co-eternity of the Son and the Father,[77] as well as the manifestation brought about by the Son in virtue of his personal property. The Word is the perfect expression of the Father's glory since he proceeds eternally from the Father "as splendor proceeds from light."[78] This is why, in the divine economy of creation and grace, the Word manifests his Father.

In Trinitarian terms, St. Thomas explains that the Father, Son, and Holy Spirit are one single light,[79] as they are one single wisdom and one same truth. If we consider the nature of divine light, it appears as single. But we can also understand light as implying an origin, for light *(lumen)* is diffused through radiance *(lux)*. And so, when we reunite the notion of origin and that of manifestation, we can associate the light with a personal property.[80] In his commentary on *The Divine Names* of Pseudo-Dionysius, St. Thomas recapitulates his explanations as follows:

> Metaphorically, light designates truth. We can therefore say that the Son and the Holy Spirit are one single light, for they are one truth. But we can also say that they are two lights, when what we mean by the expression *two lights* is two rays coming forth from a single light *(duos radios ab uno lumine procedentes)* like two blossoms *(sicut per duos flores)*, for each of them proceeds from the Father; and this does not exclude the fact that the Holy Spirit proceeds from the Son.[81]

The Father is thus the "source of light,"[82] or the "fontal light,"[83] in that he communicates the divine essence to the Son and the Holy Spirit. Since, according to St. Thomas, light also designates truth,[84] the Father appears as the ultimate personal source of truth. The Son and the Holy Spirit, receiving all their being from the Father by their eternal procession, are then designated as two lights proceeding from the Father. This is the meaning of the expression in the *Credo*: The Son is "light from light" because he is eternally engendered from the substance of the Father, which

---

Representations of Christ in the Texts and Images of the Order of Preachers, ed. Kent Emery and Joseph Wawrykow (Notre Dame, IN: Notre Dame University Press, 1998), 139–56.

77 Cf. *ST* I, q. 34, a. 2, ad 3; q. 42, a. 2, ad 1; *In Ioannem* 1:1 (#41 and 42).

78 *In Ioannem* 17:24 (#2261): "Filius est a Patre ab aeterno, sicut splendor a luce."

79 *Contra errores Graecorum,* Part I, ch. 3.

80 Ibid.

81 *In Dionysii de divinis nominibus,* ch. 2, lect. 4 (#182).

82 *In 2 Cor* 4:4 (#125): "Deus Pater est fons totius luminis" (St. Thomas explains here the meaning of "the illumination of the gospel of the glory of Christ, who is the image of God").

83 Ibid.: "fontanosum lumen," "fontanosa lux."

84 Cf. *In Ioannem* 14:6 (#1868).

he receives in its fullness. To be more precise, the Son is signified by the expression "splendor of light," which indicates his personal origin, for *splendor* designates the brilliance coming forth from light, the sunburst immediately proceeding from the luminous source.[85] Since the Son is the Father's Word, the concept of the Father's intellect, he is therefore "the splendor of the wisdom whereby the Father knows himself,"[86] he "proceeds from the Father as splendor proceeds from light."[87] As for the Holy Spirit, St. Thomas compares him with a "ray of light," along with the Son.[88] Developing the metaphor, he also considers the Holy Spirit as the "warmth" that proceeds from the light and spreads abroad the benefits of light: The Holy Spirit proceeds from the Son and communicates the Son's gifts.[89] The Trinitarian use of the image of light, for our purpose, is thus set at the intersection of a twofold communication of truth: the intra-Trinitarian communication of truth through the eternal processions, and its communication in the divine economy.

The Word, Source of Truth

St. Thomas has explained that the Son of God, insofar as he is the *Word* (that is, in virtue of his personal property), expresses the Father and all creatures contained within the Father's mind: The Word manifests the fullness of the mystery of the Father. He has also shown that the Son, insofar as he is God, is the supreme Truth. He has clarified the Trinitarian aspect of this by noting that the Son, because he is engendered by the Father, is the Truth that proceeds from the Truth. The analysis of the notion of *word* has shown the special affinity between the Word and Truth, which is the basis for the appropriation of Truth to the Word. If we take into account the causality of divine truth,[90] and the doctrine of exemplarity (participation), all the elements are assembled to develop a filial theology of truth. In fact, the uncreated truth is the cause of a twofold truth *(faciens duplicem veritatem)*, that is, a twofold consonance between the mind and reality. Firstly, it is the source of the *truth of things*: Things are true insofar as they are conformed to the ideas of the divine intellect. Secondly, it is the source of the *truth in the mind of creatures*: "It makes truth in our souls."[91] This line of thought

85 Cf. *In Heb* 1:3 (#26).

86 Ibid.

87 *De potentia*, q. 2, a. 3, sed contra 3.

88 Cf. *In Dionysii de divinis nominibus*, ch. 2, lect. 4 (#182).

89 Cf. *Super Primam Decretalem* (Leonine edition, vol. 40 E, 33–34).

90 Cf. *ST* I, q. 14, a. 8.

91 *In Ioannem* 18:38 (#2365). The divine truth, the first truth, lies in the identity of God's intellect and being. Created things are true in virtue of their conformity to the divine intellect; and truth is found in the created intellect through its participation in uncreated truth. Divine truth is thus the source of truth in things, and

leads to a supplementary reason (an economic motive) for appropriating truth to the person of the Son: He is the Word through whom things are true and by whom truth is communicated to the minds of creatures.[92] This last point, regarding which St. Thomas's texts are particularly abundant, merits our special attention because of its repercussions in the study of creation and salvation. The influence of the Word in the knowledge of truth is exerted in two connected areas: that of the knowledge of truth through the natural light of reason (a sharing in the Word), and that of knowledge of truth through grace, in which the Word is not only shared through a common participation but also personally "possessed" by those who receive him. I shall illustrate this teaching by a few texts drawn principally from St. Thomas's commentary on the Fourth Gospel.

The Universal Influence of the Word in All Knowledge of Truth

In making use of his doctrine on the causality of divine science and on participation, St. Thomas constantly attributes the communication of all knowledge and all truth to the Son. All human knowledge is, in varying degrees, a participation in divine knowledge. Now the Son is the Word of the Father, the concept of the Father's intellect knowing himself. This is why "all our knowledge is derived from the Word."[93] St. Thomas stresses the universal extent of this participation when he presents the theme of illumination by the Word. We are not departing from the knowledge of truth since, by definition, illumination is the manifestation of a known truth to another person. The term "light," when applied to the mind, means the "manifestation of truth" *(manifestatio veritatis)*; and hence "to illuminate (to enlighten: *illuminare*) means nothing else but to communicate to others the manifestation of the known truth."[94] Properly speaking, illumination or enlightment refers not to any kind of knowledge, but only to knowledge in relation to God. Hence, in the strict sense, "illumination is the manifestation of the truth in reference to God, who illuminates every mind."[95]

---

the source of truth in the minds of men and angels. Truth in the minds of men and angels is caused and "measured" by God's uncreated truth. See *ST* I, q. 16, a. 6; *De veritate,* q. 1, a. 4 and 5.

92 *In Ioannem* 18:38 (#2365).

93 Ibid., 8:55 (#1284): "Quia omne imperfectum a perfecto initium sumit, inde est quod *omnis nostra cognitio a Verbo derivatur.*"

94 *ST* I, q. 106, a. 1: "Lumen secundum quod ad intellectum pertinet nihil aliud est quam quaedam manifestatio veritatis. [. . .] Unde illuminare nihil aliud est quam manifestationem cognitae veritatis alteri tradere."

95 Ibid., q. 109, a. 3: "Illuminatio proprie est manifestatio veritatis, secundum quod habet ordinem ad Deum, qui illuminat omnem intellectum." Here St. Thomas explains illumination by means of truth. Elsewhere, he presents truth by means of

The illuminating influence of the Word is not limited to the supernatural knowledge given by grace, but is concerned first with the natural light of the human intellect.[96] Thus, for example, the verses from John 1:4–5—*And the life was the light of men, the light shines in the darkness, and the darkness has not overcome it*—can be understood either as the inflowing of natural knowledge or the communication of grace.[97]

> Everything which is what it is by participation is derived from what is such by its essence; just as everything afire is so by participation in fire, which is fire by its very nature. Then since the Word is the true light by his very nature, everything that shines must do so through him, insofar as it participates in him. And so he *enlightens every man coming into this world.* [. . .] For all men coming into this visible world are enlightened *(illuminantur)* by the light of natural knowledge through participating in this true Light [namely, the Word], which is the source of all the light of natural knowledge participated in by men.[98]

This applies equally to wisdom, and St. Thomas again makes the same affirmation when he is considering *truth.* His reference to the *Ambrosiaster,* in this context, is well-known: All truth, regardless of who declares it, comes from the Holy Spirit.[99] But before applying it to the Holy Spirit, St. Thomas clarifies the universal causality of the Word. After having explained that the Word is the light,[100] he continues: "Whatever truth is

---

the theme of illumination: "Veritas enim est illuminatio intellectus" (*In Ioannem* 8:44 [#1250]). The two themes are mutually interconnected.

96 Cf. *ST* I–II, q. 109, a. 1, ad 2: "The natural light bestowed upon the soul is God's enlightenment *(illustratio Dei),* whereby we are enlightened *(illustramur)* to know what pertains to natural knowledge."

97 *In Ioannem* 1:4 (#95).

98 Ibid., 1:9 (#127 and 129): "Omne enim quod est per participationem, derivatur ab eo quod est per essentiam suam tale; ut omne ignitum est hoc per participationem ignis, qui est ignis per suam naturam. Quia ergo Verbum est lux vera per suam naturam, oportet quod omne lucens luceat per ipsum, inquantum ipsum participat. Ipse ergo *illuminat omnem hominem venientem in hunc mundum.* [. . .] Quia homines omnes venientes in hunc mundum sensibilem illuminantur lumine naturalis cognitionis ex participatione huius verae lucis, a qua derivatur quicquid de lumine naturalis cognitionis participatur ab hominibus."

99 I *Sent.,* dist. 19, q. 5; *ST* I–II, q. 109, a. 1, ad 1; *ST* II–II, q. 172, a. 6, arg. 1; *In Titum* 1:13 (#32); and so on. Cf. Pseudo-Ambrose, *Commentaria in epistolam ad Corinthios primam* (PL 17, 245 B): "Quicquid enim verum a quocumque dicitur, a Sancto dicitur Spiritu."

100 *In Ioannem* 1:4 (#97): "The Evangelist, speaking of the Word, not only says that he is Life but also Light."

known by anyone is due to a participation in that Light which shines in the darkness; for every truth, no matter by whom it is spoken, comes from the Holy Spirit."[101] In these explanations, the effect of the universal action of the Holy Spirit is referred to the enlightening influence of the Word.

The Holy Spirit is at the source of all truth because he communicates the light of the Son, the Word of the Father. The gift of this light has to do firstly with man's intellectual faculty (the superior part of the human soul), which participates in the Word.[102] It also has to do with the exercise of the intellect under the influence of the Word. When we say that all truth comes from the Holy Spirit or that all knowledge of the truth participates in the Word, this should be understood of the infusion of the natural light of knowledge as well as of the divine action that moves the intelligence to know and speak the truth. This universal action should not be confused with the knowledge of grace given by the Word and by the Holy Spirit when they dwell in the souls of the saints.[103] Nevertheless, in all cases knowledge, wisdom, and truth are derived from the Word himself:

> Whatever light and whatever wisdom exists in men has come to them from participating in the Word.[104]
>
> By his intellect, God is not only the cause of all things that naturally subsist, but all intellectual knowledge is also derived from the divine intellect [. . .]. Necessarily, then, it is by the Word of God, who is the "reason" of the divine intellect, that all intellectual knowledge is caused. Accordingly, we read in John [1:4]: *The life was the light of men.* For the Word himself, who is life and in whom all things are life, as a light, makes the truth manifest to the mind of men.[105]

---

101 Ibid., 1:5 (#103). Cf. ibid., 5:32 (#805): "The human word has no truth unless it is supported by God."

102 Ibid., 1:4 (#101): "For we would never be able to look upon the Word and light itself except through a participation in it; and this participation is in man and is the superior part of the soul, that is, the intellectual light *(lux intellectiva).*"

103 *ST* I–II, q. 109, a. 1, ad 1: "Every truth by whomsoever spoken is from the Holy Spirit as bestowing the natural light [of knowledge], and moving us to understand and speak the truth, but not as dwelling in us by sanctifying grace, or as bestowing any habitual gift superadded to nature." Cf. II *Sent.*, dist. 28, q. 1, a. 5.

104 *In Ioannem* 1:26 (#246): "Quicquid lucis et sapientiae est in hominibus, provenit eis ex participatione Verbi."

105 *SCG* IV, ch. 13 (#3495): "Deus autem non solum est causa per intellectum suum omnium quae naturaliter subsistunt, sed etiam omnis intellectualis cognitio ab intellectu divino derivatur, sicut ex superioribus patet. Oportet igitur quod per Verbum Dei, quod est ratio intellectus divini, causetur omnis intellectualis cognitio. Propter quod dicitur Ioan. 1,4: *vita erat lux hominum:* quia scilicet ipsum Verbum, quod vita est, et in quo omnia vita sunt, manifestat, ut lux quaedam, mentibus hominum veritatem."

In this way, the divine Word causes all truth known by men;[106] his influence extends to the conception of all human "words" and to the formation of every speech.[107] The action of the Holy Spirit is directly connected with this prerogative of the Word, for the Holy Spirit communicates what he receives from the Father and his Word.

The Influence of the Word in the Knowledge of Grace

St. Thomas likewise attributes to the influence of the Word inspired words[108] (the prophets were sent, and they spoke "through participation in the Word")[109] and interior teaching.[110] In this context, it is to the knowledge *of God*, in faith, that St. Thomas pays the greatest attention. The Word of God is "the root and source of all knowledge of God"; in believers, all other supernatural knowledge is derived from this knowledge of God given by the Word.[111] The Word of God, in virtue of his personal property, manifests the Father: We have already noted several passages in St. Thomas explaining that such manifestation of the Father properly belongs to the Word. Further, human participation of the Word in the knowledge of God develops according to the growth of the image of the Triune God: an image by creation, an image by grace, and an image in glory.[112] Participation in the Word is thus accomplished through a progressive assimilation. Already given in the natural knowledge of God, this assimilation to the Word is realized to a much higher degree by the knowledge of grace, which is none other than divinization:

> Human wisdom consists in knowing God. But this knowledge flows to us from the Word, because to the extent that we share in the Word of God, to that extent do we know God.[113]

---

106 Cf. *In Ioannem* 18:38 (#2365): The Word "makes truth in our souls."

107 Ibid., 1:1 (#33): "There is one absolute Word, by participation in which all persons having a word are called 'speakers.'" Cf. ibid. 14:7 (#1879): "Every created word is some likeness of that Word."

108 Ibid., 5:38 (#820): "Christ is the natural Word of God. Every word inspired by God is a participated likeness of this Word."

109 Ibid., 10:8 (#1384). Ibid., 1:18 (#221): "In the past, the Only Begotten Son manifested knowledge of God through the prophets, who made him known to the extent that they shared in the eternal Word *(inquantum aeterni Verbi fuerunt participes).*"

110 Ibid., 13:13 (#1775).

111 Ibid., 17:25 (#2267–68).

112 Cf. *ST* I, q. 93, a. 4. The growth of the image follows the same rhythm as the growth of filiation (*ST* I, q. 33, a. 3).

113 *In Ioannem* 17:25 (#2267): "Humana autem sapientia in Dei cognitione consistit. Haec autem cognitio ad homines derivatur a Verbo; quia inquantum homines participant Verbum Dei, intantum Deum cognoscunt."

> To the extent that something approaches to a likeness of the Word of the Father, to that extent the Father is known in it, and to that extent it is in the image of the Father.[114]
>
> One is called a son of God insofar as one shares in the likeness of his natural Son. And one knows [God] in the measure in which one has a likeness to him, since knowledge is attained through assimilation.[115]

The act of understanding consists in a union, an assimilation. The knowing subject somehow makes the perfections that belong to other beings exist within himself. When the mind knows, "that which is known is in a certain way in the knower," because "the form of the known is in the knower."[116] When it knows, the mind intentionally "becomes" the thing known.[117] Such union with the known thing abides in the intimacy of the word within the intellect itself. This is how St. Thomas will explain the presence of God in the saints: God is present in those who know and love him, to the extent that he is known and loved. We will return to this later. For now, we should note one of the consequences of this teaching. Natural knowledge of the truth results in a very imperfect participation in the Word. It is in receiving the Word himself through grace that we "possess" the truth, for it is then that the Word, namely Truth, is personally received by man, who may delight in him:

> The Word of God is truth itself. And since no one can know the truth unless he adheres to the truth, it is necessary that anyone who desires to know the truth adhere to this Word.[118]
>
> Although there is no one who does not have some truth from God, they alone have the truth and the Word abiding in them whose knowledge has progressed to the point where they have reached a knowledge of the true and natural Word.[119]

114 Ibid., 14:7 (#1879): "Inquantum aliquid accedit ad similitudinem paterni Verbi, intantum in ipso cognoscitur Pater, et similiter inquantum habet de imagine Patris."

115 Ibid., 1:18 (#216): "Intantum aliquis dicitur filius Dei, inquantum similitudinem Filii naturalis participat; et intantum cognoscit, inquantum de similitudine eius habet: quia cognitio fit per assimilationem." Aquinas here refers to 1 John 3:2: "When he comes, we will be like him, and we will see him as he is."

116 *De veritate,* q. 2, a. 2; cf. *ST* I, q. 14, a. 1.

117 "This is what makes the Philosopher say, in Book III of *De Anima,* that 'the soul is in a certain way all things'" (*ST* I, q. 14, a. 1).

118 *In Ioannem* 14:6 (#1869): "Verbum Dei est ipsa veritas. Et quia nullus potest veritatem cognoscere nisi adhaereat veritati, oportet omnem qui veritatem cognoscere desiderat, huic Verbo adhaerere."

119 Ibid., 5:38 (#820): "Cum nullus sit quin aliquam veritatem habeat a Deo, illi tantum habent veritatem, et Verbum in ipsis manens, quibus intantum cognitio proficit ut perducantur ad veri et naturalis Verbi cognitionem."

These explanations show a twofold movement. On the one hand, following a movement that we might call "descending," Truth gives himself in person when the Word comes to dwell in the hearts of those who receive him with living faith. On the other hand, following an "ascending" movement, full adherence to the truth is accomplished only by welcoming the Word himself, through grace. St. Thomas also explains this in an adjacent context dealing with revelation and with every inspired word addressed to men. These clarifications have great interest for Christology, for grasping the relation between Old and New Testaments, and in a general manner for perceiving the central position of Christ, the Word of God, in the Christian notion of revelation:

> The word of God leads to Christ, since Christ himself is the Word of God by nature. Now, every word inspired by God is a participated likeness of that Word. Therefore, since every participated likeness leads to its original, it is clear that every word inspired by God leads to Christ.[120]

We shall find the same theme (all that proceeds from a principle leads back to this principle) in the study of the action of the Holy Spirit. For the present, we should note the "verbocentrism" of Thomas's theology of the Truth. Knowledge of the truth comes from the Word and, through grace, leads back to the Word. Knowledge of the truth finds its fulfillment in faith in Christ, by virtue of the very nature of truth and by reason of the personal property of the Word.

The Mission of the Word

In the explanations regarding grace, we have already touched on the mission of the Word, that is, the sending of the Word into our hearts. Conformity to the Word, the illumination of grace by the Word, the welcoming of the truth indwelling men, and divinization, are the effects of the invisible mission of the Word. Without going into every aspect of this teaching, we should at least note the place occupied in it by knowledge of the truth in its Trinitarian dimension. In his commentary on St. John, St. Thomas sums up the structure of the divine missions in this way:

> Just as the effect of the mission of the Son was to lead to the Father, so the effect of the mission of the Holy Spirit is to lead the faithful to the Son. Now the Son, since he is begotten Wisdom, is Truth itself: *I*

120 Ibid.: "Verbum enim Dei ducit ad Christum: Nam ipse Christus est naturale Dei Verbum. Omne autem verbum a Deo inspiratum, est quaedam participata similitudo illius. Cum ergo omnis similitudo participata ducat in suum principium, manifestum est quod omne verbum inspiratum a Deo ducit ad Christum."

> *am the Way, and the truth, and the life* (Jn 14:6). And so the effect of such a mission is to make men sharers in the divine wisdom and knowers of the truth. The Son, since he is the Word, gives teaching to us; but the Holy Spirit enables us to grasp it.[121]

The divine missions are presented here under the aspect of the mutual relations between the divine Persons. The work of the Son, by virtue of his property as Word and as Son of the Father, is to manifest the Father and to lead to him. In the same way, the mission of the Holy Spirit is to manifest the Son and lead to him. The person sent leads to the one from whom he proceeds, for what issues from a principle manifests this principle.[122] The structure of the missions appears in the following way: The Holy Spirit leads to the Son and the Son leads to the Father, who is the "ultimate principle" to whom we are led back.[123] The roots of this teaching are profoundly patristic.[124] Close to St. Thomas in his phrasing, St. Albert the Great formulated it in similar terms: Each person leads to the one from whom he proceeds; our return to God takes place in the rhythm of the Trinitarian relations and is completed in the person of the Father.[125]

This Trinitarian structure is closely associated with the knowledge of truth, for the mission has for its end to "make men knowers of the truth." Each person intervenes here according to his distinctive property. We shall see further on how St. Thomas understood the effect of the mission of the Holy Spirit in relation to truth. As for the Son, he gives the truth in procuring a participation in what he is, namely begotten Wisdom, the very Truth. This participation in the Truth, a special effect of the mission of the Son, constitutes, in the proper sense of the terms, a sanctification, a divinization. It is a question of filial adoption, envisaged here under the aspect of our assimilation to the Word and Truth:

---

121 Ibid., 15:26 (#1958): "Sicut effectus missionis Filii fuit ducere ad Patrem, ita effectus missionis Spiritus Sancti est ducere fideles ad Filium. Filius autem, cum sit ipsa sapientia genita, est ipsa veritas; supra XIV [6]: *Ego sum via, veritas et vita.* Et ideo effectus missionis huiusmodi est ut faciat homines participes divinae sapientiae, et cognitores veritatis. Filius ergo tradit nobis doctrinam, cum sit Verbum; sed Spiritus Sanctus doctrinae eius nos capaces facit."

122 Ibid., 16:14 (#2107): "Omne enim quod est ab alio, manifestat id a quo est; Filius enim manifestat Patem, quia est ab ipso. Quia ergo Spiritus Sanctus est a Filio, proprium est ut clarificet eum." See ibid., 17:2 (#2185).

123 I *Sent.*, dist. 15, q. 4, a. 1: "manifestatio ipsius Patris, qui est ultimum ad quod recurrimus." Cf. ibid., dist. 14, q. 2, a. 2: "Principium ad quod recurrimus, scilicet Patrem [. . .]."

124 See, for instance, St. Irenaeus of Lyons, *Against Heresies* IV,20,5.

125 St. Albert the Great, I *Sent.*, dist. 31, a. 14, ad quaest. 2; and I *Sent.*, dist. 3, a. 17. See G. Emery, *Trinity in Aquinas,* 45.

> *Sanctify them in the truth* (Jn 17:17). *In the truth,* that is, in me, your Son, who *am the Truth* (Jn 14:6). It is like saying: Make them sharers in my perfection and my holiness [sanctity]. [. . .] Sanctify them in me, the truth *(in me veritate)*, because I, your Word, am the Truth.[126]

Being the Begotten Truth, the Truth of the Father, the Son leads to the Father and obtains for us the presence of the Father. From this standpoint, the welcoming of the truth is nothing else than the indwelling of the Holy Trinity:

> Since the Father loves the Son, as is shown by the glory he gave him, consequently, the Father loves all those in whom the Son is present; and the Son is in them insofar as they have knowledge of the truth. So the meaning is this: *I will make your name known to them* (Jn 17:26). And by the fact that they know you, I, your Word, will be in them; and by the fact that I am in them, *the love with which you love me may be in them* (Jn 17:26), that is, will be given to them, and you will love them as you have loved me. We can also explain *the love with which you have loved me may be in them* in this way: As you have loved me, so they, by sharing in the Holy Spirit, may love. And by that fact I will be in them as God in his temple, and they in me, as members in the Head: *He who abides in love abides in God, and God abides in him* (1 Jn 4:16).[127]

These explanations are remarkable and deserve our attentive observation. Because they know the truth, and in the measure in which they know the truth, the faithful receive the Son himself who dwells in them. Because of this, in virtue of the presence of the Son, which is intimately connected to this knowledge of the truth, the Father loves the disciples of the Son with the same love with which he loves his Son. The Father loves the disciples with the very love he bears the Son, because of the Truth dwelling in them. This is why the Love of the Father and the Son, namely the Holy Spirit, is given to them. Thus, because of the presence of the Son, the Father himself comes into the faithful, who adhere to the Truth.

---

126 *In Ioannem* 17:17 (#2229).

127 Ibid. 17:26 (#2270): "Quia dictum est, quod Pater diligit Filium, ut ostenditur per claritatem quam dedit ei: consequens ergo est ut diligat omnes in quibus est Filius, qui est in eis, inquantum habent veritatis cognitionem. Et sic est sensus: *Ego faciam eis notum nomen tuum;* et per hoc quod cognoscunt te, ego Verbum tuum ero in eis; et per hoc quod in eis sum, *dilectio, qua dilexisti me, in ipsis sit,* idest, ad eos derivetur, et diligas eos sicut me dilexisti. Vel aliter: *Ut dilectio qua dilexisti me,* idest, sicut tu me dilexisti, ita ipsi participando Spiritum Sanctum, diligant: et per hoc ergo ero in ipsis sicut Deus in templo, et ipsi in me, sicut membra in capite; I Io. IV [16]: *Qui manet in caritate, in Deo manet, et Deus in eo.*"

The indwelling of the divine Persons appears therefore as the blossoming of the welcome given to the Truth, or rather as *the Trinitarian dimension of the event that takes place in the adherence to the Truth.*

St. Thomas explains elsewhere that, when the Son is sent on a mission, the beneficiaries of this mission receive an imprint ("the stamping of a seal") of his personal property, a created gift whose origin or exemplar is the personal relation of the Son to the Father, in such wise that the beneficiary of the Son's mission is referred to the Father as a participant in the very mode in which the Son himself relates to the Father: "And the proper mode of reference of the Son to the Father is to be the Word who manifests him."[128] The sanctifying mission of the Son is accomplished when its beneficiaries know the Father through participating in the Son's personal property, that is, through assimilation to the begotten Wisdom and begotten Truth who manifests the Father. Otherwise put, the Son conveys a likeness or resemblance to the modality through which he is referred to the Father; this resemblance is the imprint with which the Son marks the saints, for their union to God will come about through being integrated into the personal relation that the Son has with the Father. The believers' adherence to the truth is therefore a union with the Father that comes about through sharing in the relation of the Son to the Father. Following on from St. Augustine, St. Thomas likewise explains that the Son is sent and given inasmuch as he is the "Word breathing Love" *(Verbum spirans Amorem).* The presence of Truth is inseparable from Love that the knowledge of Truth arouses. I shall return to this in discussing the action of the Holy Spirit. But we should note here, concerning the Word, that the manifestation of the Father by the Word is not limited to the present working of grace. It extends even to the beatific vision:

> In our homeland *we shall see face to face,* as we read in 1 Corinthians 13:12. Therefore, we will then be plainly told of the Father, and not in proverbs. Christ says *of the Father* (Jn 16:25: *I shall tell you plainly of the Father*), because no one can see the Father in that glory unless the Son manifests him: *No one knows the Father except the Son and any one to whom the Son chooses to reveal him* (Mt 11:27). For the Son is the true Light, and gives us the light by which we can see the Father.[129]

---

[128] I *Sent.*, dist. 15, q. 4, a. 1. Cf. *SCG* IV, ch. 21 (#3576): "The word of wisdom by which we know God and which is infused in us by God, properly represents the Son *(est proprie repraesentativum Filii).*"

[129] *In Ioannem* 17:25 (#2150): "In patria videbimus *facie ad faciem,* ut dicitur 1 Cor XIII [12], ideo tunc non in proverbiis, sed palam de Patre annuntiabitur nobis. Dicit autem *de Patre,* quia nullus potest Patrem videre in illa gloria nisi Filio manifestante; Matth. XI [27]: *Nemo novit Patrem nisi Filius, et cui Filius voluerit revelare.* Ipse enim est lux vera, dans nobis lucem, qua Patrem videamus."

The beatific vision is the immediate contemplation of the first Truth, the divine essence. But St. Thomas also envisages the Trinitarian aspects of this vision. The Son is the Light and the Truth begotten by the Father and, in virtue of this, he manifests the Father to the blessed:

> The vision of the divine essence is granted to all the blessed by partaking of the divine light which is shed upon them from the fountain of the Word of God, according to Ecclesiasticus (1:5): *The Word of God on high is the fountain of Wisdom.*[130]

The theme of the beatific vision "in the Word" *(in Verbo)* therefore signifies that the divine Truth is contemplated in the Word, because the Father has expressed all things in this Word: In the Word, the Father expresses himself, he expresses the Trinity and all creatures. The vision *per essentiam* is achieved "in the Word" because the Word manifests the full Trinitarian mystery to the blessed.[131] Here we find an outstanding application of the action of the Word, which St. Thomas has explained in connection with light, manifestation, and truth. Indeed, a reality is manifested and known in a word. Since the divine Word is the Light and Splendor of the Father, the vision of the divine essence by the blessed will take place through and in this Word.

The Father Makes Truth through His Word

To clarify the appropriation of the gift of truth to the Son, we need to consider one last point. Truth is a participation in the Word, but insofar as it is a created effect, truth has as its source the entire Trinity. In a first step, St. Thomas has explained that the appropriation of truth to the Son is based on the affinity that truth has with the very notion of "word." And when looking at it from the aspect of efficient and exemplar causality, he recognizes a *mode of action* distinctly characterizing the Word. It is this way of acting that we express when we say that the Father makes truth "through the Word":

> By his essence, Christ is the uncreated Truth, which is eternal and not made, but is begotten by the Father. But all created truths were made through him, and these are certain participations and reflections of the first Truth, which shines out in those souls who are holy.[132]

130 *ST* III, q. 10, a. 4: "Divinae essentiae visio convenit omnibus beatis secundum participationem luminis derivati ad eos a fonte verbi Dei, secundum illud Eccli. I: *Fons sapientiae verbum Dei in excelsis.*"

131 For further reflections on this, see José Luis González-Alió, "La visión beatífica como realidad trinitaria," *Scripta Theologica* 19 (1987): 597–631.

132 *In Ioannem* 1:17 (#207): "Ipse est per suam essentiam veritas increata; quae aeterna est, et non facta, sed a Patre est genita; sed per ipsum factae sunt omnes veritates

In this commentary on John 1:17 *(Grace and truth came through Jesus Christ)*, St. Thomas shows that created truth (it is a question here of truth in the order of grace) is made by the Word, that is, by the Son insofar as he is begotten of the Father. In this case, we are dealing with a proper feature (a property) of the Son. St. Thomas made this clear in his commentary on John 1:3 *(all things were made through him)*. What does it mean to be the one "through whom" the Father brings all things to be? If, in this expression *through whom*, one understands the causality of the Word with regard to creatures, then it is a question strictly of a *property of the Son*. The expression "through him," taken in this sense, does not designate the "formal principle" of the Father's action (this principle is the essential wisdom of God that is appropriated to the Son), but it designates the Word as the principle or the cause of creatures, under the aspect of his generation by the Father:

> If the *through* denotes causality from the standpoint of the thing produced, then the statement, *The Father does all things through the Son,* is not appropriation but it is proper to the Word, because the fact that he is a cause of creatures is had from someone else, namely the Father, from whom he has being.[133]

The Son is the one "through whom" the Father acts, because he is the Son and Word begotten by the Father. In the action of Father and Son, the preposition "through" signifies the *authority* of the Father, that is, the property of the Father as *principle* of the Son. The Son exists insofar as he eternally receives his being from the Father, and he acts in the same manner, that is, insofar as he eternally receives his action from the Father. Just as the Son possesses a proper and distinct mode of existence,[134] he possesses a mode of action distinctly his own. The action of the Father and Son is one, the principle of this action is also one (it is the divine nature or essence), and the effects of this action are common to Father and Son. But the "actors" (the subjects of the action) are personally distinct, and what

---

creatae, quae sunt quaedam participationes et refulgentiae primae veritatis, quae in animabus sanctis relucent."

133 Ibid., 1:3 (#76). See *ST* I, q. 39, a. 8: "The preposition 'through' *(per)* is not always appropriated to the Son but sometimes means a property of the Son, according to this verse of St. John (1:3): *All things were made through him;* not because the Son were an instrument, but because he is the principle from the principle." For more details on this, see chapter four in this volume: "The Personal Mode of Trinitarian Action in St. Thomas Aquinas."

134 On this mode of existence *(modus existendi)* proper to each divine Person, see *De potentia*, q. 2, a. 1, ad 13; q. 2, a. 5, ad 5; q. 3, a. 15, ad 17; q. 9, a. 5, ad 23.

we can call their "mode of action" is also distinct.[135] If we apply these reflections to truth, according to St. Thomas's explanations, we will see that it pertains *properly to the Son* to be *the one through whom the Father makes truth*.[136]

2. The Spirit of Truth

St. Thomas associates the Holy Spirit and Truth for three closely connected reasons. In the first place, the Holy Spirit is very Truth, insofar as he is God. In the second place, the Gospel designates him as "the Spirit of Truth" because he proceeds from the Son, who is Truth. And in the third place, the Holy Spirit is called "the Spirit of Truth" because of the effects of his action: The Holy Spirit gives truth. The third reason presupposes and integrates the two preceding ones.

The Spirit of Truth: The Personal Relationship of the Holy Spirit to the Son

From the start, St. Thomas stresses that the Holy Spirit is Truth itself, as much as that he is God. The Father, Son, and Holy Spirit are one sole Truth just as they are one Light and one only God.[137] From this viewpoint, the attribution of Truth to the Holy Spirit does not signify a distinctive trait of the Holy Spirit. It is a question, rather, of his very divinity, that is, of his consubstantiality with the Father and the Son.

The property of the Holy Spirit comes up in a second explanation. The Holy Spirit is "the Spirit of Truth" by virtue of the mode of his personal procession: He proceeds from the Truth. This aspect is particularly

---

135 II *Sent.*, dist. 13, q. 1, a. 5, corp., ad 4, and expositio textus: "The Son holds his being and his action from the Father, and this is why the Father acts through the Son. [. . .] The Son, who is acting, exists from the Father. [. . .] The Father acts through the Son, because the Son is the cause of what is accomplished in virtue of one same and indivisible power, a power that the Son possesses in common with the Father but which he receives, nonetheless, from the Father through his generation."

136 The uncreated Truth indeed remains *appropriated* to the Son; it is not proper to the Son but belongs to the entire Trinity (*ST* I, q. 39, a. 8). In regard to created truth, causality belongs equally to the whole Trinity. What allows us to speak of a proper characteristic of the Word is the personal relationship to the Father that the expression "through him" sets in the foreground. When we say that the Word is the one "through whom" the Father acts, we mean that the Son acts inasmuch as he receives his being and his action from the Father, through the eternal generation (the speaking of the Word): In the Trinity, the Word is the only Person who acts in this hypostatic mode.

137 Cf. *Contra errores Graecorum*, Part I, ch. 3; and *In Dionysii de divinis nominibus*, ch. 2, lect. 4 (#182).

emphasized in the commentary on the Fourth Gospel, but it also appears in numerous passages where St. Thomas teaches the procession of the Holy Spirit *from the Son.*

> In his words *The Spirit of Truth who proceeds from the Father* (Jn 15:26), our Lord was not altogether silent about his being the principle of the Holy Spirit, since he called him *the Spirit of Truth* after having called himself *the Truth* (Jn 14:6).[138]
>
> Because we read *the Spirit of Truth,* that is, the Spirit of the Son, we understand that the Spirit proceeds from the Son.[139]
>
> The Holy Spirit is *the Spirit of Truth* inasmuch as he proceeds from the Son who is the Truth of the Father.[140]

At first glance this exegesis might appear quite simple. The Spirit is the Spirit of Truth, and since the Son designated himself as the Truth, St. Thomas shows that the Spirit proceeds from the Son-Truth. However, such an interpretation involves a complex reflection of Trinitarian theology. In fact, to conclude that the Holy Spirit proceeds from the Son, St. Thomas introduces a fundamental principle of his Trinitarian teaching: "There is no relation in accord with which the Holy Spirit can be called 'the Spirit of the Son of God' except a relation of origin, for this is the only distinction we find in God. Therefore one must say that the Holy Spirit is the Son's Spirit by proceeding from him."[141] The theological rule invoked is that of the real distinction of the divine Persons through the sole relative opposition according to origin.[142] All relationships of one divine Person to another are based on the relations that constitute them as persons, that is, on origin. When we say that the Father is the Father of the Son, or that the Son is the Son of the Father, we signify a relationship of distinct persons: This relationship is based on the eternal generation of the Son by the Father, in virtue of which the Father and the Son are really distinct. It is the same with Thomas's exegesis of John 15:26.[143] The soteriological significance of

---

138 *SCG* IV, ch. 25 (#3622).

139 *In Ioannem* 15:26 (#2065). See ibid., 14:17 (#1916): "[Christ] adds *of Truth,* because the Spirit proceeds from the Truth." Ibid., 15:26 (#2062): "When [Christ] says *the Spirit of Truth,* he shows the Holy Spirit as related to the Son, for the Son is the Truth: *I am the Way, and the Truth, and the Life* (John 14:6). He shows the Holy Spirit as related to the Father when he says *who proceeds from the Father.* So to say that the Holy Spirit is *the Spirit of Truth,* is the same as saying that the Holy Spirit is the Spirit of the Son."

140 *In 1 Cor* 2:10 (#100).

141 *SCG* IV, ch. 24 (#3606). See G. Emery, *Trinity in Aquinas,* 227–28.

142 Ibid. See *ST* I, q. 36, a. 2.

143 *SCG* IV, ch. 24 (#3612).

this teaching is obvious: The procession a *Filio* accounts for the unity and continuity of the work of the Son and the Holy Spirit.

This theological interpretation of Scripture could claim roots in diverse sources in the tradition flowing from St. Augustine, but St. Thomas advances, rather, Greek patristic sources, by reason of the doctrinal debate with the Christian East. Conformably with the rules of theological dispute, Aquinas produces arguments or "authorities" that the Greeks could accept.[144] In regard to the expression "Spirit of Truth," he refers to two authorities in particular. The first is an extract from the letter *Salvatore nostro* of Cyril of Alexandria to Nestorius. Constantly cited, this extract appears in the *Summa contra Gentiles* in the Latin translation of the *Acts* of Ephesus: "Spiritus Veritatis nominatur et est Spiritus Veritatis et profluit ab eo, sicut denique et ex Deo Patre."[145] The second authority is a passage from the treatise *On the Holy Spirit* by Didymus the Blind, translated by St. Jerome:

> *He will not speak on his own authority* (Jn 16:13); that is, not without me or without my judgment and that of the Father, for he is not from himself but from the Father and from me. [. . .] The Holy Spirit, who is the Spirit of Truth and the Spirit of Wisdom, cannot learn words from the Son which are foreign to him, since he himself is sent forth by the Son, that is, he is the Truth which proceeds from the Truth, the Consoler from the Consoler, God the Spirit of Truth proceeding from God.[146]

St. Thomas understands these explanations to apply not only to the economy of grace (the Holy Spirit is sent by the Son) but also to the immanent relations of the Trinity (the Holy Spirit eternally proceeds from the Son), because of the correspondence between God's work in our world and his own immanent life. The "economy" (mission) is rooted in the "theology" (eternal procession) whose intimate structure it displays. This close parallel between theology and the economy is one of the elemental

144 Cf. *ST* I, q. 1, a. 8.

145 *SCG* IV, ch. 24 (#3609); cf. *De potentia,* q. 10, a. 4, ad 13. For parallel passages, see G. Emery, *Trinity in Aquinas,* 236–42; Martin Morard, "Thomas d'Aquin lecteur des conciles," *Archivum Franciscanum Historicum* 98 (2005): 211–365, at 269–70 (with the specification of Aquinas's possible sources).

146 *Catena in Ioannem* 16:13: "Didymus. Ait ergo non loquetur a semetipso; hoc est, non sine me et sine meo et Patris arbitrio: Quia non ex se est, sed ex Patre et me est. [. . .] Spiritus vero Sanctus, qui est Spiritus veritatis Spiritusque sapientiae, non potest Filio loquente audire quae nescit, cum hoc ipsum sit quod profertur a Filio, idest procedens Veritas a Veritate, Consolator manans a Consolatore, Deus de Deo Spiritus veritatis procedens" (*Catena aurea in quatuor Evangelia,* vol. 2, 540). Cf. Didymus, *De Spiritu Sancto* 34–46 (PL 23, 133–34).

features of Aquinas's pneumatology. Sent into the world by the Father and by the Son as the Spirit of Truth, the Holy Spirit proceeds eternally from the Father and the Son-Truth. This grounds the salvific work of the Holy Spirit in relation to truth.

The Spirit of Truth Manifests the Truth

In spite of the importance of the eternal procession of the Holy Spirit found in the expression "Spirit of Truth," there is yet a third aspect to which St. Thomas pays great attention. It is a question of the effect of the action of the Holy Spirit: He is the "Spirit of Truth" because he leads to the truth, he inspires and teaches the truth. This action of the Holy Spirit, like that of the Son, has a twofold aspect. It extends, on the one hand, to all knowledge of the truth (including natural knowledge); it concerns, on the other hand, the knowledge of grace that results from the sanctifying mission of the Holy Spirit.

> Every truth, by whomever it may be said, is from the Holy Spirit in the sense that he imparts the natural light and that he moves the mind to understand and utter the truth. This is not so, however, in the sense that he dwells in the soul by sanctifying grace or that he bestows some gift in the form of an enduring disposition which supplements nature; this is only so as regards the knowledge and utterance of certain truths, above all those which are a matter of faith.[147]

When St. Thomas explains the teaching given by the Holy Spirit, it is in the order of the knowledge of grace that he most frequently invokes the relationship of the Holy Spirit to the Son-Truth. Christ's promise to send the Spirit of Truth who "will guide you into all truth" or who "will teach all truth" (Jn 16:13)[148] has to do with the knowledge of grace. It is the knowledge of what is necessary for salvation, that is, the knowledge of what we must believe and do in order to be saved.[149] This promise concerns not only Apostolic times but the Church as long as it lasts: Divine

---

147 *ST* I–II, q. 109, a. 1, ad 1: "Omne verum, a quocumque dicatur, est a Spiritu Sancto sicut ab infundente naturale lumen, et movente ad intelligendum et loquendum veritatem. Non autem sicut ab inhabitante per gratiam gratum facientem, vel sicut a largiente aliquod habituale donum naturae superadditum, sed hoc solum est in quibusdam veris cognoscendis et loquendis; et maxime in illis quae pertinent ad fidem." See II *Sent.*, dist. 28, q. 1, a. 5; *In 1 Cor* 12:3 (#718); see also below, footnote 187.

148 St. Thomas knew the two versions: "Docebit vos omnem veritatem" and "deducet vos in omnem veritatem" (see, for example, the *Catena* on John 16:13 [vol. 2, 540]).

149 *ST* I–II, q. 106, a. 4, ad 2; cf. *In Ioannem* 16:13 (#2099–104).

providence governs the Church through the Holy Spirit so that she may not err in matters of faith. The truth and infallibility of the Church's teaching in matters of faith are guaranteed by the Holy Spirit, who teaches "all truth."[150]

> Since the Holy Spirit is *the Spirit of Truth* insofar as he proceeds from the Son who is the Truth of the Father, he breathes the truth to those to whom he is sent, just as the Son, sent by the Father, makes them know the Father.[151]

The Holy Spirit is the Spirit "*of Truth* because he proceeds from the Truth and because he utters the truth."[152] The action of the Holy Spirit as manifestating the truth is thus seen to be directly connected with his eternal procession, which furnishes its profound reason: "This Spirit leads to knowledge of the Truth because he proceeds from the Truth, who says, *I am the Way, and the Truth and the Life.*"[153] St. Thomas sums up this reading in his commentary on John 16:13: "Since the Holy Spirit is from the truth, it is for him to teach the truth and to render [those he teaches] like his principle."[154] These explanations are based on a principle already encountered in connection with the Son-Truth: When an agent receives its being from another, its action manifests this other. In formal terms, St. Thomas explains that "everything which is from another manifests that from which it is";[155] or, "What acts in virtue of another tends in its effect to manifest that other, for the action of a principle which is from a principle manifests this principle."[156] When applied to the Son and to the Holy Spirit, this metaphysical rule leads Aquinas to the following explanations: "The Son manifests the Father, because he is from the Father. And so

150 *Quodlibet* IX, q. 8, a. 1.

151 *In 1 Cor* 2:10 (#100): "Quia enim Spiritus Sanctus est Spiritus veritatis, utpote a Filio procedens, qui est veritas Patris, his quibus mittitur inspirat veritatem, sicut et Filius a Patre missus notificat Patrem." These explanations rest on John 14:26 ("But the Counselor, the Holy Spirit, whom the Father will send in my name, he will teach you all things") and on Matthew 11:27 ("No one knows the Father except the Son and any one to whom the Son chooses to reveal him").

152 *In Ioannem* 14:17 (#1916): "Addit autem *veritatis*, quia a veritate procedit et veritatem dicit."

153 Ibid.: "Iste Spiritus ducit ad cognitionem veritatis, quia procedit a veritate, quae dicit supra eodem: *Ego sum via, et veritas, et vita.*"

154 Ibid., 16:13 (#2102): "Cum enim sit a veritate, eius est docere veritatem, et facere similes suo principio."

155 Ibid., 16:14 (#2107): "Omne enim quod est ab alio, manifestat id a quo est."

156 Ibid., 17:2 (#2185): "Agentis cuiuslibet quod agit ab alio, intentio est reducere suum effectum in causae manifestationem, nam ex actione principii quod est de principio, manifestatur ipsum principium."

because the Holy Spirit is from the Son, it is his property to manifest him."[157] This work of manifestation is based on the divine relationships of the Son and the Holy Spirit: "As God, Christ has the Holy Spirit as manifesting himself, inasmuch as the Spirit proceeds from him."[158] Here we again find the order and nature of the missions of the divine Persons: The Holy Spirit manifests the Son and the Son manifests the Father. Since the Son is Truth itself, it is then by teaching the Truth that the Holy Spirit manifests the Son.[159]

The Mode of the Holy Spirit's Action in Teaching the Truth

St. Thomas has explained that the Son is the source of all manifestation of the truth and that his mission consists in making the truth known. He has also explained that the mission of the Holy Spirit consists in teaching the Truth. So the action of the Son and the action of the Holy Spirit are identical: to make the truth known. The Holy Spirit teaches no other truth than Christ, nor does he teach a truth higher than that which the Son teaches.[160] Rather, he transmits and inscribes in the hearts of the faithful the truth that he receives from the Son in proceeding from him. The Holy Spirit "came to manifest Christ who, since he is the Truth, ought to have been manifested only by the Truth."[161] St. Thomas notes, however, a distinction in the mode of action of the Spirit.

On the one hand, the Holy Spirit receives his action from the Father and the Son, while the Son receives his from the Father only. Since the Spirit holds his being and his action from the Son, the effect of the Holy Spirit's mission is to render men like the Son-Truth. In other words, "The Holy Spirit teaches insofar as he makes us participate in the wisdom of the Son."[162] This aspect expresses the *order* of the divine Persons: It is in sending the Holy Spirit that the Son obtains for us the interior knowledge of faith.[163]

---

157 Ibid., 16:14 (#2107): "Filius enim manifestat Patrem, quia est ab ipso. Quia ergo Spiritus Sanctus est a Filio, proprium est ut clarificet eum."

158 Ibid., 3:34 (#543): "Inquantum vero Deus, habet Spiritum Sanctum ut manifestantem tantum, secundum quod ab eo procedit." St. Thomas adds that, as man, the incarnate Son has the Holy Spirit as Sanctifier *(ut sanctificantem).* In both cases, that is, as God and as man, Christ has the Holy Spirit "without measure," though in a different way.

159 Ibid., 16:14 (#2105).

160 In his *Catena* on Luke 12:10 (vol. 2, 178), St. Thomas cites this clarification under the name of St. Athanasius: "non tamquam doctrina Spiritus dogma Filii superet."

161 *In Ioannem* 1:32 (#271): "Venit enim Spiritus sanctus ad manifestandum Christum, qui cum sit veritas, non nisi per veritatem manifestandus erat."

162 Ibid., 14:26 (#1960): "Docet, inquantum nos facit participare sapientiam Filii."

163 Ibid., 17:26 (#2269). The Son makes the Father known by sending the Holy Spirit.

Believers are "sanctified in the truth" (Jn 17:17) when they receive the Holy Spirit whom the Father and the Son send them, thus giving them "knowledge of the truth of faith" that sanctifies.[164]

On the other hand, the way in which the Holy Spirit teaches the truth can be distinguished from the way in which the Son teaches the truth.[165] The Son, as we have seen, teaches the truth by granting men to participate in, or to be assimilated to, his personal property of Word, Wisdom, and Splendor of the Father. As for the Holy Spirit, his action of teaching the truth is especially connected with love, which constitutes his distinctive personal property:

> In us, love of the truth arises when we have conceived and considered truth. So also in God, Love proceeds from conceived Truth, which is the Son. And just as Love proceeds from the Truth, so Love leads to the knowledge of the truth: *He will glorify me because he will receive from me and declare it to you* (Jn 16:14). And therefore Ambrose says that any truth, no matter who speaks it, is from the Holy Spirit. *No one can say Jesus is Lord except by the Holy Spirit* (1 Cor 12:3); *When the Paraclete comes, whom I shall send to you from the Father, the Spirit of truth* (Jn 15:26). To manifest the truth fits the property of the Holy Spirit, for it is love that leads to the revelation of secrets.[166]

---

164 Ibid., 17:17 (#2229).

165 In his commentary on John (ibid., 14:16 [(#1912]), St. Thomas explicitly notes this distinct mode of action in connection with the name *Paraclete*: "The Son and the Holy Spirit are Consolers and Advocates in a different way *(alia et alia ratione)*, if we consider what is congruent to each person. Christ is called an Advocate because as a human being he intercedes for us to the Father; the Holy Spirit is an Advocate because he makes us ask. Again, the Holy Spirit is called a Consoler inasmuch as he is formally Love *(inquantum est amor formaliter)*. But the Son is a Consoler inasmuch as he is the Word *(inquantum est Verbum)*. The Son is a Consoler in two ways: because of his teaching and because the Son gives the Holy Spirit and incites love in our hearts. Thus the word 'another' *('another Paraclete')* does not indicate a different nature in the Son and in the Holy Spirit. Rather, it indicates the different mode in which both of them are each an Advocate and a Consoler *(designat alium modum quo uterque est consolator et advocatus)*." For more details, see chapter four in this volume: "The Personal Mode of Trinitarian Action in St. Thomas Aquinas."

166 *In Ioannem* 14:17 (#1916): "Sicut in nobis ex veritate concepta et considerata sequitur amor ipsius veritatis, ita in Deo concepta Veritate, quae est Filius, procedit Amor. Et sicut ab ipsa procedit, ita in eius cognitionem ducit; infra cap. XVI [14]: *Ille me clarificabit, quia de meo accipiet* et cetera. Et ideo dicit Ambrosius, quod omne verum a quocumque dicatur a Spiritu sancto est. 1 Cor 12:3: *Nemo potest dicere, Dominus Iesus, nisi in Spiritu Sancto*; infra XV [26]: *Cum venerit Paraclitus, quem ego mittam vobis Spiritum veritatis.* Manifestare autem veritatem convenit proprietati Spiritus Sancti. Est enim amor qui facit secretorum revelationem."

St. Thomas envisages here the source of the manifestation of truth, that is, the Trinitarian "reason" for the manifestation of truth: On the one hand, Love proceeds from Truth; on the other hand, it is because of his Love that God gives us his Truth.[167] But Aquinas also clarifies the role of love in welcoming the Truth. Love causes men to seek the truth, to fix their attention on the truth and to give it a welcome. It is love that renders man capable of receiving the truth.[168]

> The one who comes [to Christ] through a knowledge of the truth must hear, when God speaks within: *I will hear what the Lord God will speak within me* (Ps 84:9); and he must learn, through affection. The one who comes [to Christ] through love and desire *(If any one thirsts, let him come to me and drink* [Jn 7:37]) must hear the word of the Father and grasp it, in order to learn and be moved in his affections. For that person learns the word who grasps it according to the meaning of the speaker. But the Word of the Father breathes forth Love. Therefore, the one who grasps the word of God with the fervor of love, learns.[169]

The Son is sent invisibly into the soul only when the grasp of truth brings with it the affection of charity.[170] As for the Holy Spirit, he teaches the truth insofar as, bestowing grace, he pours out charity, and through it grants a man to seek the truth and to grasp it in love. St. Thomas explains it anew by giving the example of the sense of taste, through which we can perceive the savor of things.

---

167 *SCG* IV, ch. 21 (#3578): "To reveal one's secrets to one's friend is the proper mark of friendship. [. . .] Therefore, since by the Holy Spirit we are established as friends of God, fittingly enough it is by the Holy Spirit that men are said to receive the revelation of the divine mysteries." Being Love in person, the Holy Spirit is the first Gift "through which all other gifts are given" (*ST* I, q. 38, a. 2).

168 *In Ioannem* 14:17 (#1918–19). See footnote 121 above.

169 Ibid., 6:45 (#946): "Nam qui venit per cognitionem veritatis, oportet eum audire, Deo inspirante, secundum illud Ps. LXXXIV [9]: *Audiam quid loquatur in me Dominus Deus,* et addiscere per affectum, ut dictum est. Qui vero venit per amorem et desiderium, ut dicitur infra VII [37]: *Si quis sitit, veniat ad me, et bibat,* et hunc oportet audire verbum Patris, et capere illud, ad hoc ut addiscat, et afficiatur. Ille enim discit verbum qui capit illud secundum rationem dicentis; Verbum autem Dei Patris est spirans Amorem: Qui ergo capit illud cum fervore amoris, discit."

170 *ST* I, q. 43, a. 5, ad 2: "The Son is the Word; not, however, just any word, but the Word breathing Love *(spirans Amorem)*. This is why Augustine says that 'the Word as I want the meaning understood is knowledge together with love' [*De Trinitate* IX,10,15]. Consequently not just any enhancing of the mind indicates the Son's being sent, but only that sort of enlightening that bursts out forth into love." On this theme, see Raimondo Spiazzi, "Conoscenza con amore in Sant'Agostino e in San Tomaso," *Doctor communis* 39 (1986): 315–28.

> Christ says: *He [the Paraclete] will teach you all things* (Jn 14:26), because no matter what a person may teach by his exterior actions, he will have no effect unless the Holy Spirit gives an understanding from within. For unless the Spirit is present to the heart of the listener, the words of the teacher will be useless: *The breath of the Almighty makes him understand* (Job 32:8). This is true even to the extent that the Son himself, speaking by means of his human nature, is not successful unless he works from within by the Hoy Spirit. [. . .] One does not learn without the Holy Spirit teaching. The one who receives the Holy Spirit from the Father and the Son knows the Father and the Son and comes to them. The Spirit makes us know all things by inspiring us from within, by directing us and lifting us up to spiritual things. Just as one whose sense of taste is tainted does not have a true knowledge of flavors, so one who is tainted by love of the world can not taste divine things: *The sensual man does not perceive those things of the Spirit of God* (1 Cor 2:14).[171]

The first effect of the mission of the Holy Spirit is, then, to render men "capable of the truth,"[172] by raising them up to divine realities through grace and charity, and by "softening the hearts of the hearers."[173] St. Thomas again illustrates this action of love in a markedly suggestive way by means of the image of a lantern or a lamp *(lucerna)*:

> Just as a lamp cannot give light unless there is a fire blazing within it, so a spiritual lamp does not give any light unless it is first set ablaze and burns with the fire of love. Therefore, to be ablaze comes first, and the giving of light depends on it, because knowledge of the truth is given due to the blazing of love: *If any one loves me, he will keep my word, and my Father will love him, and we will come to him, and make our home with him* (Jn 14:23); and *I have called you friends, because everything I*

---

[171] *In Ioannem* 14:26 (#1958 and 1959): "Dicit ergo *ille vos docebit omnia,* quia quaecumque homo doceat extra, nisi Spiritus Sanctus interius det intelligentiam, frustra laborat: Quia nisi Spiritus adsit cordi audientis, otiosus erit sermo doctoris, Iob XXXII [8]: *Inspiratio omnipotentis dat intelligentiam;* et intantum, quod etiam ipse Filius organo humanitatis loquens, non valet, nisi ipsemet interius operetur per Spiritum Sanctum. [. . .] Non discit non docente Spiritu Sancto, quasi: Ille qui recipit Spiritum Sanctum a Patre et Filio, ille Patrem cognoscit, et Filium, et ad eos venit. Facit autem nos scire omnia interius inspirando, dirigendo, et ad spiritualia elevando. Sicut enim qui habet gustum infectum non habet veram cognitionem de saporibus, ita et qui infectus est amore mundi, non potest gustare divina, secundum illud 1 Cor 2:14: *Animalis autem homo non percipit ea quae sunt spiritus Dei.*"

[172] Ibid. See footnote 121 above.

[173] Ibid., 15:27 (#2066): "Emolliendo audientium corda."

have heard from my Father I have made known to you (Jn 15:15); *You who fear the Lord, love him, and your hearts will be enlightened* (Sir 2:10 according to the Vulgate). For fire has two properties: it both burns and shines. Its blazing signifies love.[174]

There is, therefore, a twofold relationship between charity and truth. It expresses the order of the mission of the Son and of the Holy Spirit under two complementary aspects. On the one hand, truth flowers in charity. From this standpoint, we can note a participation in the very order of the Trinitarian processions. As the divine Word breathes Love, the knowledge of truth arouses love. In receiving the truth that "bursts out forth into love," we receive it according to the very pattern of its Trinitarian model. On the other hand, charity exerts a fundamental influence on the mind that knows and receives the truth. And from this standpoint, the movement of the will precedes the illumination of the mind by truth. It is through the ardor of charity that knowledge of the truth is given, for charity moves the mind to grasp the truth and give it its assent.[175] This is also the path of our access to the Trinitarian mystery, according to St. Thomas's teaching on the effect of the mission of the Holy Spirit: The Holy Spirit, who is Love, leads us to the Word and Truth of the Father.

To show how the Holy Spirit teaches the truth, St. Thomas makes equal use of the theme of "impulse" or "impulsion of love," by means of which, in the *Summa contra Gentiles*, he exposes the personal property of the Holy Spirit. When he explains that the Holy Spirit is personally Love, he does not intend to say that the act of love should be attributed exclusively, in a proper manner, to the Holy Spirit. He intends love, rather, as the "imprint" *(impressio)* that arises in the will and "moves" the will toward

---

174 Ibid., 5:35 (#812), on Jesus' words about John the Baptist ("He was a lamp, blazing and shining"): "Sicut lucerna lucere non potest nisi igne accendatur, ita lucerna spiritualis non lucet nisi prius ardeat et inflammetur igne caritatis. Et ideo ardor praemittitur illustrationi, quia per ardorem caritatis datur cognitio veritatis; infra XIV [23]: *Si quis diligit me, sermonem meum servabit, et Pater meus diliget eum: et ad eum veniemus, et mansionem apud eum faciemus;* infra XV [15]: *Vos autem dixi amicos, quia omnia quae audivi a Patre meo, nota feci vobis.* Eccli. II: *Qui timetis Deum, diligite illum, et illuminabuntur corda vestra.* Nam ignis duo habet: scilicet quod ardet et splendet. Ardor autem ignis significat dilectionem." St. Thomas proposes elsewhere the image of a window, which, when the blinds are closed, prevents the sunlight from entering the house: In order to see the sunlight, one must open the blinds (Ibid., 12:39 [#1697]).

175 *ST* II–II, q. 4, a. 2 and a. 3. On this interconnection of intellect and will (truth and love), see Michael S. Sherwin, *By Knowledge and by Love: Charity and Knowledge in the Moral Theology of St. Thomas Aquinas* (Washington, DC: Catholic University of America Press, 2005); Benoît Duroux, *La psychologie de la foi chez saint Thomas d'Aquin* (Paris: Téqui, 1963).

the beloved good. It is this immanent imprint of love that, by analogy, permits one to grasp the distinctive property of the Holy Spirit.[176] It is equally by means of this *interior principle of impulse* proper to love that St. Thomas accounts for the name "Spirit" given to the third person of the Trinity. Since the good that is loved is present in the will of the lover as drawing him toward itself (the one whom I love is present to my will as inclining me toward him), and since such an impulse refers to the "spirit" in living beings,[177] "it is therefore fitting that God proceeding by the mode of love should be called *Spirit,* as subsisting in virtue of a 'spiration.'"[178] This theme clarifies the preceding explanations while at the same time offering a synthesis of them:

> Since the word *spiritus* suggests a kind of impulsion, and since every motion produces an effect in harmony with its source (as heating makes something hot), it follows that the Holy Spirit makes those to whom he is sent like the one whose Spirit he is. This is why, being the Spirit of Truth, he teaches all truth.[179]

We find here the various aspects of the action of the Holy Spirit teaching the truth: his relation of origin to the Son-Truth, the assimilation to the principle from whom he proceeds, and the loving impulse that characterizes his personal property. St. Thomas can thus explain that the Holy Spirit "teaches the truth" without confounding his mode of acting with that of the Word but in connecting this work of the Spirit, the Paraclete, with the distinct characteristics of his person.

---

[176] *SCG* IV, ch. 19; *ST* I, q. 37, a. 1. See G. Emery, *Trinity in Aquinas,* 102–4 and 153–56; Emmanuel Durand, "Au principe de l'amour: *formatio ou proportio*?" *Revue Thomiste* 104 (2004): 551–78.

[177] *SCG* IV, ch. 19 (#3566): "Amatum in voluntate existit ut inclinans, et quodammodo impellens intrinsecus amantem in ipsam rem amatam; impulsus autem rei viventis ab interiori ad spiritum pertinet." Cf. *ST* I, q. 37, a. 1.

[178] *SCG* IV, ch. 19 (#3566): "Convenit Deo per modum amoris procedenti ut *Spiritus* dicatur eius, quasi quadam spiratione existente." Cf. *ST* I, q. 36, a. 1: "Among corporeal beings the term 'spiritus' appears to signify an impulse and motion *(impulsionem quamdam et motionem)*; we give the name 'spiritus' to breath and to wind. Now it is distinctive of love that it move and urge the will of the lover towards the beloved *(quod moveat et impellat voluntatem amantis in amatum)*."

[179] *In Ioannem* 15:25 (#2062): "Quia hoc nomen spiritus quamdam impulsionem importat, omnis autem motus habet effectum convenientem suo principio, sicut calefactio facit calidum: consequens est ut Spiritus Sanctus eos, in quos mittitur, similes faciat ei cuius est Spiritus: Et ideo, cum sit Spiritus veritatis, docet omnem veritatem."

To Do the Truth

The action of the Holy Spirit, inseparable from that of the Son, appears in the practical aspect of truth as well. "To do the truth" *(facere veritatem)*, according to St. Thomas, is to act in a virtuous manner insofar as this action is submitted and conformed to the order of the divine intellect. It is by reason of this virtuous action that we speak of "the truth of life."[180] This *veritas vitae* does not designate the truth as it is in the intellect, but the truth "in things" in reference to an intellect, not only to the human intellect but firstly to that of God: "Truth as applied to 'life' is used in a particular sense, inasmuch as a man fulfills in his life that to which he is ordained by the divine intellect."[181] To live in the truth is to live uprightly.[182] "Truth consists not only in thoughts and words, but also in deeds *(in factis)*."[183] This is why "to adhere to the truth" means not only knowing the truth speculatively but also living in conformity with God's design.[184] This "truth of life" belongs to the criteria for the understanding of God's revelation:

> The statements and commands found in Sacred Scripture can be interpreted and understood from what the saints have done, since it is the same Holy Spirit who inspired the prophets and the other authors of Sacred Scripture and who moves the saints to act. For, as it is said in 2 Peter 1:21, *Moved by the Holy Spirit holy men spoke from God*; and in Romans 8:14, *All who are led by the Spirit of God are sons of God.* Thus, Sacred Scripture should be understood according to the way Christ and the other saints observed it [in their deeds].[185]

---

180 *ST* I, q. 17, a. 1: "Operatio virtuosa veritas vitae nominatur." This consideration of the truth as a virtue comes from Aristotle: see *ST* II–II, q. 109, a. 3, ad 3.

181 Ibid., q. 16, a. 4, ad 3: "Veritas autem vitae dicitur particulariter, secundum quod homo in vita sua implet illud ad quod ordinatur per intellectum divinum."

182 *ST* II–II, q. 109, a. 3, ad 3: "The truth of life is that of a man who lives aright in himself." Cf. IV *Sent.*, dist. 46, q. 1, a 1, qla 3, ad 1: "The truth of life consists in one's acting in conformity with what reason teaches"; IV *Sent.*, dist. 46, q. 1, a. 1, qla 3, ad 3: "Insofar as our actions are likened to the intellect, as what is regulated relates to what regulates, we can speak of the truth of life."

183 *In Ioannem* 3:21 (#495): "Veritas enim non solum in cogitatione et dictis consistit, sed et in factis."

184 *In Rom* 2:8 (#198).

185 *In Ioannem* 18:23 (#2321): "Dicta et praecepta sacrae Scripturae ex factis sanctorum interpretari possunt et intelliguntur, cum idem Spiritus Sanctus qui inspiravit prophetis et aliis sacrae Scripturae auctoribus, moverit sanctos ad opus. Nam, sicut II Petr. I [21] dicitur, *Spiritu Sancto inspirati locuti sunt sancti Dei homines*; ita Rom. VIII [14] dicitur: *Qui Spiritu Dei aguntur, hi sunt filii Dei.* Sic sacra Scriptura intelligenda est secundum quod Christus et alii sancti servaverunt."

Uprightness and the truth of life are attributed to the Holy Spirit for the same reason that led to attributing to him the knowledge of speculative truth: By his loving impulse, the Holy Spirit is the source of a motion of the will. Further, this truth of life does not concern only what is necessarily required for salvation. It extends also to works of perfection, to the evangelical counsels, and to various works of mercy.[186] Commenting on the verse, *No one can say "Jesus is Lord!" except by the Holy Spirit* (1 Cor 12:3), St. Thomas explains:

> *To say something in the Holy Spirit* can be understood in two ways. (1) In one way, it can mean: in the Holy Spirit moving but not possessed. For the Holy Spirit moves the hearts of certain men to speak, although he does not dwell in them [. . .]. According to this, therefore, it must be understood that no one can say anything true, unless moved by the Holy Spirit, who is the Spirit of truth, of whom it is said in John (16:13): *When the Spirit of truth comes, he will guide you into all the truth.* Hence Ambrose says in the Gloss on this verse [1 Cor 12:3]: *Every truth by whomsoever spoken is from the Holy Spirit.* This applies especially to matters of faith, which are had by a special revelation of the Holy Spirit. Among these is the fact that Jesus is Lord of all things. [. . .] (2) In another way someone speaks in the Holy Spirit moving and possessed. And according to this, what is said here can be verified, but in such a way that to speak refers not only to the mouth but also to the heart and the deed. [. . .] No one, therefore, can say *Jesus is Lord* unless he possesses the Holy Spirit, that is, in such a way that he confesses him not only with his lips but also reveres him as Lord in his heart and obeys him as his Lord in his works.[187]

The Holy Spirit is thus the source of truth in all its dimensions: the truth of mind and word, the truth of the heart, but also the truth of action

---

[186] *ST* II–II, q. 43, a. 7, ad 4; cf. IV *Sent.*, dist. 38, q. 2, a. 4, qla 2, ad 1.

[187] *In 1 Cor* 12:3 (#718): "Dicere aliquid in Spiritu sancto, potest intelligi dupliciter. Uno modo in Spiritu Sancto movente, sed non habito. Movet enim Spiritus Sanctus corda aliquorum ad loquendum, quos non inhabitat [. . .]. Secundum hoc ergo intelligendum est quod nullus potest dicere quodcumque verum, nisi a Spiritu Sancto motus, qui est Spiritus veritatis, de quo dicitur Io. XVI [13]: *Cum autem venerit ille Spiritus veritatis, docebit vos omnem veritatem.* Unde et in Glossa Ambrosius, hoc in loco dicit: *Omne verum a quocumque dicatur, a Spiritu Sancto est.* Et specialiter in illis quae sunt fidei, quae per specialem revelationem Spiritus sancti sunt habita, inter quae est quod Iesus sit omnium dominus [. . .] Alio modo loquitur aliquis in Spiritu Sancto movente et habito. Et secundum hoc etiam potest verificari quod hic dicitur, ita tamen quod dicere accipiatur non solum ore, sed etiam corde et opere. [. . .] Nemo, ergo nisi habendo Spiritum Sanctum, potest dicere Iesum dominum, ita scilicet quod non solum hoc ore confiteatur, sed etiam corde revereatur ipsum ut dominum et opere obediat ipsi quasi domino."

conformed to the known truth. These elements could be completed by the notion of "the truth of the practical intellect," which comes from "conformity with righteous appetite."[188] Such truth is found in the practical intellect insofar as it directs the action; it depends on the conformity of the intellect with a right desire, and pertains to the virtue of prudence.[189] In this domain again, it is the action of the Holy Spirit that is at stake, since rectitude of desire is caused by the Holy Spirit.[190] These explanations, which extend the sense of "to speak the truth," show that St. Thomas envisages *the wholeness and integrity of the Christian life* under the action of the Holy Spirit, in the light of truth.

3. Conclusion

It is not enough to affirm that the thought of St. Thomas Aquinas on truth contains important Trinitarian developments. We must go further and recognize that Thomas's teaching on truth is directly connected with his doctrine of the Triune God, while paying attention to the double-mapping of our path to the Trinitarian mystery: what belongs to all three persons by virtue of their common divinity, and what pertains to each person in his distinctive property. Aquinas's teaching on truth reaches its full meaning in the doctrine of the immanent Trinity and in the exposition of the Trinitarian economy (creation, grace, and glory). Our inquiry showed that the Trinitarian economy is put in the foreground. Aquinas's commentary on St. John gives special prominence to the Trinitarian dimension of the communication of truth through the mission of the Son and of the Holy Spirit, to such an extent that the theology of truth appears as a theology of salvation history.[191]

Aquinas's Trinitarian teaching on truth is centered on the Word. All true knowledge comes from the Word and, through the Holy Spirit, leads to the Word. The appropriation of Truth to the Son is a central aspect of this view. This appropriation, however, is only one aspect of a far vaster teaching. St. Thomas considers with the greatest attention the relationship of

---

188 *ST* I–II, q. 64, a. 3; cf. *ST* I–II, q. 57, a. 5, ad 3: "Verum autem intellectus practici accipitur per conformitatem ad appetitum rectum."

189 See the insightful analysis by Camille de Belloy, "La vérité de l'agir selon saint Thomas d'Aquin," *Revue Thomiste* 104 (2004): 103–25.

190 St. Thomas attributes to the Holy Spirit our rectitude of desire and appetite; see, for example, *ST* II–II, q. 83, a. 5, ad 1; and *In Rom* 8:26 (#693). The gifts that perfect the affectivity are appropriated to the Holy Spirit by reason of the mode of his procession as Love; cf. *ST* I, q. 39, a. 8.

191 For further reflections on this issue, see Serge-Thomas Bonino, "La théologie de la vérité dans la *Lectura super Ioannem* de saint Thomas d'Aquin," *Revue Thomiste* 104 (2004): 141–66.

word and truth, in man and in God. He associates it with a sheaf of themes in the midst of which he takes into account Trinitarian faith in the Son: the generation of the Word by the Father, the light, the manifestation, the splendor, and so on. He thus shows the role of the Son in the gift of truth, in the domain of natural knowledge as well as in that of grace. The Son, as the Truth of the Father, manifests and reveals the Father. The Son communicates knowledge of the Father in the realm of faith today, and he will not cease to manifest the Father in the beatific vision. The Holy Spirit does not intervene in second place but is at the first level of this teaching. Proceeding eternally from the Son-Truth, by whom he is also communicated to men, the Holy Spirit is the principle of all participation in the Son-Truth, in the order of natural knowledge and that of grace. By the impulse of love that he communicates, the Holy Spirit leads us to seek the truth and adhere to it; he disposes men to receive the truth and inscribes it upon their hearts. Those whom he establishes as "knowers of the truth," he enables to "do the truth" by virtuous action, thus causing the truth to flower in all its dimensions. At its summit, this welcome of the Truth is nothing else than the indwelling of Father, Son, and Holy Spirit in the saints, that is, the most intimate participation in Trinitarian life.

How does it happen that St. Thomas's teaching on truth is sometimes presented while omitting these profound Trinitarian dimensions? We have to recognize that, in more than one place, St. Thomas treats certain aspects of truth without invoking faith in the Trinity. More than other theologians of his time (St. Bonaventure in particular), he clearly distinguishes between the realms of faith and philosophical reason. In St. Thomas, the teaching on the transcendentals is integrated with Trinitarian faith only through important clarifications and distinctions. We have already noted that, in order to grasp the profundity of his Trinitarian teaching on truth, it is necessary to turn to his biblical commentaries, especially that on St. John. In this field, the teaching of his synthesizing works (*Commentary on the Sentences*, disputed questions *De veritate*, the *Summa contra Gentiles*, and the *Summa theologiae*) attains its full clarity only when in conjunction with them the biblical commentaries have been read. Here we touch on a problem of interpretation of the writings of St. Thomas. If we consider the biblical commentaries as an appendix to his theological works, we might be tempted to situate the relationships of truth to the Trinity at a secondary level. But if we consider the reading of Scripture as the primary task of the theologian that St. Thomas was, recognizing that the synthesizing works are themselves linked with this reading of Scripture, we are bound to recognize that the Trinitarian dimension is at the heart of his teaching on truth.

CHAPTER 4

The Personal Mode of Trinitarian Action in St. Thomas Aquinas

WHEN SCHOLASTIC theologians explore the economic act of the Trinity, they frequently refer to the doctrine of appropriations.[1] They understand by "appropriation" the attribution to one divine Person of features common to the whole Trinity, in order to illumine better the distinct properties of the Father, of the Son, and of the Holy Spirit.[2] It is in this way, for example, that the Scholastics of the thirteenth century generally considered the attribution of creation to the Father ("I believe in God, the Father almighty, creator of heaven and earth") or sanctification to the Holy Spirit ("I believe in the Holy Spirit, the Lord, the giver of life").[3] Resting on a complex analysis of the divine attributes, the theory of appropriations possesses a realism that Albert the Great, for example, describes by explaining that Trinitarian appropriation is founded "on the side of the reality itself" and not solely in our mind.[4]

---

1 English translation by Matthew Levering; this essay appeared in *The Thomist* 69 (2005): 31–77.

2 St. Bonaventure, *Breviloquium* I, ch. 6 (*Opera omnia,* vol. 5 [Quaracchi: Editiones Collegii S. Bonaventurae, 1891], 214–15).

3 St. Thomas, *ST* I, q. 45, a. 6, ad 2. The aim of appropriation is not to diminish the personal features of the Trinity (as is sometimes suggested by modern criticism) but, on the contrary, to make the persons more manifest to believers (*ST* I, q. 39, a. 7).

4 St. Albert the Great, I *Sent.*, dist. 34, a. 5 (*Opera omnia,* ed. Auguste Borgnet, vol. 26 [Paris: Vivès, 1893], 171). Following his master, St. Thomas explains: "From the standpoint of the reality, the likeness of the appropriated attribute to the person's property makes the congruity of the appropriation, *a congruence which would be there even if we did not exist*" (I *Sent.*, dist. 31, q. 1, a. 2). See Gilles Emery, *La théologie trinitaire de saint Thomas d'Aquin* (Paris: Cerf, 2004), 369–98.

However, today the theory of appropriations provokes reservations among many theologians, who accuse it of obscuring the personal dimension of the Trinitarian act or running the risk of being a mere linguistic game.[5] The appropriative method would be quite unsatisfying if one regarded the divine act as pertaining exclusively to the divine essence and the Trinitarian dimension as dependent only on an appropriation. In other words, appropriation would be badly understood if one used it in order to cover up or "disguise" a monist conception of divine action.

Is appropriation, however, the sole explication of the Trinitarian dimension of the divine act? Is it not necessary, rather, to recognize a mode of acting *proper* to each divine Person, beyond the appropriations? Certain oft-repeated clichés in this domain aim at opposing the Thomist tradition to the Greek tradition (with the latter recognizing a distinct mode of acting of the hypostases in the single operation of the Trinity).[6] In fact, the texts show that Thomas Aquinas upholds a personal, proper modality of the act of the Father, of the Son, and of the Holy Spirit. It is this teaching, too little known even today, that I wish to present here, by situating it in its doctrinal context.

The structure of this study will be as follows. I will describe first the fundamental principle of the thought of St. Thomas concerning the Trinitarian act: The Father creates and does everything by his Son in the Holy Spirit (section 1). This principle governs the speculative thesis of the "causality of the Trinitarian processions" that St. Thomas develops in a proper and original way (section 2). This affirmation of the personal dimension of the Trinitarian act raises a question (section 3): Is it necessary to recognize a "proper role" or a "distinct action" of each divine Person? In order to attempt to respond to this question, I propose to consider first the exegesis of John 1:3, in which St. Thomas shows that to be the one "through whom" the Father does all things is a *proper* feature of the Son (section 4). This exegesis rests on the Trinitarian doctrine of the distinct "mode of existence" of each divine Person. Because the mode of action reflects the mode of being, it is necessary to recognize a distinct *mode* of action of each divine Person (section 5). This teaching can be illustrated by the exegesis of many biblical passages. As an example, I propose to consider the way in which St. Thomas shows that the Son and the Holy Spirit both exercise the role of Consoler, but in distinct *modes* (section 6). In all these explanations, however, St. Thomas maintains

[5] See Yves Congar, *Je crois en l'Esprit Saint* (Paris: Cerf, 1995), 346–61; for examples of a sharper criticism, see Catherine Mowry LaCugna, *God for Us: The Trinity and Christian Life* (San Francisco: HarperCollins, 1991), 99–101; Anne Hunt, *The Trinity and the Paschal Mystery: A Development in Recent Catholic Theology* (Collegeville: The Liturgical Press, 1997), 113–14, 176.

[6] See, for example, Henri Barré, *Trinité que j'adore: Perspectives théologiques* (Paris: Lethielleux, 1965), 150.

quite firmly the unity of the divine action and the unity of the Trinity as the source of created effects: The doctrine of perichoresis permits him to show the profoundly personalist character of the rule of the unity of action of the Trinity (section 7). This unity of action does not signify that, in the life of faith, believers have a relation only to the undivided Trinity; there is rather, in the life of grace, a relationship of believers to each divine Person in his distinction. This relationship is found not at the "entitative" level by which we are ontologically referred to the Trinity as cause, but at the level of the "intentional" or "objective" union with the divine Persons; from this standpoint, the gifts of grace refer us to the divine Persons in their distinctiveness (section 8). This theological path is complex, but it is necessary if we are to render a faithful account of the thought of Thomas Aquinas.

1. The Father Creates and Accomplishes All Things by His Son in the Holy Spirit

The properties of the divine Persons clarify not only their distinction and their subsistence in the immanence of the Trinity, but equally their act in the world. With respect to the Father, Thomas Aquinas shows that paternity designates primarily the intra-Trinitarian relation of the Father to the Son and secondarily the relation that God the Father holds with the world according to diverse degrees of participation (paternity toward creatures lacking reason and toward creatures made to the image of God, divine paternity according to nature and according to grace): It is by participating in the relation that the Son holds with his Father that creatures have God for their Father.[7] In his study of the Son, Thomas establishes that the *Word*, by virtue of his personal property, possesses a relationship toward creatures, because the Father accomplishes all things by his Word. The very name of *Word* signifies the Son in his exemplar and efficient causality; it permits one to understand the foundation of the manifestation of the Father as accomplished by the Son.[8] The study of the name Son as well as the theme of the *Image* (a proper name of the Son) clarifies equally the creative and the salvific action of the Son.[9] One can hardly summarize, at one stroke, this vast teaching. Let us recall the master idea that guides Aquinas's explanations:

> Whoever makes something must preconceive it in his wisdom, which is the form and pattern of the thing made: as the form preconceived in the mind of an artisan is the pattern of the cabinet to be

[7] St. Thomas, *ST* I, q. 33, a. 3.

[8] Ibid., q. 34, a. 3: The Word of God, inasfar as he is the Word *(Verbum)*, expresses and causes creatures.

[9] See, notably, *ST* III, q. 3, a. 8; *SCG* IV, ch. 11 (#3474), ch. 12 (#3483), ch. 13, and ch. 42.

> made. God makes nothing except through the conception of his intellect, which is the eternally conceived Wisdom, that is, the Word of God and Son of God. Accordingly, it is impossible that God should make anything except through his Son. And so Augustine says, in his *De Trinitate*, that the Word is the Art full of the living patterns of all things. Thus it is manifest that all things which the Father makes, he makes through the Son.[10]

This action of the Father "through his Word" concerns creation (the Word is the expression and the productive source of creatures), providence, the manifestation of the Father and his revelation, salvation, and the gift of filiation—in brief, the whole creative and salvific divine act. In every case, Thomas Aquinas explains the action of the Son by means of his property of *Word*, *Son*, and *Image*, that is, by means of what characterizes him distinctly in the Trinity.

In a similar manner, the personal property that manifests the distinction and the eternal existence of the Holy Spirit permits one also to account for his act in the economy of creation and grace. It is by means of the property of *Love* that Thomas Aquinas explicates the action of the Holy Spirit in creation, in the exercise of providence, in the movement of creatures, in vivification, sanctification, and the life of grace. Being personally *Gift*, the Holy Spirit is given to the saints and abides in them; he communicates the presence of the Father and of the Son, showering the Church with his gifts.[11] Let us note, here again, the guiding idea of this teaching:

> Even as the Father utters himself and every creature by the Word he begets, inasmuch as the Word begotten completely expresses the Father and every creature, so also he loves himself and every creature by the Holy Spirit, inasmuch as the Holy Spirit proceeds as Love for the primal goodness, the motive of the Father's loving himself and every creature.[12]

---

10 *In Ioannem* 1:3 (#77): "Quicumque enim aliquid facit, oportet quod illud praeconcipiat in sua sapientia, quae est forma et ratio rei factae: sicut forma in mente artificis praeconcepta est ratio arcae faciendae. Sic ergo Deus nihil facit nisi per conceptum sui intellectus, qui est sapientia ab aeterno concepta, scilicet Dei Verbum, et Dei Filius: et ideo impossibile est quod aliquid faciat nisi per Filium." The English translation (here with modifications) is taken from Thomas Aquinas, *Commentary on the Gospel of John,* Part 1, trans. James A. Weisheipl and Fabian R. Larcher (Albany, NY: Magi Books,1980); Part 2, trans. James A. Weisheipl and Fabian R. Larcher (Petersham, MA: St. Bede's Publications, 1999).

11 See, notably, the *SCG* IV, chs. 20–22.

12 *ST* I, q. 37, a. 2, ad 3: "Sicut Pater dicit se et omnem creaturam Verbo quod genuit, inquantum Verbum genitum sufficienter repraesentat Patrem et omnem creaturam; ita diligit se et omnem creaturam Spiritu Sancto, inquantum Spiritus

This explanation implies that the Love by which the Father and the Son are mutually united is also the Love by which they associate us in their communion: "The Father and the Son are loving each other and us by the Holy Spirit or Love proceeding."[13] The theological exposition of divine action rests thus on the study of the persons in their common essence and in their properties.[14] In his analysis of the names *Word, Love,* and *Gift,* Thomas shows that these names bear a relationship to creatures.[15] He specifies that the divine Person (the Father, the Son, the Holy Spirit) is related to creatures not directly according to the pure relation of origin that it holds within the eternal Trinity, but under the aspect by which this person includes the divine essence:

> The name *person* includes the nature indirectly: A person is an individual substance of intelligent nature. Thus the name of a divine person does not imply a reference to the creature according to the personal relation [of this person], but such a name does imply a reference to the creature according to what belongs to the nature [of this person]. However, nothing prevents such a name, as including the essence in its signification, from bearing a relationship to the creature. Just as it is proper to the Son that he be the Son, so also it is proper to him that he be *God begotten* or *Creator begotten.* That is how the name Word bears a relationship to creatures.[16]

One finds in these explanations the structure of *relation* and the elements of the Thomistic notion of *person,* applied to the Trinitarian economy. Relation, we note briefly, bears a double aspect: (1) it is pure

Sanctus procedit ut Amor bonitatis primae, secundum quam Pater amat se et omnem creaturam." It is the reason why the name "Love" *(Amor),* as a proper name of the Holy Spirit, not only includes intra-Trinitarian relationship but also can imply a reference to creatures: "By the Holy Spirit, the Father loves not only the Son but himself and us as well" (ibid.).

13 *ST* I, q. 37, a. 2: "Pater et Filius dicuntur diligentes Spiritu Sancto vel Amore procedente et se et nos."

14 On the Trinitarian dimension of divine economic actions, see G. Emery, *Trinity in Aquinas,* 33–70 and 171–75.

15 *ST* I, q. 34, a. 3, ad 1 (on the name *Word*); see q. 37, a. 2, ad 3 *(Love)*; q. 38, a. 1, ad 4 *(Gift).*

16 *ST* I, q. 34, a. 3, ad 1: "In nomine personae includitur etiam natura oblique, nam persona est rationalis naturae individua substantia. In nomine igitur personae divinae, quantum ad relationem personalem, non importatur respectus ad creaturam, sed importatur in eo quod pertinet ad naturam. Nihil tamen prohibet, inquantum includitur in significatione eius essentia, quod importetur respectus ad creaturam: sicut enim proprium est Filio quod sit Filius, ita proprium est ei quod sit genitus Deus, vel genitus Creator. Et per hunc modum importatur relatio ad creaturam in nomine Verbi."

relationship to an other, and (2) it possesses existence in a subject. The first aspect constitutes the proper notion or *ratio* of relation (relationship to another), and the second aspect accounts for the being *(esse)* of a real relation. These two aspects are required for every real relation. In God, the first aspect consists in the pure relationship of person to person according to origin (paternity, filiation, spiration, procession). As regards the second aspect, the divine relation is identified with the very being of the divine essence; it *is* this divine essence, it is God.[17] The combination of this double aspect allows one to conceive of the divine Person as a relation that subsists: The person is distinct under the aspect of relationship to another according to origin (the first aspect of relation), and it subsists in virtue of the divine being that it formally includes and with which it is identified (second aspect of relation).[18] It is this analysis that Thomas applies to the relationship that the divine Persons hold with creatures. We will examine more closely these two aspects of relation.

Following Thomas Aquinas, the relationship to creatures does not intervene in the first aspect of the divine relation, that is, in the aspect of the pure relationship to another that constitutes the "proper reason" of the relation. Under this first aspect, the intra-Trinitarian relation is a pure relationship of person to person according to origin. The divine Person, distinguished and constituted by a relation, is not distinguished and constituted by a relationship to creatures, but by the relation it holds with another divine Person. To introduce the relationship to creatures in this first aspect would amount to thinking that the very existence of the Trinity (the real distinction of persons) depended on the action of God in the world, as if the world intervened to make a divine Person exist. Such a view of things would imply a pantheist conception of the Trinity or would lead to the difficulties of "Arianism" and of "Sabellianism" which understood the procession of persons along the lines of an action of God in the world.[19] One could no longer account for the divinity of the persons and their eternal distinction.

The relationship to creatures, however, is included in the second aspect of the divine relation, that is, in relation insofar as it "includes" the divine essence and possesses the being of the divine essence. The divine essence contains the ideas of the creatures that preexist in it, and it is the source or the cause of creatures (exemplar, efficient, and final cause). These elements have been explained in the treatise of the essential attributes that concern the divine operation (the knowledge of God, his will and love, his power). It is by his essence that God creates: by his wisdom, by his will and his love,

---

[17] Ibid., q. 28, a. 2; *De potentia*, q. 8, a. 2.

[18] *ST* I, q. 29, a. 4; *De potentia*, q. 9, a. 4. On this doctrine of divine relation, see G. Emery, *Trinity in Aquinas,* 139–44.

[19] *ST* I, q. 27, a. 1.

by his mercy, by his power.[20] In other words, God creates because he is God and *insofar as he is God.* This is why the relationship to creatures belongs not in the personal relation as pure "relationship to another" (first aspect of relation), but rather in relation under the aspect of its divine being (second aspect of relation). And what one explains in terms of *relations* applies also to *person.* The divine Person bears a relationship to creatures not under the aspect of his pure relationship toward another divine Person, but rather under the aspect of his divinity. The Holy Spirit saves, the Son creates, because the Son and the Holy Spirit are *divine* Persons, that is, because they are God and inasmuch as they are God.[21]

This is what St. Thomas explains regarding the names *Word, Love,* and *Gift*: The relationship to creatures belongs not in the "personal relation" (pure relation to another), but in the divine essence that the person "includes" (the person is the divine essence). It is in this manner that the Son is the "begotten Creator": The word *begotten* signifies the Son in his relationship to the Father, and the word *Creator* signifies the Son in his divine being. The notion of "divine Person" gathers or includes these two aspects (the relationship to another and the divine subsistence, that is to say the two aspects of relation). In Aquinas, the theological understanding of the relationship that a divine Person holds with the world implies the fundamental elements of the speculative synthesis on relation and person.

In affirming that the relationship to creatures pertains to the divine essence common to the three persons, and not to the pure relationship of person to person, has Thomas obscured the personal features of the Trinitarian economy? Has he suggested that the essence alone (and not the person as such) is involved in the creation and the economy of grace? No, because the person is not constituted solely by the relationship to another, but also by the essence in virtue of which it is a person. This is why Thomas explains that the relationship to creatures is indeed "included" in the notion of divine Person, or that it belongs "in second place" in the proper name of the divine Person. When Christians confess that the Son is the Word, or when one recognizes that the Holy Spirit is Love and Gift, the relationship to creatures is present in these personal names "in the way that essence enters the meaning of 'person.'"[22] In explaining that the relationship to the created world concerns the divine essence, Thomas clearly holds that this relationship belongs to the *person,* since the essence formally pertains to the person *as person.*

---

20 Ibid., q. 14, a. 8; q. 19, a. 4; q. 20, a. 2; q. 21, a. 4; q. 25.

21 Cf. *In Ioannem* 3:5 (#444); 10:35 (#1460); 17:3 (#2187); and so on.

22 *ST* I, q. 38, a. 1, ad 4 (about the name Donum proper to the Holy Spirit): "Nec tamen per hoc quod importatur respectus ad creaturam oportet quod sit essentiale, sed quod aliquid essentiale in suo intellectu includatur, *sicut essentia includitur in intellectu personae,* ut supra dictum est."

In order to better grasp the personal dimension of the creative and salvific act, it is necessary therefore to take an additional step. In the relationship to creatures, what "role" should one grant to what each person possesses as a personal property? How does the property of each person belong in the action of the Trinity in the world? Before answering this question, let us note briefly the theme of the "causality of the Trinitarian processions" that extends the above reflections.

2. The Causality of the Trinitarian Processions

Beginning with his first synthesis of theology, the *Commentary on the Sentences*, Thomas Aquinas formulated this central thesis: "The eternal processions of the persons are the cause and the reason *(causa et ratio)* of the entire production of creatures."[23] The words *cause* and *reason* are completed by other terms specifying the Trinitarian foundation of creation. The procession of persons is the source or origin *(origo)*,[24] the principle *(principium)*,[25] and the model *(exemplar)*[26] of the procession of creatures. This affirmation is presented as a theological exegesis of biblical texts concerning the action of the Son and of the Holy Spirit. One finds it almost twenty times in the Thomistic corpus, in the same terms[27] or in related formulations: "The temporal procession of creatures derives from the eternal procession of the persons,"[28] "the going forth of persons in the unity of essence is the cause of the going forth of creatures in the diversity of essence."[29]

St. Thomas was able to find this theological thesis in his master, St. Albert the Great.[30] It is also manifestly inspired by St. Bonaventure who, without expressly formulating this thesis, likewise taught that the proces-

23 I *Sent.*, dist. 14, q. 1, a. 1: "Processiones personarum aeternae sunt causa et ratio totius productionis creaturarum."

24 Ibid., dist. 32, q. 1, a. 3: "Processio divinarum personarum est et quaedam origo processionis creaturarum."

25 Ibid., dist. 35, divisio textus: "[. . .] de processione divinarum personarum in unitate essentiae, quae est principium creaturarum et causa."

26 Ibid., dist. 29, q. 1, a. 2, qla 2; *De potentia*, q. 10, a. 2, sed contra 2.

27 I *Sent.*, dist. 10, q. 1, a. 1; ibid., dist. 14, q. 2, a. 2; ibid., dist. 26, q. 2, a. 2, ad 2; ibid., dist. 27, q. 2, a. 3, ad 6; *De potentia*, q. 10, a. 2, arg. 19 et ad 19; *ST* I, q. 45, a. 6, corp. et ad 1; q. 45, a. 7, ad 3.

28 General Prologue of the *Scriptum* on the *Sentences*: "Sicut trames a fluvio derivatur, ita processus temporalis creaturarum ab aeterno processu personarum." See *Super Boetium de Trinitate*, prol.

29 I *Sent.*, dist. 2, divisio textus: "Exitus enim personarum in unitate essentiae, est causa exitus creaturarum in essentiae diversitate."

30 St. Albert, I *Sent.*, dist. 20, a. 3, sed contra; I *Sent.*, dist. 29, a. 2, sed contra 2 (*Opera omnia*, ed. Auguste Borgnet, vol. 25 [Paris: Vivès, 1893], 191; vol. 26 [Paris: Vivès, 1893], 76).

sion of the Son and that of the Holy Spirit possess a causality and an exemplarity with regard to creatures: The "extrinsic diffusion" of the good (the act of God in the world) has for its reason the "intrinsic diffusion" of the sovereign Good in the divine Persons, in a manner in which the first reality is the cause of all the secondary realities that derive from it. However, neither Albert nor Bonaventure developed the creative causality of the Trinitarian processions in a manner comparable to Thomas. The systematic exploitation of this thesis appears as a characteristic feature of his theology. The Trinitarian processions are the exemplary, efficient, and final source of the procession of creatures (creation and grace), the motive of the creative action on the part of God, and the principle of creatures in the ontological order and in the order of intelligibility.[31] A correct and integral understanding of God's action in the world requires knowledge of the procession of the divine Persons.[32]

In these explanations, creation is not attributed in a proper or exclusive manner to a single divine Person. God is creator in virtue of his essence, which is common to the three persons: The three persons are one single Creator God.[33] The creative "causality" is not therefore attributed in a proper manner to one divine Person, but Thomas relates it to the *Trinitarian processions.* The word *procession* means the origin—the coming to being, the way to the existence—of a reality from its principle.[34] In considering in an analogous manner the Trinity and creation under the aspect of procession (the Son and the Spirit *proceed* eternally, and creatures also *proceed* from God, although on a completely different order), Thomas uses a concept that permits one to grasp analogously the *communication of being.* Creation and the economy of grace are not connected solely to a particular divine Person but to the Trinity: Thomas emphasized the influence of the whole "Trinitarian process."

"Procession" in the Trinity signifies the personal communication of the plenitude of the divinity: The Father communicates eternally the plenitude of his divinity to the Son; with the Son, he communicates it to the Holy Spirit. When one speaks of "procession" in God, one considers the persons under the dynamic aspect of the eternal communication of the divinity. With regard to creation, in an entirely different order, "procession" consists in a participation of creatures in being and in the divine perfections (as

31 Gilles Emery, *La Trinité créatrice* (Paris: Vrin, 1995). For a shorter account, see idem, *Trinity in Aquinas,* 33–70.

32 St. Thomas, *ST* I, q. 32, a. 1, ad 3: "Cognitio divinarum personarum fuit necessaria nobis dupliciter. Uno modo, ad recte sentiendum de creatione rerum."

33 Ibid., q. 45, a. 6.

34 I *Sent.*, dist. 13, q. 1, a. 1: "Dicitur processio eductio principiati a suo principio." *ST* I, q. 40, a. 2: "Origo autem alicuius rei [. . .] significatur [. . .] ut via quaedam a re vel ad rem." The *procession* or *origin* is signified in the mode of an act (ibid.).

communicated by God's action in the world). It is at this level of the communication of a participation of divine perfections, implying the doctrine of analogy, that Trinitarian causality is situated. The communication of the entire divine essence in the Trinity is the cause and the reason of the communication of a participation of the divine essence to creatures in a radically different order: "The going forth of persons in the unity of essence is the cause of the going forth of creatures in the diversity of essence."[35] As one easily ascertains, it is a question of the distinction and the relationship between the immanent action (Trinitarian processions) and the transitive action (action of God in the world): The first is the "reason" of the second.[36]

Thomas Aquinas provided successively two interpretations of this "causality" of Trinitarian processions, the first in his *Commentary on the Sentences* and the second in the *Summa theologiae.* One discovers here a deepening of understanding. In his first work, Thomas explains that, in order to understand the action of divine Persons, it is necessary to take account of two complementary rules: (1) the efficiency of the divine essence, and (2) the causality of the eternal procession of the persons. "The procession of divine Persons is also a certain origin of the procession of creatures, since everything that is first in some genus is the cause of what comes after; but the efficiency with regard to creatures is nevertheless attributed to the common essence."[37] This double principle is invoked in order to explain in what manner "the Father and the Son love us *by the Holy Spirit.*" It permits one also to show in what way "the Father speaks all things *by his Word.*" The divine act is not explained solely by the divine nature, that is, by the essential knowledge and will of the Trinity. It is explained also by the Trinitarian processions, which are the reason of the works that God accomplishes in the world: The Word is the efficient model of all communication that God accomplishes by his wisdom, and the Holy Spirit is the reason of all communication that God accomplishes by the generosity of his love. The Word is the sole person who, in God, proceeds by mode of intellect: He is thereby the uncreated model and reason of the procession of works of wisdom accomplished by God. The Holy Spirit is the sole person who, in God, proceeds by mode of love: He is thereby the reason of the procession of creatures that come forth from God by the mode of a divine gift. Under this aspect, the creative causality

35 I *Sent.*, dist. 2, *divisio textus.*

36 In his *SCG* II, ch. 1 (#854), after having distinguished between "immanent actions" and "transitive actions," Aquinas explains: "Oportet quod prima dictarum operationum sit ratio secundae et eam praecedat naturaliter, sicut causa effectum."

37 I *Sent.*, dist. 32, q. 1, a. 3: "Processio divinarum personarum est et quaedam origo processionis creaturarum; cum omne quod est primum in aliquo genere sit causa eorum quae sunt post; sed tamen efficientia creaturarum essentiae communi attribuitur."

("efficiency") belongs to the divine essence, but the reason of this causality ("reason of the efficiency") pertains to the procession of the Son and to the procession of the Holy Spirit in virtue of the proper and distinct mode of these processions.[38] Creation is the common work of the three persons, acting by their essence, and each person is involved in this act according to his personal property.

In the *Summa*, Thomas explains the exemplarity and the causality of the Trinitarian processions, with more precision, by means of his doctrine of person and relation. This explanation bears the mark of the progress of his Trinitarian theology. Whereas, in his first work, he based his Trinitarian doctrine on the notion of *procession*, he organizes it more resolutely in the *Summa* around the notion of *person*, following the two aspects of divine relation that we have described above (the relationship to another and the divine essence):

> The divine Persons, according to the formal feature of their procession, have a causality respecting the creation of things. For as was said above (q. 14, a. 8; q. 19, a. 4) when treating of the knowledge and will of God, God is the cause of things by his intellect and will, like an artist is the cause of works of art. Now an artist works through the word conceived in his mind, and through the love of his will bent on something. Hence also God the Father made the creature through his Word, which is his Son; and through his Love, which is the Holy Spirit. In this way also the processions of the persons are the reasons of the production of creatures, inasmuch as they include the essential attributes of knowing and willing.[39]

This explanation invokes the analogy of intelligence and will. It is a question, once again, of making explicit the relationships that the immanent

---

38 Ibid. It is a question of the "reason of the efficiency not with regard to the agent but with regard to creatures" ("ratio efficientiae non ex parte efficientis sed ex parte effectorum"). In other words, the Trinitarian processions are not the cause of God's action (they do not cause God to act), but they are the cause of creatures.

39 *ST* I, q. 45, a. 6: "Divinae Personae secundum rationem suae processionis habent causalitatem respectu creationis rerum. Ut enim supra ostensum est, cum de Dei scientia et voluntate ageretur, Deus est causa rerum per suum intellectum et voluntatem, sicut artifex rerum artificiatarum. Artifex autem per verbum in intellectu conceptum, et per amorem suae voluntatis ad aliquid relatum, operatur. Unde et Deus Pater operatus est creaturam per suum Verbum, quod est Filius; et per suum Amorem, qui est Spiritus Sanctus. Et secundum hoc processiones Personarum sunt rationes productionis creaturarum, inquantum includunt essentialia attributa, quae sunt scientia et voluntas." On the continuity and evolution of this teaching in Aquinas, see Gilfredo Marengo, *Trinità e Creazione: Indagine sulla teologia di Tommaso d'Aquino* (Rome: Città Nuova, 1990).

acts (Trinitarian processions) maintain with the acts that proceed toward an exterior reality (creation and salvation). The seeming simplicity of the example of the artist should not deceive. This analogy implies a very powerful metaphysical reflection on the transcendental principles of action. For our purpose, it is the conclusion that deserves attention: The personal processions are the reason or "the cause of creation"[40] inasmuch as they "include" the essential attributes of knowledge and will. Thomas no longer exploits two complementary rules, as in his *Commentary on the Sentences*, but rather *one single theological principle*: The personal procession of a divine Person includes the essence. This explanation is attached to the doctrine of person and relation, whose results are henceforth applied to the divine act. In the divine action, the essence is not on one side, with the personal properties on the other side. Everything converges in the relation (conceived as based on the procession) and in the person who formally gathers the aspect of the distinction and the aspect of the essence.[41] The persons create and act in the world in virtue of the processions (that is, the Father acts through the Son whom he begets and in the Holy Spirit whom he spirates with the Son), insofar as the processions include the essence (as the relations also do)—that is, because the personal processions are *divine*. We find again precisely the path of explication that Thomas followed when he examined the property of the Word, of Love, and of Gift.

3. The Question of the Proper Role of Persons

The theological manifestation of the creative and salvific act of divine Persons brings us back to our first question: In the divine act, what "role" should one recognize for that which each person possesses in a proper manner? Following the teaching of Thomas Aquinas, two solutions should be avoided. Let us examine them briefly.

A first path toward a (unsatisfying) solution responds that there is no proper mode in the action of a divine Person, because the persons act solely according to that which is absolutely common to them—namely, the divine nature, which is the principle of their act. This solution takes

---

[40] *ST* I, q. 45, a. 6, ad 1: "Processiones divinarum Personarum sunt causa creationis, sicut dictum est."

[41] It is in this sense that, in his *Commentary on the Sentences* (I *Sent.*, dist. 26, q. 2, a. 2, ad 2), St. Thomas explained: "All procession and multiplication of creatures are caused by the procession of the distinct divine persons" ("ex processione personarum divinarum distinctarum causatur omnis creaturarum processio et multiplicatio"), in order to show the creative influence of the divine *relations*. The divine relation, however, does not have such a causality insofar as it consists of a reference to another (the "ratio" of the relation), but rather inasmuch as it is divine (the "being" of the relation): "ex hoc quod est relatio divina" (ibid.).

account of the Orthodox rule of the unity of energy of the three persons, or the Augustinian principle of the indivisibility of the works of the Trinity *ad extra*. The distinction of persons would then be involved in their eternal relationships but not in the act that they exercise in our favor. This explanation has been supported by some authors in modern Scholasticism, and one finds it in certain Trinitarian treatises of the twentieth century.[42] It led to connecting the economy of creation and grace to the "One God" *(De Deo uno)*, thereby pushing aside the role of the Trinitarian plurality for understanding the divine act. Likewise, it also weakened the value of the doctrine of appropriations in making of these appropriations the only way to grasp the Trinitarian dimension of the divine act.

The rule of the unity of action of the Trinity is fundamental, and the reader of Thomas Aquinas must not fail to observe its importance: It is found at the heart of the Trinitarian treatise.[43] Creation and grace are not the exclusive work of a single person, but instead the three persons are all together the source, by reason of their common divine nature. Not to recognize this would lead one to reject the Trinitarian consubstantiality. At the same time, appropriation is a valuable method, the foundations of which have been clearly underlined by Aquinas.[44] The mistake of this first response does not therefore consist in an error about the principles invoked (the unity of the divine act and the appropriations), but rather in the *exclusivity* that it attributes to them, as if the rule of the unity of operation constituted, by itself, all the explication, the single key for understanding the action of the Trinity. Aquinas's theology does not present such an exclusivity. The constant presence of the Trinitarian act in the study of the properties clearly shows this. In other words, the rule of the indivisibility of the Trinity in its act *ad extra* is perfectly exact and fundamental, but its application is excessive if one pretends to reduce to it all the aspects of the action of the divine Persons.

A second path of response, reacting vigorously against the preceding one, affirms that each divine Person exercises a proper action in our favor. The thought of many theologians today seems to be favorable to this manner of conceiving the act of the divine Persons. Such thought attempts then to specify the "personal causality," the "proper activity," the "proper function," or the "specific role" of each divine Person.[45] Grace, for example, would be attributed specifically to the Holy Spirit, as if it fell properly to the

42 Among the clearest examples of this line of thought, see Paul Galtier, *L'habitation en nous des trois personnes* (Rome: Pontificia Università Gregoriana, 1949). The central thesis of this work is the following: No action of a divine Person is really personal; in the economic action of the Holy Spirit, nothing belongs properly to him.

43 Cf. notably *ST* I, q. 32, a. 1; q. 45, a. 6.

44 I *Sent.*, dist. 31, q. 1, a. 2; see footnote 4 above.

45 As representative of this second line of thought, see Heribert Mühlen, *Der Heilige Geist als Person* (Münster: Aschendorff, 1963); idem, "Person und Appropriation.

Holy Spirit (unlike the other persons) to procure this grace. The same line of thought emphasizes, concerning the gift of adoptive filiation, that filiation makes us children of the person of the Father to the exclusion of the other divine Persons. The thesis of a "(quasi-)formal causality" of a divine Person is often advanced in such accounts, notably in the case of the grace of the Holy Spirit.[46] The Holy Spirit, personally given to the saints, would himself exercise the role of (quasi-)immanent principle of the human acts of faith and charity. One could thus explain the distinct work of persons and, more profoundly, the properly personal foundation of the Trinitarian gifts.[47]

In addition to the problem of the confusion of God and the world raised by the theory of a divine "formal causality" (because a *form* is, by definition, inherent to a creature, it is one of its constitutive ontological elements, it enters into real composition with the creature),[48] the thesis of the proper action of one divine Person presents a difficulty that is insurmountable with regard to the principles of Thomistic theology. To reserve an action and a divine gift to one person rather than to another is to put in question the unity of the Trinity both in its essence and in its relations. It is a question of a principle absolutely fundamental in Thomas Aquinas: The three persons act by a single action or operation,[49] in virtue of their

Zum Verständnis des Axioms: In Deo omnia sunt unum, ubi non obviat relationis oppositio," *Münchener Theologische Zeitschrift* 16 (1965): 37–57. The Trinitarian thought of Mühlen, a leading theologian on this question, had a very large influence.

46 The vocabulary of the "quasi-formal" causality of divine Persons is not unknown among the Scholastics. Albert the Great, for instance, employs it in order to designate the Holy Spirit as the one by whom we love God and neighbor. But he specifies immediately that neither the habit nor the act of charity are "by essence" the Holy Spirit: Rather, they are effects of the Holy Spirit. See St. Albert, *Summa theologiae* I, tract. 8, q. 36, ch. 3, in *Opera omnia*, Editio Coloniensis, vol. 34/1 (Münster: Aschendorff, 1978), 282. We thus find again the affirmation of the inseparable causality of the Trinity, with the doctrine of appropriations (ibid., tract. 7, q. 32, ch. 2 [*Opera omnia,* vol. 34/1, 254]).

47 For an exposition on this theme, in the wake of Karl Rahner, see Klaus Obenauer, *Thomistische Metaphysik und Trinitätstheologie* (Münster: Lit Verlag, 2000); cf. my critical review in *Revue Thomiste* 101 (2001): 614–17.

48 Thomas Aquinas clearly emphasizes the *exemplarity* of the Holy Spirit in the gift of charity, but without considering the Holy Spirit as a formal inherent cause in the saints, and without excluding the Father and the Son: "Oportet ponere charitatem esse habitum creatum in anima; quae quidem efficienter est a tota Trinitate, sed exemplariter manat ab amore qui est Spiritus Sanctus" (I *Sent.*, dist. 17, q. 1, a 1, corp.; cf. *ST* I–II, q. 110, a. 1; *ST* II–II, q. 23, a. 2). If we were to consider the Holy Spirit as the formal cause of charity, this would imply that the saints had a divine being or were hypostatically united to the Holy Spirit, a thesis that, of course, Aquinas rejects (I *Sent.*, dist. 17, q. 1, a 1, sed contra 3).

49 See, for example, *SCG* IV, ch. 25 (#3625): "The Three Persons are one principle of creatures and they produce creatures by a single action *(una actione).*"

common nature, and consequently the effects of the divine action always have for their source the entire Trinity.[50] The incarnation of the Son—that is, the assumption of human nature by the person of the Son—does not constitute an exception to this rule. Aquinas distinguishes between the *act* of assuming (*actus assumentis*: the uniting of the human nature to the Word of God) and the *term* of the assumption (*terminus assumptionis*: the person of the Word to whom the human nature is united), and states: "What belongs to the *act* of assuming is common to the three persons; but what pertains to the *term* belongs to one person in such a way that it does not belong to another. For the three persons caused the human nature to be united to one person, the Son."[51] Theological reflection on the Trinitarian economy can never be led against this rule, which comes into play as a fundamental aspect of the question.

In sum, the attempt to highlight the Trinitarian dimension of the divine act appears in the following perspective: The rule of the essential unity of the three persons furnishes a determinative criterion, but Aquinas does not claim that such a rule constitutes the sole aspect of the Trinitarian act. Rather, he distinguishes a proper mode of action of each divine Person. This teaching on the Trinitarian mode of action deserves closer examination.

4. "All Things Were Made through Him": A Property of the Son

The three persons act inseparably in virtue of their common divine nature, and each effect has for its source the entire Trinity. But, in this common action, each person acts in the distinct mode of his relation with the other persons. This thesis, before we come to its foundations, can be illustrated by Aquinas's teaching on the creative act of the Word. In his exegesis of John 1:3 *(All things were made through him)*, St. Thomas explains that the Word is the one through whom *(per quem)* the Father does all things. He then offers a more extended reflection on the act of the Son: What does the fact of being the one "through whom" the Father does all things mean? It can be understood in two ways.[52]

1. If one takes "through whom" to refer to the "formal principle" *(causa formalis)* of the action—that is, the principle of the act of the Father (the "in virtue of which" the Father acts)—then it is necessary to recognize

50 See, for example, *ST* III, q. 23, a. 2.

51 Ibid., q. 3, a. 4: "Quod est actionis in assumptione commune est tribus personis; sed id quod pertinet ad rationem termini convenit ita uni personae quod non alii. Tres enim personae fecerunt ut humana natura uniretur uni personae Filii."

52 *In Ioannem* 1:3 (#76).

there the divine essence. The Father, like the Son and like the Holy Spirit, acts through his essence, since it is through its nature that a being acts.[53] Thomas speaks here of "formal" principle in order to avoid all idea of an "efficient" principle, because nothing, including any person, pushes or moves the Father to act in the manner of an efficient cause.[54] As regards the "formal" principle of the Father's action, Aquinas holds that neither the Son nor the Holy Spirit is such a "principle" of action of the Father, because the Son and the Holy Spirit do not have a relation of principle with regard to the Father: The Trinitarian *order* does not permit one to see, in the Son or the Holy Spirit, a principle of being of the Father, or a principle of action of the Father. If one takes the expression "through whom" to refer to the formal principle, it would therefore be appropriated to the Son, because God the Father acts through his essential wisdom, which is appropriated to the Son:

> If the *through* denotes a formal cause, as when the Father operates through his wisdom, which is his essence, he operates through his wisdom as he operates through his essence. And because the wisdom and power of the Father are attributed to the Son, as when we say Christ, *the power of God* and the wisdom of God (1 Cor 1:24), then by appropriation we say that the Father does all things through the Son, that is, through his wisdom.[55]

It is for this reason that, in themselves, the biblical formulas *from whom, through whom,* and *in whom* (see Rom 11:36) are not proper to a person, but rather are appropriated.[56] With these explanations, one has obviously moved away from the apparent sense of John 1:3, but one has made an important specification: To say that the Father acts *through the Son* is not to make the Word a principle of the act of the Father. The Father does not receive his act from the Son. One cannot say that the Father acts "through the Son" as one says of a man that he acts "by his mind" or "by his nature." In this sense, the Father acts

---

53 In this context, "nature" *(natura)* means the inner principle of action and hence the specific essence of a being (*ST* III, q. 2, a. 1; cf. *ST* I, q. 29, a. 1, ad 4).

54 *In Ioannem* 1:3 (#76): "Sic ergo cum dicitur *omnia per ipsum facta sunt*; si ly *per* denotet efficientem causam, seu moventem Patrem ad operandum, dicendum est quod Pater nihil operatur per Filium, sed per seipsum omnia operatur."

55 Ibid. (#76): "Si vero ly *per* denotet causam formalem, sic cum Pater operetur per sapientiam suam, quae est sua essentia, operatur per suam sapientiam, sicut operatur per suam essentiam; et quia sapientia et virtus Patris attribuitur Filio, 1 Cor 1:24, dicimus: *Christum Dei virtutem, et Dei sapientiam,* ideo appropriate dicimus quod Pater omnia operatur per Filium, idest per sapientiam suam."

56 *ST* I, q. 39, a. 8.

through himself or through his essence. St. Augustine had already noted that when one holds that "the Father is wise by his begotten wisdom," one cannot mean that the Son is the cause of the wisdom of the Father (one would arrive at this "absurd" conclusion: The Father would not be wise by himself but by his Son, and the Father would therefore have his essence from the Son). The Father and the Son are one single wisdom as they are one single essence. The Son is not the wisdom by virtue of which the Father is wise, but he is the "begotten Wisdom" coming forth from the Father.[57] The same reflections are applied to the *act* of the Father.

2. However, if in the formula "through him" of John 1:3 one understands the causality of the Word with regard to creatures,[58] then it is a question strictly of a *property of the Son.* This is without doubt the more manifest sense of John 1:3. Taken in this sense, the expression "through him" designates not the principle of the action of the Father (this would lead us back to the first consideration), but the principle or the cause of creatures, and it is here that one should recognize a *proper feature* of the Word, going beyond appropriation:

> If the *through* [in Jn 1:3: *All things were made through him*] denotes causality from the standpoint of the thing produced, then the statement, *The Father does all things through the Son,* is not appropriation but it is proper to the Word, because the fact that he is a cause of creatures is had from someone else, namely, the Father, from whom he has being.[59]

The Son is the one "through whom" the Father acts because he is the Son and Word begotten by the Father. In the act of the Father through the Son, the preposition "through" refers to the *auctoritas* of the Father,

---

57 St. Augustine, *De Trinitate* VII,1,1–2; ibid. XV,7,12 (Sancti Aurelii Augustini, *De Trinitate libri* XV, ed. W. J. Mountain, 2 vols. [Turnhout: Brepols, 1968]: vol. 1, 244–49; vol. 2, 475–77). St. Thomas, I *Sent.*, dist. 32, q. 2, a. 1; *ST* I, q. 34, a. 1, ad 2.

58 In this second sense, the preposition "per" does not refer to a causality toward the Father's act *(ex parte operantis)*, but it means a causality toward creatures *(ex parte operati)* that are made by the Father "through his Word." See II *Sent.*, dist. 13, q. 1, a. 5. See above footnote 38.

59 *In Ioannem* 1:3 (#76): "Si vero ly *per* denotet causalitatem ex parte operati, tunc hoc quod dicimus Patrem omnia operari per Filium, non est appropriatum Verbo, sed proprium eius, quia hoc quod est causa creaturarum, habet ab alio, scilicet a Patre, a quo habet esse." One sees here that, for St. Thomas, the verse of John 1:3 is not limited to creation in a strict sense but concerns the divine action in the world.

that is, the property of the Father as principle of the Son. The Son *exists* in receiving eternally his being from the Father, and he *acts* in receiving eternally his act from the Father. The action of the Father and the Son is one; the principle of this action is also one (it is the divine power and nature); the effects of the action are common to the Father and to the Son. But the *actors* (the subjects of the act: *"operantes"*) are personally distinct, and their *mode of action* is also distinct.[60] Thomas writes likewise in the *Summa theologiae*:

> In some instances the preposition *through* applies to a median cause, for example, in the statement that a smith works through his hammer. And so the preposition through is not always appropriated to the Son but sometimes means a property of the Son, according to this verse of St. John (1:3): *All things were made through him;* not because the Son is an instrument, but because he is the principle from the principle.[61]

Such is the path by which Thomas Aquinas gives weight to the distinction of the persons in their act. The formula *principium de principio* refers to the person of the Son as the principle begotten by the Father. The Son exists from the Father and, accordingly, acts by receiving his being and his power of action from the Father: The Son acts *as* the "principle from the principle." This means no subordination but only the relation of origin by which the Son is referred to the Father. This distinction does not divide the action of the Trinity, or its power, or the principle of action, which are common to the three persons by reason of their one nature. It also does not concern the effects of the action: These effects come forth from the three persons in virtue of their one action. One could also, indeed, show this by the doctrine of perichoresis: The Father is in the Son, the Son is in the Father, the Holy Spirit is in the Father and in the Son, and reciprocally. For this reason, the action of the three persons is inseparable. Thomas Aquinas explains,

---

60 Cf. II *Sent.*, dist. 13, q. 1, a. 5, ad 4: "It is by reason of the Father's *auctoritas* towards the Son, inasmuch as the Son holds his being and his action from the Father, that the Father acts through the Son." In Trinitarian context, the word *auctoritas* means the relationship of a divine Person as principle or source of another person (see *ST* I, q. 33, a. 1, ad 2; I *Sent.*, dist. 29, q. 1, a. 1; *De potentia*, q. 10, a. 1, arg. 17 and ad 17).

61 *ST* I, q. 39, a. 8: "Haec vero praepositio *per* designat quidem quandoque causam mediam; sicut dicimus quod faber operatur per martellum. Et sic ly *per* quandoque non est appropriatum, sed proprium Filii, secundum illud Ioan. I, *omnia per ipsum facta sunt*; non quia Filius sit instrumentum, sed quia ipse est principium de principio."

for example: "The Son acts by reason of the Father who dwells in him by a unity of nature."[62] The profundity of the perichoresis is such that, in the act of the Son, the Father himself acts, and the Holy Spirit acts in them, inseparably. The action of the Son and of the Holy Spirit is not therefore different from that of the Father, since the persons act in indwelling the one in the other, according to their mutual immanence and thus by one same operation.

In this common action, however, each person acts according to the mode of his relative personal property. This mode of action does not express anything other than the personal property. One sees this well in the explanations regarding the act of the Father through his Word. The distinct mode of the action of the Son (the Son is the Word *by whom* or *through whom* the Father acts) does not consist in an exclusive relationship of the Son as regards creatures; rather, it consists in the proper relationship that the Son has with his Father within the Trinity. The same applies to the action of the Holy Spirit: The Son acts through the Holy Spirit, in such a way that what is done by the Holy Spirit is also done by the Son.[63] In other words, this proper mode lies in the intra-Trinitarian relation of person to person, and not in a different relation with creatures.

This is exactly what Thomas explains, from another point of view, with regard to the names *Word*, *Love*, and *Gift*: In the Trinitarian act, the personal distinction does not belong on the side of the relationship to creatures, but rather on the side of the intra-Trinitarian relation. And if, when drawing these two aspects together, one brings the personal intra-Trinitarian relation to the forefront, then one can understand what is meant by the "proper mode of act" of the divine Persons. The Father creates the world and saves humankind through the Son in the Spirit: This mode of acting through the Son in the Spirit is proper to the Father. It belongs properly to the Son to be the one through whom the Father creates and accomplishes all things: In the Trinity, the Son is the only one who acts in this way, as befits his property of Son, Word, and Image of the Father. And it belongs properly to the Holy Spirit to be the one by whom or through whom the Father and the Son act, in virtue of his property of Love and Gift. This is what Thomas explains when he shows that "the Father utters all creatures by his Word" and that "the Father and the Son love us by

---

62 *In Ioannem* 14:12 (#1898): "Filius operatur propter Patrem in se manentem per unitatem naturae."

63 *In Eph* 2:18 (#121): "Sic autem habemus accessum ad Patrem per Christum, quoniam Christus operatur per Spiritum Sanctum. [. . .] Et ideo quidquid fit per Spiritum Sanctum, etiam fit per Christum."

the Holy Spirit,"[64] or when he teaches that "the processions of the persons are the cause of the procession of creatures."[65] These expressions have a *proper*, not (only) appropriated, sense. Appropriation is not our only resource for understanding the Trinitarian dimension of the divine act.

5. Personal Mode of Being and Personal Mode of Acting

These observations are confirmed by many aspects of the teaching of Thomas Aquinas, notably by the relationship between the mode of being and the mode of acting of the persons, as well as by the distinction of the persons in their same action on behalf of creatures (creation and grace). A being acts according to what it is. As one is, so one acts. The mode of acting *(modus operandi)* is grounded in the mode of being *(modus essendi)*, which it manifests.[66] Now, if the being of the three persons is identical, their *mode of being* is distinct. This mode of being consists in the manner according to which a person possesses the divine essence, in accordance with his relative property (fatherhood, sonship, procession): "Though the same nature is in Father and Son, it is in each by *a different mode of existence*, that is to say, with a different relation."[67] The essence of the three persons is one, but each person possesses this divine essence (more precisely, each person "is" this divine essence) according to a distinct relation. Thus, the divine nature is found in each person according to a proper and distinct manner that consists of the personal relation of each person. St. Thomas explains it with great clarity:

> Just as the three persons have one and the same essence, it is not in each under the same relation or with the same mode of existence.[68]
>
> Though the same nature is in the Father, Son and Holy Spirit, it has not the same mode of existence in each one of the three, and

---

[64] *ST* I, q. 34, a. 3; q. 37, a. 2, ad 3.

[65] I *Sent.*, dist. 32, q. 1, a. 3.

[66] Cf. *ST* I, q. 89, a. 1: "As nothing acts except insofar as it is actual, the mode of action *(modus operandi)* in every agent follows from its mode of existence *(modus essendi)*." See *ST* I, q. 50, a. 5; *ST* I, q. 75, a. 2: "Only what actually exists acts, and its manner of acting follows from its manner of being."

[67] *De potentia*, q. 2, a. 1, ad 13: "Licet eadem natura sit in Patre et Filio, est tamen secundum alium modum existendi, scilicet cum alia relatione."

[68] Ibid., q. 2, a. 5, ad 5: "Sicut una et eadem est essentia trium personarum, non tamen sub eadem relatione, vel secundum eumdem modum existendi est in tribus personis." This distinct "mode of existence" applies to the essence in each divine Person and hence to all divine attributes (here all-mightiness) in each divine Person.

> when I say "mode of existence" I mean in respect of the relation. Nature is in the Father as not received from another, but in the Son it is as received from the Father.[69]
>
> Although the Godhead is wholly and perfectly in each of the three persons according to its proper mode of existence, yet it belongs to the perfection of the Godhead that there be several modes of existence in God, namely, that there be one from whom another proceeds yet proceeds from no other, and one proceeding from another. For there would not be full perfection in God unless there were in him procession of the Word and of Love.[70]

The teaching on the "modes of existing" restates the Cappadocian Trinitarian doctrine: Each divine hypostasis is characterized by a *tropos tès huparxeôs* (literally, *mode of existence*).[71] Medieval Western theologians had access to this teaching through the Latin translation of John Damascene.[72] In Aquinas's view, the "mode of existence" defines the concrete content of the proper hypostatic subsistence of the divine Person. Each person exists in a distinct manner according to a relation. This means that the personal property designates the relational mode of being proper to each person: The Father exists in the mode of the unbegotten source, the Son exists in the mode of filiation insofar as he receives his existence from the Father through generation, the Holy Spirit exists in the mode of Love who proceeds from the Father and the Son. Each person is characterized therefore by a relative mode of existence (the content of the "proper mode of existence" lies in the personal relation). This distinct mode does not disappear

---

69 Ibid., q. 3, a. 15, ad 17: "Licet eadem natura sit Patris et Filii et Spiritus Sancti, non tamen eumdem modum existendi habet in tribus, et dico modum existendi secundum relationem. In Patre enim est ut non accepta ab alio, in Filio vero ut a Patre accepta."

70 Ibid., q. 9, a. 5, ad 23: "Licet tota et perfecta divinitas sit in qualibet trium personarum secundum proprium modum existendi, tamen ad perfectionem divinitatis pertinet ut sint plures modi existendi in divinis ut scilicet sit ibi a quod alius et ipse a nullo, et aliquis qui est ab alio. Non enim esset omnimoda perfectio in divinis nisi esset ibi processio Verbi et Amoris."

71 See Basil of Caesarea, *On the Holy Spirit* 18,46 (critical edition by Benoît Pruche: Basile de Césarée, *Sur le Saint-Esprit,* "*Sources Chrétiennes* 17 bis" [Paris: Cerf, 1968], 408–9); *Letter* 235,2 (critical edition by Yves Courtonne: Saint Basile, *Lettres,* vol. 3 [Paris: Belles-Lettres, 1966], 45); idem, *Homily* 24,6 (PG 31, 613).

72 *De fide orthodoxa* I,8. See St. John Damascene, *De fide orthodoxa: Versions of Burgundio and Cerbanus,* ed. Eligius M. Buytaert (Louvain: E. Nauwelaerts; Paderborn: Schöningh, 1955), 35: "Etsi enim Spiritus Sanctus ex Patre procedit, sed non generabiliter, sed processibiliter. Alius modus existentiae est hic, incomprehensibilis et ignotus, sicut et Filii generatio. Ideoque omnia quaecumque habet Pater, eius sunt, praeter ingenerationem, quae non significat substantiae differentiam neque dignitatem, sed modum existentiae."

in the action of the persons; it remains present and qualifies intrinsically this act. The distinct mode of acting bears the same noteworthiness and the same profundity as does the mode of existing.

A precision should be made: In the Trinity, the personal distinction does not modify the divine being or nature as such, or the power of acting, or the action. But the three persons are distinct under the aspect of the *mode* of being of the divine essence in them and, consequently, under the aspect of the *mode* of acting corresponding to the mode of being. The distinction of these modes concerns therefore the proper relation of the person, that is, the intra-Trinitarian relationship of person to person according to origin. Each person exists and acts in accordance with his relation to the other persons. This mode of being and of acting expresses the order *(ordo)* of the persons, since the real plurality of the divine Persons rests in this order. For Thomas Aquinas, indeed, the personal distinction is not based solely on the difference of origin of the Son and the Holy Spirit (generation and spiration), nor even on the mode of the procession of the Son and Holy Spirit (mode of nature or intellect, mode of will or love), but on the *order of origin* within the Trinity: The Son has his existence from the Father, the Holy Spirit has his existence from the Father and the Son.[73] This order of origin consists solely in the fact that a person has his existence from another, without any priority or posteriority.[74] It is this order that ultimately grounds personal plurality. "It is necessary that there is procession from procession, and that one of the persons who proceed comes forth from the other: This is what makes a real difference in God."[75] The mode of existence in divine Persons and their distinct mode of action consist therefore in this personal order according to origin, that is, in the relation of origin. This is what Thomas explains in saying that it belongs properly to the Son to be the one "through whom" the Father acts.

In order to account for the Trinitarian dimension of creation and grace, it is therefore necessary to consider the persons who act—the subjects of the action (the "agents")—by paying more attention to the mutual *relation* of these persons. Concerning the relationship of the Father and the Son, Aquinas states:

> It is from the Father that the Son has being and acting, and this is why the Father acts through the Son.[76]

---

[73] St. Thomas, *De potentia*, q. 10, a. 2; *SCG* IV, ch. 24 (#3615–16).

[74] *ST* I, q. 42, a. 3.

[75] *De potentia*, q. 10, a. 2, ad 7: "Et sic oportet processionem esse ex processione, et procedentem ex procedente; hoc autem facit realem differentiam in divinis."

[76] II *Sent.*, dist. 13, q. 1, a. 5, ad 4: "Filius a Patre habet et esse et operari, ratione cujus Pater per Filium operatur."

> The Son, who is acting, exists from the Father.[77]
>
> We say that the Father acts through the Son, because the Son is the cause of what is accomplished in virtue of one same and indivisible power, power that the Son possesses in common with the Father but which he receives, nevertheless, from the Father by his generation.[78]

This relative order has been illumined by means of the property signified by the name *Word*: In naming the Son *Word*, we identify him as the "operative cause" of the works that the Father accomplishes by him.[79] The exegesis of John 1:3 also specified this point: The Son is a subject of action (an *operans*) distinct from the Father.[80] The Father acts "through the Son" because the Father, in the eternal generation, gives to the Son the divine essence and power by which the Son acts.

The explanations of the action of the Holy Spirit show his personal distinction in a comparable way. The Father and the Son, spirating the Holy Spirit, give to the Holy Spirit the divine essence and, with it, the power of acting. This is the reason why the Father and the Son act "in the Holy Spirit" or "through the Holy Spirit."[81] The Father and the Son are, in this regard, the principle of the act that the Holy Spirit performs, insofar as they communicate to him the divine power of acting.[82] Thomas makes explicit this teaching by means of the property signified by the personal names *Love* and *Gift*. In recognizing the Holy Spirit as Love and Gift (these names express his distinct property), we signify him as the principle of the effects that the Father and the Son accomplish through him, that is, as the Love by which the Father and the Son love us and procure for us their gifts.[83]

In sum, "Whatever the Son does he has from the Father."[84] And likewise, the Holy Spirit acts by receiving his action from the Father and the Son, because he receives from them the divine nature. It is from the Father and from the Son that the Holy Spirit receives being and the power of acting,

---

77 Ibid., dist. 13, expositio textus: "[. . .] Filius, qui est operans, a Patre est."

78 Ibid., dist. 13, q. 1, a. 5, corp.: "Sic dicimus Patrem per Filium operari, quia est causa ipsorum operatorum una et indivisibili virtute cum Patre, quam tamen a Patre nascendo recepit."

79 *ST* I, q. 34, a. 3.

80 Cf. *In Ioannem* 1:3 (#85).

81 *De potentia*, q. 10, a. 4.

82 *Contra errores Graecorum* II, ch. 4: "The Son is the principle by whom the Holy Spirit acts *(principium operandi Spiritui Sancto)*, because the Son gives the power of action to the Holy Spirit." This communication of the power of action belongs to the spiration of the Holy Spirit by the Father and the Son, and it explains that "the Son acts through the Holy Spirit" (ibid.). Cf. *De potentia*, q. 10, a. 4.

83 *ST* I, q. 37, a. 2, ad 3; q. 38, a. 2.

84 *In Ioannem* 15:26 (#2061): "Filius quidquid operatur, habet a Patre."

and it is thus that he accomplishes his actions. When commenting on John 16:13 *(He will not speak from himself)*, St. Thomas explains that

> Just as the Son does not act from himself but from the Father, so the Holy Spirit, because he is from another, that is from the Father and the Son, will not speak from himself, but whatever he will hear by receiving knowledge as well as his essence from eternity he will speak.[85]

The three persons act in one same action, but each performs this action in the distinct mode of his personal relation, that is, according to his proper "mode of existing" in accordance with the Trinitarian order. The Father acts as source of the Son and of the Holy Spirit, the Son acts as Word of the Father, the Holy Spirit acts as Love and Gift of the Father and the Son. We are not in the domain of an appropriation, but rather in the domain of a *property* of the person, as Thomas expressly explains with regard to the Word. The proper mode of the persons' acting, we repeat, does not give rise to an exclusive action of one person in the world, but rather it concerns the hypostatic relation (the relation of divine Person to divine Person) always implied in the action that the Three perform in creating the world and saving humankind.

6. An Example of Doctrinal Exegesis: The Son and the Holy Spirit as Paraclete

We already noted above the way in which St. Thomas finds in John 1:3 the property that characterizes the mode of acting of the Son. This teaching can equally be illustrated by other explanations that allow one to apprehend better the Son's mode of acting. One of the most illumining examples is the exegesis of John 14:16 on the name "Paraclete": *I will pray the Father and he will give you another Paraclete.* The interpretation of St. Thomas shows his concern, in specifying the distinct modality of the action of each person, to maintain the unity of the action of the divine Persons in virtue of their common nature. The exegesis on this verse also manifests the unity of speculative theology and biblical exegesis in St. Thomas, as well as the tight bonds that unite Trinitarian theology and Christology.

St. Thomas explains that *Paraclete* means the "advocate" or the "consoler."[86] It is thus a name that designates the Holy Spirit in his economic

[85] Ibid., 16:13 (#2103): "Sicut enim Filius non operatur a semetipso sed a Patre, ita Spiritus Sanctus, quia est ab alio, scilicet a Patre et Filio, non loquetur a semetipso sed quaecumque audiet, accipiendo scientiam sicut et essentiam ab aeterno, haec loquetur."

[86] Ibid., 14:16 (#1911–12): "Sed attende quod hoc nomen Paraclitus est graecum, et significat consolatorem [. . .]. Spiritus Sanctus est consolator et advocatus." In his

act. This act of the Holy Spirit consists in the mission that he receives from the Father and the Son: to dwell amongst the disciples so as to obtain the presence of Father and Son for them, to lead the disciples to the full understanding of Christ's teaching, to bear witness to them on behalf of the Son. In a first step, St. Thomas explains briefly why this name is ascribed to the Holy Spirit. The term *Paraclete* fits well for designating the Holy Spirit "since he is the Spirit of Love": He is the love that procures spiritual consolation, joy, intercession.[87] The attribution of the name *Paraclete* to the Holy Spirit is therefore justified by the affinity between the *action* of the Holy Spirit and his *personal property* (Love):[88] Love is the principle of action signified by the name "Paraclete." In a second step, however, St. Thomas notes that the New Testament does not exclusively restrict the name *Paraclete* to the Holy Spirit. Indeed, when the fourth gospel designates the Holy Spirit by the name *Paraclete* (Jn 14:16–17, 26; 15:26; 16:7), it specifies that the Spirit is "*another* Paraclete" (Jn 14:16): Christ is also named *Paraclete* (1 Jn 2:1). This raises a question under the form of an "objection":

> The word *Paraclete* imports an action of the Holy Spirit. Therefore, by saying *another Paraclete*, a difference in nature seems to be indicated, because different actions indicate different natures. Thus the Holy Spirit does not have the same nature as the Son.[89]

The principle invoked by this objection is very clear: A being acts in virtue of what it is, that is, according to its nature, because the nature is the principle of action. For this very reason, action makes manifest the nature of a being: "For the clearest indication of the nature of a thing is taken from its works."[90] St. Thomas often invokes this metaphysical law in order to show the divinity of the Son and the Holy Spirit: "When we want to know whether a certain thing is true, we can determine it from two aspects: its nature *(natura)* and its power *(virtus)*. For true gold is that which has the species of true gold; and we determine it if it acts like true gold."[91] Such is the principle that guides the "soteriological argument" that St. Thomas draws

---

exegesis, Aquinas also often associates with the Holy Spirit words stemming from *deprecator* (intercessor).

87 Ibid., 14:16 (#1911): "Cum sit Spiritus Amoris; amor autem facit spiritualem consolationem et gaudium."

88 On Love (following the analogy of the "impression" or the "affection of love") as the personal property of the Holy Spirit according to Aquinas, see *ST* I, q. 37; cf. G. Emery, *Trinity in Aquinas,* 153–56.

89 *In Ioannem* 14:16 (#1912).

90 Ibid., 10:38 (#1466).

91 Ibid., 17:3 (#2187).

from the Fathers of the Church:[92] Because the Son does the works proper to God (to pardon sins, to judge, to save, and so on), this shows that he is true God. In the same manner, St. Thomas shows the divinity of the Holy Spirit from the works that the Holy Spirit produces: Because he accomplishes the works proper to God (to sanctify, to deify), the Holy Spirit is God. Here is a brief example of this doctrinal exegesis often practiced by St. Thomas: "He from whom men are spiritually reborn is God; but men are spiritually reborn through the Holy Spirit, as it is stated [in Jn 3:5]; therefore, the Holy Spirit is God."[93] One easily perceives the governing idea of this teaching: The action is the sign that allows one to identify the nature of the one who acts. The objection raised regarding the name *Paraclete* rests on these explanations: Since the Holy Spirit is "another" Paraclete, and since this name *Paraclete* signifies an action, does the gospel suggest that the Holy Spirit exercises another action than the Son, and therefore that the Spirit is of another nature than the Son? So would the action of the Spirit-Paraclete be different than that of the Son-Paraclete? Or, inversely, would the action of the Spirit be conflated with the action of the Son-Paraclete? The doctrinal stakes of the question are thus manifest: How can we account for the action of the Son and the Holy Spirit while avoiding the pitfalls of "Arianism" and "Sabellianism"? St. Thomas's response deserves to be pondered over in depth.

> I reply that the Holy Spirit is a Consoler and Advocate, and so is the Son. John says that the Son is an Advocate: *We have an advocate with the Father, Jesus Christ the righteous One* (1 Jn 2:1). In Isaiah we are told that he is a Consoler: *The Spirit of the Lord has sent me to comfort those who mourn* (Isa 61:1). Yet the Son and the Holy Spirit are Consolers and Advocates in a different way *(alia et alia ratione)*, if we consider what is congruent to each person. Christ is called an Advocate because, as man, he intercedes for us to the Father; the Holy Spirit is an Advocate because he makes us ask.
>
> Again, the Holy Spirit is called a Consoler inasmuch as he is formally Love *(inquantum est amor formaliter)*. But the Son is a Consoler inasmuch as he is the Word *(inquantum est Verbum)*. The Son is a Consoler in two ways: because of his teaching and because the Son gives the Holy Spirit and incites love in our hearts. Thus the word *another* does not indicate a different nature in the Son and in the Holy Spirit. Rather, it indicates the different mode in which each of them is an Advocate and a Consoler *(designat alium modum quo uterque est consolator et advocatus)*.[94]

---

[92] See, for example, St. Athanasius of Alexandria, *De synodis* 51 (PG 26, 784).

[93] *In Ioannem* 3:5 (#444). On the same soteriological argument, see ibid., 10:35 (#1460) and 17:3 (#2187); *SCG* IV, ch. 17 (#3528).

[94] *In Ioannem* 14:16 (#1912).

The effects of the action of the Son and of the Holy Spirit in helping the disciples are identical: It is consolation, joy, forceful witnessing, adhesion to the word of God, assurance in prayer. But if the *action* of the Son is like that of the Spirit (under this heading, both of them are Paraclete), this action takes a distinct mode. The solution of St. Thomas comprises two moments: The first concerns the term *Advocate* and the second the word *Consoler* (these two terms both specify an aspect of the name *Paraclete*). Following the first approach, the distinct mode of the act of the Son is characterized by the action of his humanity. Indeed, to speak properly, "to intercede" or "to pray" is the action of a rational creature, inferior to the divine nature.[95] Thus, it is in his humanity *(secundum quod homo)* that the Son intercedes for us before the Father. In this case, because of the hypostatic union, it is a question of the proper action of the Son, inasmuch as this action has for its formal principle the humanity proper to the Son incarnate. The actions accomplished by the humanity of Christ are properly attributed to his divine Person, because the person is the subject of actions performed either in virtue of his divine nature or in virtue of his human nature.[96] One can extend this response to all the acts that Christ accomplishes in his humanity. Insofar as the action of the Word incarnate implies the cooperation of his humanity as a proper instrument, conjoined and free, this theandric action belongs properly to the person of the Son. By reason of his personal humanity, only the Son is born of the Virgin Mary, preaches, suffers, dies, rises from the dead, ascends, intercedes for us before the Father. As regards the Holy Spirit, his action as *Advocate* is of another order. Indeed, the Holy Spirit does not exercise personally a created action,[97] but he is the cause of a human action: The Holy Spirit "intercedes" insofar as he is the source of the prayer of the saints. In short, this first exegesis of the name Advocate can be summarized in the following way: "The Son is said to ask or to pray according to his assumed nature, that is, not according to his divine nature but according to his human nature. The Holy Spirit is said to ask because he prompts us to ask."[98]

In a second moment in his commentary on John 14:16, St. Thomas considers the name *Consoler* as signifying an action of the Son and the Holy Spirit according to their divine personal property. In this case, the personal mode of the action of the Son does not concern only his humanity, but it refers in the first place to his divinity. The Son "consoles" in the

95 *ST* II–II, q. 83, a. 10: "Prayer is an act of reason by which a superior is petitioned."

96 *ST* III, q. 16, a. 4; cf. q. 19, a. 1.

97 This would imply an "Arian" or "Macedonian" understanding of the Holy Spirit, because "to intercede or to ask is the act of an inferior" ("postulare enim est minoris"): *In Rom* 8:26 (#692).

98 *ST* II–II, q. 83, a. 10, ad 1.

mode of his divine and incommunicable personal property, which is being the *Word* of the Father. In this regard, the Son gives teaching and spreads the Holy Spirit: This belongs to the Word *as Word*. Indeed, it is by reason of his property of Word of the Father that the Son reveals the truth and makes known the Father, because he is personally the expression of the whole wisdom of the Father;[99] he proceeds as the "begotten Wisdom" of the Father.[100] For this reason, St. Thomas states, "Since the doctrine of anyone is nothing else than his word, and the Son of God is the Word of God, it follows that the doctrine of the Father is the Son himself."[101] At the same time, it is by reason of his property of Word, that is, inasmuch as he is the divine Word, that the Son spirates the Holy Spirit: "The Son is the Word; not, however, just any word, but the Word breathing Love."[102] It is in this manner that the Son procures the knowledge of God by faith: The Son interiorly teaches believers "by giving them the Holy Spirit."[103] Such is the completely personal mode by which the Son, according to his property of Word, is the *Consoler* by his teaching.

On the part of the Holy Spirit, the mode of action comes from his personal property as *Love*. The Holy Spirit is properly and personally the Love who proceeds from the Father and the Son. Existing personally as Love (St. Thomas accounts for this personal property through the analogy of the "impression" or the "affection" of love in the will), the Holy Spirit acts in the mode of the Love of the Father and the Son, in communicating to human beings the impulsion of love that gives them their union to God: He spreads charity, that is, communicates a participation in his personal property, obtaining consolation and joy (which belongs formally to the Spirit as Love).[104]

In this way, St. Thomas can explain that the Son and the Holy Spirit, possessing the same nature, exercise the same action: to console. They receive therefore, under this aspect, the same name: *Consoler*. This is, moreover, the reason why the name *Consoler* is appropriated. It is not proper to a

99 *SCG* IV, ch. 13 (#3495); *In Ioannem* 1:9 (#127–29); ibid. 17:25 (#2267): "Human wisdom consists in knowing God. But this knowledge flows to us from the Word, because to the extent that we share in the Word of God, to that extent do we know God."

100 *ST* I, q. 34, a. 1, ad 2; *SCG* IV, ch. 12 (#3484).

101 *In Ioannem* 7:16 (#1037): "Cum doctrina uniuscuiusque nihil aliud sit quam verbum eius, Filius autem Dei sit Verbum eius: sequitur ergo quod doctrina Patris sit ipse Filius."

102 *ST* I, q. 43, a. 5, ad 2: "Filius autem est Verbum, non qualecumque, sed spirans Amorem"; cf. *ST* I, q. 36, a. 2; I *Sent.*, dist. 15, q. 4, a. 1, ad 3.

103 *In Ioannem* 17:26 (#2269): "Alia cognitio est interior per Spiritum Sanctum; et quantum ad hoc dicit *Et notum faciam*, scilicet eis dando Spiritum Sanctum."

104 *SCG* IV, ch. 21 (#3578) and ch. 22 (#3586); *In Ioannem* 14:26 (#1959).

person, as the New Testament attests, but each person exercises this action according to his proper mode *(alius modus)*. The Son consoles in accordance with his property of Word: He is the Word through whom the Father consoles and who, with the Father, sends the Holy Spirit. The Holy Spirit consoles in a manner that corresponds to his property of Love: He is the Gift through whom the Father and Son console us and give us a share in their Love. The proper mode of the personal action does not imply that the effect is exclusively proper to one person (the created effect, like the divine action that produces that effect, is appropriated);[105] rather, this mode concerns the relative property of the persons, that is, the intra-Trinitarian relation of person to person: The Son acts inasmuch as he is begotten as Word of the Father, the Holy Spirit acts inasmuch as he is personally Love proceeding from the Father and his Word, and the Father acts through the Son whom he begets and in the Holy Spirit whom he spirates with the Son.

7. Immanent Trinity, Economic Trinity, and Perichoresis

In explaining that the distinction of the mode of action applies on the side of the relation of divine Person to divine Person (personal property), and not on the side of effects of the divine action, is St. Thomas truly able to show the personal dimension of the relationships that the divine Persons have with us? In other words, does this doctrine honor sufficiently the aspect *quoad nos* of the Trinitarian act in its personal dimension? We have already indicated above the reasons why Thomist thought can accept neither that a created effect be attributed in a proper manner to one divine Person to the exclusion of others, nor that an action in the world belongs to one person rather than to another. But the objection remains, because it could seem that the Thomist explication has divided the Trinity by a kind of dichotomy: on the one hand, the intra-Trinitarian relations in which one observes a personal distinction and a distinct mode of action, and on the other, the relations to creatures in which the personal distinction no longer intervenes directly and cedes its place to the unity of the Trinity.

This difficulty can be formulated in terms derived from Karl Rahner: Does not St. Thomas's explanation divide the "immanent Trinity" and the "economic Trinity"? Indeed, following the thought of St. Thomas, the distinct mode of action of the persons consists in their eternal personal properties and not in a different relation of persons with creatures. In this case,

105 Appropriation is based precisely upon the affinity between the effect (or, rather, the essential attribute to which this effect is referred) and the relative property of the divine Person.

can one still affirm that "the economic Trinity is the immanent Trinity and vice versa"? Does not the Rahnerian *Grundaxiom* imply that the solution of St. Thomas ought to be avoided?

In reality, the teaching of St. Thomas leads rather to the following position: The Trinity acts in the world, reveals itself and gives itself ("economic Trinity"), as it is in itself ("immanent Trinity"). In themselves, in the intra-Trinitarian life, the divine Persons are distinguished by their relative properties: The Trinitarian plurality arises neither from a difference of essence nor from a different relationship of persons toward something exterior to the Trinity;[106] instead, it arises from relations of origin, in the measure in which one person proceeds from another. In the same way, when the persons act in the world, they are distinguished neither by a difference of essence nor by a different relationship to creatures; instead, they are distinguished by their mutual relations, in the measure in which the persons who act are each referred to the others. This point bears repeating: In the "immanent Trinity," the real distinction of persons arises only from their personal relations and consists in these opposed relations;[107] in the same way, in the "economic Trinity," the distinction of persons who act resides entirely in these mutual relations according to origin. This is what is expressed by the affirmation of the "relative mode of acting" of the persons within their common action for us. Precisely where, at first glance, one could have suspected a division of the "immanent Trinity" and the "economic Trinity," it is instead necessary to recognize that *St. Thomas coherently maintains the identity of the Trinity in itself and in its act for us.*

This teaching can be illustrated by the doctrine of the missions and, even better, by that of perichoresis. The sending of the Son and of the Holy Spirit in grace ("invisible mission"), according to St. Thomas, consists in a twofold relation: the relation of origin of the person sent (intra-Trinitarian relation) and a relation to the created effect.[108] The first relation is the eternal relation that constitutes the person of the Son and of the Holy Spirit. The second relation implies a created effect that is appro-

---

106 This is the reason why speculative Trinitarian theology, in St. Thomas, is founded on the doctrine of the *immanent* processions: If one began from the act of God in the world (transitive action), Arianism and Sabellianism could no longer be avoided; cf. *ST* I, q. 27, a. 1.

107 *Quodlibet* XII, q. 1, a. 1: "Veritas fidei habet quod in divinis solum est distinctio quae est secundum relationes oppositas."

108 *ST* I, q. 43, a. 1: "In ratione missionis duo importantur: quorum unum est habitudo missi ad eum a quo mittitur; aliud est habitudo missi ad terminum ad quem mittitur. [. . .] Missio igitur divinae Personae convenire potest, secundum quod importat ex una parte processionem originis a mittente; et secundum quod importat ex alia parte novum modum existendi in aliquo." Cf. *ST* I, q. 43, a. 2 and a. 5.

priated to the person sent, in virtue of an affinity between the created effect (wisdom, charity) and the personal property of the Son and of the Holy Spirit. Thus, the mission of the divine Person includes his eternal procession, to which it adds a created effect in virtue of which this person is made present in a new manner (one then speaks of the "temporal procession" of the divine Person).[109] The Son and the Holy Spirit are sent according to their relation of origin: The person sent is the person *proceeding*, the person *inasmuch as he proceeds*. The completely *proper* character of the invisible mission of the Son and of the mission of the Spirit does not primarily reside in the created effect (this effect, common to the whole Trinity, is appropriated to one person), but instead resides in the eternal personal relation that the mission includes: The Son is sent in being turned toward the Father who begets him; the Holy Spirit is sent and given according to his relation to the Father and the Son who spirate him.

Extending these reflections, St. Thomas explains that the "visible mission" of the persons, that is, the incarnation of the Son and the manifestation of the Spirit by sensible signs, consists in a twofold manifestation: the manifestation of the eternal procession of the person sent, and the manifestation of a plenitude of grace that flows forth visibly, in the presence of witnesses, in order to establish the Church in faith and charity through word and sacrament.[110] Here again, the proper foundation of the "visible mission" is taken from the eternal property of the person: The visible mission manifests the Holy Spirit insofar as he is personally Love and Gift (this is his relative property),[111] that is, insofar as he is the "sanctifying Gift" of the Father and the Son; as regards the Son, he is sent insofar as he is, according to his property, the principle and the giver of the Holy Spirit, that is to say, insofar as he is "the author of sanctification."[112] The Son is manifested by the holy humanity that he assumes; this holy humanity, participating instrumentally in the power of the divinity, works to procure salvation. The human act of Christ *collaborates* with his divine act and *reveals* the person of the Son in his personal traits (it is sign and instrument), because this human act manifests the Son *as Son of the Father and as Giver of the Spirit*. The proper characteristics of the act of the Son and

---

109 *ST* I, q. 43, a. 2, ad 3: "Missio includit processionem aeternam, et aliquid addit, scilicet temporalem effectum." Cf. I *Sent.*, dist. 14, q. 1 and q. 2: The created gift of charity is a disposition (dispositive cause) to receive the uncreated Gift, that is, the Holy Spirit himself (efficient, exemplar, and final cause).

110 I *Sent.*, dist. 16, q. 1, a. 1 and a. 2.

111 Cf. *ST* I, q. 37 and q. 38.

112 Ibid., q. 43, a. 7: "Nam Spiritui Sancto, inquantum procedit ut Amor, competit esse sanctificationis donum; Filio autem, inquantum est Spiritus Sancti principium, competit esse sanctificationis huius auctorem." Cf. ibid., ad 4.

of the Holy Spirit, in their mission, are thus taken principally from the eternal relation that this mission makes manifest.

The doctrine of perichoresis offers a synthesis of this teaching. St. Thomas explains that the divine Persons are mutually "each in the other" according to a threefold point of view. Each person is interior to the others: (1) in virtue of their common essence, because where there is the essence of a person, there is the person himself; (2) in virtue of their relations, because each relative implies in itself its correlative; (3) in virtue of the processions, because these processions are "immanent": The person who proceeds dwells in the person from whom he proceeds.[113] The latter two aspects permit one in addition to understand the *reciprocity* of the divine Persons. Indeed, under the aspect of the unity of essence, the Father is in the Son in the same way as the Son is in the Father, that is, by identity of nature, because each person possesses the same divine nature.[114] Nevertheless, under the aspect of relations, the mutual presence of persons assumes the *proper mode* of the relation. This mode is not interchangeable but distinct in reciprocity. The Son is in the Father insofar as he is related to the Father as his Son, just as the Father is in the Son insofar as he is his Father. Paternity and filiation thus imply *two distinct modes of presence in reciprocity*: "On the side of the relation, the mode [of presence of the Father in the Son and of the Son in the Father] is *different*, according to the different relationship of the Father to the Son and of the Son to the Father."[115] The same point holds when one considers the persons under the aspect of origin: The Father is in the Son insofar as he begets the Son, the Son is in the Father insofar as he is begotten by the Father; the Holy Spirit is in the Father and the Son insofar as he proceeds from them, just as the Father and the Son are in the Holy Spirit insofar as they spirate him.[116] The relations are not limited therefore to "distinguishing" the persons by reason of the "opposition" that they

113 Ibid., q. 42, a. 5. St. Thomas explains, with regard to the procession of the Son, that "the Son came forth from the Father from all eternity in such a way that the Son is still in the Father from all eternity. And so when the Son is in the Father, he comes forth, and when the Son comes forth he is in the Father: So the Son is always in the Father and always coming forth from the Father" (*In Ioannem* 16:28 [#2161]).

114 I *Sent.*, dist. 19, q. 3, a. 2, ad 3: "Si accipiatur Pater esse in Filio propter unitatem essentiae, eodem modo est Pater in Filio et Filius in Patre: Et tunc haec praepositio 'in' non importabit aliquam relationem realem, sed tantum relationem rationis, qualis est inter essentiam et personam, secundum quam essentia dicitur esse in persona."

115 Ibid.: "Si autem hoc accipiamus ex parte relationis, tunc est alius modus, ut dictum est, secundum diversam habitudinem Patris ad Filium, et Filii ad Patrem." In this case, the relations are really distinct (fatherhood and sonship).

116 Ibid., dist. 19, q. 3, a. 2, ad 1: "Unde Filius est in Patre sicut originatum in originante, et e converso Pater in Filio sicut originans in originato."

have, but the relations are also the reason of the *unity* of the persons that they distinguish.[117] Relation thus grounds the Trinitarian communion.

Perichoresis sheds light not just on the being and the relations of the Trinity in itself, but also on the act of the Trinity within this world. In the first place, the mutual "being in" of the persons implies their common act. Just as the persons *exist* indivisibly, they *act* inseparably: The Father who acts is in the Son and in the Holy Spirit, the acting Son is in the Father and in the Holy Spirit, the Spirit who acts is in the Father and in the Son, in such a way that their action is common and that the effects of this action are also common. The action of persons in the world cannot be different, since each acts by having the others in him and by being in the others. Likewise, the effects cannot be related to a single person, because the three persons act mutually "one in the other." But the persons are not conflated: The Son acts in being turned toward the Father by his filiation and in being turned toward the Holy Spirit by spiration (the Son acts *a Patre* and *per Spiritum Sanctum*), the Father acts in being turned toward the Son by his paternity and toward the Holy Spirit by spiration (the Father acts *per Filium* and *per Spiritum Sanctum*), and the Holy Spirit acts in being turned toward the Father and the Son by his procession (the Holy Spirit acts *a Patre* and *a Filio*). Such is the proper "mode" by which each person is distinctly in the other and acts distinctly in the other under the aspect of personal relation. Perichoresis shows the depth of the communion of persons (unity and distinction) in their act.

Working inseparably in the economy, the three divine Persons are therefore also inseparably *present*. This presence concerns, in the first place, the mysteries of the Son of God in his flesh: In Christ, the Son incarnate, the whole Trinity is made present to humankind, by reason of the divine consubstantiality and by reason of the Trinitarian relations. The presence of the Trinity is also given when the Son and the Holy Spirit are sent into the souls of saints ("invisible mission" of the divine Person). The Father is not "sent," because he does not have a principle; he is rather the one who sends the Son and the Holy Spirit. Nevertheless, the Father comes to dwell in the hearts of the saints, along with the Son and the Spirit whom he sends. In both cases, perichoresis accounts for the coming and for the presence of the three persons together:

> The Father is in the Son, the Son is in the Father, and both are in the Holy Spirit. For this reason, when the Son is sent, the Father and the

---

117 Relations account for the unity and for the real distinction in the Trinity: "Quamvis Pater sit in Filio per unitatem essentiae, et quantum ad intellectum relationis; tamen relatio, inquantum habet rationem oppositionis, distinguit Patrem a Filio secundum suppositum" (ibid., dist. 21, q. 1, a. 2, ad 4).

> Holy Spirit come also, simultaneously. This takes place in the Son's advent in the flesh, as he says himself in John 8:16: *I am not alone, but I and the Father who sent me.* This holds also when he comes into the soul [of saints], as he likewise says himself in John 14:23: *We will come to him, and we will make our home with him.* This is why the coming and the inhabitation belong to the whole Trinity.[118]

Due to perichoresis, the coming of the Son in the economy of salvation is a presence not only of the Son, but also of the whole Trinity. This is the reason why the incarnation and the mysteries of the life of Christ are a *revelation of the Trinity.* And, in the gift of grace, the perichoresis of divine Persons is extended to us. When the Holy Spirit is given with the charity that he spreads, when the Son comes to inhabit human beings by living faith, it is the whole Trinity that is made inseparably present, as much in virtue of the common essence of the persons as in virtue of their relations. The mutual indwelling of the divine Persons, explicated by the doctrines of processions, relations, and essence (the pillars of Trinitarian doctrine), thus illumines the two aspects of the Trinitarian act: (1) the inseparable unity of the action of the persons, the unity of their presence in the economy, and the unity of their effects; (2) the personal dimension of the Trinitarian act, which is rooted in the proper mode of being of the persons and in their mode of action according to their distinctive property.

8. Our Relation in Grace to Each Divine Person: Objective Union

In the explications that we have undertaken to this point, we have principally considered the *causal action* of the Trinity, that is, the divine Persons as efficient and exemplar source of the gifts of nature and of grace. Under this aspect, St. Thomas invites us to recognize the unity of the Trinity, because the three persons exercise together one single causal action. This is why the created effects, considered in an "ontological" or "entitative" manner, refer us to the three persons in their inseparable causality.[119]

---

118 Ibid., dist. 15, q. 2, ad 4: "Cum Pater sit in Filio, et Filius in Patre, et uterque in Spiritu Sancto, quando Filius mittitur, simul et venit Pater et Spiritus Sanctus; sive intelligatur de adventu Filii in carnem, cum ipse dicat, Ioan. 8:16, *Solus non sum, sed ego, et qui misit me Pater,* sive intelligatur de adventu in mentem, cum ipse dicat, Ioan. 14:23, *Ad eum veniemus, et mansionem apud eum faciemus.* Et ideo adventus vel inhabitatio convenit toti Trinitati."

119 Recall that the divine action or the created effect can be appropriated to one person in particular, but this appropriation finds its place within the common causality of the whole Trinity.

Does not, however, the experience of faith give us a relation with each divine Person in particular? Consequently, is it not necessary to recognize that grace enables us to enter into relation not only with the unity of the Trinity, but with each person in his distinct personality? St. Thomas responds clearly: Yes, when the Son and the Holy Spirit are sent to the saints in grace, the saints come to "enjoy" each person in his personal property. But this relation to the Father, to the Son, and to the Holy Spirit in their distinct personality is no longer situated at the level of the *causality* of the Trinity (the ontological or entitative aspect): It concerns the *intentional* or *objective* engagement with the divine Persons, who are really "given" and "possessed" by the beneficiaries of grace.

St. Thomas explains that, by grace, the Trinity dwells in the human being "as the known is in the knower and as the beloved is in the one who loves."[120] The Trinity, in the distinction of persons, is given to human beings as "object" of acts of supernatural knowledge (faith, beatific vision) and as "object" of charitable acts (charity, fruition). The divine Persons are no longer understood only as the cause of the effects that they procure in us, but rather they are given and present "as the object of the operation is present in the one who operates."[121] The word *object* in this context should be rightly understood. It does not indicate any depersonalization of God (in the manner in which, today, one may distinguish a relationship to another in terms of "subject" or "object"). The word *object* is taken here in its formal sense and designates what is directly attained or apprehended by an action, the reality toward which the activity or the "operation" is carried out by an acting subject. When applied to God, this word means that, by the habits or the acts of wisdom and of charity, human beings attain, apprehend, or "possess" the divine Persons inasmuch as they are united to these persons by knowledge and love. This is why, in order to designate this relation to the divine Persons, the Thomist tradition speaks of the "objective" presence of the Trinity, or of the "intentional" presence of the divine Persons (the terms *intentional* or *spiritual* designate, by opposition to *natural*, the mode of being that a reality assumes in the subject who knows it and who loves it).[122]

One can summarize the explications of St. Thomas in the following manner. The whole Trinity, in one same action, is the source or the cause

120 *ST* I, q. 43, a. 3. This new relation to the divine Persons does not pertain to the order of nature (creation), but exclusively to that of grace.

121 Ibid., q. 8, a. 3: "sicut objectum operationis est in operante"; cf. I *Sent.*, dist. 37, q. 1, a. 2; dist. 37, *expositio primae partis textus*: "per modum objecti."

122 The vocabulary of intentionality is of philosophical origin; it comes from Arab authors (Averroes); see the note of Fr. René-Antoine Gauthier in *Sentencia libri de anima*, Leonine edition, vol. 45/1, 169.

of sanctifying grace (grace is appropriated to the Holy Spirit, by reason of the affinity that grace possesses to the property of the Holy Spirit as Love and Gift of the Father and the Son). The whole Trinity is the source or the cause of our filial adoption (adoption is appropriated to the Father as its author, to the Son as its model, and to the Holy Spirit as to the one who inscribes it in our hearts).[123] The whole Trinity is the cause of the gifts of wisdom and of love (the gifts that illumine the intellect are appropriated to the Son, while the gifts that inflame charity are appropriated to the Holy Spirit).[124] But salvation consists in the reception of the *divine Persons themselves*: the presence of the Son and of the Holy Spirit who are sent, and the presence of the Father who comes to indwell the hearts of his children with the Son and the Holy Spirit whom he sends.[125] The created gifts caused by the Trinity (sanctifying grace, wisdom, charity) are a disposition conferred upon human beings to make them capable of receiving the divine Persons who are themselves really given and substantially present.[126] In order to designate this relationship to divine Persons, St. Thomas speaks of "fruition" *(frui, fruitio)*.[127] This word designates the union of love with the divine Persons who are the ultimate end of the human being and in whom the human being finds his happiness.[128] St. Thomas is very clear: By grace, "we enjoy *(fruimur)* the property of each person."[129] To enjoy the divine Persons, or to "possess" *(habere)* the divine Persons,[130] is to be "conformed" to the Son and to the Holy Spirit who are sent to us, and to be united to the divine Persons as "object" of knowledge and of love, that is, to be caught up in the divine Persons known and loved by faith (and then by the vision) and by charity (fruition).

The doctrine of the image of the Trinity in the human being develops the same points. It is in knowing and loving the divine Persons that we are conformed to these persons, and it is then that the image of the Trinity in the human being attains its highest degree (image of grace and of glory). According to Aquinas's teaching, the perfect image of God in the human

---

123 *ST* III, q. 23, a. 2, ad 3.

124 *ST* I, q. 43, a. 5, ad 1, ad 2 and ad 3.

125 Cf. ibid., q. 43, a. 4.

126 I *Sent.*, dist. 14, q. 2, a. 1, qla 1; dist. 14, q. 2, a. 2, ad 2; dist. 15, q. 4, a. 1; cf. *ST* I, q. 43, a. 3, corp., ad 1 and ad 2. The just receive not only created gifts, but the uncreated Gift himself. The divine Person is the "cause" and the "end" of his created gifts. This is why the gift of the Holy Spirit himself is absolutely primary *(simpliciter prius)* in relationship to his created gifts (ibid., dist. 14, q. 2, a. 2, qla 2).

127 *ST* I, q. 43, a. 3; cf. *ST* I, q. 38, a. 1.

128 I *Sent.*, dist. 1, q. 2; dist. 14, q. 2, a. 2, ad 2; cf. *ST* I–II, q. 11.

129 I *Sent.*, dist. 1, q. 2, a. 2, ad 2: "Proprietate uniuscujusque personae fruimur."

130 *ST* I, q. 43, a. 3.

being is accomplished when the human being is *conformed* to the Trinity (assimilation to the divine Persons) by his *acts* of knowledge and of love ("objective" union)—that is, when the human being, configured to the Word and to the Holy Spirit who are sent, is united to the Trinity known and loved.[131] It is in this "objective" order that the fruition of the divine Persons and the indwelling of these persons in the heart of the human being is realized. The divine Persons are not ontologically mixed with the creature, but the creature is enabled to be united to the divine Persons, who are really present in the mode of a known and loved "object."

In this context, St. Thomas speaks of our "experience" of the Son and of the Holy Spirit in their proper personality. This teaching extends that of St. Augustine. The bishop of Hippo had explained that the Son is sent into the soul of the saints when he is "known as having his origin in the Father"; in the same way, the Holy Spirit is sent when he is known as proceeding from the Father and from the Son.[132] In his mission, the divine Person is manifested; the Son and the Holy Spirit are made known by the gifts that represent them and that are appropriated to them.[133] And when the person is thus manifested, the person is given in his personal relation. The Son is made known in his relation to the Father: In faith, he is received as the one sent from the Father and as the Son of the Father. Similarly, the Holy Spirit is made known in his relation to the Father and to the Son: He is received as the Spirit of the Father and the Son. As regards the Father, he is known as the source of the Son and the Holy Spirit, whom he sends into our hearts.[134] This knowledge of the divine Person in his personal distinction belongs to the very notion of "mission."[135] In order to make explicit such a grasp of the persons in their mission, St. Thomas speaks of an "experimental knowledge" of the Son and of the Holy Spirit. The expression, in St. Thomas, is not rare in this context: One finds it many times, as much in the *Commentary on the Sentences* as in the *Summa*, and always in reference to the love that makes knowledge perfect.[136] This knowledge is an experience of

---

131 *ST* I, q. 93, a. 7–8: The image of God is found in the human being according to the acts that have God for their object.

132 St. Augustine, *De Trinitate* IV,20,29 (ed. W. J. Mountain, vol. 1, 199).

133 St. Thomas, I *Sent.*, dist. 15, q. 4, a. 1, ad 1.

134 Ibid., dist. 15, q. 4, a. 1; cf. dist. 14, q. 2, a. 2.

135 Ibid., dist. 15, q. 2, ad 5; dist. 15, q. 4, a. 1, ad 1.

136 Ibid., dist. 14, q. 2, a. 2, ad 3; dist. 15, q. 2, ad 5; dist. 15, *expositio textus*; dist. 16, q. 1, a. 2; *ST* I, q. 43, a. 5, ad 2. On this theme, see in particular Albert Patfoort, "*Cognitio ista est quasi experimentalis* (I *Sent.*, dist. 14, q. 2, a. 2, ad 3m)," *Angelicum* 63 (1986): 3–13; idem, "Missions divines et expérience des Personnes divines selon S. Thomas," *Angelicum* 63 (1986): 545–59; Jean-Pierre Torrell, *Saint Thomas Aquinas,* vol. 2: *Spiritual Master* (Washington, DC: Catholic University of America Press, 2003), 94–98.

the divine Person present and acting, a "fruitful knowledge" *(fruitio)* of the person sent. This theme of "experimental knowledge" makes explicit the union given by the mission of the Son and of the Holy Spirit, that is, the union to the Son and to the Holy Spirit inasmuch as we are "conformed" or "assimilated" to them through our acts (or through our habitus) of supernatural knowledge and charity.

According to these explanations, therefore, it is necessary to distinguish the "ontological" aspect of grace and the "intentional" aspect of the gifts of wisdom and charity rooted in habitual grace.[137] Under its "ontological" or "entitative" aspect, that is, considered in itself (in the subject to which it is given), habitual grace is the effect of the action of the whole Trinity and refers us therefore to the Trinity in the unity of the three persons.[138] But under their "intentional" aspect, when one considers them in their dynamism, that is, from the side of the *object* toward which they lead us (the "objective" manifestation of known and loved divine Persons), the gifts of grace (wisdom and charity) "conform" us to the Son and to the Holy Spirit and refer us to the three persons inasmuch as these persons are distinct from each other and are apprehended in their proper singularity, one as Father, the second as only-begotten Son, the third as Holy Spirit come forth from the Father and the Son.[139]

9. Conclusion

Aquinas firmly recognizes the unity of action of the divine Persons, the unity of their principle of action and the unity of their relationship to created effects. Appropriations come into the picture at this level: that of the action itself (for example, to create, to vivify, to sanctify, to comfort), that of the principles of action (power, wisdom, will) and of created effects (for example, being, grace, adoptive filiation, consolation), which, being common to the three persons, are nevertheless attributed specially to one person in virtue of an affinity with the exclusive property of this person. But Aquinas also clearly maintains a *relational mode of acting* of each person, a proper and distinct mode that consists in the personal intra-Trinitarian relationship qualifying intrinsically the act of the Father, Son, and Holy

137 For further discussion, see Charles Journet, *L'Église du Verbe Incarné: Essai de théologie spéculative,* vol. 2: *Sa structure interne et son unité catholique* (Saint-Maurice: Éditions Saint-Augustin, 1999), 454–68.

138 III *Sent.*, dist. 4, q. 1, a. 2, qla 1: "Gratia quae in nobis est, est effectus essentiae divinae, non habens respectum ad distinctionem personarum." It is here that the appropriations find a place.

139 Under this aspect, it is no longer a question of appropriation, but of a relation to the three divine Persons, each one being apprehended in his proper and distinct personality.

Spirit. The recognition of a *proper* mode of acting of each divine Person gives more value to the doctrine of appropriation, because appropriation of essential features rests precisely on the relative property that characterizes the distinct mode of existence and act of the Father, Son, and Holy Spirit. By accounting for the personal dimension of the divine action, the proper mode of acting of the persons grounds the Trinitarian structure of the economy: All comes forth from the Father, through the Son, and in the Spirit.

At another level, in the order of the objective union to the Trinity known and loved (and no longer only in the order of the causality of the divine act), St. Thomas shows that the gifts of grace enable human beings to enter into relation with each person in particular, that is to say, each person apprehended in a proper and distinct way.

In highlighting the proper features of the act of the Son and of the Holy Spirit, this doctrine gives a particular prominence to the person of the Father: Being the source in the Trinity, the Father is the "ultimate term"[140] to which the Holy Spirit and the Son lead human beings. Creation and salvation are accomplished in the rhythm of the Trinitarian relations.

---

140 I *Sent.*, dist. 14, q. 2, a. 2.

CHAPTER 5

The Ecclesial Fruit of the Eucharist in St. Thomas Aquinas

CONTEMPORARY THEOLOGY has generally sought, in ecclesiology as well as in sacramental theology, to highlight the relationship between the Church and the Eucharist.[1] The work of Henri de Lubac is well-known for its important achievements in this rediscovery, especially with respect to the now famous formula: "The Church makes the Eucharist, but the Eucharist also makes the Church."[2] This organic relationship between the Eucharist and the Church, whose unity flows from the Eucharist itself, is at the heart of St. Thomas Aquinas's theology of the Eucharist. Thomist authors generally have not failed to recognize this fact.[3] Thus it was with St. Thomas that Cardinal Journet showed that the grace or effect produced by the Eucharist is "the secret unity of the Church."[4] The ecclesial fruitfulness of the Eucharist, a

1 Translation by Therese C. Scarpelli of "Le fruit ecclésial de l'Eucharistie chez saint Thomas d'Aquin," *Nova et Vetera* (French) 72 (1997): 25–40. Translation published in *Nova et Vetera* (English) 2 (2004): 43–60.

2 Henri de Lubac, *Méditation sur l'Église* (Paris: Aubier, 1953), 113; cf. 129: "Au sens le plus strict, l'Eucharistie *fait l'Église*." A critical study of this double relationship in the writings of Henri de Lubac is found in Paul McPartlan, *The Eucharist Makes the Church: Henri de Lubac and John Zizioulas in Dialogue* (Edinburgh: T&T Clark, 1993), 1–120.

3 Aloysius M. Ciappi, "Eucharistia: Sacramentum unitatis Ecclesiae apud D. Thomam et posteriores theologos OP," in *La Eucaristía y la Paz. XXXV Congreso eucarístico internacional 1952: Sesiones de estudio*, vol. 1 (Barcelona: Planas, 1953), 282–86.

4 Charles Journet, *L'Église du Verbe Incarné*, vol. 2 (Paris: Desclée de Brouwer, 1951), 671; see idem, "Le mystère de la sacramentalité," *Nova et Vetera* (French) 49 (1974): 161–214, especially 203–4.

theme present in the teaching of the Council of Trent,[5] was especially highlighted in the Second Vatican Council: The sacrament of the Eucharist *represents* and *effects* the unity of the faithful, who form one single body or one single people in Christ.[6]

The Church celebrates the Eucharist, and the Eucharist effects the Church's unity. These two statements are not at exactly the same level. Priority must be given to the second statement, which expresses the mystery of the Church and reveals its very soul: The Eucharist, the sacrifice of Christ, makes the Church. I will sketch here the teaching of St. Thomas regarding this second statement.

1. The Ecclesial Dimension in All Aspects of the Sacrament

The ecclesial dimension first appears in all aspects of St. Thomas's analysis of the sacrament, whose symbolism and efficacy require, in a dynamic way, the adoption of a three-level structure: first, the sign itself; then the intermediary reality that is at once the sign and the first effect of the sacrament; and finally the reality of grace effected and signified by the sacrament. The great Scholastics (for example, St. Albert and St. Bonaventure) agree in the general application of this structure and acknowledge the mystical Body as the fruit of the grace of the Eucharist.[7] Thus the principal elements of the doctrine that Thomas inherits are already in place, but the unfolding of this doctrine in his own theology deserves special examination.

The Sensible Sign of the Eucharist (sacramentum tantum)

On the level of sign, Thomas likes to recall an image from the *Didache*, developed in the west by Cyprian and then by Augustine, from whom Thomas derives it:

---

[5] This fact is rarely emphasized in studies, but the reader will be easily convinced by examining several documents, notably the *Decree on the Most Holy Sacrament of the Eucharist* (Session XIII, October 11, 1551) in the Preamble, ch. 2 and ch. 8, as well as the *Teaching on the Most Holy Sacrifice of the Mass* (Session XXII, September 17, 1562) in ch. 7; cf. *Decrees of the Ecumenical Councils*, vol. 2, ed. Norman P. Tanner (Washington, DC: Georgetown University Press: 1990), 693–97 and 735.

[6] Dogmatic Constitution, *Lumen Gentium*, #3, 11, and 26; *Christus Dominus,* #11 and 15; *Unitatis Redintegratio,* #2 and 15. Among the numerous works devoted to this topic, one can refer to the study of the texts and their sources (Fathers, liturgy, Magisterium) by Bruno Forte, *La Chiesa nell'Eucaristia: Per un'ecclesiologia eucaristica alla luce del Vaticano II* (Naples: M. D'Auria, 1988).

[7] St. Albert the Great, IV *Sent.*, dist. 8, a. 11–13; St. Bonaventure, IV *Sent.*, dist. 8, pars 2, a. 2, q. 1.

> Our Lord has proffered his Body and his Blood in those things which, from a multitude, are reduced to unity, since the bread is one single reality made of many grains; while the wine is one single [drink] made of many grapes.[8]

Here, Thomas echoes Augustine's commentary on John: "O mystery of goodness, O sign of unity, O bond of charity!"[9] The bread and wine, which constitute the matter of this sacrament, are here seen as the sign of that which the Eucharist effects: From a multitude, the Eucharist brings forth a single reality *(ex multis unum).*

This first aspect of the Eucharist—which Thomas frequently recalls[10]—is not inconsequential, since the sacrament effects that which is represented or signified, that is, the true Body of Christ and the unity of the mystical Body. Thus in Thomas, this ecclesial signification serves to show that the sacrament effectively produces such a grace.[11] Other liturgical acts are mentioned in this context: for example, the commingling of water in the wine, which signifies the mystical Body, "the uniting of the members to their Head," or "the uniting of the Christian people to Christ."[12] Similarly, the breaking of the bread signifies the distribution of graces in the Church and the various states of the mystical Body (glorious,

---

8 St. Thomas, *ST* III, q. 79, a. 1. See St. Augustine, *In Iohannis Evangelium* 6:56, *Tractatus* 26,17 (Aurelius Augustinus, *In Iohannis Evangelium Tractatus CXXIV,* Corpus Christianorum, Series Latina 36 [Turnhout: Brepols, 1954], 268); idem, *Sermo* 227 (PL 38, 1100); idem, *Sermo* 272 (PL 38, 1247–48). Cf. *Didache* IX,4 (*Sources Chrétiennes* 248 [Paris: Cerf, 1978], 177); St. Cyprian, *Epist.* 63,13; 69,5 (Cyprianus Episcopus, *Epistularium,* Corpus Christianorum, Series Latina 3C, 408–9 and 476–77). See Marie-François Berrouard, "Le symbolisme du pain et du vin," in *Oeuvres de Saint Augustin,* vol. 72 (Paris: Desclée de Brouwer, 1972), 822–23. For the history of this Eucharistic symbol, see Adalbert G. Hamman, *Études patristiques* (Paris: Beauchesne, 1991), 93–100.

9 St. Thomas, *ST* III q. 79, a. 1; cf. St. Augustine, *In Iohannis Evangelium* 6:50–52, *Tractatus* 26,13 (p. 266); cf. *Tractatus* 26,17 (p. 268).

10 St. Thomas, IV *Sent.*, dist. 8, q. 1, a. 1, qla 1, arg. 2; dist. 11, q. 1, a. 1, qla 1, arg. 2; dist. 11, q. 2, a. 1, qla 2; dist. 11, q. 2, a. 2, qla 1, arg. 4; *ST* III, q. 74, a. 1; q. 75, a. 2, arg. 3; q. 79, a. 1; q. 79, a. 2; *Catena in Matthaeum* 26, lect. 7 (vol. 1, 384); *In Ioannem* 6:52 (#960); *In 1 Cor* 11:24 (#654); *Reportationes ineditae Leoninae in 1 Cor* 11:23; see below, footnotes 79 and 81.

11 *ST* III, q. 79, a. 1. This argument is only made after three other reasons, but this does not necessarily mean that we must interpret it as a marginal or extrinsic motif as Bruno Forte argues in "Contributo ad uno studio del rapporto fra l'Eucaristia e la Chiesa in S. Tommaso d'Aquino," in *Tommaso d'Aquino nel suo settimo centenario,* vol. 4 (Naples: M. D'Auria, 1974), 409–20, cf. 410–13. Moreover, this symbolism is present everywhere in the works of Thomas, right into the office of *Corpus Christi.*

12 IV *Sent.*, dist. 11, q. 2, a. 4, qla 1; *ST* III, q. 74, a. 6 and a. 7.

militant, and awaiting the resurrection).[13] The ecclesial symbolism associated with food will be further developed with respect to the *res* of the Eucharist, since through communion the faithful are transformed into that which they eat: the Body of Christ. St. Thomas therefore holds firmly to the representing of the ecclesial reality (the unity of the mystical Body) by the Eucharistic species, which, as the sacramental matter, contribute to signifying and producing the grace of the Eucharist.

The Sacramental Body of Christ (res et sacramentum)

Thomas next emphasizes the ecclesial dimension in relation to the first effect of the sacrament, which is the *corpus verum*, the Eucharistic Body of Christ (and his Blood). At the heart of the sacramental organism, the Eucharist substantially comprises all the treasure, *the spiritual good of the whole Church*; it comprises *the whole mystery of our salvation.*[14] Thus in his *Commentary on the Sentences*, Thomas invokes the ecclesial efficacy of the Eucharist to demonstrate that Christ is truly present there:

> It is fitting that there be a sacrament in which Christ is contained not only by participation, but by his essence, in order that thus the union of the Head to his members may be perfect *(ut sit perfecta coniunctio capitis ad membra).*[15]
>
> The perfection of the sacraments of the New Law demands that there be a sacrament in which Christ is joined and united to us in reality *(in quo Christus nobis realiter coniungatur et uniatur)*, and not merely through participation in his virtue, as in the other sacraments.[16]

Thomas invokes the same argument to show the fittingness of the institution of the Eucharist. The Eucharist, considered under the aspect of the *verum corpus*, is "the sacrament which, really containing the Head conformed to his members, unites the mystical Body to its Head."[17]

> The perfection of the body requires that the members be united to their head; but by this sacrament the members of the Church are

---

13 IV *Sent.*, dist. 12, q. 1, a. 3, qla 3, corp. et ad 1; *ST* III, q. 83, a. 5, ad 7–9 (on the *corpus triforme* of Amalarius).

14 *ST* III, q. 65, a. 3, ad 1; q. 83, a. 4; cf. IV *Sent.*, dist. 49, q. 4, a. 3, ad 4.

15 IV *Sent.*, dist. 10, q. 1, a. 1. Thomas receives this approach from Albert the Great (IV *Sent.*, dist. 10, a. 1, sed contra 2; *Opera omnia,* ed. Auguste Borgnet, vol. 29, 244). In the *Summa theologiae*, this specifically ecclesiological argument will be replaced by a theme drawn from the perfection of the sacrifice of the New Covenant (*ST* III, q. 75, a. 1).

16 IV *Sent.*, dist. 9, q. un., a. 1, qla 1. Cf. ibid., sed contra 2; *ST* III, q. 65, a. 3.

17 IV *Sent.*, dist. 8, q. 1, a. 3, qla 2, ad 1.

united to their Head *(membra Ecclesiae suo capiti coniunguntur)* [. . .]; it was therefore necessary that this sacrament be instituted.[18]

Insisting on the truth of Christ contained in the Eucharist, Thomas constantly reminds us that the true Body of Christ is also the sign, the representation, the likeness, the exemplar, and the figure of his mystical Body, which is the Church; in other words, it is the sign and the cause of that which the Eucharist procures.[19] He never fails to attribute to the *corpus verum* the fundamental structure of the *res et sacramentum*: The true Body of Christ is at once *signum* and *res.* As sign, the Body of Christ denotes unity, the gathering of a multitude of members in unity. Ecclesial realism appears deeply rooted in Eucharistic realism. Thus, showing the fittingness of the institution of this sacrament, Thomas closely links the substantial *conversion* of the bread and wine into the Body and Blood of Christ (transubstantiation) and our own *conversion* in Christ, which is the end *[finis]* of the transubstantiation:[20] "It was fitting that this sacrament, in which the incarnate Word is contained in order to unite us to himself, be proposed to us under the figure of food, not so that he may be converted into us by his union with us, but rather so that, by our union with him, we may be converted into him *(nos in ipsum convertens)*."[21] Here we reach the third level, that of the sacramental grace proper to the Eucharist.

***The Fruit of the Eucharist* (res tantum)**

Thomas formulates the proper effect of the sacrament in terms of nutrition or food *(cibus).* Here, however, the food is not transformed into the one who eats it, but rather the one eating is changed *(convertitur)* into the food that he eats. This understanding is clearly a development of Augustine's thought.[22] The effect proper to the Eucharist, as Thomas expresses it, is the transformation *(transformatio)* of man into Christ by love, the transmutation *(transmutatio)* of the one who eats into the food that is eaten, our *conversio* into Christ, a union or *adunatio* of man to Christ: in other words, incorporation into Christ.[23] Such is the meaning of the *communio* or

18 Ibid., dist. 8, q. 1, a. 3, qla 1, sed contra 1.

19 All these phrases are Thomas's own: III *Sent.*, dist. 12, q. 3, a. 1, qla 1, arg. 1; dist. 13, q. 2, a. 2, qla 2, arg. 2 and ad 2; IV *Sent.*, dist. 12, q. 1, a. 3, qla 3, ad 1; dist. 13, expositio textus; *ST* III, q. 82, a. 9, arg. 2; In Eph 4:13 (#217).

20 This is not an exaggerated term: The use of the faithful is the end *(finis)* of this sacrament (*ST* III, q. 74, a. 2); cf. *ST* III, q. 74, a. 2, ad 2: "finis effectus."

21 IV *Sent.*, dist. 8, q. 1, a. 3, qla 1; cf. dist. 9, q. un., a. 2, qla 4.

22 St. Augustine, *Confessions* VII,10,16, quoted for instance in IV *Sent.*, dist. 8, q. 1, a. 3, qla 1; *ST* III, q. 73, a. 3, ad 2; *In Ioannem* 6:55 (#972).

23 St. Thomas, IV *Sent.*, dist. 8, q. 1, a. 3, qla 1, ad 3 ("transmutari"); dist. 9, q. un., a. 2, qla 4 ("Christo incorporari"); dist. 12, q. 2, a. 1, qla 1 ("conversio"); dist. 12,

synaxis, which characterizes the Eucharist: "We enter into communion with Christ through the Eucharist; we share in his Flesh and in his Godhead; we enter into communion and are mutually united by it."[24]

With St. John Damascene, St. Thomas likewise speaks in this context of an "assuming of the divinity of Christ" effected by the Eucharist (divinization).[25] In St. Thomas, the ecclesial dimension of Eucharistic grace is present to a remarkable degree, as is shown by other expressions that can be collected from the *Summa theologiae.* The breadth of Thomas's vocabulary is worth noting. He refers to the effect that the Eucharist brings about (the *res* signified and not contained) as the mystical Body of Christ *(Corpus Christi mysticum)*, or the unity of this mystical Body *(unitas corporis mystici)*; the society of the Body of Christ and of his members *(societas corporis et membrorum suorum)*, the union of the members with the Head, or the mutual union of the members of Christ with one another; the Church of the saints and the faithful, the society of the saints *(societas sanctorum)*, or the Church constituted of diverse faithful *(Ecclesia ex diversis fidelibus)*; very often: the unity of the Church *(unitas ecclesiastica)*; the unity signified by the bread and the wine, or simply unity itself; the spiritual nourishment received through union with Christ and his members; peace and unity *(pax et unitas)*; union with Christ or with God; transformation into Christ; the unity of the many in Christ *(multi unum in Christo)*; the incorporation of people into Christ; the union *(unio)* or the reunion *(adunatio)* of the Christian People with Christ; communion *(communicatio)* with Christ and mutual communion of the faithful among each other.[26] For this reason, the Eucharist is called "sacrament of unity (of the Church)" *(sacramentum unitatis [ecclesiasticae])*, or "sacrament of unity and of peace" *(sacramentum unitatis et pacis)*, peace being understood as the union of wills that charity

---

q. 2, a. 2, qla 1 ("transformatio"); ibid., qla 3 ("unio"); *De articulis fidei et Ecclesiae sacramentis* II (Leonine edition, vol. 42, 255: "adunatio"; "homo Christo incorporatur"); and so on.

24 *ST* III, q. 73, a. 4; quote from John Damascene, *De fide Orthodoxa,* ch. 86,15 [IV,13] (St. John Damascene, *De fide orthodoxa: Versions of Burgundio and Cerbanus,* ed. Eligius M. Buytaert [Louvain: E. Nauwelaerts; Paderborn: Schöningh, 1955], 317). Cf. IV *Sent.*, dist. 8, q. 1, a. 1, qla 3 (with a text from Dionysius).

25 *ST* III, q. 73, a. 4: "The assuming" *(metalepsis)* is indeed a name for the Eucharist itself.

26 All these expressions, a complete list of which would be extremely long, are collected from the treatise on the Eucharist (*ST* III, q. 73–83). On this topic, see Godefridus Geenen, "L'adage *Eucharistia est sacramentum ecclesiasticae unionis* dans les oeuvres et la doctrine de S. Thomas d'Aquin," in *La Eucaristía y la Paz,* 275–81; Felicísimo Martínez, "La Eucaristía y la unidad de la Iglesia en Santo Tomás de Aquino," *Studium* 9 (1969): 377–404.

brings about.[27] The Eucharist thus produces the same effect as did the coming of the Son into our world; it bestows on man all the goods that Christ gave to the world through his passion; it applies the work of our redemption. In short, it confers the whole mystery of our salvation.[28]

In the same way, Thomas also reserves for the Eucharist the name "sacrament of charity" *(sacramentum caritatis)*, because it represents charity and procures a growth in charity, a strengthening of life in the Spirit, and a most sweet and delectable spiritual refreshment.[29] The charity procured by the Eucharist is not limited to the *habitus*, but extends even to "charity in its act *(quantum ad actum)* which is stimulated by this sacrament."[30] But we are not speaking here of a reality different from the preceding one. It is not as though there were an ecclesial effect of the sacrament on the one hand, and a personal and individual effect on the other hand, added to or juxtaposed with the first. In fact, the same reality of grace, that is, the incorporation of the person into Christ, is at once both the food of personal spiritual refreshment and, by its very nature, the building up of the Church, whose unity, founded in faith (Baptism and Confirmation), is strengthened and completed by charity. The close connection between the personal and ecclesial dimensions of the Eucharist, founded in incorporation into Christ, has been particularly well expressed by Cajetan:

> When we hear that the fruit *(res tantum)* of the sacrament is grace, and that that which is to be received is the unity of the Church or the mystical Body of Christ, we do not see two separate realities there, since it is all nothing more than the grace of God in his faithful.[31]

The Eucharist thus strengthens the unity of the mystical Body by intensifying man's union with Christ and the mutual union of the members. The spiritual perfection of the individual is the perfection of this person as a member of the Church, and such perfection is charity. We are now at the heart of Thomas's vision of the Church. Baptism, the sacrament of faith,

---

27 *ST* III, q. 67, a. 2; q. 73, a. 2, sed contra; q. 73, a. 4; q. 80, a. 5, ad 2; q. 82, a. 2, arg. 3 and ad 3; q. 83, a. 4, corp. and ad 3. Cf. Adolph Hoffmann, "Eucharistia ut sacramentum pacis secundum S. Thomam," in *La Eucaristía y la Paz*, 163–67.

28 *ST* III, q. 79, a. 1; q. 83, a. 1 and 4.

29 Ibid., q. 73, a. 3, ad 3; q. 74, a. 4, arg. 3; q. 78, a. 3, arg. 6 and ad 6; q. 79, a. 4, ad 3; q. 80, a. 5, ad 2 (sacrament of charity); cf. q. 78, a. 3, ad 6: "Hoc autem est sacramentum caritatis quasi figurativum et effectivum"; ibid., q. 79, a. 1, ad 1; q. 81, a. 1, ad 3 (increase of habitual grace); ibid., q. 79, a. 1, corp. and ad 2; q. 81, a. 1, ad 3 (delectation and sweetness); and so on.

30 Ibid., q. 79, a. 4. This is the reason for the Eucharist's effacement of venial sins.

31 Cajetan, *In Tertiam Partem Summa theologiae,* q. 73, a. 1 (Leonine edition, vol. 12, 139).

builds up the Church by incorporating the baptized into Christ and building them into one unified Church. Baptism and Confirmation effect the initial incorporation into the Church that the Eucharist nourishes and completes.[32] And in baptism, the unifying power of the Eucharist is already at work. In fact, of its very nature baptism contains the desire or the *objective hunger* for the Eucharist—not necessarily proceeding from the psychological conscience—the desire to spiritually ingest *(manducare)* Christ, the desire for the transformation into Christ given in the act of faith completed in charity.[33] The Eucharist is therefore dynamically included in all the other sacraments to such an extent that without this "objective hunger" for the Eucharist, no effect of grace can be obtained. To put it another way, the hunger for the Eucharist belongs organically to salvation.[34] A profound reason for this truth is supplied by the *res* of the Eucharist: "The effect of this sacrament is the unity of the mystical Body without which salvation cannot exist."[35] At this deep level, the fullness of the fruit of the Eucharist is identical with the Church. Thomas can therefore explain:

> Since in spiritually eating the Flesh of Christ and in spiritually drinking his Blood we become participators in the Church's unity which is caused by charity [. . .], he who does not eat thus is outside the Church and consequently outside charity, and therefore does not have life in himself.[36]

In Thomas, this close connection between Church and Eucharist is supported by two major theological motifs. The first pertains to the sacraments. Thomas sees the efficacy of the sacraments and the grace given through them as a function of incorporation into Christ: It is by incorporating man into Christ (and thus building up the Church) that the sacraments and the Eucharist produce the life of grace. The second motif pertains to Thomas's understanding of the Church as essentially subsisting

32 *ST* III, q. 39, a. 6, ad 4; q. 73, a. 3. See Martin Morard, "L'Eucharistie, clé de voûte de l'organisme sacramentel chez saint Thomas," *Revue Thomiste* 95 (1995): 217–50.

33 *ST* III, q. 73, a. 3. Texts and analyses on this topic are found in Jean-Marie R. Tillard, "Le *votum Eucharistiae*: l'Eucharistie dans la rencontre des chrétiens," in *Miscellanea Liturgica in onore di S.E. il Cardinale Giacomo Lercaro*, vol. 2 (Rome/Paris: Desclée, 1967), 143–94.

34 *ST* III, q. 80, a. 11: "Et ideo sine voto percipiendi hoc sacramentum, non potest homini esse salus."

35 Ibid., q. 73, a. 3: "Res sacramenti est unitas corporis mystici, sine qua non potest esse salus."

36 *In Ioannem* 6:54 (#969): "Ille enim spiritualiter carnem Christi manducat et sanguinem bibit qui particeps fit ecclesiasticae unitatis, quae fit per caritatem; Rom. XII,5: *Omnes unum corpus estis in Christo.* Qui ergo non sic manducat, est extra Ecclesiam, et per consequens extra caritatem; ideo non habet vitam in semetipso."

in the life of Christ's grace given by the Holy Spirit; that is, faith operating through charity.[37] It is therefore in terms of faith and charity that Thomas illumines what it means to belong to the Church and explains its unity, just as it is in terms of faith and charity that he explains the fruit of the grace of the Eucharist. Both the Church and the Eucharist are seen under the aspect of incorporation into Christ. Thus, commenting on John 6:57, Thomas designates the fruit of the Eucharist (the *res signata tantum*) as "incorporation into the mystical Body by the union of faith and charity."[38] Likewise, in his homilies on the *Credo*, for example, Thomas explains the unity of the Church by means of faith, hope, and charity, the three theological virtues on which this unity is founded, and through which it is procured.[39] Here we find a profound "osmosis" between the interior dimension of the mystery and its accomplishment through the rite, achieved by an inclusion of the sacramental world and the nature of the Church with respect to the theological virtues.

2. Christology and Pneumatology

The power of the Eucharist, Thomas explains, derives primarily and principally from the fact that it contains the Word made flesh,[40] into whom the one who communicates spiritually is "converted." As we have seen, this personal and ecclesial effect has as its sign and cause the double level of the *sacramentum tantum* (the Eucharistic species with the words of consecration) and the *res et sacramentum* (the true Body and Blood of Christ), these two elements coming together in the unity of the sacrament itself (the first concurring in producing grace only by virtue of the second).[41] More precisely—leaving aside here the universal value of the Eucharist as sacrifice offered, which deserves to be considered on its own—it is the spiritual ingestion of the Body and the Blood of Christ that produces this spiritual effect: "The unity of the mystical Body is the fruit of the true Body of Christ which was received."[42]

Thomas bases his teaching on numerous scriptural passages, notably John 6:57 [6:56]—*He who eats my flesh and drinks my blood remains in me, and I in him*—and 1 Corinthians 10:17—*Since there is one single bread, we*

37 Yves Congar, *Esquisses du Mystère de l'Église* (Paris: Cerf, 1941), 59–91: "L'idée de l'Église chez saint Thomas d'Aquin."

38 *In Ioannem* 6:57 (#976); cf. ibid., 6:64 (#993).

39 *In Symbolum Apostolorum Expositio,* a. 9 (#973–975); cf. *ST* III, q. 8, a. 3.

40 *ST* III, q. 79, a. 1: "Effectus huius sacramenti debet considerari, primo quidem et principaliter, ex eo quod in hoc sacramento continetur, quod est Christus"; cf. *In Ioannem* 6:55 (#973).

41 IV *Sent.*, dist. 8, q. 1, a. 1, qla 1, ad 2.

42 *ST* III, q. 82, a. 9, ad 2: "Unitas corporis mystici est fructus corporis veri percepti."

are one single Body, all we who have part in this single bread.[43] He also highlights the theme of the Church's birth from the side of the crucified Christ, from which flow water and blood (Jn 19:34),[44] representing the sacraments by which the Church is built *(fabricata)*, instituted *(instituta)*, consecrated *(consecrata)*, or saved *(salvata)*.[45] The effect of the Eucharist is that of Jesus' passion, whence the sacraments acquire their efficacy and to whose fruits they give access.[46] Church and sacrament are here inextricably tied by their source: "Christ has suffered his passion, out of charity, in order to unite himself to the Church as a spouse."[47]

In order to illuminate the transforming and unifying power of the Eucharist, Thomas also draws on the explanation of Cyril of Alexandria that defends the incarnation of the Word with respect to the passion of Jesus:

> The life-giving Word of God, uniting himself to his own Flesh, makes it life-giving as well. It was thus fitting that he should unite himself in a certain way to our bodies by his holy Flesh and by his precious Blood which we receive as a living benediction in the bread and wine.[48]

The Eucharist derives its power from the life-giving power of the Flesh of the incarnate Word. In the Eucharist, the life-giving Flesh of the Logos comes to unite itself to our own, to confer on it immortal life. Having sanctified his own Flesh, the Word sanctifies the believer who, through spiritual

---

43 See, for instance, IV *Sent.*, dist. 8, q. 1, a. 3, qla 1, sed contra; *ST* III, q. 73, a. 2, sed contra; q. 74, a. 1; q. 75, a. 1; *In Ioannem,* ch. 6, lect. 7.

44 We have found eight occurrences of this theme in the treatise on the Eucharist in the *Tertia pars*: q. 74, a. 6; q. 74, a. 7, arg. 2, corp., ad 2 and ad 3; q. 74, a. 8, arg. 1 and corp.; q. 79, a. 1.

45 All these expressions are Thomas's own: IV *Sent.*, dist. 1, q. 1, a. 4, qla 3, sed contra 1; dist. 18, q. 1, a. 1, qla 1; *ST* I, q. 92, a. 3; *ST* III, q. 62, a. 5, sed contra; q. 64, a. 2, ad 3; q. 66, a. 3, arg. 3 and ad 3; q. 66, a. 4, arg. 3 and ad 3; *In Ioannem* 19:34 (#2458). For the many patristic sources of this theme (which Thomas develops especially with reference to Augustine and Chrysostom), see Sebastian Tromp, "De nativitate Ecclesiae ex corde Iesu in Cruce," *Gregorianum* 13 (1932): 489–527; Alban A. Maguire, *Blood and Water: The Wounded Side of Christ in Early Christian Literature* (Washington, DC: Catholic University of America Press, 1958).

46 *ST* III, q. 62, a. 5; cf. IV *Sent.*, dist. 8, q. 1, a. 1, qla 3; *ST* III, q. 79, a. 1: "Et ideo effectum quem passio Christi fecit in mundo, hoc sacramentum facit in homine."

47 IV *Sent.*, dist. 26, q. 2, a. 1, ad 3: "Caritatem, per quam pro Ecclesia sibi in sponsam coniungenda passus est" (about marriage; *Opera omnia*, vol. 11 [Paris: Vivès, 1882], 72).

48 *ST* III, q. 79, a. 1. Thomas quotes this passage more at length in *Catena in Lucam* 22:19 (Marietti edition, vol. 2, 286); cf. Cyril, *In Lucam* 22:19 (PG 72, 907–12). On this topic, see Jean-Marie R. Tillard, *L'Eucharistie Pâque de l'Église* (Paris: Cerf, 1964), 60–83.

and sacramental communion, unites himself to this divinized Flesh of Christ. This fundamental reference to the Word appears in the explanation of the efficacy of the words of consecration: They retain their power from the fact that they are, properly speaking, the words of the incarnate Word. It is through the words of the incarnate Word, pronounced by the priest acting in the Person of Christ, that the substantial change takes place: "The sacrament is accomplished by the words of Christ."[49] Does this fundamentally Christological understanding obscure the action of the Holy Spirit? This question, over and above the problem of the epiclesis, directly concerns the relationship between the Eucharist and the Church.

Thomas's attention to the pneumatological dimension of the sacrament must be clearly acknowledged: "The Body is in this sacrament [. . .] in a spiritual manner *(spiritualiter)*, that is, in an invisible manner and by the power of the Holy Spirit."[50] The words pronounced by the priest are the instrument through which passes the power of the Holy Spirit.[51] From a Trinitarian point of view, Thomas explains the unity of the action of Christ and of the Holy Spirit in the Eucharist, by means of the theme of the Son's operating through the Holy Spirit (understood in close connection with the *Filioque)*: Christ the Priest accomplishes the Eucharistic conversion by the Holy Spirit. It is in this manner that Thomas appropriates transubstantiation to Christ, who operates, and at the same time to the Holy Spirit, through whom Christ acts.[52] As for the grace of configuration and of incorporation into Christ, that is, the personal and ecclesial fruit of the Eucharist, Thomas attributes it to the Holy Spirit by full right.[53] Commenting on John 6 in the context of the Eucharist, Thomas explains: "He who eats and drinks spiritually becomes a participator in the Holy Spirit, by whom we are united to Christ in the union of faith and charity, and through whom we become members of the Church."[54] Thomas first underlines the presence of the Holy Spirit, who works this spiritual communion, in the Flesh of the incarnate Word himself. The following passage of his commentary on John is worth examining for the very evocative illumination it provides on the pneumatology of Thomas's Eucharistic doctrine:

---

49 *ST* III, q. 78, a. 1, sed contra; q. 75, a. 7, arg. 3; q. 78, a. 2, arg. 2; q. 78, a. 4, sed contra. St. Ambrose, *De sacramentis* IV,4,14–IV,5,23 (Ambroise de Milan, *De sacramentis, De mysteriis, Sources Chrétiennes* 25 bis [Paris: Cerf, 1961], 108–15). Cf. Pierre-Marie Gy, *La liturgie dans l'histoire* (Paris: Cerf, 1990), 211–21.

50 *ST* III, q. 75, a. 1, ad 1.

51 Ibid., q. 78, a. 4, ad 1.

52 IV *Sent.*, dist. 10, *expositio textus*: "Appropriatur [transsubstantiatio] Filio sicut operanti, quia ipse est sacerdos et hostia; Spiritui autem Sancto sicut quo operatur, quia ipse est virtus de illo exiens ad sanandum (Luke 6:19)."

53 *ST* III, q. 63, a. 3, ad 1; *In Ioannem* 6:57 (#976).

54 *In Ioannem* 6:55 (#973; cf. #972).

> The Flesh of Christ is capable of accomplishing many things in many ways insofar as it is united to the Word and to the Spirit *(ut coniuncta Verbo et Spiritui)*. [. . .] If we abstract divinity and the Holy Spirit, this Flesh is no more powerful than any other flesh; but if the Spirit and divinity are present, this Flesh is capable of accomplishing many things because it makes those who take it live in Christ: in fact, it is through the Spirit of charity that man lives in God. [. . .] If you attribute this effect of the Flesh to the Spirit, and to the divinity united to the Flesh, then it procures eternal life, as we see in Galatians 5:25: *If we live in the Spirit, let us walk also in the Spirit.* And this is why Christ adds: *The words which I have spoken to you are Spirit and life* (Jn 6:64 [6:63]). We must therefore refer them to the Spirit united to the Flesh; and understood thus, they are life, which is to say, the life of the soul. For in the same way as the body lives by a bodily life through a bodily spirit, so the soul lives by a spiritual life through the Holy Spirit: *Send forth your Spirit and they will be created* (Ps 103:30).[55]

These texts, to which many others could be added,[56] show us that Thomas's Eucharistic theology, far from being reduced to a "christomonism," upholds the presence of the Spirit at all levels: in the Flesh of the Lord, in his Eucharistic Body, and in his ecclesial Body, for which the Spirit procures, through faith and charity, that unity that constitutes the fruit of the Eucharist. The Eucharist nourishes and strengthens the communion of the faithful with the Lord and with one another, by the *communicatio* of the Body and Blood of Christ. It is indeed by the power of the Holy Spirit that this communication of the incarnate Word strengthening the members of his Body in unity is accomplished.[57]

3. The Eucharist and Forgiveness

At the heart of the deepening of ecclesial unity that it effects, the Eucharist contains a purifying power as well as a demand for reconciliation, to which Thomas draws attention. In the *Summa theologiae*, after having dis-

[55] *In Ioannem* 6:64 (#993). The source of this exegesis is found in Augustine, *Tractatus* 27,5–6 *On the Gospel of John* (*In Iohannis Evangelium Tractatus CXXIV*, 271–72).

[56] See, notably, Jean-Pierre Torrell, *Saint Thomas Aquinas,* vol. 2: *Spiritual Master,* trans. Robert Royal (Washington, DC: Catholic University of America Press, 2003), 175–99: "The Heart of the Church."

[57] *In 2 Cor* 13:13 (#544): "Communicatio vero divinorum fit per Spiritum Sanctum. . . . Et ideo Spiritui Sancto attribuit communicationem." On this topic see Jean-Marie R. Tillard, "La marque de Thomas d'Aquin sur le dialogue oecuménique," in *Ordo sapientiae et amoris: Hommage au Prof. J.-P. Torrell, OP,* ed. Carlos-Josaphat Pinto de Oliveira (Fribourg: Éditions Universitaires, 1993), 625–54, especially 643–53.

cussed the grace of the Eucharist and its eschatological implications, Thomas devotes to this theme the majority of the articles in the question dealing with the effects of the Eucharist (*ST* III, q. 79). At the root of the sacramental symbolism of food, belonging to Christ by grace appears as an indispensable precondition for the fruitful reception of the sacrament: The Eucharist is a *spiritual food* for the growth of the living (that is, those who live by grace). Nevertheless, the Eucharist contains within itself a reconciliating power that can be described as total: "This sacrament possesses of itself the virtue of remitting all sins by the passion of Christ who is the source and cause of remission of sins."[58] Therefore no obstacles to the vivifying power of the Eucharist can exist on the part of the sacrament, but only on the part of the recipient, who can be incapable of perceiving its fruit. Grace does not constrain man, but each must enter into it freely.[59]

Furthermore—and I want here to emphasize this aspect—Thomas understands the relationship between the Eucharist and sin in terms of the fruit of ingesting the Eucharist: that is, in terms of union with Christ (and, through Christ, with the Father) and of the mutual communion among the faithful. "Whoever takes this sacrament signifies by that very act that he is united to Christ and incorporated into his members, which occurs through faith informed [by charity], and this is incompatible with mortal sin."[60] Thomas discusses the incompatibility between the state of mortal sin and the fruitful reception of the Eucharist explicitly in the light of "the mystical Body of Christ which is the society of the saints."[61] The Eucharist, the sacrament of consummation, nourishes and deepens the communion of the Church, in its two dimensions of relation to the Head and fraternal unity of the members. The Eucharist presupposes in its members an already constituted ecclesial communion, of which it is the sacrament. The absence of this communion, if it exists, impairs the *signification* of the sacrament and the *reality* of its effect. In pneumatological terms, Thomas elsewhere explains that "the Spirit is only given to those who are in Christ Jesus [. . .]: The Holy Spirit does not come to the man who is not united to Christ the Head."[62] The sacrament of Penance is ordered precisely to true and full participation in the Eucharist, in the totality of its ecclesial nature.

---

58 *ST* III, q. 79, a. 3: "Virtus huius sacramenti potest considerari dupliciter. *Uno modo, secundum se. Et sic hoc sacramentum habet virtutem ad remittendum quaecumque peccata, ex passione Christi, quae est fons et causa remissionis peccatorum.*"

59 Nevertheless, Thomas adds that this sacrament can remit mortal sin, either by the "hunger" or "longing" *(votum)* for the Eucharist, or, if the sinner is neither attached to nor conscious of his sin, by the fervor of charity that the Eucharist confers (*ST* III, q. 79, a. 3).

60 *ST* III, q. 80, a. 4.

61 Ibid.

62 *In Rom* 8:2 (#605).

Similarly, at the depth of this fundamental theological perception we can grasp the forgiveness of "light" sins, which the Eucharist achieves. In effecting fervent charity, it purifies the members of the Church by uniting them more closely to Christ and to one another. In other words, it is by intensifying their union with Christ and their fraternal charity that the Eucharist purifies the members of the Church of their venial sins. And again, it is by effecting union with Christ that the Eucharist fortifies the spiritual vitality of the Church's members in protecting or preserving them from future sins.[63] Indeed, Thomas brings the ecclesial dimension of forgiveness into special prominence, in the light of the Eucharist and of the incorporation into Christ that this sacrament effects.

4. The Eschatological-Ecclesial Implications of the Eucharist

Finally, the ecclesial effect appears in the eschatological dimension of the Eucharist. It is the sacrament of our pilgrimage toward the Fatherland, the sacrament of hope.[64] This eschatological dimension is written into the structure of all the sacraments. For Thomas, the sacraments are at once commemorative signs (Passion of Christ), demonstrative signs (present gift of grace), and announcing signs (future glory). They bear the historical event of the Passion (and Resurrection) of Jesus, whence they procure the fruit of grace in the present moment, while announcing the fulfillment whose seed they possess. For Thomas, this eschatological signification is not reduced to a secondary aspect or a mere periphery to the sacrament, but rather belongs to it formally and expressly.[65]

This eschatological effect, which the Eucharist prefigures in the manner of an anticipatory *(praefigurativum)* sign, constitutes its ultimate effect *(ultimus effectus)*,[66] which the sacrament "does not produce immediately but which it signifies": the spiritual ingestion of God in the face-to-face vision and perfect charity found in eternal life.[67] Thomas develops it

---

63 *ST* III, q. 79, a. 4 and a. 6.

64 Ibid., q. 75, a. 1; q. 79, a. 2.

65 Ibid., q. 60, a. 3. See Jean-Marie R. Tillard, "La triple dimension du signe sacramentel (À propos de Sum. Theol., III, 60, 3)," *Nouvelle Revue Théologique* 83 (1961): 225–54; Pierre-Marie Gy, "Avancées du traité de l'Eucharistie de S. Thomas dans la *Somme* par rapport aux *Sentences*," *Revue des Sciences Philosophiques et Théologiques* 77 (1993): 219–28, cf. 225.

66 *ST* III, q. 74, a. 6.

67 IV *Sent.*, dist. 9, expositio textus. The theme of spiritual ingestion *(spiritualis manducatio)* through beatific vision and charity, evoked in this passage, is developed with regard to the angels in *ST* III, q. 80, a. 2.

notably in regard to the name *viaticum*, which designates the Eucharist,[68] but references to it are found throughout the treatise on the Eucharist. He explains it thus: The Eucharist delivers us from whatever hinders our entry into glory; it prepares the obtaining of glory, the blessed enjoyment of God in the Fatherland, the eternal inheritance, the entrance into the Kingdom of heaven and into eternal life, the glory of the soul and the resurrection of the body.[69] Here the ecclesial implications of the sacrament are even more clearly outlined: The Eucharist signifies the union of God's children, through Christ, with the Father and with the Church triumphant; it announces the "transfer" into the Church triumphant.[70] Following Augustine, Thomas here links the patristic theme of the "medicine of immortality" with the theme of the Church in glory:

> *My Flesh is truly food* (Jn 6:56) *[and my Blood drink].* Since men expect that food and drink will cause them to be no longer hungry or thirsty, this result is truly achieved only by this food and this drink which makes those who take it immortal and incorruptible, in the companionship of the saints where total and perfect unity and peace will reign.[71]

The connection between the enjoyment of God and the unity of the society of the saints expresses, from the aspect of hope, the double dimension of the ecclesial communion recalled earlier with regard to the *res tantum* of the sacrament. "In the glory of heaven, two things will most delight good men: the enjoyment of the Godhead and the common society of the saints; for there is no joyful possession without society."[72] As for the resurrection, it too appears as a fruit of the life-giving power of the Eucharist. Following the *Ambrosiaster*, Thomas explains that the life of the soul flows into the body for salvation in this present life, and for incorruptibility in the life of glory.[73] At a deeper level, the eschatological implications of the Eucharist are founded on the incarnate and resurrected Word who is contained therein: True God and true man, the Word-made-flesh resurrects and vivifies both souls and bodies through his risen flesh.[74]

---

68 *ST* III, q. 73, a. 4.

69 These are the phrases that Thomas uses in *ST* III, q. 73, a. 4; q. 73, a. 6, arg. 3; q. 74, a. 6; q. 78, a. 3, corp. and ad 3; q. 79, a. 1, ad 3; q. 79, a. 2; q. 80, a. 2, ad 1; q. 83, a. 5, ad 9.

70 *ST* III, q. 83, a. 4, ad 9; cf. IV *Sent.*, dist. 13, *expositio textus.*

71 *ST* III, q. 79, a. 2; cf. Augustine, *Tractatus* 26,17 *On the Gospel of John (In Iohannis Evangelium Tractatus CXXIV,* 268).

72 *In Heb* 12:22 (#706). Cf. *ST* I–II, q. 4, a. 8.

73 *ST* III, q. 79, a. 1, ad 3; cf. q. 74, a. 1; Ambrosiaster, *In 1 Cor* 11:26 (PL 17, 243).

74 *In Ioannem* 6:55 [6:54] (#973); cf. *ST* III, q. 56, a. 1 and a. 2.

Once again, at the heart of the ecclesial gift of the Eucharist, we discover the action of the Holy Spirit. Commenting on John 6, Thomas explains: "The Holy Spirit makes the unity of the Church: *One single Spirit and one single Body* (Eph 4:4)—he who is the *pledge of our eternal inheritance* (Eph 1:14). Wonderful, then, are the benefits of this food which gives eternal life to the soul; but they are wonderful also because they likewise give life to the body. [. . .] The Spirit makes us merit the resurrection."[75]

5. Theology, Preaching, and Liturgy

Thomas carried these themes of "academic" or scholarly theology into his liturgical writings and preaching activity. Among other examples, we may take as witnesses the sermon *Homo quidam fecit cenam magnam* (sermon of the second Sunday after Trinity Sunday), of which a good edition exists,[76] as well as the liturgy of Corpus Christi, whose attribution to Thomas is well-established.[77]

The sermon *Homo quidam fecit cenam magnam* is devoted to the theme of spiritual refreshment. Here Thomas clearly emphasizes the ecclesial effect of the Eucharist, that is, the unity of the mystical Body, in relation to the faith and charity by which God dwells in the hearts of the faithful. In particular, this sermon confirms that the theme of refreshment and delectation is understood properly in direct reference to the Church. Eucharistic symbolism is likewise presented here in its anamnetic dimension (Passion of Christ), in its present reality, and in the hope of its future fulfillment (the beatitude of eternal life):

> The present effect [of the Eucharist], signified and not contained, that is, the unity of the Church, is delectable. What is there indeed which causes more joy than this unity? *How good and pleasant it is for brothers,* etc. (Ps 132:1). This Supper produces the greatest delectation, whether one looks to the past, to the present, or to the future. [. . .] It unites us to God and makes us dwell in God. This is why it

---

[75] *In Ioannem* 6:55 [6:54] (#972–73).

[76] Louis J. Bataillon, "Le sermon inédit de saint Thomas *Homo quidam fecit cenam magnam.* Introduction et édition," *Revue des Sciences Philosophiques et Théologiques* 67 (1983): 353–69.

[77] Pierre-Marie Gy, "L'Office du Corpus Christi et S. Thomas d'Aquin. Etat d'une recherche," *Revue des Sciences Philosophiques et Théologiques* 64 (1980): 491–507; Pierre-Marie Gy, "L'Office du Corpus Christi, oeuvre de S. Thomas d'Aquin," in *La Liturgie dans l'histoire* (Paris: Cerf, 1990), 223–45; Jean-Pierre Torrell, *Saint Thomas Aquinas,* vol. 1: *The Person and His Work,* trans. Robert Royal (Washington, DC: Catholic University of America Press, 1996), 129–36.

> is said in John 6:57 [6:56]: *He who eats my flesh and drinks my blood [. . .] remains in me,* that is to say, by faith and charity, *and I in him,* by grace and the sacrament.[78]

We cannot look here in detail at the various elements of the liturgy of Corpus Christi. A brief outline of several examples allows us nevertheless to discern a remarkable continuity between Thomas's teaching labors and his liturgical works. In the office *Sacerdos,* we can immediately note the signification of the Church's unity by the multiple grains and grapes from which are confected the single bread and wine of the Eucharist; we can likewise observe there the eschatological signification of the Eucharist, that is, the immortality and incorruptibility of eternal life, for which we hope as the perfect *societas sanctorum* where peace and unity will reign fully (Augustine on John 6:55).[79] We also find there the theme of the divinization of the faithful accomplished by the only Son, as well as the theme of purification from sins. And Thomas takes care to link the Eucharist to the action of the Holy Spirit: It is to the Spirit that the Acts of the Apostles attributes the fidelity of the first Church breaking bread in the grace of Pentecost.[80]

The ecclesial signification of the gifts is manifested in the Secret of the Mass *Cibavit*: "Grant, Lord, to your Church, the gifts of unity and peace which are signified as a mystery by these offerings."[81] As for the eschatological-ecclesial dimension, it is present throughout Thomas's liturgical

---

78 Latin text in the edition given by Fr. Bataillon, "Le sermon inédit," 362. Note that the eschatological signification is presented, as in the *Summa theologiae* and in the Office of Corpus Christi, in reference to the food eaten by Elias for his journey to Horeb (1 Kgs 19:8; ibid., 363).

79 Lesson from Matins (a homily of Augustine): St. Thomas, *Opera omnia,* Vivès edition, vol. 29, 339; idem, *Opuscula theologica,* Marietti edition, vol. 2, 278. Cf. P.-M. Gy, "L'Office du Corpus Christi," 233–34, note 28. Also see the texts quoted from the ms. *Paris B.N. lat 1143,* copied at the beginning of the study of each section of the office in Ronald J. Zawilla, *The Historiae Corporis Christi attributed to Thomas Aquinas: A Theological Study of Their Biblical Sources* (Diss. University of Toronto, 1985).

80 Legenda *Immensa divinae largitatis* from Matins: *Opera omnia,* Vivès edition, vol. 29, 336–37; *Opuscula theologica,* Marietti edition, vol. 2, 276–77. See the text in P.-M. Gy, "L'Office du Corpus Christi," 244–45 (cf. 233, note 28). The Holy Spirit appears in many other parts of the office, starting with the antiphon of the Magnificat in the first Vespers for the feast: "O quam suauis est, domine, spiritus tuus" (in Zawilla, *The Historiae,* 216).

81 "Ecclesie tue, quesumus Domine, unitatis et pacis propicius dona concede, que sub oblatis muneribus mistice designantur. Per Dominum nostrum" (in Zawilla, *The Historiae,* 319; cf. St. Thomas, *Opera omnia,* Vivès edition, vol. 29, 342; *Opuscula theologica,* Marietti edition, vol. 2, 281).

works, but appears notably at the end of the sequence *Lauda Sion*.[82] Fr. Gy, emphasizing this movement to eschatology, surmises that "one would hardly find the like in any contemporary theologians."[83] The attention paid to this eschatological dimension is fully consistent with the deep movement of St. Thomas's theology toward the vision of God, toward the plenary revelation of the mysteries in the fulfillment of the Church: This is exactly what Thomas put at the heart of his doctrine of the Eucharist. This too brief liturgical and homiletic sketch certainly deserves a more thorough study. But it confirms the theological, spiritual, and pastoral importance that Thomas accorded, in every field in which he was active, to the theme of the unity of the Church that the Eucharist effects.

The theology of St. Thomas bears witness to a profound connection between the Eucharist and the Church, which his theology takes into consideration at every level on which he analyzes this sacrament, under the aspects of both its signification and its efficacy. His doctrine of the Church's unity as the *res* of the Eucharist draws deeply from the Fathers, and from Augustine in particular. This "osmosis" between Eucharistic realism and the realism of the Church involves the major themes of his Eucharistic doctrine, especially his understanding of the efficacy of the sacrament through incorporation and conversion in Christ, as well as his grasp of the mystery of the Church according to this same theme of incorporation by means of faith and charity, in its double dimension of union with Christ and of fraternal unity among the members by the action of the Holy Spirit. In St. Thomas the Eucharist appears in its fullness as the very soul of ecclesial life. *Tantum ergo sacramentum!*

82 "Tu nos bona fac videre/In terra viventium./Tu qui cuncta scis et vales/Qui nos pascis his mortales/Tuos ibi commensales/Coheredes et sodales/Fac sanctorum civium.-Amen" (*Opera omnia,* Vivès edition, vol. 29, 342; *Opuscula theologica,* Marietti edition, vol. 2, 281).

83 P.-M. Gy, *La liturgie dans l'histoire,* 277.

CHAPTER 6

Reconciliation with the Church and Interior Penance: The Contribution of Thomas Aquinas on the Question of the *Res et Sacramentum* of Penance

SACRAMENTAL PENANCE, which provides remission of sins, brings reconciliation with the Church and with God.[1] Today, numerous theologians agree in recognizing more clearly that reconciliation with the Church constitutes the "first effect" of the sacrament of penance or its "proper effect," which brings reconciliation with God (second effect) to the Christian sinner. Grounded in the study of the history of penance (the patristic theme of "peace with the Church"), this thesis constitutes one focus of contemporary reflection on this sacrament.[2] Having arrived at maturity in the movement for the rediscovery of the ecclesial dimension of the sacraments, which Vatican II sanctioned, today this thesis is one key to understanding the sacrament in its ecclesial

[1] Translation by Robert E. Williams, SSI, of "La réconciliation avec l'Église et la pénitence intérieure: l'apport de Thomas d'Aquin sur la question du *res et sacramentum* de la pénitence," in *Praedicando et docendo: Mélanges offerts à Liam Walsh OP*, ed. Barbara Hallensleben and Guido Vergauwen (Fribourg: Éditions Universitaires, 1998), 31–47. English translation published in *Nova et Vetera* 1 (2003): 283–302.

[2] Colman E. O'Neill, "Les Sacrements," in *Bilan de la théologie du XXe siècle*, ed. Robert Vander Gucht and Herbert Vorgrimler, vol. 2 (Tournai, Paris: Casterman, 1971), 457–500, cf. 493–98; Herbert Vorgrimler, *Buße und Krankensalbung*, "Handbuch der Dogmengeschichte IV/3" (Freiburg/Basel/Wien: Herder, 1978), 195–96; Reinhard Messner, *Feiern der Umkehr und Versöhnung*, "Gottesdienst der Kirche, Handbuch der Liturgiewissenchaft 7/2, Sakramentliche Feiern 1/2," (Regensburg: Friedrich Pustet, 1992), 185–86. Already Karl Rahner was able to produce a substantial list of theologians who accepted this determination of the *res et sacramentum* (*Theologische Schriften*, vol. 8 [Einsiedeln/Zürich/Köln: Benzinger Verlag, 1967], 449–50): H. de Lubac, M. Schmaus, E. Schillebeeckx, J. Ratzinger, Y. Congar, and many others.

dimension. It may be expressed thus: "Reconciliation with God by means of reconciliation with the Church."[3]

From the very beginnings of this approach, it was integrated into the Scholastic analysis of the sacrament's structure; reconciliation with the Church, therefore, was defined as the "*res et sacramentum* of penance."[4] We find this to be the case with most of the theologians who hold to the sacraments' causality along with its three elements: the sacramental sign itself *(sacramentum tantum)*; the intermediate effect in the order of signification-causality, which is already a reality brought about by the sacrament *(res et sacramentum)*; and finally, the ultimate effect, that is, sacramental grace or the "fruit" of the sacrament *(res tantum)*. From this standpoint, then, reconciliation with the Church replaces the "inner penance" that for Thomas Aquinas and many medieval theologians constituted this *res et sacramentum* of penance. This chapter examines reconciliation with the Church under the aspect of *res et sacramentum*. It aims at making a comparison of these two approaches to the intermediate sign-effect of penance in hopes of establishing that the Thomistic doctrine of "inner penance" offers a theological framework for a better understanding of the relation between "reconciliation with God" and "reconciliation with the Church."

1. Reconciliation with the Church

It was Bartomeu M. Xiberta, a Spanish Carmelite, who first presented a systematic treatment of the statement: "Reconciliation with the Church is the *res et sacramentum* of penance [. . .], the proper and immediate effect of sacramental absolution." This thesis forms the subject of his doctoral dissertation defended in 1921 at the Gregorianum in Rome.[5] In a rather

---

3 Bernard Rey, *Pour des célébrations pénitentielles dans l'esprit de Vatican II* (Paris: Cerf, 1995), 177. The author endeavors to position the ecclesial community ("Church of sinners") as the subject of the collective action of reconciliation (see especially 163–65): In my view, this thesis raises many problems.

4 So, for example, Jean-Hervé Nicolas, *Synthèse dogmatique: De la Trinité à la Trinité* (Fribourg: Éditions Universitaires, 1985), 1050–52. Without prejudice to the other names of this sacrament, in this essay I will keep using the term "penance," which joins together the virtue and the sacrament. Let us remember that the word "penance" *(paenitentia)* does not come from the idea of pain *(poena)*. It was used very early on by Christians: To do penance *(paenitentiam agere)* translates *metanoia*, the deep down conversion of which the Gospel speaks and from which the sacrament gets this name; Pierre-Marie Gy, "La documentation sacramentaire de Thomas d'Aquin," *Revue des Sciences Philosophiques et Théologiques* 80 (1996): 425–31; cf. 428 for the *res et sacramentum* of penance (Thomas and Rahner).

5 Bartomeu M. Xiberta, *Clavis Ecclesiae: De ordine absolutionis sacramentalis ad reconciliationem cum Ecclesia* (Rome: Pontificia Università Gregoriana, 1922). We are using the reproduction of the 1922 text by J. Perarnau in *Miscellania Bartomeu M.*

traditional manner, his argument is built upon the witness of Scripture and Tradition, and then confirmed by a study of the Scholastic doctors.[6] The proposition, or rather the demonstration, of Xiberta is not put forward as a criticism of St. Thomas Aquinas, since the author appeals to him, along with other Scholastics (St. Bonaventure in particular), in support of his thesis.[7] At the most, Xiberta observes, the radical distinction between the individual forum and the social forum, on which his opponents base themselves by invoking St. Thomas, is not decisive. As regards the scope of his thesis, in his preface, as at the end of his study, Xiberta underlines its apologetical dimension: To hold in a historically sound way that reconciliation with the Church is the *res et sacramentum* of penance is to possess the means that allows us to establish the *sacramental* dignity of the penance practiced in the Church (relationship between the "divine element" and the "human element") against those who see in it only an ecclesiastical institution.[8] If Xiberta deserves the honor of this first historico-doctrinal study, we must nevertheless grant the initiative to the Jesuit theologian Maurice de la Taille, director of Xiberta's thesis, who taught that the *res et sacramentum* of penance consists in "the extinction of [the sinner's] debt to the Church" *(extinctio debiti erga Ecclesiam).* For Father de la Taille, sacramental absolution is first of all *(per prius)* the Church's acceptance of the satisfaction the penitent offers after having confessed his sins (satisfaction performed or intended to be performed): This relieving of the debt owed to the Church signifies the relieving of the debt owed to Christ.[9] Between Xiberta's apologetical dimension and the

---

Xiberta, Analecta sacra Tarraconensia 45/2 (Barcelona: Biblioteca Balmes, 1972 [1973]), 241*–341* (with the original paging indicated by brackets).

6 "Reconciliatio cum Ecclesia est res et sacramentum sacramenti paenitentiae" (B. M. Xiberta, *Clavis Ecclesiae,* [12]; cf. [96]); "proprium et immediatum fructum absolutionis sacramentalis" (p. [11]). "Ostendere conabor reconciliationem cum Ecclesia nedum abesse ab effectibus sacramenti, esse potius proprium et immediatum fructum. [. . .] Nos vere ostendere conabimur infusionem gratiae deletivae peccati esse finem sacramenti eiusque excellentissimum effectum, ordine tamen causalitatis intercedere alium effectum immediate significatum et causatum per sacramentum, videlicet reconciliationem cum Ecclesia" (pp. [11]-[12]).

7 Ibid., [89]: "Iuxta Angelicum [. . .] reconciliationis vero per sacramentum proprium est reconciliare cum Ecclesia." We will take a look at the position of St. Thomas later.

8 The author names Wycliff, Luther, and "most of the heretics" who follow them, as well as certain "Modernists" (B. M. Xiberta, *Clavis Ecclesiae,* [3]–[4]; cf. [94]–[95]).

9 Maurice de la Taille, *Mysterium Fidei de Augustissimo Corporis et Sanguinis Christi Sacrificio atque Sacramento* (Paris: Beauchesne, 1921), 581. The Eucharistic context of de la Taille's teaching should be noted. For de la Taille's influence on Xiberta's thesis, see H. Vorgrimler, *Buße und Krankensalbung,* 195, note 46.

stress de la Taille puts on the "debt of sin," the theme of reconciliation with the Church is still rather far from the theological interpretation it will have later. But it underlines quite clearly the role of the Church as mediator in the signification and granting of forgiveness.

Among the works of major influence, we cannot overlook Henri de Lubac's *Catholicism*, which marks a decisive stage in the work of restoring value to the sacraments' social dimension within Catholic dogma. Already *Catholicism* offers the main elements of reflection: a close analogy between baptism and penance, identical nature of the "disciplinary institution" and the "means of inner purification," priority of reconciliation with the Church as the immediate effect of penance and "efficacious sign" of reconciliation with God. "There can be no return to the grace of God without a return to the communion of the Church."[10] In De Lubac's quick summary, which provides a whole theological program for the sacrament of penance, there is, however, no mention of *res et sacramentum*, nor is there any need for it.

Later historical studies—those of B. Poschmann in particular—will only confirm Xiberta's thesis (which Poschmann explicitly took as his model)[11] and there is no reason to dwell on them here. We should point out, however, that on the historical level, as on the theological level, Poschmann offers a radicalization of Xiberta's thought. Poschmann explains that on the historical level the penitential teaching of the early Church can be understood only in light of Xiberta's thesis.[12] For Poschmann, on the theological level, only the concept of reconciliation with the Church as the immediate effect of penance allows the sacrament to preserve its full meaning (necessity of the sacramental intervention of the Church); it alone allows us to see penance as an authentic judicial process (an aspect to which Poschmann pays much attention).[13] Once the central place of *pax cum Ecclesia* in early penance has been well established (this is what the historical studies do), it still remains to be shown that it amounts to precisely the *res et sacramentum* of penance. For this we need, besides history, a speculative analysis of the sacrament. Poschmann provides its outline: Reconcilia-

---

10 Henri de Lubac, *Catholicism: A Study of Dogma in Relation to the Corporate Destiny of Mankind* (New York: Longmans, Green and Co., 1950), 37–38.

11 Bernhard Poschmann, *Paenitentia secunda: Die kirchliche Buße im ältesten Christentum bis Cyprian und Origenes, Eine dogmengeschichtliche Untersuchung* (Bonn: P. Hanstein, 1940), 12.

12 Ibid., note 1 ("nur von ihr aus"). The thesis of Xiberta is clearly formulated: "Daß 'die Rekonziliation mit der Kirche *res et sacramentum* des Bußsakraments' sei" (ibid.).

13 Bernhard Poschmann, "Die innere Struktur des Bußsakraments," *Münchener Theologische Zeitschrift* 1/3 (1950): 12–30, cf. 25 and 29.

tion with the Church constitutes a *res*—that is, the thing signified and the immediate effect of the sacramental action—but it is also the *sign* of reconciliation with God. The Church gives her forgiveness to the converted sinner, and God has promised his forgiveness to whomever the Church forgives. Already that was precisely Xiberta's explanation. Furthermore, if we ask what efficacy reconciliation with the Church has in regard to sacramental grace (the *res tantum*), Poschmann's answer is, a certain "right" to receive God's grace. But we could also imagine that there is no reason to add a supplementary effect to reconciliation with the Church since this latter *includes* peace with God, forgiveness, and grace.[14] Hence we may ask ourselves if the framework of *res et sacramentum* really allows us to take into account the historical thesis touted by Poschmann.

Poschmann comes across as more critical of Thomas Aquinas and the Middle Ages overall. As a matter of fact, it is the subsequent controversy about contrition and attrition that he thinks got off on the wrong track by misunderstanding *pax Ecclesiae* as the "first goal" and the "indispensable means" of reconciliation with God. Poschmann points out that if Thomas Aquinas had presented reconciliation with the Church, and not inner penance, as the *res et sacramentum*, the development of penitential doctrine would have taken a wholly different path.[15] For in this case "the sacrament then keeps its irreplaceable importance, even with the most perfect contrition, and there would have been no need to have recourse to imperfect repentance to insure its right to exist."[16] Perhaps such an observation applies to Duns Scotus or to those theologians denounced in Blaise Pascal's tenth *Provinciale*, but certainly not to the position of Thomas Aquinas, as we shall see later. Nowhere do we find that St. Thomas had to "raise the ante on the requirements for repentance, resulting in an extrasacramental justification,"[17] for the good reason that Thomas's effort consists in tying together as closely as possible personal contrition and the

---

14 Ibid., 21.

15 Bernhard Poschmann, *Buße und letzte Ölung* (Herder: Freiburg im Breisgau, 1950), 111: "Hätte Thomas mit der altkirchlichen Auffassung als 'res et sacramentum' der Buße statt der 'paenitentia interior' die reconciliatio mit der Kirche herausgestellt, dann würde die Entwicklung der Bußlehre einen anderen Weg genommen haben."

16 Ibid.: "Ist die 'pax ecclesiae' nächstes Ziel und unumgängliches Mittel zur Versöhnung mit Gott, dann behält das Sakrament auch bei der vollkommensten Reue seine unersetzliche Bedeutung, und es wäre nicht nötig gewesen, auf die unvollkommene Reue zu rekurrieren, um ihm die Existenzberechtigung zu sichern."

17 Ibid.: "Erst recht wäre kein Anlaß gewesen, im Gegensatz zu Thomas und den Scholastikern, die Anforderungen an die vollkommene, die Rechtfertigung außersakramental bewirkende Reue so zu übersteigen, daß sie für den normalen Christenmenschen fast auszuscheiden scheint."

sacramental dimension: The contrition Thomas speaks of is contrition at work in the Church's sacramental process.

On the speculative level, C. Dumont tried to determine more precisely the proper structure of this *res et sacramentum.*[18] He points out that in order for us to be able to consider reconciliation with the Church as the *res et sacramentum* of penance, we have to uncover more than a relation of extrinsic analogy or simple likeness between it and grace; and we must also be able to establish a distinction. This observation leads us to exclude immediately an understanding of reconciliation only in its juridical nature, and to retain the penitent's *real participation* in the community in which he is reintegrated: The penitent becomes an "active member" in the Church once again. For Dumont, reconciliation with the Church and grace remain nevertheless distinct since grace designates a larger field of relations (the whole aspect of salvation), while integration into the Church "only introduces a necessary historical moment."[19] With this analysis Dumont gains a technical explanation that allows him to give an account of the *res et sacramentum,* but with an important consequence: a separation between grace and the Church, which have neither the same intensity nor the same depth. (Along with other nuances in his understanding of the Church, J.-H. Nicolas resolves this difficulty by explaining that the notion of sacrament is not univocal: Here the *res et sacramentum* is so closely bound up with the *res tantum* that it can hardly be separated from it.)[20]

As for the relationship of causality that reconciliation with the Church has with grace, Dumont explains it in terms of "disposing causality" (thus, in reference to Hervaeus Natalis, coming up short of Thomas Aquinas's mature thought).[21] Faced with this difficulty, he maintains the identity of the twofold affirmation: The penitent is received into the Church because God gives him back his grace, or, reciprocally, divine friendship is given back to the penitent because he is taken back into ecclesiastical communion.[22] Consequently, extending the remarks of his predecessors, Dumont points out that this reconciliation with the Church allows us to show the *necessity of the sacramental avowal* made to the Church's minister (Council of Trent), since we have here a reconciliation *within* the Church and a resumption of responsibility by the reconciling Church. The thesis of reconciliation with the Church as the *res et sacramentum* of penance is pro-

---

18 C. Dumont, SJ, "La réconciliation avec l'Église et la nécessité de l'aveu sacramentel," *Nouvelle Revue Théologique* 81 (1959): 577–97.

19 C. Dumont, "La réconciliation avec l'Église," 586.

20 J.-H. Nicolas, *Synthèse dogmatique,* 1051. But then we are still faced with the problem of the distinction.

21 C. Dumont, "La réconciliation avec l'Église," 586–87 and note 18.

22 Ibid., 587.

moted anew, not without relevance, in order to defend Catholic teaching on the sacrament.

It cannot be denied, however, that the most important attempt at a synthesis belongs to Karl Rahner. Rahner definitely accepts the thinking of Thomas Aquinas on several key points, particularly the place of the penitent's actions, with the priest's absolution, at the heart of the sacramental sign, as well as the instrumental efficient causality of the sacrament thus constituted.[23] Moreover, Rahner is unwilling to give up on finding a *res et sacramentum*, a "middle term" between the sign and the effect of penance: It is reconciliation with the Church, which respects both history (the patristic theme of *pax et communio cum Ecclesia*) and reality itself. Through his reconciliation with the Holy Community, the sinner, who has been reintegrated into the Church, acquires a new participation in the Spirit of the Church *(res et sacramentum)* that forgives and grants "peace with God" *(res tantum)*.[24] This explanation, which stresses the necessity of the priest's absolution for there to be a reconciliation with the Church, is based upon a close parallel with baptism. In a way analogous to the baptismal character (the stable integration into the Church of which the baptized person is made a member), the *res et sacramentum* of penance consists in the restoration of the living bond with the Church.[25]

Rahner does not simply replace one theological explanation with another, but he fits the thinking of Thomas into his views. On the one hand, he shows that for Thomas (as for Bonaventure) the sacrament really produces reconciliation with the Church. On the other hand, he upholds "inner penance" as the effect produced or reinforced by the sacrament, while stressing that authentic "inner penance" (contrition) includes the desire to refer oneself to the ministry of the Church. True repentance includes the will to be reconciled with the Church in such a way that it bears the twofold aspect of reconciliation with God and with the Church.

> The sacrament reconciles with the Church the sinner who approaches the Church with his "inner penance" as the will to be reconciled with the Church. Through this, the sinner has a right to the "infusio gratiae" that allows him to achieve fully this "inner penance" by which he is able essentially to make his own the grace that is offered to him,

---

23 Karl Rahner, "Vergessene Wahrheiten über das Bußsakrament," in *Theologische Schriften*, vol. 2 (Einsiedeln/Zürich/Köln: Benzinger Verlag, 1964), 143–83, cf. 161–71. In particular, Rahner challenges the assimilation of the thought of Thomas Aquinas to that of Duns Scotus.

24 Ibid., 180–81.

25 Ibid., 180–82. See Karl Rahner, "Das Sakrament der Buße als Wiederversöhnung mit der Kirche," in *Theologische Schriften*, vol. 8 (Einsiedeln/Zürich/Köln: Benzinger Verlag, 1967), 447–71, cf. 468.

in such a way that it becomes proper to him in a sanctifying and justifying fashion and he is thereby freed from his personal sins.[26]

By designating reconciliation with the Church as the *res et sacramentum* of penance, Rahner takes inner penance with its existential fabric and orients it toward an immediate relationship with the Church in her visibility and her sanctifying dimension.

Rahner's thesis is grounded more profoundly in the sacramentality of the Church (the Church as primordial sacrament, *Ursakrament*) and the understanding of the sacraments as "self-achievements" *(Selbstvollzüge)* of the Church. This approach clarifies first of all the "duality" that we see in every sacrament, as well as in the Church: the sign *(sacramentum)* and the reality of grace *(res)*. From this point of view, every *res et sacramentum* consists essentially in an ecclesial reality. Since Rahner has recourse to the comparison with baptism and the Eucharist, which showcase the ecclesial aspect in a particularly clear manner,[27] it is fitting that we should consider the *res et sacramentum* in these two sacraments in particular.

For Rahner, as we have said, baptism's *res et sacramentum* consists of incorporation into the Church *(das Eingegliedertsein, die Gliedschaft)* in a stable and lasting way. Rahner excludes from this state the question of the "ontological status" of the baptismal character: whether it is thought of as simply a "bespeaking" *(Beanspruchtheit)* on the part of the Church, or if its fundamental aspect is an ontological grounding in the person (the quality or "spiritual power" that makes us apt for acts of worship and of Christian life, in the Thomistic tradition); all this is no longer of any importance to him.[28] Here, as in the case of penance, the proper grounding of the *res et sacramentum* in the process of sacramental justification is reinterpreted in order to adapt it to the ecclesial scheme of things. Rahner adds weight to his choice by a critique of the Scholastic position: Without this "bespeaking" by the Church, we can give only an artificial explanation to the role of

[26] K. Rahner, "Das Sakrament der Buße als Wiederversöhnung mit der Kirche," 469: "Das Sakrament versöhnt mit der Kirche den Sünder, der mit seiner 'paenitentia interior' als Willen zur Versöhnung mit der Kirche eben dieser Kirche entgegenkommt; der Sünder hat dadurch das Recht auf jene 'infusio gratiae,' die es ihm ermöglicht, jene 'paenitentia interior' zu vollziehen, durch die er imstande ist, die ihm verliehene Gnade existentiell so sich anzueignen, daß sie in einer ihn heiligenden und rechtfertigenden Weise seine eigene wird und er so von seinen persönlichen Sünden befreit ist."

[27] K. Rahner, "Vergessene Wahrheiten," 179–80.

[28] Karl Rahner, *Kirche und Sakramente* (Freiburg: Herder, 1960), 78–79. This thesis claims to be a return to the origins of the concept of "character," without which, according to Rahner, the theory of character would remain "arbitrary" (ibid.); cf. idem, "Vergessene Wahrheiten," 180, note 1.

sign that belongs to the character. Put another way, only the social dimension of the *res et sacramentum* allows us to establish its role of *sacrament*, for a sign requires *visibility*.[29] The argument has weight (besides, it did not escape the Scholastics), but Rahner's objection cannot be the deciding factor. St. Thomas Aquinas put forward the following response: The character is a sign through reference to the sensible rite of the sacrament's celebration whereby it is imprinted[30] (likewise, inner penance will have to be understood in reference to outward penance). In other words, the nature of sign and the "visibility" belong to the character not as if this made up an independent reality, but rather when character is taken *in the unity of the sacrament with its three moments* (namely, *sacramentum, res et sacramentum, res tantum*) by which it is referred to the visible sacramental sign. The social dimension (present at each level of the analysis of the sacrament) doubtlessly does not oblige us to follow Rahner in such a definite fashion.

The case of the Eucharist, which Rahner treats first in his *Kirche und Sakramente*, is still more interesting. Without questioning the truth of Christ's Body and Blood, Rahner nevertheless refuses to see in it the *res et sacramentum* of the Eucharist. For Rahner this consists in a "deeper integration into the unity of the Mystical Body," a renewed incorporation that is the first effect and the efficacious cause of the other effects of the Eucharist.[31] For whoever would continue to hold that the true Body and Blood of Christ (the "Real Presence") is the *res et sacramentum*, Rahner has the following objection: Even if we hold that the *verum Corpus* is the sign of its grace insofar as the Church possesses it as the sign of her own unity (which is necessary in this case), we would still have to be able to account for the ordering of the effects *(res)* of the Eucharist and the primary place *(vorgeordnete Wirkung)* that belongs here to the Church's unity.[32] Rahner's view is profound, and the stress he lays upon ecclesial unity is altogether fundamental. Still, one can say that the position of Thomas Aquinas (here Rahner mentions the Eucharist as "the sacrament of the Church's unity," which is found in Thomas) in fact goes further than Rahner's. Thomas firmly holds that the *verum Corpus* is the *res et sacramentum* of the Eucharist, but he does not consider the unity of the Church as one effect that procures other sacramental graces. There is not on one side an ecclesial effect of the sacrament, and on the other side a personal and individual effect. It is clearly *the same reality of grace*, incorporation into Christ given to the person, which is both the food of spiritual rebuilding and at

29 K. Rahner, *Kirche und Sakramente,* 78–80.

30 St. Thomas, *ST* III, q. 63, a. 2, ad 4: "Character habet rationem signi per comparationem ad sacramentum sensibile a quo imprimitur."

31 K. Rahner, *Kirche und Sakramente,* 74.

32 Ibid., 75.

the same time, by its very nature, the building up of the Church, whose unity is strengthened and achieved through charity.[33]

Reconciliation with the Church is a constituent of the ecclesial action of reconciliation with God. It is immediately obtained through the sacrament. The sinner receives forgiveness in his ecclesial reintegration. Grounded in Scripture and the practice of the early Church, this statement highlights very well the ecclesial dimension of the sacrament and meets the desires of contemporary thinking. From the start, it is also associated with the "defense" of several aspects of Catholic teaching (sacramentality, necessity of confession, necessity of absolution by a priest). However, its formulation in terms of *res et sacramentum* entails several difficulties: the distinction between the intermediate element and the *res* of the sacrament, the likening of the penitential framework to that of baptism, the nature of reconciliation with the Church in the person of the penitent, its "causality" in regard to sacramental grace (reconciliation with God), the modifications the very notion of *res et sacramentum* has undergone, as well as the articulation (Rahner) of this concept along the main lines of Thomas Aquinas's treatment of penance. This is what we will now examine.

2. Inner Penance in St. Thomas Aquinas

Inner Penance

The framework of Thomas Aquinas's thinking is summarized in the following statement: "Even in Penance there is something which is *sacramentum tantum*, that is, the actions done by the penitent sinner as well as by the absolving priest. Now, the *res et sacramentum* is the inner penance of the sinner, while the *res tantum*, which is not sacrament, is the remission of sin. The first of these, taken integrally, is the cause of the second; the first and the second are the cause of the third."[34]

This framework of understanding calls for several observations. First, it puts an important stress on the "outward" acts performed personally by

---

[33] Cajetan has expressed this unity well: "When we hear that the fruit *(res tantum)* of the sacrament is grace, and that what is to be received is the unity of the Church or the Mystical Body of Christ, we do not understand by that that there are two diverse realities since all that is nothing else but God's grace in his faithful" (Cajetan, *In Tertiam,* q. 73, a. 1; Leonine edition, vol. 12, 139). See chapter five in this volume, "The Ecclesial Fruit of the Eucharist in St. Thomas Aquinas."

[34] St. Thomas, *ST* III, q. 84, a. 1, ad 3: "Etiam in paenitentia est aliquid quod est sacramentum tantum, scilicet actus exercitus tam per peccatorem paenitentem, quam etiam per sacerdotem absolventem. Res autem et sacramentum est paenitentia interior peccatoris. Res autem tantum et non sacramentum est remissio peccati. Quorum primum totum simul sumptum est causa secundi; primum autem et secundum sunt causa tertii."

the penitent (expression of contrition, confession, and satisfaction), obviously in relation with the inward acts of conversion. Here penance is taken in the Gospel sense of "to do penance" *(agere paenitentiam)*, the sensible character of which permits identification with an authentic *sacramentum*.[35] These acts make up the "matter of the sacrament," while the priest's action (absolution) constitutes its "form." This anthropological grounding of the matter of the sacrament provides the starting point for a theological analysis of the sacrament: What the penitent does, in action and word, signifies a holy reality.[36] Thomas will go so far as to write that the *penitent in person* constitutes the "matter" of this sacrament.[37] In agreement with the Thomistic teaching on the *res et sacramentum*, the latter will be understood with immediate reference to the sacramental sign (namely, the penitent's acts with the priest's absolution). This stress is all the more important because, unlike the theologians who went before him (and numerous theologians who followed), Thomas attributes a real instrumental efficiency to the sacrament, and hence to the personal activity of the penitent (taken with the absolution given by the priest), as regards the giving of grace. It seems that no theologian held this before him, and Thomas himself, in his early writing on the *Sentences*, speaks only of a disposing instrumental causality.[38] In the *Summa*, however, it is no longer a question of a mere disposition to grace by the activity of the penitent and of the priest, but indeed of a real instrumental efficacy.[39] By virtue of Christ's passion, which acts in it, the sign or sacrament works effectively, as instrument, to obtain grace.

Next we should note that the production of the *res et sacramentum* belongs to the first element, the sacramental sign *taken integrally*. In other words, the penitent's acts of conversion do not have this efficacy except under the sway of their form, the priest's sacramental absolution. Thus,

35 IV *Sent.*, dist. 22, q. 2, a. 3, qla 3, ad 2; *ST* III, q. 90, a. 2, arg. 1, ad 1.

36 *ST* III, q. 84, a. 1; remember that St. Thomas defines a sacrament as follows: "signum rei sacrae inquantum est sanctificans homines" (ibid., q. 60, a. 2).

37 *De forma absolutionis*, chap. 4 (Leonine edition, vol. 40 C, 40): "Ipse autem peccator confitens est sicut materia in hoc sacramento."

38 Thomas was not the first to make the penitent's actions the matter of the sacrament (that was already the opinion of Hugh of St.-Cher and of Bonaventure), but nobody made them an efficacious cause of grace.

39 IV *Sent.*, dist. 22, q. 2, a. 1, qla 1, ad 2; cf. qla 2. *ST* III, q. 86, a. 6; cf. q. 64, a. 1. See Bruno de Vaux St.-Cyr, *Revenir à Dieu: Pénitence, conversion, confession* (Paris: Cerf, 1967), 151–78. For Thomas's progress on instrumental causality, see Jean-Pierre Torrell, "La causalité salvifique de la résurrection du Christ selon saint Thomas," *Revue Thomiste* 96 (1996): 179–208, cf. 186–92; Hyacinthe Dondaine, "A propos d'Avicenne et de saint Thomas. De la causalité dispositive à la causalité instrumentale," *Revue Thomiste* 51 (1951): 441–53. For what follows I am indebted to Fr. Hyacinthe Dondaine's unpublished course on penance given at Le Saulchoir.

Abelard's thesis whereby the penitent's contrition remits sins, and that of Hugh of St. Victor, who held that the priest's absolution remits them, are combined by Thomas into a more satisfactory position.[40] In giving its full value to the thesis of an authentic instrumental efficacy, Thomas's effort consists in showing the unity of the sacramental action and of personal conversion understood within the workings of the divine grace of forgiveness in the Church.

Therefore, the *sacramentum*, considered as a whole, produces the intermediate element, the *res et sacramentum*, defined as "inner penance." What are we dealing with? Inner penance designates first of all contrition,[41] which by its aim extends to all "parts" of penance since it overlaps equally confession (avowal of sins) and satisfaction, insofar as these are included virtually, or *in voto*, in full contrition.[42] In the *Summa*, St. Thomas specifies that contrition belongs to inner penance, and it implies the intention to confess and give satisfaction.[43] We may define contrition, for its part, as sorrow or remorse for sins committed, with the intention of removing the consequence of sin, which is the offense committed against God.[44] Thus understood, inner penance is at once *signified* and *obtained*

---

40 Paul Anciaux, *La théologie du sacrement de pénitence au XIIe siècle* (Louvain: E. Nauwelaerts, 1949), 275–302; Pierre Adnès, "Le rapport de la contrition et de l'absolution chez saint Thomas et les théologiens médiévaux," in *S. Tommaso Teologo*, ed. Antonio Piolanti, Studi Tomistici 59 (Vatican City: Libreria Editrice Vaticana, 1995), 301–9. In the judgment of K. Rahner, this understanding of the causality of the acts of the person and of absolution provides "the conceptual assimilation of an authentic tradition going back to the patristic age" ("Vergessene Wahrheiten," 165–66; cf. 162–64).

41 *In Rom* 11:29 (#927): "Duplex est paenitentia: interior et exterior. Interior quidem consistit in contritione cordis, qua quis dolet de peccatis praeteritis."

42 IV *Sent.*, dist. 22, q. 2, a. 1, qla 2, ad 3: "Tres partes paenitentiae sunt et in paenitentia exteriori et in interiori; quia confessio et satisfactio quae videntur tantum ad exteriorem paenitentiam pertinere, inveniuntur in interiori paenitentia quantum ad propositum et praemeditationem eorum." Thomas is not the first author to posit inner penance as *res et sacramentum*. That was already the position of Peter Lombard, of St. Bonaventure, and of many others. Rather, Thomas's originality lies in the efficacy he sees in this contrition and its place within the process of sacramental penance.

43 *ST* III, q. 90, a. 2, ad 1: "[Contritio] virtualiter autem pertinet ad paenitentiam exteriorem, inquantum scilicet implicat propositum confitendi et satisfaciendi"; ibid., a. 3, ad 2: "contritio continet virtute totam paenitentiam." On inner penance and contrition, see Eric Luijten, *Sacramental Forgiveness as a Gift of God: Thomas Aquinas on the Sacrament of Penance* (Leuven: Peeters, 2003), 149–51; Giuseppe Perini, "La penitenza interiore in S. Tommaso d'Aquino," in *Indubitanter ad Veritatem: Studies Offered to Leo J. Elders*, ed. Jörgen Vijgen (Budel: Damon, 2003), 322–39.

44 IV *Sent.*, dist. 17, q. 2; cf. *ST* III, q. 85, a. 1, ad 3; q. 85, a. 5 and a. 6.

by the actions of the penitent and the minister.[45] Inner penance may be considered under two aspects. On the one hand, inasmuch as it is an act of virtue, it is the origin of the outward penitential action *(sic interior paenitentia est omnino causa exterioris)*. On the other hand, inasmuch as it falls within a sacramental ecclesial gesture, that is, as part of the sacrament of penance, inner penance *acts efficaciously* for the healing of sin; as such, it is obtained by the outward action of the penitent and of the priest.[46]

The framework of the *res et sacramentum* appears here in broad daylight: Inner penance is *res* (effect) in relation to the priest's absolution and the penitent's outward acts, which signify it; it remains somehow "proportionated" to the penitent's acts. It is likewise a sign in relation to the forgiveness of sins, in reference to the outward action with which it forms a whole. Lastly, it is the efficacious cause of the forgiveness of sins, together with the penitent's personal action and the priest's absolution, taken once again as an organic whole.[47]

What is at stake in this conception is clear. For Thomas, there can be no forgiveness of sins without an authentic inner conversion of the heart.[48] We are miles away from a forgiveness obtained *ex opere operato* without the deep-down participation of the penitent (here Thomas returns to the early doctrine). At the same time, this inner penance obtains forgiveness within the ecclesial action since it obtains its effect with penitential acts through

45 Ibid., dist. 22, q. 2, a. 1, qla 2: "Interior paenitentia est res exterioris paenitentiae; sed ut significata tantum per actus paenitentis; ut significata autem et causata per actus eosdem, adjuncta absolutione ministri."

46 Ibid., ad 1: "Paenitentia interior potest considerari dupliciter. Uno modo prout est quidam actus virtutis; et sic interior paenitentia est omnino causa exterioris; sicut etiam in aliis virtutibus actus interiores sunt causae exteriorum. Alio modo prout est actus operans ad sanationem peccati; et sic pertinet ad paenitentiae sacramentum; et ita interior paenitentia non est causa exterioris, sed effectus vel signatum ipsius: non enim habet efficaciam operandi contra morbum peccati, nisi ex suppositione propositi exterioris paenitentiae et absolutionis desiderio."

47 Faced with the difficulty of conceiving the kind of causality that belongs to inner penance with regard to sacramental grace, some Thomists and other theologians have been led to posit an "ornament of the soul" *(ornatus animae)* as *res et sacramentum*, a mysterious counterpart to the baptismal character. "Magna videtur altercatio de ornatu," Cajetan too observes (*In Tertiam*, q. 84, a. 1–2; Leonine edition, vol. 12, 288). We must, however, point out that inner penance is not the cause of charity; it is the cause of the remission of sins, which is the proper effect of the sacrament.

48 *ST* III, q. 86, a. 2; cf. q. 84, a. 5, ad 3. As a virtue, inner penance consitutes a fundamental disposition of Christian life, which is not limited to the celebration of the sacrament (ibid., q. 84, a. 8). As "contrition of the heart" for sin committed, inner penance is required for the fruitful reception of baptism; see *In Rom* 11:29 (#927); cf. *ST* III, q. 68, a. 6, ad 3.

absolution.[49] This analysis of penance places the conversion experience at the heart of the process of justification. Cooperating with the divine action, to which all initiative belongs, the virtuous act of penance engages faith, hope, charity, and filial fear.[50] Thomas makes the scheme of Christian justification and sacramental forgiveness coincide. When all is said and done, he knows only *one Christian penance*: a virtuous labor undertaken in a sacramental action where grace is at work.[51]

As for the *res* of the Sacrament, obtained by means of the *res et sacramentum,* Thomas designates it as "the remission of sins." Such is the proper effect of the sacrament of penance, expressed by the words of absolution (the sacrament effects exactly what it signifies, and Thomas follows this signification closely). This forgiveness of sins obtains the "reconciliation of friendship" *(reconciliatio amicitiae)* that best characterizes (better, in fact, than the category of strict justice, in Thomas's judgment) the underlying intention of penance.[52]

The sacrament is shown here fundamentally as the "means" to rid the offense that thwarts the friendship God wishes to establish with his children. It is also with this theme of restored friendship that Thomas develops the pneumatological character of penance. The fruit of the sacrament, obtained through the power of Christ's passion (passion "for the remission of sins"),[53] is due to the Holy Spirit, since he is Love in person and Communion in the bosom of the Trinity, the underlying reason for the entire economy of salvation and mercy: "Since it is through the Holy Spirit that we are made friends of God, it is therefore through Him that God remits our sins."[54]

Even outside the sacramental celebration, contrition includes the intention of confessing and the desire for absolution (intention to "submit oneself to the keys of the Church"). This is the reason we would not willingly speak of the forgiveness of sins through a contrition that is "extrasacramental" (Poschmann). And such is the reason why Thomas has no difficulty holding

---

49 *ST* III, q. 84, a. 1, ad 3 ("primum autem et secundum sunt causa tertii"); IV *Sent.*, dist. 22, q. 2, a. 1, qla 2. It is in this sense that inner penance constitutes the "immediate cause" of the remission of sins (ibid., sed contra 2).

50 *ST* III, q. 85, a. 5; q. 86, a. 6, ad 2: "The forgiveness of sin is accounted the effect not only of the virtue of penance, but also, and that chiefly, of faith and charity." Compare with the teaching on justification in *ST* I–II, q. 113.

51 Hyacinthe F. Dondaine, *La pénitence,* typewritten course (Le Saulchoir), 81.

52 *ST* III, q. 90, a. 2. This remark is important because for Thomas the virtue of penance is a species of justice. But here the theological virtues enrich and elevate justice (q. 85, a. 3, ad 4).

53 Even more: The effect of penance is obtained "insofar as we are united to Christ suffering for our sins" (*SCG* IV, chap. 72 [#4071]).

54 *SCG* IV, chap. 21 (#3582), in reference to Proverbs 10:12, John 20:22, and Matthew 13:21.

that confession to a layman under such conditions may be "somehow sacramental."[55] Lastly, the framework of the sacrament does not in itself require a temporal simultaneity of its components. Certainly "perfect contrition" may be given at the moment of the sacrament's celebration, but it may just as well precede it (Thomas deems this case the most common). In this case, through the desire *(votum)* of the sacrament, that is, by the virtue of the "keys of the Church" that already acts in the penitent's contrition, such perfect contrition may procure the forgiveness of sins *(remissio culpae)* even before the priest's absolution is actually given.[56] This shows the very deep connection between contrition and absolution in Aquinas's thought. Forgiveness of sins is given neither by absolution *alone* nor by contrition *alone*, but by contrition *and* absolution as a whole, that is, by the "virtue of the keys" acting in contrition. This teaching clearly shows that, in the sacrament of penance, God acts at the very heart of human freedom: Forgiveness of sins follows from the penitent's inner conversion under the sway of absolution. Here, obviously, the doctrine matches Christian experience, which bears witness to the complexity of the undertaking and to its character that may vary according to personal dispositions. To show this, Thomas does not hesitate to assert an anticipated causality of the complete sacrament (absolution already acts in the penitent's contrition).[57] In any case, St. Thomas insists that pardon for sin does not take place without an act of the virtue of

---

55 IV *Sent.*, dist. 17, q. 3, a. 3, qla 2, ad 1: "Nihilominus confessio laico ex desiderio sacerdotis facta, sacramentalis est quodammodo, quamvis non sit sacramentum perfectum, quia deest ei id quod est ex parte sacerdotis."

56 *Quodlibet* IV, q. 7, a. 1 (Leonine edition, vol. 25/2, 330): "Sacramenta dupliciter operantur, uno modo secundum quod exhibentur in actu, alio modo secundum quod habentur in uoto. [. . .] Et idem est etiam in sacramento penitencie, quod consummatur in dispensatione ministri absoluentis: cum enim aliquis actu absoluitur, consequitur plenarie sacramenti effectum; set, si ante quam absoluatur, habeat hoc sacramentum in uoto, quando scilicet proponit se subicere clauibus Ecclesiae, iam uirtus clauium operatur in ipso, et consequitur remissionem culpae. Si quis tamen in ipsa absolutione inciperet conteri et claues Ecclesie habere in uoto, in ipsa absolutione sacerdotis culpa ei dimitteretur per graciam, que infunditur in hoc sacramento sicut et in aliis sacramentis noue legis. Vnde quandoque contingit quod aliqui non perfecte contriti, uirtute clauium graciam contritionis consecuntur, dum modo non ponant obicem Spiritui sancto."

57 Ibid.; see Daniel Ols, "Saint Thomas a-t-il soutenu l'existence d'une causalité efficiente anticipée dans l'économie sacramentelle?" in *S. Tommaso Teologo*, ed. Antonio Piolanti, Studi Tomistici 59 (Vatican City: Libreria Editrice Vaticana, 1995), 285–97. In his Commentary on the *Sentences*, Thomas distinguishes between the disposing action of contrition as a virtue and the instrumental action of contrition as part of the sacrament (IV *Sent.*, dist. 17, q. 2, a. 5, qla 1, corp.). In the *Summa* he stresses more strongly the relationship of all true contrition with the ministry of the Church ("keys of the Church") by which the virtue of penance is ordered to the Passion of Christ that remits sins (*ST* III, q. 86, a. 6, ad 3; cf. corp.).

penance,[58] and he adds that "true contrition cannot exist without the desire to submit oneself to the keys of the Church, [. . .] so that in contrition, the fault is forgiven."[59]

Reconciliation with God and Reconciliation with the Church

For St. Thomas the term "reconciliation" *(reconciliatio)* designates the restoration of friendship after the hindrance to friendship has been done away with. Thus reconciliation appears as the sinner's return in grace into the heart of God. Penance, whose *object* is the sin that the penitent wants to work on eliminating, is wholly oriented toward reconciliation with God, which is its *end*.[60] We are far removed from any reduction of reconciliation to the juridical: At its root reconciliation pertains to the love of charity.[61] Reconciliation is closely associated with *satisfaction* (a part of penance) since it aims precisely at the reconciliation of the offended friend's heart: reconciliation with God and reconciliation with our neighbor.[62] Along with contrition and confession, satisfaction works for the remission of sin and of the punishment due to sin, as well as for "reconciliation with the members of the Church."[63] Thus reconciliation is at the terminus of the penitential exercise of conversion, just as it is first in God's saving plan.[64]

What place does St. Thomas give to reconciliation with the Church? If we look at the instances where the terms *reconciliatio* and *reconciliare* occur in the treatise on the sacraments in the *Commentary on the Sentences*

---

58 *ST* III, q. 86, a. 2, ad 1: "There is no remission of sins [. . .] without an actual change of the will, which is the effect of penance"; cf. ibid., corp.: "It is impossible for a mortal actual sin to be pardoned without penance, if we speak of penance as a virtue."

59 *Quodlibet* IV, q. 7, a. 1, ad 3 (Leonine edition, vol. 25/2, 330–31): "Nunquam potest esse uera contritio sine uoto clauium Ecclesie [. . .] et ideo in contritione culpa remittitur."

60 IV *Sent.*, dist. 14, q. 1, a. 1, qla 4, ad 2. This distinction between the object and the end allows Thomas to explain the difference between penance and the theological virtues. Thomas fully accepts that "penance reconciles with God," but only the theological virtues have God as their "object."

61 IV *Sent.*, dist. 15, q. 1, a. 5, qla 2, corp.: "Reconciliatio autem nihil aliud est quam amicitiae reparatio"; cf. a. 1, qla 2, arg. 1: "Reconciliatio, cum sit amoris, ad caritatem pertinet."

62 Ibid., dist. 15, q. 1, a. 1, qla 2, arg. 1 and ad 1; dist. 15, q. 1, a. 5, qla 2; dist. 15, q. 4, a. 7, qla 1, arg. 3 and ad 3; dist. 16, q. 1, a. 1, qla 2; *ST* III, q. 85, a. 3, arg. 1. Let us recall that for Thomas works done without charity cannot count as satisfaction since then the motive for their acceptance by God would be wanting (IV *Sent.*, dist. 15, q. 1, a. 3, qla 2). It is charity (friendship) that accounts for the worth of satisfaction.

63 *In 1 Cor* 11:27 (#690), in the context of participation in the Eucharist.

64 IV *Sent.*, dist. 18, q. 1, a. 2, qla 3.

and the *Summa theologiae*, first we must say that this vocabulary shows up quite often in an ecclesial context. Here Thomas is drawing on the heritage of the patristic vocabulary, passed on by Augustine in particular, and by the texts cited in Gratian's *Decretals*. This reconciliation, which finds its place at the end of the process of penance,[65] is attached especially to admission to the Church's sacraments ("reconciliation with the Church") and above all to Eucharistic communion, which requires "peace with the Church."[66] The texts pay special attention here to the reconciliation of the dying, of persons engaged in an activity incompatible with the dignity of baptized persons, of apostates, heretics, priests degraded from their order, all with a heavy ecclesial content.[67] In this context, "reconciliation with the Church" is closely tied with the activity of the ministers.[68] Here we must highlight two aspects.

In a way similar to what we have been able to observe in the contemporary rediscovery of the theme of reconciliation with the Church, Thomas here brings out the necessity of the activity of the Church's ministers:

> Through the sacraments man is not only reconciled to God, but he must also be reconciled to the Church. Now, he can only be reconciled to the Church if the Church's sanctification reaches him. [. . .] But in penance the sanctification of the Church does not reach a man except through the minister. [. . .] He is not yet reconciled to the Church in such a way that he can be admitted to the sacraments of the Church unless he has first been absolved by a priest.[69]

---

65 ibid., dist. 14, q. 1, a. 5, qla 3; *ST* III, q. 80, a. 6.

66 IV *Sent.*, dist. 9, q. 1, a. 5, qla 3, sed contra 2 and corp.; dist. 14, q. 1, a. 5, qla 3; dist. 17, q. 3, a. 3, qla 2, ad 3; dist. 17, q. 3, a. 3, qla 3; *ST* III, q. 80, a. 6.

67 IV *Sent.*, dist. 25, q. 1, a. 2, sed contra 1; *ST* III, q. 80, a. 6; q. 82, a. 8, sed contra.

68 Ibid., dist. 14, q. 1, a. 1, qla 2; dist. 17, q. 3, a. 3, qla 2, ad 3. Just as Thomas interprets the canonical penance of the ancient Church in light of the solemn penance of the Middle Ages (IV *Sent.*, dist. 14, q. 1, a. 5, qla 3), just so he is incapable of giving a correct account of the role that the early practice reserved to the bishop in reconciliation (IV *Sent.*, dist. 20, *divisio textus* and *expositio textus*). We should point out that he finds himself in the same difficulty when it comes to the ancient doctrine of the non-repeatability of penance (*ST* III, q. 84, a. 10). Indeed, his reflection starts from a very concrete point: the sacramental practice he knows, "penance as it is practiced in the Church" (*ST* III, q. 84, a. 1).

69 IV *Sent.*, dist. 17, q. 3, a. 3, qla 2, ad 3: "Per sacramenta homo non solum Deo, sed etiam Ecclesiae oportet quod reconciliatur. Ecclesiae autem reconciliari non potest nisi sanctificatio Ecclesiae ad eum perveniat. [. . .] Sed in paenitentia Ecclesiae sanctificatio non pervenit ad hominem nisi per ministrum. [. . .] Non tamen adhuc Ecclesiae reconciliatus est, ut ad sacramenta Ecclesiae admitti debeat, nisi prius a sacerdote absolvatur." Cf. ibid., dist. 14, q. 1, a. 1, qla 2.

Reconciliation with the Church is understood essentially in reference to the Church's sanctifying function and the grace of communion that constitutes it (in relation to the Eucharist especially). Here we are approaching the theme of the Church as sacrament developed by Rahner in this context.[70] It is not surprising, then, to learn that it is in connection with the Eucharist that Thomas prefers to treat the ecclesial dimension of penance: "Whoever receives this sacrament (the Eucharist) shows thereby that he is united to Christ and incorporated in his members, which is achieved through faith informed [by charity], and nobody can have that together with mortal sin."[71] St. Thomas considers this incompatibility between the state of mortal sin and the fruitful reception of the Eucharist explicitly in the light of the "Mystical Body of Christ, which is a society of saints."[72] The Eucharist nourishes the communion of the Church in its two dimensions of relationship with Christ and fraternal unity of the members. The absence of this communion, if it occurs, wounds the *signification* of the sacrament and the *reality* of its effect. The sacrament of penance is as a matter of fact ordered to true and full participation in the Eucharist, the sacrament of charity and of the Church's unity. Here we find reconciliation with God achieved at the very heart of the ecclesial communion. In Thomas, it is around the divine friendship that is charity (faith formed by charity) that the themes of the Church, of contrition, of the sacrament of penance, and of the Eucharist are bound together. At this level, it is quite difficult to assign priority to reconciliation with the Church or to reconciliation with God; in reality, the two coincide.[73]

However, St. Thomas endeavors vigorously to show that the proper virtue of the sacrament does not extend only to reconciliation with the Church, but indeed reaches to reconciliation with God. On this point he disagrees with Bonaventure. As already seen, the Franciscan Doctor, also, holds that inner penance is the *res et sacramentum* of the sacrament of penance. He likewise states that the sacrament reconciles with God and

---

[70] For this relationship between Eucharist, ecclesial mediation, and reconciliation, see ibid., dist. 13, q. 1, a. 3, qla 2.

[71] *ST* III, q. 80, a. 4.

[72] Ibid. For Thomas, all the sacraments are ordered to the Eucharist, which bestows its underlying unity on the sacramental organism (ibid., q. 65, a. 3). Now the Eucharist is a major source of Thomas's ecclesiological thinking.

[73] In Thomas's view of the Church, which is at once moral, sacramental (Eucharistic), pneumatological, and theocentric, first place belongs to the grace of the Holy Spirit that incorporates into Christ (cf. especially *ST* I–II, q. 106, a. 1; *ST* III, q. 8, a. 3). See Yves Congar, "L'idée de l'Église chez saint Thomas d'Aquin," in *Esquisse du mystère de l'Église* (Paris: Cerf, 1941), 59–91. The theme of inner penance as *res et sacramentum* finds its full meaning within this vision of the Church as a body of faith and charity whose soul is the Holy Spirit.

the Church. But he distinguishes more sharply these two aspects of penance: (1) sacrament that reconciles with God; and (2) sacrament of the Church.[74] This distinction crystallizes in the question of the scope of the "power of the keys" exercised by the Church's ministers. In his function of "descending mediation," the priest has the power to grant reconciliation with the Church; such is the goal that is proportionate to his status as human minister. But in his function of "ascending mediation" (reconciliation with God), the priest can only *ask for* the grace on behalf of the sinner. This is how St. Bonaventure explains the alternation of words that beseech and words that indicate a fact in the rite of absolution. Thus, St. Bonaventure goes on, if we wish to speak properly, we must say that the power of the keys confided to the Church *does not go so far as the suppression of the fault* since it reaches this only by way of prayer and petition *(per modum deprecantis)*, while it actually extends to reconciliation with the Church, in regard to which it is in the position of being able to share *(per modum impertientis)*. Consequently, if a priest absolves a penitent, it is because he judges that God has first of all absolved him of his fault; only God can absolve. The priest's absolution *presupposes* divine forgiveness.[75]

As we have seen, St. Thomas's position veers in another direction. Thanks to his notion of instrumental causality, he can assign a "divine effect" to the action of the penitent and the priest without undermining God's prerogatives ("principal cause"). Through the personal cooperation of the penitent and by the action of Christ working through the minister, the fault that attacked the divine friendship is forgiven. He therefore gives full weight to the personal action of the penitent and to the Church's mediation: The sacramental sign (the penitent's acts and the priest's absolution), with inner penance, is the *(instrumental) cause* of the remission of sins.[76] Given this fact, he no longer has to distinguish between the realm of reconciliation with the Church and that of reconciliation with God in the remission of fault *(culpa)*. In the same sense he will hold firmly to the indicative formula of absolution, since the sacrament effects what it signifies: "I absolve you."[77]

---

[74] St. Bonaventure, IV *Sent.*, dist. 22, a. 2, q. 2: The three elements of the sacrament's makeup *(sacramentum, res et sacramentum, res)* are distributed successively under these two aspects.

[75] St. Bonaventure, IV *Sent.*, dist. 18, pars 1, a. 2, q. 1; cf. ad 3: The priest can obtain grace for the sinner, but he does not give it: Absolution from guilt belongs only to God. This concept will persist in the Scotist theory of the divine "pact."

[76] St. Thomas, *De forma absolutionis,* chap. 2,11 (Leonine edition, vol. 40 C, 37); *ST* III, q. 84, a. 1, ad 3; cf. q. 62, a. 1.

[77] *ST* III, q. 84, a. 3; the meaning *(perfectior expositio)* is: "Ego te absolvo, idest, sacramentum absolutionis tibi impendo" (ibid., ad 5).

3. Conclusion

St. Thomas's thought is therefore distinguished by his taking into account the personal action of the penitent in all its depth, together with the minister's action, to obtain efficaciously the remission of sins and, through this, a return to divine friendship in the bosom of the Church. Of this unique Christian penance, contrition, called forth by charity, is the heart: Penance is a conversion of love, an inner transformation, and reconciliation is a *gift of love.* Hence, in the sacramental action, the penitent's person and ecclesial mediation converge in a profound unity. For Thomas Aquinas, this is what is at stake in inner penance as *res et sacramentum.*

According to Thomas Aquinas—and this is another benefit of his thought—inner penance and contrition entail an internal relationship with the ministry of the Church and with Eucharistic communion, that is, the communion of the Church. We have seen that Rahner, while making reconciliation with the Church the *res et sacramentum* of penance, sought to maintain the merits of the Thomistic doctrine of contrition. We can now see how this doctrine of contrition is entirely capable of taking on the ecclesial dimension of the *res et sacramentum* of penance, which historical studies have restored to value. Thomas himself points us in the direction of understanding the *res et sacramentum* of penance as a *personal engagement* ("inner penance") grasped in the ecclesial action and recognized or ratified by the Church, *so that it implies readmission to the public worship of the Church.* Such is the *res et sacramentum* of penance.[78] Accordingly, reconciliation with the Church is the Church's recognition of the penitent's inner conversion to God. We have seen that this understanding has the advantage of respecting the proper framework of the *res et sacramentum.* But, no matter if we keep this framework in all its details, it especially allows us to understand reconciliation with the Church as part of the renewal of life to which the Gospel calls the disciples of Christ and which marks the concrete participation in the communion of grace that the Church is. The Thomistic doctrine of contrition and the understanding of the *res et sacramentum* of penance truly aims at this depth of divine friendship of which the Church is the sacrament.

---

78 C. E. O'Neill, "Les Sacrements," 497. The author points out further—but that goes beyond our subject—that such an understanding can provide an interpretation suggestive of "devotional confession" and also clarifies the doctrine of indulgences ("contrition granted ecclesial aid").

CHAPTER 7

A Note on St. Thomas and the Eastern Fathers

THE CONFRONTATION between the thought of St. Thomas Aquinas and the doctrines issuing from Eastern Orthodoxy runs through the history of Thomism, most often in the form of a controversy.[1] This confrontation often unfolds in two contradictory ways. For certain theologians, the thought of St. Thomas offers a solid foundation for deepening doctrinal union with the East.[2] Other theologians judge that the future of theological dialogue between Catholics and Orthodox will happen through the withdrawal or disappearance of Thomism, perceived exclusively as an obstacle to ecumenical progress.[3] In reality, recent research shows that there is no irreducible opposition between the thought of St. Thomas and the Orthodox tradition such as one finds, for example, in Maximus the Confessor—despite an important *difference of perspective* in the manner of considering the mystery of God and his relation to the world (this difference illustrates well the process of estrangement between the East and West): The two approaches may reveal a profound fundamental convergence.[4]

---

1 Translation by Jennifer Harms and Fr. John Baptist Ku, OP. A former version of this essay appeared in French: "Saint Thomas d'Aquin et l'Orient chrétien," *Nova et Vetera* (French) 74/4 (1999) 19–36.

2 See, for instance, Marie-Joseph Le Guillou, *Préface* to Juan Miguel Garrigues, *Maxime le Confesseur: La charité, avenir divin de l'homme* (Paris: Beauchesne, 1976), 7.

3 Jean-Claude Larchet, "La Question du Filioque," *Le Messager Orthodoxe* 129 (1997/2): 3–58. For this reason, Larchet rejoices in "the loss of influence of Thomist theology in the course of the last decades," as offering a new hope for the doctrinal rapprochement of the West and the East (p. 58).

4 See the remarkable book of Antoine Lévy, *Le créé et l'incréé chez S. Maxime le Confesseur et S. Thomas d'Aquin: Aux sources de la querelle palamienne* (Paris: Vrin,

In trying to clarify the question somewhat, it is worth investigating first of all St. Thomas himself, in order to discern the relationship that his theological reflection establishes with Eastern traditions. The "dialogue" of St. Thomas with the Christian East covers a large area that touches on diverse domains. This chapter offers only a brief survey of the relationship that St. Thomas's theology establishes with the Eastern Fathers, that is, with the Eastern Christian authors of Antiquity.

1. The Active Interest in Greek Patristic Writings

St. Thomas paid great attention to the Greek Fathers.[5] His interest surpasses that of most of his Latin contemporaries working in the West.[6] This is all the more remarkable because St. Thomas, aside from a few rudimentary expressions, did not know Greek. Lacking therefore an immediate access to Greek texts, he employed other means. The first of these consisted in recourse to available Latin translations. This is how, for example, from the time of his *Catena in Matthaeum* and *Summa contra Gentiles* forward, St. Thomas elaborated his Christology by means of a direct, firsthand reading of the *Acts* of the Councils of Ephesus and Chalcedon in the Latin collection of conciliar texts usually known as the *Collectio Casinensis* (this name comes from a manuscript of Monte Cassino, though St. Thomas might have consulted another manuscript of the same text).[7] In the same way, he renewed Latin theology by his reading of the *Acts* of the Second Council of Constantinople, without limiting himself to the canons of this fifth ecumenical council. This knowledge visibly makes its mark in the structure of St. Thomas's Christology, which issues from the doctrine of these councils. Martin Morard was able to show that the use of

---

2006); cf. Anna N. Williams, *The Ground of Union: Deification in Aquinas and Palamas* (Oxford: Oxford University Press, 1999).

5 Rosario Scognamiglio, "Presenza dei Padri Greci in S. Tommaso," in *Istituto San Tommaso: Studi 1995*, ed. Dietrich Lorenz and Stefano Serafini (Rome: Pontificia Università San Tommaso d'Aquino, 1995), 17–44.

6 It is necessary to specify: *in the West.* Latin theologians, notably Dominicans and Franciscans, were also present in the East and showed a deep interest in the Greek Fathers; such interest was supported by their knowledge of the Greek language and of Byzantine theology. Note that the concern for a better understanding of Eastern thought was shared by many other contemporary authors in the West; as an example within the Dominican Order, see Humbert of Romans's *Opus Tripartitum*, in *Fasciculus Rerum Expetendarum et Fugiendarum Prout ab Orthuino Gratio Presbytero editus est*, ed. Edward Brown (London: Chiswell, 1690), 185–228.

7 On the *Collectio Casinensis* and its use by St. Thomas, see the essential study of Martin Morard, "Thomas d'Aquin lecteur des conciles," *Archivum Franciscanum Historicum* 98 (2005): 211–365, at 218–29 and 344–51.

the *Acts* of Constantinople II, which furnished Aquinas with a dossier important for apprehending the stakes of Nestorianism in particular, designates St. Thomas as a pioneer: He was the first Latin Scholastic truly to exploit Constantinople II in Christology and in exegesis.[8] His knowledge of the Third Council of Constantinople is no less evident.[9]

Aside from the available translations he was able to procure, St. Thomas employed a second means, as he indicates himself in the dedication at the head of his patristic *Catena* on the Gospel of Mark: "In order that the exposition of the saints [the Fathers] may be more complete and continuous, I have had translated into Latin some of the commentaries of the Greek Doctors, and I have inserted several passages *(plura)* of these commentaries among the commentaries of the Latin Fathers."[10] The result is impressive and deserves to be recalled: In this work of patristic compilation, we count fifty-seven Greek authors (of whom some, such as Theophylactus, were almost unknown in the West before their use by St. Thomas) in comparison to twenty-two Latin authors.[11]

This permits us to note two characteristics of the theological activity of St. Thomas. First, the exegesis and commentaries of St. Thomas Aquinas are nourished as much by the Greek Fathers as by the riches of the Latin West. In a conscious and explicit way, St. Thomas does not intend to compose only a Latin theology, but a Christian "ecumenical" theology, if one may so name it, which would fully integrate the contribution of the Eastern Fathers into the heart of the Catholic patrimony. To

8 Martin Morard, "Une source de saint Thomas d'Aquin: le deuxième concile de Constantinople (553)," *Revue des Sciences Philosophiques et Théologiques* 81 (1997): 21–56; this most instructive study shows what St. Thomas owes to the Acts of this council. See Martin Morard, "Thomas d'Aquin lecteur des conciles," 297–305.

9 See St. Thomas, *ST* III, q. 18 and q. 19. References to Constantinople III appear in Aquinas's late works, from the time of 1271; cf. Martin Morard, "Thomas d'Aquin lecteur des conciles," 305–16. See Jean-Pierre Torrell in St. Thomas d'Aquin, *Somme théologique: Le Verbe incarné,* vol. 3: 3a, *Questions 16–26* (Paris: Cerf, 2002), 422–32.

10 St. Thomas, *Catena in Marcum, Epistola dedicatoria* (Marietti edition, vol. 1, 429): "Et ut magis integra et continua praedicta sanctorum expositio redderetur, quasdam expositiones Doctorum graecorum in latinum feci transferri, ex quibus plura expositionibus latinorum Doctorum interserui." The last phrase suggests that Aquinas had translated more Greek texts than he used in his *Catena aurea.*

11 Jean-Pierre Torrell, *Saint Thomas Aquinas,* vol. 1: *The Person and His Work,* trans. Robert Royal (Washington, DC: Catholic University of America Press, 1996, 2005), 139; cf. Carmelo G. Conticello, "San Tommaso ed i Padri: La Catena aurea super Ioannem," *Archives d'histoire doctrinale et littéraire du moyen âge* 57 (1990): 31–92.

designate the Eastern Fathers, St. Thomas sometimes uses the expression "the Doctors of the Greeks" *(doctores graecorum)*, especially when he wants to designate the Fathers recognized as such by the Byzantine theologians.[12] But the Greek Fathers are not only Doctors of Eastern Christianity: They are Fathers of the whole Church *(doctores Ecclesiae)*,[13] they are "*our* doctors" *(doctores nostri)*.[14] Secondly, St. Thomas is an *active initiator*, a promoter of this Latin rediscovery of the Eastern patrimony: He ordered translations, and it seems that he even ordered more translations than he directly used.

2. Principal Greek Authors

Who were the principal Greek patristic sources of St. Thomas? Before addressing their theological content, it is useful to note first of all the material presence of the Greek Fathers in Aquinas's work, which in itself reveals the high regard he had for the Eastern heritage.[15] If we hold ourselves to direct citations, first place goes to St. John Chrysostom, many of whose works St. Thomas uses, particularly the *Homilies on the Gospel of Matthew* and *On John*. St. John Chrysostom is, after St. Augustine, the Father of the Church cited most abundantly by St. Thomas (before St. Jerome, St. Ambrose, or St. Gregory the Great, who nevertheless are counted among the major sources of the Latin West). It is principally through him that the patristic exegesis of the "school" of Antioch influenced St. Thomas. It is necessary to observe in this regard that the Eastern Father most employed by St. Thomas is not an Alexandrian, despite the undeniable affinities of St. Thomas's thought with the Alexandrian patristic tradition.

One is not surprised to find in second place (but only in second place) Pseudo-Dionysius the Areopagite, the famous neo-Platonist Christian, the study of whom was already flourishing in Paris before St. Thomas, and on whose work St. Albert the Great undertook to write a complete commentary. St. Thomas himself wrote a commentary on Pseudo-Dionysius's treatise on the *Divine Names* and abundantly exploited his other works *(The Celestial Hierarchy, The Ecclesiastical Hierarchy, Letters)*. He is a major source of the neo-Platonism in St. Thomas, of apophaticism in our access to the mystery of God, and also of a great number of practices and patristic doctrines, notably in the liturgical and sacramental realm. It is thanks to Dionysius, for

12 See, for example, *SCG* IV, ch. 24 (#3609).

13 Ibid.

14 *De potentia*, q. 10, a. 2.

15 For the statistical data, taken from the *Index thomisticus*, see Leo J. Elders, "Santo Tomás de Aquino y los Padres de la Iglesia," *Doctor Communis* 48 (1995): 55–80 (detailed statistical table on 66).

example, that St. Thomas understood that between the priest and the bishop there is a distinction not only of jurisdiction but of order.[16]

Next in our ranking of Eastern authors, perhaps a surprise, we find Origen, the only Greek Christian author prior to the Council of Nicaea who receives great attention from St. Thomas.[17] Of Origen, St. Thomas knows and makes particular use of *On First Principles* (in Rufinus's translation) and the *Commentary on St. John.* St. Thomas has recourse to Origen principally in his exegetical works; he receives him, however, in a critical way when he detects in his works theologically erroneous statements (the origin of souls, universal reconciliation at the end of time) or a philosophical heritage that puts the faith in danger: Because of the ambiguities of his attachment to a Platonic conception of hypostases with "graded" existence, Origen is considered by St. Thomas, following Epiphanius of Salamis and St. Jerome, as the "father of Arius."[18] This did not stop him from often retaining the "mystical" exegesis of Origen, which constitutes an important source of St. Thomas's practice of the spiritual senses of Scripture.

After Chrysostom, Pseudo-Dionysius, and Origen, St. John Damascene occupies a central position in the library of St. Thomas; the Damascene could be included among the Eastern (pre-)Scholastic theologians, but in reality he represents, for the East as for the West, a synthesis of Greek patristic theology (the councils, Gregory Nazianzen and Gregory of Nyssa, Cyril of Alexandria, Leontius of Byzantium, Maximus the Confessor, without forgetting the importance of Nemesius of Emesa for the theology of creation and anthropology). In St. John Damascene, St. Thomas draws principally from the *Exposition of the Faith*, the third part of his great *Fount of Knowledge.* The influence of the Damascene is particularly apparent in the treatise on the incarnation of the Word, and it often guides St. Thomas's reflection on particular themes, as one can see, for example, in the question on the adoration of Christ and the veneration of icons.[19] In

---

16 For St. Thomas, however, this distinction of *ordo* is limited to the relation of the bishop to the mystical Body of Christ that is the Church. Even if the doctrine of the three degrees of orders (episcopate, presbyterate, and diaconate) is not fully integrated, St. Thomas perceived here an important aspect of patristic and Eastern ecclesiology. See Joseph Lécuyer, "Les étapes de l'enseignement thomiste sur l'épiscopat," *Revue Thomiste* 57 (1957): 29–52.

17 Numerous texts of Origen circulated in the Middle Ages, notably in exegetical *Catenae.* But the fact remains remarkable: The name of Origen appears approximately 1,094 times in the work of St. Thomas. This represents a material presence almost equal to that of St. Ambrose of Milan, and greater than that of St. Hilary of Poitiers, for example.

18 *Super Boetium de Trinitate,* q. 3, a. 4 (Leonine edition, vol. 50, 116).

19 *ST* III, q. 25. This question offers a striking example of the influence of St. John Damascene, who constitutes St. Thomas's principal source here.

the material order of explicit citations by St. Thomas, one observes next the presence of St. Cyril of Alexandria, St. Basil of Caesarea, St. Athanasius, St. Gregory of Nyssa, Eusebius of Caesarea, St. Gregory Nazianzen, and so forth.

Overall, St. John Chrysostom is the Greek Father most employed by St. Thomas in his exegetical works. The importance of Chrysostom, with whom St. Thomas read Scripture, cannot be overestimated; in certain works (*Catena* on Matthew and Mark) the patriarch of Constantinople prevails even over the bishop of Hippo. This is a remarkable fact in the literature of Latin theology in the thirteenth century. However, concerning reflections organized in a synthetic manner, it is to St. John Damascene that St. Thomas turns the most often; such is the case, for example, in the dogmatic treatises on the Trinity and on Christ in the *Summa theologiae.*

The indications given up to this point show the presence of the Greek Fathers on a general level, certainly suggestive, but for the most part of a material order. When one considers the theological content, one must attest that this presence does not lose its importance. Some examples will permit us to illustrate and to better grasp the influence of the Greek Fathers in the theology of St. Thomas.

3. Three Examples of Influence

The significance of a theological source is not limited to its singular occurrence, nor to its original content in the form of a citation. It takes on all its meaning in the doctrinal exposition that gives it value. One can in effect envision St. Thomas's theological sources in two ways. On one level, one can consider the original content of a cited text, that is, the particular thought of the author cited or invoked by St. Thomas. On a second and more profound level, one must consider the use that St. Thomas makes of this author, the interpretation that he gives—that is, what the theological source *becomes* when it enters into the body of St. Thomas's reflection. In order to designate this second level, one could speak of an "elaborated" or "extended" influence. In any case, the significance of a theological source (especially concerning the Fathers of the Church) is not limited to the material aspect of a citation. Thus, since theological sources draw their whole meaning from the heart of the doctrinal elaboration that puts them to use (the second level), I propose to consider here some examples of "extended" influence.

The Concept of "Instrument"

The concept of *instrument* in Christology offers without doubt one of the best illustrations of such extended influence. It is a veritable key to Christology and to the doctrine of salvation in the thought of St. Thomas, who regards the humanity of Christ as "the instrument of his divinity." St. Thomas explicitly develops this doctrine in making reference to St. John Damascene, whom he cites regularly on this subject: "The flesh of Christ is the organ *(organon)* of his divinity."[20] This teaching is derived from St. Cyril of Alexandria and from St. Athanasius of Alexandria, who was one of the first to make frequent use of it in Christology.[21] In developing this theme of the humanity of Christ as instrument of his divinity, St. Thomas indicates that the human nature of Christ possesses a proper action, distinct from the act of the divine nature (conforming to the dogma formulated by the Third Council of Constantinople): In the person of the incarnate Word, the divine nature uses the human nature in order to procure our salvation, in a manner comparable to that by which an agent uses an instrument.

The concept of "instrument" *(instrumentum, organum, organon)*, in such a context, should be understood in an analogical manner: St. Thomas makes

20 John Damascene, *De fide orthodoxa,* book III, ch. 15, cited, for example, in *ST* III, q. 2, a. 6, arg. 4; q. 7, a. 1, arg. 3; q. 19, a. 1; q. 48, a. 6, and so on. The context of this affirmation, in the particular passage of St. John Damascene, is the theandric operation of Christ that procures salvation for us, that is, the divine and human actions that belong to Christ by virtue of his two natures. St. John Damascene, *De fide orthodoxa: Versions of Burgundio and Cerbanus,* ed. Eligius M. Buytaert (Louvain: E. Nauwelaerts; Paderborn: Schöningh, 1955), 228–43. For this concept in St. Thomas, see Jean-Pierre Torrell, *Saint Thomas Aquinas,* vol. 2: *Spiritual Master,* trans. Robert Royal (Washington, DC: Catholic University of America Press, 2003), 126–31; idem, "La causalité salvifique de la résurrection du Christ selon saint Thomas," *Revue Thomiste* 96 (1996): 179–208; Eduardo M. Taussig, *La humanidad de Cristo como instrumento según Santo Tomás de Aquino* (Rome: Pontificia Università San Tommaso, 1990); Elio Monteleone, *L'umanità di Cristo "strumento della divinità": Attualità ed evoluzione del pensiero di Tommaso d'Aquino* (Acireale, 1999); Paul G. Crowley, "*Instrumentum divinitatis* in Thomas Aquinas: Recovering the Divinity of Christ," *Theological Studies* 52 (1991): 451–75; Theophil Tschipke, *L'humanité du Christ comme instrument de salut de la divinité* (Fribourg: Academic Press, 2003).

21 For a survey of the patristic teaching, see T. Tschipke, *L'humanité du Christ,* 35–85. See, for example, St. Athanasius, *On the Incarnation,* trans. a Religious of CSMV. (Crestwood, NY: St. Vladimir's Orthodox Theological Seminary, 1993), §8, 34: "[The Word] prepared this body in the Virgin as a temple for himself, and took it for his very own, as the instrument through which he was known and in which he dwelt." We encounter here two major themes of the Alexandrian Christology that St. Thomas develops: substantial (hypostatic) appropriation, and the humanity-instrument. "The Word of God thus acted consistently in assuming a body and using a human instrument to vitalise the body" (St. Athanasius, *On the Incarnation,* §45, 82).

every effort to free it from any mechanical or material representation. He explains that the humanity of Christ constitutes a completely unique instrument, since it is a matter of a humanity that is *living*, *free*, and *united* to the divine nature in the person of the Word. But in speaking of an instrument, one can show that under the influence of the divine nature, the human nature of Christ (his human act) collaborates with his divine action on our behalf, and that the humanity of Christ thus contributes in a real way to procuring our salvation, by giving its own mark to our salvation, as an instrument leaves its mark on the effect it procures. In technical terms, St. Thomas explains that the humanity of Christ is the "instrumental efficient cause" of grace, of the forgiveness of sins, of the divinization of human beings—in brief, of all that we mean by the word "salvation." It is *efficient cause* because it is a truly effectual source of our new life; it is *instrumental*, because it procures this properly divine effect through the motion of the divine nature and by participation in the divine operation.

This exposition of the concept of instrument presupposes a very lively perception of the unity without confusion of God and man in Christ. The understanding of the Eucharist illustrates this well: By our communion in the Body and Blood of Christ, we receive the vivifying power with which the humanity of Christ is endowed and which it transmits, which it extends to us, by virtue of its union with the divinity of the Word. With St. Cyril of Alexandria, St. Thomas explains that "God's life-giving Word by uniting himself with his own flesh, made it to be productive of life. And so it was right that he should be united somehow with our bodies through his sacred flesh and precious blood, which we receive as a life-giving blessing in the bread and wine."[22]

This doctrine, which St. Thomas did not possess at the beginning of his career and which progressively matured in his reflection, permits him to set forth two central realities. First, it permits him to explain that a created reality, which the humanity of Christ is, is truly the effectual source of salvation: Such a created reality can thus be a co-principle of the properly (exclusively) divine effects of salvation and grace. God alone can grant salvation and grace; nevertheless, in the manner of an instrument, the humanity of Christ *participates effectively* in the granting of salvation, in "producing" it (instrumental efficient cause). This gives an exceptional value to the human action of Jesus in the gift of salvation to men. It is the key to St. Thomas's interpretation of our salvation by the passion of Christ on the Cross.[23] But St. Thomas applies this doctrine equally to *all the acts*

---

22 *ST* III, q. 79, a. 1. This passage of St. Cyril is more extensively cited by Thomas in the *Catena in Lucam* 22:19 (Marietti edition, vol. 2, 286); cf. St. Cyril, *In Lucam* 22:19 (PG 72, 907–12).

23 *ST* III, q. 48, a. 6.

in the life of Christ: his passion, but also his resurrection, his ascension, and in a general way all that Christ lived in his flesh.[24]

In a similar manner, St. Thomas applies this concept of instrument (instrumental efficient cause) to the sacraments, in an understanding of sacraments that no theologian before him had proposed in such a precise manner, and that would not be adopted by some other schools. Bonaventurian theology, for example, could hardly accept that a created reality (the sacrament) be *effectively* an imparting cause of grace. In contrast, for St. Thomas in his mature works, not only is the sacrament a disposition to the grace that God grants by virtue of a pact or promise, but the sacrament effectively *causes* the grace in its role as instrument. The difference does not concern the reality of the grace procured *ex opere operato*, but rather it concerns the means of accounting for the proper influence of the sacrament. It is the value of the created reality assumed into the divine order that is at stake here. This teaching continues to possess great importance in the doctrine of the sacraments, for example as regards the sacrament of penance. For St. Bonaventure, the priest who absolves has the power to reconcile efficaciously to the Church (this is the effect proportionate to the activity of a created cause) and to ask for grace for the sinner, but the minister does not exercise the role of effective giver of grace (God alone reconciles the sinner to God); this role the minister exercises only as concerns reconciliation with the Church. St. Thomas, for his part, can assign a "divine effect" to the action of the minister and also to that of the penitent, thanks to his concept of instrumental causality, and he can therefore unite in the same act reconciliation with God and reconciliation with the Church.[25] It is a matter, here again, of a remarkable valuation of man's collaboration with the divine work.

The second important consequence is the following: For St. Thomas, all grace, all divinization, is Christic; all life of communion with God and of fraternal charity bears the imprint of the humanity of Christ, which deploys its influence therein. This is the reason why grace renders us similar to Christ and conforms us to him, in the manner by which an effect bears and transmits the mark of the instrument by which it was procured. This doctrine, one notes, clarifies in an exceptional way our knowledge of the mystery of Christ and the sacraments. In the same way it can offer the best path to a deeper penetration of current questions on the Christian

---

24 Ibid.: "All Christ's actions and sufferings operate instrumentally in virtue of his Godhead for the salvation of men." See in particular *ST* III, q. 56 (resurrection) and q. 57, a. 6 (ascension).

25 See chapter six in this volume, "Reconciliation with the Church and Interior Penance: The Contribution of Thomas Aquinas on the Question of the *Res et Sacramentum* of Penance."

theology of religions, notably when one reflects on the unique salvific value of the humanity of Christ, in its singularity and historical integrity. This is a key to Christology that St. Thomas owes to his study of St. John Damascene and to the theme of the *organon* in the work of the Alexandrian Fathers, which he developed in an original way with the Aristotelian philosophical tools of causality.

The Hypostatic Union

The mode of union of God and man in Christ constitutes a central question of the speculative theology of St. Thomas. This question appears in the *Summa theologiae* immediately after that of the fittingness of the Incarnation at the beginning of the *Tertia Pars*: Its results determine the whole of Christology. It is necessary first of all to note that, among the patristic sources invoked in this question of capital importance, one observes twice as many Greek authors as Latins, St. John Damascene being the most often invoked (twice as often as Augustine). Reading the question does not contradict these material indications: St. Thomas does not provide a Latin theology here, but theology *tout court*, indeed truly more Greek than Latin if one considers its inspiration. Who are the Greek patristic sources? John Damascene first of all, then Cyril of Alexandria (Council of Ephesus) and the councils of Chalcedon and Constantinople II, as well as St. Gregory Nazianzen. In this list, the predominant role goes to the Christology of St. Cyril, be it in the words of the Alexandrian himself or in its later elaboration at Constantinople II and by St. John Damascene.

One can observe then that the structure of St. Thomas's Christology, governed by the study of the mode of union of humanity and divinity in Christ, is fundamentally a Greek structure—more precisely that of St. Cyril of Alexandria—but is deepened and expanded, so as to be able to integrate the Latin tradition (St. Augustine, St. Leo, with the special emphasis they put on the full integrity of Christ's human nature).[26] Of course, the teaching of the Councils (Ephesus, Chalcedon, Constantinople II, and Constantinople III) plays a determining role. Just as Cyril has a very strong sense of the unity of the person or hypostasis of Christ, so does St. Thomas: His Christology, against all Nestorianism, starts with the person or hypostasis of the Word, who unites to himself a human nature. Cyril conceives the union according to the hypostasis as a substantial *appropriation* by which the Word

---

26 Ciriaco Scanzillo, "Influssi di S. Cirillo d'Alessandria nella Cristologia di S. Tommaso," in *Tommaso d'Aquino nel suo settimo centenario*, vol. 4: *Problemi di teologia* (Naples: Edizioni Domenicane Italiane, 1976), 187–220. The fundamental study on the Greek Fathers in St. Thomas's Christology is, still today, that of Ignaz Backes, *Die Christologie des hl. Thomas von Aquin und die griechischen Kirchenväter* (Paderborn: Schöningh, 1931).

makes humanity his own; St. Thomas follows him even in this vocabulary.[27] For St. Cyril, the Word incarnate acts by his own Spirit, which he poured out in his humanity; this is a theme dear to Cyril, as the ninth anathema added to his third letter to Nestorius notably testifies;[28] likewise for St. Thomas the fullness of grace of Christ flows from the action of the Spirit, which the Word himself sends to his humanity.[29]

One could easily multiply examples. Thus, at the beginning of his career, St. Thomas noted that some theologians conceived of the incarnation of the Word as follows: A man, composed of a soul and a body, was assumed by the Word from the first instant of his conception, in such a way that by this union the Word became man. This is the famous theory of *homo assumptus*, common in the Antiochene theology (Theodore of Mopsuestia) from which Nestorius issued and which, before reappearing in the twentieth century, likewise enjoyed some favor among some early medieval Latin Scholastics.[30] This Christological theory of *homo assumptus* is not the one that St. Thomas follows, but in his *Commentary on the Sentences* he specifies, like most of his contemporaries (St. Bonaventure, for example), that "it is not heretical."[31] From the *Summa contra Gentiles* onward, his

27 *SCG* IV, ch. 41 (#3794): "Let the Word be set down as subsisting in a human nature as in one made his very own *(in sibi propria facta)* by the Incarnation; and in consequence that body is truly the body of the Word of God, and the soul in like manner, and the Word of God is truly man" (trans. Charles J. O'Neil [Notre Dame, IN: University of Notre Dame Press, 1975], 195). On this reprising of the theme of *oikeiôsis* from the Alexandrian Fathers by St. Thomas, see Herman M. Diepen, *La théologie de l'Emmanuel* (Paris: Desclée de Brouwer, 1960), 3–47; the historical survey leads Diepen to conclude: "Saint Thomas brings us back to our point of departure, Saint Cyril of Alexandria and his doctrine of the Christological *appropriation*" (47). Cyril furnishes Thomas with the foundation of his speculative Christology.

28 The theme of the "proper Spirit" (the Holy Spirit is Christ's own Spirit) is connected to the lively perception of the unity of Christ by St. Cyril; his doctrinal adversaries are not mistaken there; see André de Halleux, *Patrologie et œcuménisme: Recueil d'études* (Leuven: University Press/Peeters, 1990), 367–95: "Cyrille, Théodoret et le *Filioque*." Although here it is a matter of Christology and not the Trinitarian question of the procession of the Holy Spirit, which becomes a debate only much later, we are nonetheless at the source of divergent views regarding the relationship between Christ and the Spirit that are not without influence on the question of the eternal procession of the Holy Spirit.

29 Cf. *ST* III, q. 7, a. 13: The mission of the Son is presupposed to the mission of the Spirit; the plenitude of grace in Christ, of which the principle is the Holy Spirit, results from the union of the humanity of Christ to his divinity.

30 For a description of this theory, see *ST* III, q. 2, a. 6.

31 III *Sent.*, dist. 6, q. 1, a. 2 (ed. Maria Fabianus Moos [Paris: Lethielleux,1933], 230). At stake is the first opinion regarding the mode of union, set forth by Peter Lombard. On this first teaching of St. Thomas and the other texts on this question,

position is quite different: This theory of the incarnation, in the judgment of St. Thomas, is not Catholic because it definitively conceives of the humanity of Jesus as a human being endowed with a proper hypostasis or subsistence besides the Word, which would constitute two supposits in Christ: This theory of the *homo assumptus* falls necessarily under the error of Nestorius.[32] It is not difficult to identify the reason for this change: St. Thomas noticed the similarity of this doctrine with that of Nestorius in reading the Acts of Ephesus, especially anathemas 2, 4, and 8 of St. Cyril, which he cites on the subject. The judgment is just as clear-cut in the *Summa theologiae*, which advances another source, testifying once again to the Greek documentation of St. Thomas: This Christological theory of the *homo assumptus* (two hypostases or subsistences in one person) was condemned by the Fathers at the second Council of Constantinople. St. Thomas has recourse here to the Council's examination of the writings of Theodore of Mopsuestia (the controversy on the "Three Chapters"). For St. Thomas, it is a matter of a heresy that benefited for too long among Latin theologians from the forgetting of the ancient Councils.[33]

The Literal Senses of Sacred Scripture

Numerous examples could illustrate still further the authority that St. Thomas attributed to the Greek Fathers. One concerning the plurality of the literal senses of Scripture does not perhaps constitute a theological question of primary importance, but it reveals very well the impact of patristic theology on St. Thomas's hermeneutics. Can one same passage of Scripture contain many literal senses? No one denies the plurality of the spiritual senses that display the Christological, ecclesiological, moral, and eschatological riches of Scripture; it is a matter rather of the first sense intended by the biblical author, that is, of the literal sense that grounds the spiritual senses. The question gave rise to numerous studies. Certain texts of St. Thomas would quite clearly suggest a positive response; but such a response was rejected by other theologians in the name of St. Thomas's own theological project: A plurality of literal senses would weaken the solidity of scriptural doctrine, notably in dogmatic material.[34] Before

---

see Francis Ruello, *La christologie de S. Thomas d'Aquin* (Paris: Beauchesne,1987), 102–21 and 383–94; Hyacinthe Dondaine, "Qualifications dogmatiques de la théorie de l'Assumptus-homo dans les oeuvres de S. Thomas," *Revue des Sciences Philosophiques et Théologiques* 30 (1941–42): 163–68.

32 *SCG* IV, ch. 38.

33 *ST* III, q. 2, a. 3 and a. 6; see the disputed question *De unione Verbi incarnati*, a. 2; and above, footnote 8.

34 An overview of the principal texts of St. Thomas and of the studies that have been devoted to them can be found in Mark F. Johnson, "Another Look at the Plurality of the Literal Sense," *Medieval Philosophy and Theology* 2 (1992): 117–41.

developing the theory in questions specially dedicated to the normative value of different authorities in theology, St. Thomas meets this problem in his practice of biblical interpretation. The recognition of a plurality of literal senses comes from his use of patristic exegesis, and especially from the equal authority he assigns to Greek and Latin Fathers.

The most extensive discussion appears in the examination of the question of whether the creation of formless matter preceded the creation of things in time. This question has to do with the exegesis of the first verses of Genesis, where it is written that "the earth was without form and void" (Gn 1:2) before God said, "Let there be" (Gn 1:3ff.).[35] Was there then an earth or matter without form ("formless") before God created things in their distinction and in their proper species? Aquinas discusses two divergent exegeses. Following St. Augustine, God created all things simultaneously; there is no temporal priority between the creation of "formless" matter and the making of distinct creatures, but only a priority of reason or of nature.[36] The motive behind this view is simple: Matter cannot exist concretely without a form that allows it to exist and to be this or that; "formless matter" has no existence. For his part, St. Basil of Caesarea rejects this type of philosophical exegesis, which he could have known through the Alexandrians: For Basil, the succession of events narrated in the first chapter of Genesis possesses a temporal reality; the creation of formless matter preceded the creation of each distinct thing in time. Formless matter, in the biblical text, does not signify a total absence of form, but rather a formed matter that does not yet possess its full completion and beauty.[37]

The opinion of St. Thomas, like that of his master St. Albert, leans clearly toward Augustine's solution, more conformed to reason. Even so, he refuses to exclude the solution of St. Basil, because of the authority that he attributes to the Cappadocian Father, and he puts it on the same level as that of Augustine. But if the two exegeses are possible, must one conclude that the theologian cannot determine the literal sense of this passage? It is here that the principle of interpretation developed by St. Thomas

[35] *De potentia*, q. 4, a. 1.

[36] St. Augustine, *De Genesi ad litteram* I,15,29. Cf. St. Thomas, *De potentia*, q. 4, a. 1, arg. 1.

[37] St. Basil, *In Hexaemeron* II,1 (PG 29, 29). Along with St. Basil, Aquinas mentions St. John Chrysostom and St. Ambrose (see *ST* I, q. 66, a. 1). In *De potentia*, q. 4, a. 1, he specifies: "Et hoc intellexit magnus Basilius, Gregorius et sequaces eorum"; it is not clear to which "Gregory" St. Thomas refers here: Was he thinking of St. Gregory of Nyssa (cf. *In Hexaemeron*, PG 44, 80), or of St. Gregory Nazianzen (as the Marietti edition suggests), or of St. Gregory the Great? In any case, Aquinas considers St. Basil as the leading author for such an interpretation, as the *De potentia* shows.

intervenes: "Every truth that can be adapted to the sacred text in accordance with the context, is the sense of Holy Scripture."[38]

Thus St. Thomas is brought to recognize that Scripture can bear many senses under a single "letter." It is manifestly a matter of the literal sense, since Thomas considers here the sense that corresponds to the intention of the author and that permits the defense of the truth, which belongs properly only to the literal sense. We find ourselves then in the presence of two literal senses; if one thinks that the redactor of Genesis could not have had these two senses in mind, the objection does not bother St. Thomas: "Even if commentators [the Fathers] adapt certain truths to the sacred text that were not understood by the author, without doubt the Holy Spirit understood them, since he is the principal author of Holy Scripture."[39] This thesis illustrates the principle that St. Thomas receives from the Fathers: "It is by the same Spirit that the Scriptures were written and interpreted."[40] If the theologian receives this double sense of Genesis 1:2ff., it is because he recognizes the same authority in St. Augustine and in St. Basil, in the Latin Father and in the Greek Father, who, despite their differences, have both preserved and transmitted the Scriptures "without blemish."

Certainly St. Thomas does not attribute an infallible authority to the Fathers when they speak on their own. This unquestionable authority belongs to the canonical Scriptures alone.[41] He knows when to reject that which does not seem true in the patristic writings and when to propose a favorable interpretation that seeks to save a part of the truth.[42] But it is not rare, when several patristic interpretations are in play, to see the great respect he bears for the Greek doctors.

Perhaps the most beautiful testimony, despite its brevity, concerns St. Gregory Nazianzen, in a passage where St. Thomas recognizes the value of

---

[38] *De potentia*, q. 4, a. 1: "Unde omnis veritas quae, salva litterae circumstantia, potest divinae Scripturae aptari est eius sensus." St. Thomas explained earlier in the same article: "The other [exegetical rule] is not to reduce Scripture to one sense so as to exclude other senses that contain truth and that can be applied to Scripture in accordance with the context."

[39] Ibid.: "Unde si etiam aliqua vera ab expositoribus sacrae Scripturae litterae aptentur, quae auctor non intelligit, non est dubium quin Spiritus Sanctus intellexerit, qui est principalis auctor divinae Scripturae."

[40] *Quodlibet* XII, q. 16 (Leonine edition, vol. 25/2, 421): "Ab eodem Spiritu scripture sunt exposite et edite."

[41] Ibid.; cf. *ST* I, q. 1, a. 8, ad 2.

[42] Yves Congar, "Valeur et portée oecuméniques de quelques principes herméneutiques de saint Thomas d'Aquin," *Revue des Sciences Philosophiques et Théologiques* 57 (1973): 611–26. We note, however, that the question *De potentia* 4,1 does not concern a "reverential exposition."

an interpretation that he does not make his own, but that he acknowledges "on account of the teaching of Gregory Nazianzen, whose authority in Christian doctrine is so great that no one has ever presumed to attack his teaching, any more than that of Athanasius."[43] At issue here is whether the angels were created before the corporeal world; Thomas thinks that the simultaneous creation of spiritual and corporeal creatures is more probable, although Gregory Nazianzen (whose teaching Aquinas knows through John Damascene)[44] thinks that the angels were created first. This remarkable consideration of Gregory Nazianzen in Thomas Aquinas is a good example of the importance he gave to the *sententia doctorum graecorum*.[45]

For St. Thomas, the *ressourcement* of theology necessarily requires the study of the Greek Fathers as much the Latin Fathers. He proposes to develop neither a "Western" nor an "Eastern" theology, but a Catholic theology that benefits from the foundations laid by the patristic tradition recognized in its fullness. This objective of ecumenical Catholic fullness is at the heart of the project to which St. Thomas continues even today to invite his readers.

43 *ST* I, q. 61, a. 3: "propter sententiam Gregorii Nazianzeni, cuius tanta est in doctrina christiana auctoritas, ut nullus unquam eius dictis calumniam inferre praesumpserit, sicut nec Athanasii documentis." Aquinas refers here to St. Jerome (or, rather, Rufinus).

44 Ibid., arg. 1.

45 Ibid., ad 1.

CHAPTER 8

The Unity of Man, Body and Soul, in St. Thomas Aquinas

THE NOTION of man as a composite of soul and body often raises concern over the possibility of dualism.[1] Over the last few decades, the debate has crystallized on the notion of the soul and in particular its incorruptibility. For example, it is not unusual for treatises on eschatology to place an opposition between the resurrection and the doctrine of the immortality of the soul, as though these were two irreconcilable views of man and his destiny.[2] We are thus faced with only one alternative: either to adopt a "Greek" anthropology, which is supposed to separate the soul from the body, or to embrace the biblical anthropology, in which man is a bodily person existing in indissoluble unity.[3] Even the liturgy has become somehow reluctant to use the word "soul."[4]

This critical attitude toward the idea of "soul" is often presented as a rejection of modern rationalism, which views man's soul and body as two substances (Descartes). But is it really necessary to understand the soul and body in this way? The thought of St. Thomas Aquinas is particularly

[1] Translation by Therese Scarpelli of "L'unité de l'homme, âme et corps, chez saint Thomas d'Aquin," *Nova et Vetera* (French) 75/2 (2000): 53–76. Latins texts have been translated into English by Fr. Damien Logue, OCD.

[2] Gisbert Greshake and Jacob Kremer, *Resurrectio mortuorum: Zum theologischen Verständnis der leiblichen Auferstehung* (Darmstadt: Wissenschaftliche Buchgesellschaft, 1986), 240–55.

[3] See, for instance, François-Xavier Durrwell, *Regards chrétiens sur l'au-delà* (Paris: Mediaspaul, 1994), 78–87.

[4] Joseph Ratzinger, *Eschatology: Death and Eternal Life,* trans. Michael Waldstein with Aidan Nichols, OP (Washington, DC: Catholic University of America Press, 1988), 105.

illuminating in this area.[5] In responding to the problems of other thinkers, St. Thomas laid the groundwork for a deeply unified understanding of man that sacrifices neither the essential link between soul and body nor the primacy of the spiritual soul in man, and that can therefore account for the unity within the human person, soul and body.

1. A Heritage Tinged with Dualism

The Platonic Inheritance from Some Fathers of the Church

St. Thomas's patristic sources presented him with a conception of man that often has a somewhat dualistic flavor. The following are two examples, one from the Latin West, the other from the East. For St. Augustine, in the West, "man, as he appears to men, is a rational soul making use of a mortal and earthly body."[6] His definition gives primary importance to the soul, identifying the body as an instrument of the soul: Man is a soul making use of a body. The soul thus appears as a complete substance, a finished being, with the capacity to govern a body. As Augustine says, man is "a rational soul having a body."[7] Later texts, for instance in the *City of God*,[8] give greater value to the role of the body, but medieval tradition often retained Augustine's more dualistic explanations: The soul is a substance using a body that, to a certain extent, is exterior to the soul. "If you want a definition of the soul and if you ask me: What is the soul? I answer without difficulty. For to me the soul seems to be a certain substance endowed with reason and capable of governing a body."[9] A similar notion is found in the East, to which St. John Damascene (though with other nuances) bears witness: "The soul is a living essence, simple, incorporeal, invisible in its

---

5 Among the best studies, I would like to mention in particular the brief synthesis presented by Norbert Alfons Luyten, "L'homme dans la conception de S. Thomas," in *L'anthropologie de saint Thomas* (Fribourg: Éditions universitaires, 1974), 35–53.

6 St. Augustine, *De moribus Ecclesiae Catholicae* I,27,52: "Homo igitur, ut homini apparet, anima rationalis est mortali atque terreno utens corpore" (*Œuvres de saint Augustin,* vol. 1, ed. B. Roland-Gosselin [Paris: Desclée de Brouwer, 1936], 98).

7 St. Augustine, *In Iohannis Evangelium* 5:26, Tractatus 19,15 (Aurelius Augustinus, *In Iohannis Evangelium Tractatus CXXIV*, Corpus Christianorum, Series Latina 36 [Turnhout: Brepols, 1954], 199).

8 St. Augustine, *De civitate Dei* XIII,24,1; XIX,3; see St. Thomas, *ST* I, q. 75, a. 4, sed contra.

9 St. Augustine, *De quantitate animae* XIII,22: "Si autem definiri tibi animum vis, et ideo quaeris quid sit animus; facile respondeo. Nam mihi videtur esse substantia quaedam rationis particeps, regendo corpori accommodata" (*Œuvres de saint Augustin,* vol. 5, ed. Pierre de Labriolle [Paris: Desclée de Brouwer, 1939], 272).

proper nature to bodily eyes, immortal, reasoning and intelligent, formless, making use of an organised body, and being the source of its powers of life, and growth, and sensation, and generation."[10] Here we recognize the two constitutive elements in the anthropological dualism of the Platonic tradition:[11] (1) the notion of the soul as an essence or substance with its own complete self-existence; and (2) instrumentalism, that the soul as an essence that makes use of a body.

Nemesius of Emesa's famous analogy illustrates this notion of man: The soul is to the body what the pilot is to the ship he guides. St. Thomas describes Platonic anthropology in these same terms: "Plato and his followers asserted that the intellectual soul is not united to the body as form to matter, but only as mover to movable, for Plato said that the soul is in the body as a sailor in a ship."[12] According to St. Thomas, then, Platonic anthropology is characterized by two features: First, the soul is united to the body as the spiritual mover or pilot of a corporeal reality; second, man is not a whole composed of soul and body, but a soul that makes use of a body. This understanding of man is precisely what St. Thomas is constantly rejecting.[13] The hylomorphism that he imbibed from Aristotle requires him to do so, for two reasons. First, the assertion that man is his soul eliminates matter and the body from the definition of man. Second, the instrumentalist notion of the relationship between soul and body is unable to guarantee the essential character of the link between the two, since the denial of substantial union between soul and body entails that this union can only be accidental.

The Eclecticism of St. Thomas's Contemporaries

St. Thomas's contemporaries expressed this problem, inherited from the Fathers, in an anthropology that views man as a composite of two substances:

---

[10] St. John Damascene, *An Exposition of the Orthodox Faith (De fide orthodoxa)* II,12. This definition gives more weight to the unity of the human person.

[11] See, for example, Plato, *Alcibiades* 129e–130c.

[12] St. Thomas, *SCG* II, ch. 57; *Quaestio disputata de spiritualibus creaturis,* a. 2: "Plato used to say [. . .] that man is not a composite of soul and body, but a soul making use of a body, so that the soul is in the body just as a sailor is in a ship" (Leonine edition, vol. 24/2, 26–27: "Unde dicebat Plato, ut dictus Gregorius refert, quod homo non est aliquid compositum ex anima et corpore set est anima utens corpore, ut intelligatur esse in corpore quodammodo sicut nauta in naui"). Cf. Nemesius of Emesa, *De natura hominis,* ch. 3 (Némésius d'Emèse, *De natura hominis: Traduction de Burgundio de Pise,* ed. G. Verbeke and J. R. Moncho [Leiden: Brill, 1975], 51–52). Like all other Scholastics, Aquinas ascribes the *De natura hominis* of Nemesius of Emesa to St. Gregory of Nyssa; see Emil Dobler, *Falsche Väterzitate bei Thomas von Aquin: Gregorius, Bischof von Nyssa oder Nemesius, Bischof von Emesa?* (Fribourg: Éditions universitaires, 2001).

[13] See, especially, *ST* I, q. 75, a. 4.

one spiritual and immortal, the other corporeal. Each of these two principles is treated as a substance, a reality in itself. This problem can be easily recognized in the great Franciscan theologians against whom St. Thomas argues. For instance, Alexander of Hales's *Summa theologiae* explains that the soul is not merely the form of the body: It is a reality in itself *(ens in se)*, a substance in absolute terms *(substantia simpliciter)*, engaged in a relationship with the body that is comparable to that of the mover and the moved.[14] The same is true for St. Bonaventure:

> The soul is not only a form, but it is also a reality in itself *(hoc aliquid)*; this is why it is not only united to the body as the perfection of this body, but also as its mover. [. . .] God composed man of the natures that are most distant from each other, united in one single person and in one single nature: These are the body and soul. The one is a corporeal substance, the other, namely the soul, is a spiritual and immaterial substance. They are the things that are most distant from each other in the category of substance.[15]

Here we find the two characteristic keynotes of Platonic anthropology: the understanding of the soul as substance and the notion of the mover that makes it possible to define more precisely the relationship of the soul to the body.

Aristotle's anthropology, which is more clearly essential to St. Thomas, looks quite different. According to the Stagyrite's famous formula, "The soul is the form of a natural body having life potentially within it. But the formal substance is entelechy; therefore, the soul is the entelechy of a body of this nature" (*On the Soul* II,1; 412 a 20–23). The soul is the act of the living body. To designate the state of completion that constitutes the

---

14 *Summa fratis Alexandri,* Liber II, inq. 4, tract. 1, sect. 1, q. 1, caput 2 (Alexander de Hales, *Summa theologica,* vol. 2 [Quaracchi: Editiones Collegii S. Bonaventurae, 1928], #321, 385–86). For the historical context, see Edouard-Henri Wéber, *La personne humaine au XIIIe siècle: L'avènement chez les maîtres parisiens de l'acception moderne de l'homme* (Paris: Vrin, 1991), 74–198.

15 St. Bonaventure, *Breviloquium* II, ch. 9–10 (*Opera omnia,* vol. 5 [Quaracchi: Editiones Collegii S. Bonaventurae, 1891], 227–28): "Ex his apparet, qualiter finis beatitudinis necessitatem imponit praedictarum conditionum ipsi animae ad beatitudinem ordinatae. Quoniam autem ut beatificabilis est immortalis; ideo, cum unitur mortali corpori, potest ab eo separari; ac per hoc non tantum forma est, verum etiam hoc aliquid; et ideo non tantum unitur corpori ut perfectio, verum etiam ut motor. [. . .] Ut igitur in homine manifestaretur Dei potentia, ideo fecit eum ex naturis maxime distantibus, coniunctis in unam personam et naturam; cuiusmodi sunt corpus et anima, quorum unum est substantia corporea, alterum vero, scilicet anima, est substantia spiritualis et incorporea; quae in genere substantiae maxime distant."

being-in-act, Aristotle speaks of entelechy (ultimate actuality): The soul is the first entelechy of the living body. Since the soul is the form of the living body, which organizes the body and enables it to execute its actions, it follows that the soul and the body are not two different things. "That is why we can wholly dismiss as unnecessary the question whether the soul and the body are one: It is as meaningless as to ask whether the wax and the shape given to it by the stamp are one, or generally the matter of a thing and that of which it is the matter" (*On the Soul* II,1; 412 b 6–9). The soul is thus inseparable from the body (*On the Soul* II,1; 413 a 4). Aristotle's position, however, poses a problem for Christians: Can the soul survive the body that it informs? Aristotle's texts can be interpreted in different ways.[16] It remains true that the idea of a perishable soul can claim Aristotelian origin, since the Stagyrite did not consistently take the final decisive step to identify the soul (form) with the immortal intellect.[17] This explains why Christians suspected Aristotle of naturalism while being easily seduced by the Platonic position, since the latter acknowledges the soul's heavenly origin and highlights its spiritual nature, its kinship with that which is beyond the world, and its immortality.

Thus, even while borrowing elements of Aristotelian anthropology, many of St. Thomas's contemporaries preserve the Platonic notion that the soul is a substance in itself. This paradoxical position is held by St. Thomas's teacher, St. Albert: "The soul may be considered in two ways: first according to the being which it has in itself, and thus it is not defined in relation to the body; and second in relation to the body." Therefore it follows that "the soul can be understood in two ways: according to that it is a soul, i.e., the act and mover of the body; and according to that it is a certain substance which is contained in the category of substance."[18] The eclecticism of this anthropology is patent: "Considering the soul in itself *(secundum se)*, we adopt the opinion of Plato. But considering it as the

---

[16] Giovanni Negro, "Soul and Corporeal Dimension in the Aristotelian Conception of Immortality," *Gregorianum* 79 (1998): 719–42. See St. Thomas, *Quaestio disputata de spiritualibus creaturis,* a. 2.

[17] Augustin Mansion, "L'immortalité de l'âme et de l'intellect d'après Aristote," *Revue Philosophique de Louvain* 51 (1953): 444–72.

[18] St. Albert the Great, *Über den Menschen: De homine,* ed. Henryk Anzulewicz and Joachim R. Söder (Hamburg: Meiner, 2004), 58: "Si tamen attenditur id quod est anima, tunc potest considerari duobus modis, scilicet secundum esse quod habet in se, et sic non diffinitur in comparatione ad corpus, vel secundum comparationem ad corpus. [. . .] Anima dupliciter potest diffiniri, scilicet secundum quod est anima, idest actus corporis et motor, et secundum quod est substantia quaedam contenta secundum seipsam in praedicamento substantiae." Cf. St. Albert the Great, *Summa de creaturis, Secunda Pars: De homine,* tract. 1, q. 4, a. 1 (*Opera omnia,* ed. Auguste Borgnet, vol. 35 [Paris: Vivès, 1896], 34).

form of animation which it fulfils for the body, we adopt the opinion of Aristotle."[19] In this view of man, Aristotle's approach illumines the *action* of the soul, that is, the act of animating the body, while Plato's approach defines the *essence* of the soul. This position was as widespread among philosophers as among theologians.[20]

2. The Unity of the Human Person: Soul and Body

The Intellective Soul, Substantial Form of the Human Person

When St. Thomas speaks of man's soul, he is describing what he calls "the intellective soul" *(anima intellectiva)*, that is, "that principle of intellectual operation which we call the soul of man."[21]

> The intellect which is the principle of intellectual operation is the form of the human body. For that whereby primarily anything acts is a form of the thing to which the act is to be attributed; for instance, that whereby a body is primarily healed is health, and that whereby the soul knows primarily is knowledge; hence health is a form of the body, and knowledge is a form of the soul. The reason is because nothing acts except so far as it is in act; wherefore a thing acts by that whereby it is in act. Now it is obvious that the first thing by which the body lives is the soul. And as life appears through various operations in different degrees of living things, that whereby we primarily perform each of all these vital actions is the soul. For the soul is the primary principle of our nourishment, sensation, and local movement; and likewise of our understanding. Therefore this principle by which we primarily understand, whether it be called the intellect or the intellectual soul, is the form of the body.[22]

---

19 St. Albert the Great, *Summa theologiae* II, tr. 12, q. 69, membrum 2, a. 2, ad 2 (*Opera omnia,* ed. Auguste Borgnet, vol. 33 [Paris: Vivès, 1895], 16): "Animam considerando secundum se, consentiemus Platoni; considerando autem eam secundum formam animationis quam dat corpori, consentiemus Aristoteli."

20 Bernardo C. Bazán, "The Human Soul: Form and Substance? Thomas Aquinas' Critique of Eclectic Aristotelianism," *Archives d'Histoire Doctrinale et Littéraire du Moyen Age* 64 (1997): 95–126; here at 106–13.

21 St. Thomas, *ST* I, q. 75, a. 2.

22 Ibid., q. 76, a. 1: "Respondeo dicendum quod necesse est dicere quod intellectus, qui est intellectualis operationis principium, sit humani corporis forma. Illud enim quo primo aliquid operatur, est forma eius cui operatio attribuitur, sicut quo primo sanatur corpus, est sanitas, et quo primo scit anima, est scientia; unde sanitas est forma corporis, et scientia animae. Et huius ratio est, quia nihil agit nisi secundum quod est actu, unde quo aliquid est actu, eo agit. Manifestum est autem quod primum quo corpus vivit, est anima. Et cum vita manifestetur secundum diversas operationes in diversis gradibus viventium, id quo primo operamur

This explanation is founded on the understanding of human action that makes it possible to demonstrate that the soul is the form of the human body. The form of man, that is, that which determines the matter and gives man his own being, consists in the principle of the activity that is specifically human: intellectual knowledge. For St. Thomas, the principle of intellectual activity is the first principle of all other activities: biological, sensitive, motive, and so on. As this text shows, the intellective soul is man's sole substantial form, since it guarantees all the animating functions of the human person. Is St. Thomas thereby reducing man to his intellect? It should be noted that, first, Aquinas makes a clear distinction between the soul's essence *(essentia)* and its powers *(potentiae)*: The soul's essence is not the soul's powers (powers to act, such as knowledge or will); and, second, the intellect is the root of all man's spiritual activities. He defines the will as the inclination toward the reality grasped by the intellect, that is, the proper inclination of beings endowed with understanding; the same goes for freedom.[23] For St. Thomas, then, the intellective soul (endowed with its powers) appears as the spiritual principle that accounts for all the activities of man as a whole.

How can the intellective soul be understood as the form of the body? St. Thomas repeatedly explains this concept with reference to the human experience of thought and sensation. If the intellective soul were not the form of the body, I could not explain how I, a single subject, can be thinking (through the intellect), freely willing (through the will), and sensing (through the body). By definition, the principle of a being's activities (sensing, thinking) is the form. In this way the soul, the principle of the life of the body, is the principle of all our vital activities: Through the soul, man develops physically, exercises the activities of the senses, and moves. Likewise, it is through the soul that man thinks and wills. This appeal to common experience enables St. Thomas to refute some disciples of Averroes, or "Averroists" (for whom there is only one single intellect for all men),[24] as well as the Platonic notion of the intellect as the mover rather than the form of the body. For St. Thomas, a Platonic anthropology, which views the body as the instrument or organ of the soul, cannot explain

---

unumquodque horum operum vitae, est anima, anima enim est primum quo nutrimur, et sentimus, et movemur secundum locum; et similiter quo primo intelligimus. Hoc ergo principium quo primo intelligimus, sive dicatur intellectus sive anima intellectiva, est forma corporis."

23 See, especially, *SCG* IV, ch. 19; *ST* I, q. 80, a. 1; *De veritate,* q. 23, a. 1.

24 For this "monopsychism" (one single possible intellect for all men, one separated agent intellect), which St. Thomas opposes, see Alain de Libera, *Thomas d'Aquin: L'unité de l'intellect contre les Averroïstes* (Paris: Flammarion, 1994), 9–73; Richard C. Dales, *The Problem of the Rational Soul in the Thirteenth Century* (Leiden: Brill, 1995).

this common experience: When I am thinking, I am a corporeal being who is thinking. If Plato or Averroes's disciples were to be believed, the "I" who is thinking would be different from the corporeal being that I am. The act of thought could no longer be attributed to a corporeal being. The thinking Socrates would be different from the sensing Socrates: "Socrates would no longer be one."[25]

St. Thomas, then, has recourse to our common experience of unity in activity: I walk, I hear, I think, I love. If body and soul were two entities with separate existences, the same man could not be considered the single subject of these different actions. But in order for the same man to really be the subject of these different actions, he must be *one in his being*, since a being acts in virtue of what it is.[26] And the *only way* of accounting for this unity of being is to recognize that the intellective soul is the substantial form of the body, since it properly belongs to the form to communicate its being to matter. Indeed, the substantial form is that which gives a being its existence—not only its possession of such and such a characteristic, but its existence, absolutely speaking. This is the first activity of the substantial form, "to communicate its own existence to matter."[27] In order for man to be one and the same subject of all his different operations, the soul and the body must be one in existence: Only the identification of the soul as substantial form guarantees such unity. St. Thomas holds this to be the only solution that safeguards the unity of human activity and of human being.

This affirmation of the soul as the sole substantial form in man would meet with stubborn opposition. The Augustinian theologians, particularly the Franciscans, generally taught a plurality of substantial forms in man. This notion involves having other substantial forms in man besides the animating form that is the intellectual soul: that is, the vegetative form, which is the animating principle for vegetative life, and the sensitive form, which is the animating principle for sensitive life. According to this view, these intermediary forms exist and fulfill their animating function even when the intellectual soul is present: The soul is united to the body by means of these other substantial forms, and through them the rational soul exercises its animating activity in the body. This view, to which St. Bonaventure subscribes, can serve as a bastion against Aristotle's materialism. Nevertheless, it implies a spiritualism that does not escape dualism,

25 *ST* I, q. 76, a. 1; the *SCG* adds that no longer being one, man would no longer be a single being *(ens)* absolutely, but only accidentally (Book II, ch. 57 [#1328]).

26 *SCG* II, ch. 57 (#1331); the operation cannot be one if the existence is not one. That which has a different existence cannot be the subject of one and the same action.

27 *SCG* II, ch. 68 (#1450): "Quasi esse suum communicans materiae." Disputed questions *De anima*, q. 9 (Leonine edition, vol. 24/1, 79–80): "Est autem hoc proprium forme substantialis quod det materie esse simpliciter."

since it weakens the ties between body and soul by safeguarding their relationship through intermediate forms.

The debate became more heated among theologians over the question of Christ's death. If, as St. Thomas teaches, the intellectual soul is the only substantial form of the body,[28] what happened to Christ during the three days of his death? By definition, death is the separation of the soul from the body. If the soul was separated from the body, was the body at the tomb still *Christ's* body? To answer this question, some theologians had recourse to a "form of corporeity" *(forma corporeitatis)* distinct from the soul, which ensured the identity and continuity of the living body of Christ and his body in the tomb.[29] To measure the resistance that the thought of St. Thomas elicited, one should consider the various censures with which his teaching, considered as a dangerous novelty, met; most notably, it was condemned as heretic at Oxford by Robert Kilwardby and his successor John Peckham.

Nonetheless, St. Thomas's reply is extremely firm: If other substantial forms were present alongside the soul, the union of the spiritual soul to the body would ultimately be accidental, and man would no longer be one, *because his body would have another existence than that of his soul.*[30] Thus despite the opposition with which his doctrine would meet, the intellective soul as the sole substantial form remains for St. Thomas as the *only* way of accounting for the unity of man and the substantial relationship between the soul and the body. This "being-form" of the soul designates not only its function, as St. Albert tried to assert, but also its nature or essence.

Man Is Neither the Soul nor the Body, but the Composite of the Two

Man is therefore a "composite" of soul and body. First of all, this statement abolishes the view that man is identified with his soul, suggested by the Platonic tradition. The phrase "man is his soul" could have two meanings that St. Thomas avoids. (1) It could mean that "man" in the generic sense (humanity) is defined in terms of the soul, while "man" as individual (*this particular* man) is defined in terms of soul and body; the soul would therefore be the essence of the human species, while the human individual would be constituted by a soul linked to a body.[31] Thomas rejects this first position,

---

28 *ST* I, q. 76, a. 4.

29 See E.-H. Wéber, *La personne humaine au XIIIe siècle,* 113–19.

30 *ST* I, q. 76, a. 3. In that case, St. Thomas explains, there would be in us a man (in virtue of the intellective soul) and an animal (in virtue of an animal soul) which would not be one and the same being.

31 This, according to St. Thomas, is Averroes's position; cf. *Super Metaphysicam* VII, lect. 9 (#1467).

since it eliminates matter and the body from the generic definition of man. Rather, it belongs to the essence and nature of man to be corporeal: Thomas here defines man as "what is endowed with reason in a sensitive nature."[32] (2) In a radical Platonic sense, the phrase could mean that the individual man is his soul: "I am my soul." This position would imply that all the actions of a man are attributed properly to his soul alone. If I am my soul, then since I am the subject of my actions, my soul is the only proper subject of my actions. If this were true, our acts of sensation should be attributed only to our soul. St. Thomas rejects such a notion, since the act of sensation is not accomplished by the soul alone, but by the soul insofar as it is united to the body, that is, by the soul insofar as it depends on a bodily organ.[33] The soul essentially needs a body: The body is required for the reality of sense knowledge and the passions. Since the act of sensing is really the act of the man, as experience shows us, man is a being composed of soul and body.

To summarize, "man is neither his body, nor his soul."[34] St. Thomas would not have approved of the now widespread expression "I am my body." I cannot be strictly or exclusively identified with my body or with my soul; rather, I am both, in a reality that is neither one nor the other, properly speaking, but in which the one exists on account of the other.

It Is Good and Necessary for the Soul to be United to the Body

Among the beings endowed with intellect, St. Thomas explains, man holds "the lowest place." Here he is considering the human being in terms of his participation in the intelligent and free life that he receives from God. God knows all things through his own essence, and he knows creatures insofar as he is their cause and exemplar, that is, without any mediation. The angels, on the other hand, know through objective images that are infused into them by God without any sensory mediation.[35] As for men, their knowledge proceeds from their sensory experience. In man alone among all the beings endowed with intellect, intellectual knowledge begins in the senses, which present images of sensible realities to the intellect, which then disengages their intelligible content. The path that unfolds from the starting point of the senses is not alien to human nature. The human soul initially has no innate knowledge of things: It must *acquire* this knowledge by its own activity, by means of sensory experience. It therefore belongs to the nature of the human soul to know from the senses (especially the sense of

[32] *Super Metaphysicam* VII, lect. 9 (#1463): "Nam homo est quod habet rationem in natura sensitiva."

[33] *ST* I, q. 75, a. 4.

[34] *SCG* II, ch. 89 (#1752): "Non enim homo est suum corpus, neque sua anima."

[35] *ST* I, q. 55, a. 2.

touch, as St. Thomas specifies). This applies to every form of natural knowledge, and even knowledge of God. Thus the human soul is united to a human body *because the very nature of the soul requires it.*[36] The soul needs the senses so that the latter may lead it to its specific proper activities: intellectual knowledge, free will, and spiritual love. Without the senses, that is, without being united to the body, the soul could not execute its most intimate activities.[37] Here it is evident that, as the Cartesian conception of man also demonstrates, anthropology is very closely linked to the theory of knowing on which it largely depends.

It is therefore for the sake of man's integral wholeness that St. Thomas challenges the Platonic theory of knowledge. If the soul had innate knowledge of things without the senses, one would effectively have to admit that the soul has no need of the body in order to accomplish the activities that are proper to it. In contrast, St. Thomas proposes a unified vision of man. Why does a spiritual form, the soul, come to constitute with this body a corporeal mode of being that is the human mode of being? The soul is united to the body, St. Thomas explains, not so much for the sake of the body as for the sake of the soul itself: "For it cannot be said that the intellectual soul is united to the body for the sake of the body [. . .], but rather the reverse. Especially does the body seem necessary *(maxime necessarium)* to the intellectual soul, for the latter's proper operation which is to understand."[38] A beautiful passage of his *Commentary on Ephesians* explains the soul's need for the body:

> The body is made in view of the soul, and not conversely. In this way, the natural body is a certain fullness of the soul *(plenitudo animae)*. Indeed, if the members did not find their completion in the body, the soul could not fully exercise its operations. And the same applies to Christ and the Church.[39]

---

36 Ibid., q. 76, a. 5.

37 *SCG* II, ch. 83 (#1674).

38 *ST* I, q. 84, a. 4: "Non enim potest dici quod anima intellectiva corpori uniatur propter corpus: quia nec forma est propter materiam, nec motor propter mobile, sed potius e converso. Maxime autem videtur corpus esse necessarium animae intellectivae ad ejus propriam operationem, quae est intelligere." *De malo,* q. 5, a. 5: "For since the human soul is intellective in potency, it is united to the body in order that through the senses it may acquire intelligible species, by which the soul actually understands. For the union of the soul with the body is not for the sake of the body but for the sake of the soul."

39 *In Eph* 1:23 (#71): "Nam corpus est factum propter animam, et non e converso. Unde secundum hoc corpus naturale est quaedam plenitudo animae. Nisi enim essent membra cum corpore completa, non posset anima suas operationes plene exercere. Similiter itaque est hoc de Christo et de Ecclesia."

It follows that the human body, from a philosophical and theological point of view, differs from the bodies of higher animals: At the core of its being, in its raison d'être, it is the expression—or rather the indispensable partner—of a spiritual soul in the closest of unions:[40] The body is *plenitudo animae.* The body is that which situates the soul in its necessary relation to the world. Far from losing its nature on account of its link with matter, the soul is completed by the body. A spiritual creature, man is not a stranger in this world: He is at home in it. The soul itself, like man, exists at the boundary or the junction of the spiritual and material worlds. It is somewhat like the creaturely hyphen.[41]

The Human Soul Is a Subsistent Principle

By definition, form is act.[42] This definition excludes the possibility of any matter entering into the composition of the soul itself, as was suggested by St. Bonaventure, among others. Following the Jewish philosopher Avicebron, and more distantly, St. Augustine, the Franciscan master effectively taught that the soul contains some kind of matter, a spiritual matter *(materia spiritualis)*[43] that bears witness to its creaturely status. St. Thomas criticizes this conception of the soul for its metaphysical inconsistency. Since the soul is created, it includes composition: a composition not of matter and form, but of essence and participated existence. Like every creature, its essence (what it is) is not identical with its existence, which it receives from God at the moment of creation.[44]

Nevertheless, although its existence is distinct from its essence, the soul is subsistent. In virtue of what it is by the creating action of God, the soul possesses in itself something by which it remains in being. The human soul is incorruptible: It is a self-subsistent principle *(principium subsistens).* Here, St. Thomas's thought is guided by the fact that the soul is the principle of man's intellectual activity. Yet intellectual activity takes place in an incorporeal way. It is true that the soul receives from the senses the images whose intelligible content it then abstracts; in this respect, regarding the process of knowing, we know by means of the senses. But the act of intellection is not accomplished by a corporeal organ. To rephrase:

---

40 Léon Elders, *La philosophie de la nature de saint Thomas d'Aquin: Philosophie générale de la nature, Cosmologie, Philosophie du vivant, Anthropologie philosophique* (Paris: Téqui, 1994), 338.

41 *SCG* II, ch. 68 (#1453): "Anima intellectualis dicitur esse quasi quidam horizon et confinium corporeorum et incorporeorum."

42 *ST* I, q. 75, a. 5.

43 St. Bonaventure, II *Sent.*, dist. 17, q. 1, a. 2; cf. ibid., dist. 3, 1, a. 1, q. 1 (*Opera omnia,* vol. 2 [Quaracchi: Editiones Collegii S. Bonaventurae, 1895], 89–91 and 414–16).

44 *ST* I, q. 75, a. 5.

The act of intellection (and consequently the acts of will and love) is made possible by bodily organs, but does not consist in the activity of a bodily organ. St. Thomas's argument is not based on neuroscience, but it is strictly philosophical and unfolds in three stages.

First, St. Thomas notes that the soul can know all corporeal objects. It knows them to the extent that they are made present to it, since knowledge is a union effected by the presence of the known in the knowing subject. But a corporeal organ is by nature limited and limiting: It facilitates knowledge of only certain things, or certain aspects of a thing; the eye sees color, touch manifests the texture of a body, and so on. The universal scope of the objects of intellectual knowledge thus requires that this knowledge not be determined and limited by a bodily organ. The act of intellectual knowledge, then, is immaterial and does not depend on the body: It is by itself that the human intellect knows. Second, St. Thomas emphasizes the metaphysical relationship of act and being: A being acts according to what it is; it is, according to how it acts, in such a way that act expresses being and reveals being. As a result, that which executes its operation by itself, exists or subsists also by itself. Thus—and this constitutes the third step within St. Thomas's thought—the soul subsists in itself. Since it is self-subsistent, it has no principle of corruption within itself. The soul is a form that possesses the ability to subsist in itself: It exercises the act of existing as though from itself.[45]

This does not mean that the soul escapes the creaturely condition, or that it arrogates to itself a divine prerogative, as is sometimes unfortunately thought. If the soul is granted self-subsistence, it is only in virtue of God's creative act, that is, as a gift from the creative wisdom of God. According to St. Thomas, this is one of the reasons that the human soul cannot be produced by the parents. The parents' activity, insofar as they act as creatures, cannot extend to producing an immaterial and self-subsistent effect. To rephrase: The soul cannot draw its existence from material principles.[46] The nature of the soul implies, then, that it is directly produced and infused from God alone, according to a special act of God's providence. This also means that man, whose soul is created by God, is made for a direct relationship with God. This doctrine presupposes a deep metaphysical view of the cooperation between the parents and God in such an essential and free activity as procreation: The parents' procreating act is not detached from God's, but rather is inscribed in God's act as a collaboration in his work.

---

[45] Ibid., q. 75, a. 2 and a. 6. See Robert Lahaye, *Qu'est-ce que l'âme? Réponse à Claude Tresmontant* (Paris: Téqui, 1971).

[46] *ST* I, q. 118, a. 2; *De potentia*, q. 3, a. 9. Disputed questions *De anima,* q. 14.

The Soul Is a Subsistent Form, not a Substance in the Strict Sense

So far, St. Thomas has established that the intellectual soul is the form of the body, that it is man's sole substantial form, and that it is self-subsistent. But by granting that the human soul has the capacity for self-subsistence, has St. Thomas not fallen into the very dualism that he was seeking to avoid? Here we must make a crucial and all-too-often-neglected clarification: For St. Thomas, the human soul is not a substance united to another substance, that is, the body. As we have seen, the notion of two substances belongs to the Platonizing anthropology for which St. Thomas criticizes many of his contemporaries. On the few occasions when St. Thomas speaks of the human soul as a substance, he does so only in a limited sense that calls for clarification. He develops the topic thoroughly in the first disputed question *De anima*, so as to clarify the central point of his anthropology right at the outset.

In order for a thing to be a substance, that is, an individual that exists in itself and through itself *(substantia, hoc aliquid)*, it must meet two ontological conditions: (1) to subsist by itself; (2) to be complete in its own species, that is, to possess everything that is required by the nature of such a thing.[47] The soul easily fulfills the first condition, but not the second: It is not a complete reality that also happens to make use of a body (Plato). The soul does not constitute the whole essence of man, but is only the form actuating the matter. The soul is thus one part of the whole that is man. The complete substance is the human individual, not the soul; thus we can speak of the soul as a substance only in a derivative sense *(per reductionem)*. This is why, strictly speaking, the soul is not for St. Thomas a substance, but only a *subsistent form*, the form of man.

In conclusion, the outcome of these considerations expresses the unique status of the human soul: The soul possesses an independence of *existence* regarding matter (it subsists by itself), but not an independence of *essence* (it is one part of the essence of man, and not a complete substance). Man is not an incarnate spirit, but a hylomorphic composite of a kind that Aristotle himself did not even imagine. This anthropology likewise shows that in reflecting on man in the light of God, the Christian theologian does not blindly submit to philosophy; rather, philosophy is led to its ultimate conclusions through the impetus provided by faith.

---

[47] Disputed questions *De anima*, q. 1 (Leonine edition, vol. 24/1, 7): "Indiuiduum autem in genere substantie non solum habet ut per se possit subsistere, set quod sit aliquid completum in aliqua specie et genere substantie."

3. The Body and Man's Corporeal Nature

St. Thomas's understanding of the body is inseparable from his understanding of the soul as man's sole substantial form.[48] As a preliminary, we should clarify that the word "body" can be understood in two main ways: first, as a part of man distinct from the soul; second, as a whole that possesses spatial dimensions, in the same way in which we designate corporeal beings by the word "body." In the remainder of this chapter, the word "body" will generally signify a part of man whose form is the soul. St. Thomas's understanding of the human body can be typified by four characteristics, the first of which we have already encountered: The body is necessary, natural, and good for the soul; the body is united to the soul for the sake of the soul. Without reexamining this first characteristic, we must now consider the other three.

The Soul Makes the Body a Body

St. Thomas makes a generalized, startling, and perhaps somewhat provocative claim: "The soul is the very nature of the body."[49] This statement is a direct and rigorous consequence of the strict application of hylomorphism to the study of man. Matter is actualized by the substantial form: *All actuality derives from the form.*

In fact, if the body possessed any degree of actuality outside the form, it would derive its actuality from outside the soul: The body would be predetermined as a body by something other than the soul, thus reducing the unity of the soul and body to an accidental connection. This is a position that St. Thomas, opposing some Franciscan masters, seeks to avoid at all costs, and as a result, he is strenuously opposed to the notion of a *form of corporeity* different from the intellective soul. For the same reason, St. Thomas upholds the theory of a succession of substantial forms in the human embryo: In the genesis of a tiny human being, the intellective soul intervenes at the end of an embryonic process in order to take completely upon itself the entire animating function of the human composite.[50]

---

48 Bernardo C. Bazán, "La corporalité selon saint Thomas," *Revue Philosophique de Louvain* 81 (1983): 369–409.

49 I *Sent.*, dist. 3, q. 2, a. 3, ad 1: "Anima enim est natura ipsius corporis."

50 For St. Thomas, the human embryo is first animated by a vegetative soul, then by a sensitive soul: Each one stands in as the embryo's substantial form in these two first stages. From the moment that God infuses the spiritual soul into the embryo, this spiritual soul alone exclusively fulfills the function of substantial form. The sensitive form ceases to be a form; it is corrupted or absorbed into the sole substantial form, which is the spiritual soul. The succession of forms thus occurs by way of inclusive assumption after a time lapse. Following Aristotle and contemporary medical theories, Thomas estimates this time lapse to be 40 days for boys and 90 days for girls! (III *Sent.*, dist. 3, q. 5, a. 2). For many authors, today's theological anthropology can

When St. Thomas says that the soul is the form of the body, this implies that matter is a potential principle and that all the body's actuality derives from the soul. By the soul, the body exists; by the soul, the body is organized; by the soul, the body has life:

> Therefore, since the soul is the substantial form because it constitutes a human being in a determinate species of substance, there is no other substantial form intermediate between the soul and prime matter; but it is the soul itself which perfects man according to diverse levels of perfection, so that there is a body, and a living body, and a rational animal.[51]

Consequently, for St. Thomas the corpse of a dead man is no longer his body, properly speaking. The examples are macabre, but eloquent: The eye of a dead man is no more an eye than a painted eye or the eye of a statue. "Therefore, on the withdrawal of the soul, as we do not speak of an animal or a man unless equivocally, as we speak of a painted animal or a stone animal; so is it with the hand, the eye, the flesh and bones."[52] The cult of relics aptly illustrates this concept: The relics of saints, explains St. Thomas, are not the bodies that the saints possessed in their living life, since there is a clear difference in form. We venerate relics in memory of the body that was previously the temple of the Holy Spirit and that will be conformed to Christ's glorious Body in the resurrection, and on account of the soul that was united to it and that now stands in the presence of God in the beatific vision.[53] This

---

no longer uphold the time lapse idea; see Markus Schulze, *Leibhaft und unsterblich: Zur Schau der Seele in der Anthropologie und Theologie des hl. Thomas von Aquin* (Fribourg: Universitätsverlag, 1992). The precise duration of this process is not a matter of great importance for Aquinas, but the theory of a succession of forms is indisputably an essential tenet of his thought. See E.-H. Wéber, *La personne humaine au XIIIe siècle,* 161–67; Georges Cottier, "L'embryon humain et l'âme spirituelle," *Nova et Vetera* (French) 76/4 (2001): 35–51. For further discussions, see Alejandro Serani Merlo, "L'embryon humain, sa vie et son âme: Une perspective biophilosophique," *Nova et Vetera* (French) 79/1 (2004): 89–103; Louise-Marie Antoniotti, "La vérité de la personne humaine. Animation différée ou animation immédiate ?" *Revue Thomiste* 103 (2003): 547–76.

51 Disputed questions *De anima,* q. 9 (Leonine edition, vol. 24/1, 81): "Sic igitur cum anima sit forma substantialis, quia constituit hominem in determinata specie substantiae, non est aliqua alia forma substantialis media inter animam et materiam primam; set homo ab ipsa anima rationali perficitur secundum diversos gradus perfectionum, ut sit scilicet corpus, et animatum corpus, et animal rationale." See *ST* I, q. 76, aa. 3–7.

52 *ST* I, q. 76, a. 8; see the first disputed question *De anima,* and the disputed question *De spiritualibus creaturis,* a. 4.

53 *ST* III, q. 25, a. 6, corp. and ad 2.

teaching is clearly the direct conclusion that St. Thomas draws with rigorous consistency from Aristotle's assertion: "The soul is the first entelechy of an organized body." Understood thus, the body is the "fullness of the soul," according to the previously cited passage from the *Commentary on Ephesians.* The human body is not a "thing"; rather, it is the "expressive arena of the soul," the "soul's external face," whose interior principle is the soul.[54]

The Body Cannot be Reduced to Extension

Cartesian anthropology has habituated us to consider the body and soul as two substances, each with its own essential attribute: thought *(res cogitans)* and extension *(res extensa).* We thus risk reducing the body to the three dimensions of extension and movement (physical mechanism). On the one hand, St. Thomas refuses to identify the soul purely and simply with thought, as expressed in his consistent thesis of the real difference between the soul and its powers. This thesis, too, rests on his conception of the soul as a substantial form: Since the soul is a form, it is in act, not in potency. To identify soul and thought would signify that we are always engaged in the act of thinking, which experience clearly disproves. Thus St. Thomas holds that the soul is act and form (first act) as regards its essence. The soul's operations (second act: to know, to will), for their part, are really distinct from the soul's essence.[55]

On the other hand, corporeity seems to admit of a twofold interpretation. (1) Corporeity *(corporeitas)* can be considered in terms of accident, as a synonym for the dimensions of corporeal extension, that is, as the "quantitative" aspect of the body; in this case, corporeity is an accidental determination such as quantity. (2) On a deeper level, corporeity can also be considered in terms of substantial determination of this corporeal being, that is, man: Here, then, corporeity is that which makes the body to be a body, that which makes man corporeal. In this case, corporeity must be the body's substantial form, that is, the principle of actuality of the body, from which derive the dimensions of extension.[56] The body is therefore characterized by something other than extension, since extension is merely a property deriving from the substantial form of the body. This position will be expanded in the following section, but it already provides us with the basis for two preliminary conclusions. First of all, the human body is not an organized machine that stands ready to receive the breath of life; rather, that which receives life is matter (given the appropriate conditions making

---

54 Marie-Joseph Nicolas, "Le corps humain," *Revue Thomiste* 79 (1979): 357–87. Fr. Nicolas describes the human body as "le champ expressif de l'âme" or "la face extérieure de l'âme."

55 *ST* I, q. 77, a. 1.

56 *SCG* IV, ch. 81 (#4152).

matter capable to be informed by a human soul). The second conclusion is no less important: It is on account of the soul that the human body is a human body, and specifically *on account of its substantial union with the soul.* The body itself, as well as the very fact of being a body, depends on the substantial form. Thus the corporeity of fire is the substantial form of fire; the corporeity of a giraffe is its animal giraffe soul. And man's corporeity is his intellective soul. In this metaphysical perspective, the human body enjoys a unique rank among all bodies, since that which grants it to be what it is, is an immortal soul. This is the test for the philosopher's (and the theologian's) views on the human body. *Man's corporeity is his soul.* This statement can appear somewhat surprising, and it calls for closer examination.

Man's Corporeity Is His Soul

It is on account of the soul that the individual human being exists, that he is endowed with a body, and that this body is a living one. Properly speaking, corporeity *(corporeitas)* designates that by which a body is a body, that is, the form that makes the body to be what it is. Excluding all other substantial forms and rejecting in particular the notion of a "form of corporeity" distinct from the soul, St. Thomas rigorously identifies corporeity with the intellective soul. His most developed explanation of this position is found in the *Summa contra Gentiles*:

> For there are not different substantial forms in one and the same thing, by one of which it is placed in the supreme genus, for example, substance; by another in its proximate genus, for example, body or animal; and by another in its species, e.g., man or horse. Since, if the first form were to make the being substance, the following forms would be accruing to that which already is actually a definite something, and subsisting in nature; thus, the later forms would not make a definite something *(hoc aliquid)*, but would be in the subject which is a definite something as accidental forms. Therefore, corporeity, as the substantial form in man, cannot be other than the rational soul, which requires in its own matter the possession of three dimensions, for the soul is the act of a body.[57]

[57] Ibid.: "Non enim sunt diversae formae substantiales in uno et eodem, per quarum unam collocetur in genere supremo, puta substantiae; et per aliam in genere proximo, puta in genere corporis vel animalis; et per aliam in specie puta hominis aut equi. Quia si prima forma faceret esse substantiam, sequentes formae iam advenirent ei quod est hoc aliquid in actu et subsistens in natura: et sic posteriores formae non facerent hoc aliquid, sed essent in subiecto quod est hoc aliquid sicut formae accidentales. Oportet igitur, quod corporeitas, prout est forma substantialis in homine, non sit aliud quam anima rationalis, quae in sua materia hoc requirit, quod habeat tres dimensiones: est enim actus corporis alicuius."

The Church's eschatological doctrine provides the context for this explanation. How can we assert that the human person is resurrected with his *own body*? The resurrected body is certainly in a different condition from the earthly body (1 Cor 15), yet it is truly the same person's body. St. Thomas follows the teaching of the Fourth Lateran Council: "All will rise with their own bodies, which they now wear."[58] How can we explain the identity and continuity of the earthly body and the resurrected body, despite their different conditions? St. Thomas answers by making a distinction between the two previously mentioned senses of "corporeity." At the deepest level, corporeity is the substantial form of man, since *it is from the soul that the human body has all its reality as body.* St. Thomas excludes a plurality of substantial forms, clarifying further that the body has extension because *this is required by the soul.* The conclusion of this explanation clearly establishes how one can preserve the identity between the earthly body and the resurrected body:

> Therefore, although this corporeity [taken as an accident: quantity] yields to nothingness when the human body is corrupted, it cannot, for all that, be an obstacle to the body's rising with numerical identity; the reason is that corporeity taken in the first way [that is, as a substantial form: the human soul] does not yield to nothingness, but remains the same.[59]

Since the soul is by nature the form of the body, it is permanently ordered toward this body. The material and quantitative elements that constitute this body today constitute it only in virtue of the soul. In this way, the soul is defined in terms of its relationship to the body, and the body is defined by the soul. Thus the primary raison d'être of corporeal identity is found not in the matter, but rather in the soul of the human person. The identity of this subsistent soul sustains our hope in the resurrection: Glory does not destroy nature, but perfects and fulfills it.

---

58 Fourth Lateran Council, Constitution on the Catholic Faith *Firmiter*: "Qui omnes cum suis propriis corporibus resurgent, quae nunc gestant" (*Decrees of the Ecumenical Councils,* vol. 1, ed. Norman P. Tanner [Washington, DC: Georgetown University Press, 1990], 230). See Pseudo-Athanasius's *Quicumque* Symbol (Denzinger, #76); *Fides Damasi* (Denzinger, #72).

59 *SCG* IV, ch. 81 (#4152): "Alio modo accipitur corporeitas prout est forma accidentalis, secundum quam dicitur corpus quod est in genere quantitatis. Et sic corporeitas nihil aliud est quam tres dimensiones, quae corporis rationem constituunt. Etsi igitur haec corporeitas in nihilum cedit, corpore humano corrupto, tamen impedire non potest quin idem numero resurgat: eo quod corporeitas primo modo dicta non in nihilum cedit, sed eadem manet." See *Quodlibet* XII, q. 6, a. 1; *De veritate,* q. 10, a. 4, ad 3; *Quaestio disputata de spiritualibus creaturis,* a. 3, ad 14.

Similarly, for St. Thomas, the soul is the source of the essential properties of the human body: to have two hands, two feet, sense organs, and so on. Thus when St. Thomas describes the particulars of the human body, he explains them in terms of the fact that the human body is the body of a rational being. Man is endowed with hands so that he may make himself instruments to achieve the effects that he seeks; he is endowed with senses for the sake of his intellective soul, which needs to use these senses in order to exercise its peculiar activity.[60] This account is not an indication of prescientific naïvety. Rather, it expresses the wisdom of God's creative design, which unites the body and soul for the good of the soul, in conformity with the soul's vocation and following human nature. For St. Thomas, man is not a spiritual being because he has a body (which some of today's authors seem to suggest), but he has this body because he is spiritual: He is endowed with a body adapted to the exigencies of his spiritual nature.[61]

The human body, therefore, holds a unique position proper to man: It is part of a spiritual being. The dignity of the human body derives from its principle, the spiritual soul. Our body is permeated with spirituality, because its form is the rational soul, which bears the image of God.[62] For St. Thomas, the recognition of the dignity of the human body is inseparable from the recognition of the spiritual soul's union with the body of which it is the substantial form.

4. The Soul Separated from the Body and the Resurrection

The status of the soul when separated from the body by death constitutes, for numerous theologians, one of the greatest difficulties with Thomistic anthropology.[63] How can one conceive of the existence of the soul without the body without getting caught in the pitfalls of a Platonic-type anthropology?

---

60 See *ST* I, q. 76, a. 5, ad 4.

61 Norbert Alfons Luyten, *La condition corporelle de l'homme* (Fribourg: Éditions universitaires, 1957).

62 B. C. Bazán, "La corporalité selon saint Thomas," 407–8.

63 G. Greshake and J. Kremer, *Resurrectio mortuorum,* 223–36. On this question, see Anton C. Pegis, "The Separated Soul and Its Nature in St. Thomas," in *St. Thomas Aquinas 1274–1974 Commemorative Studies,* ed. Armand Maurer, vol. 1 (Toronto: Pontifical Institute of Medieval Studies, 1974), 131–58; Wolfgang Kluxen, "Anima Separata und Personsein bei Thomas von Aquin," in *Thomas von Aquino: Interpretation und Rezeption,* ed. Willehad P. Eckert (Mainz: Matthias Grünewald Verlag, 1974), 96–116; Montague Brown, "Aquinas on the Resurrection of the Body," *The Thomist* 56 (1992): 165–207.

The Separated Soul Is Deprived of the Fullness of the Person

In conformity with his strict understanding of man, St. Thomas considers that the integrity of human nature is required in order that there be a human person. Moreover, the body is essentially part of human nature. Without a body, there can no longer be a person, properly speaking, since one constitutive element of human substance is missing:

> The soul is a part of the human species; and so, although it may exist in a separate state, yet since it ever retains its natural aptitude to be united to the body, it cannot be called an individual substance, which is the hypostasis or first substance, as neither can the hand nor any other part of man; thus neither the definition nor the name of *person* belongs to it.[64]

This teaching is not exclusive to St. Thomas. We find it also in some of his contemporaries, but the reason invoked here is definitely a characteristic of Thomistic anthropology: The separated soul is no longer a person, because man is not the soul; the soul is not a substance or a hypostasis in the strict sense, since the integrity of its nature requires that it be united with the body. Even when addressing the question of Christ's soul, St. Thomas does not abandon this notion. The dead Christ does remain a person, since his person is that of the eternal Word. But during the three days of his death, Christ was no longer a man, properly speaking, because his death broke the union of soul and body that constitutes a man. St. Thomas is so strongly convinced of this that the contrary position seems to him to be heretical *(contra fidem)*: If Christ were still a man during the *triduum* of his death, he would not be truly dead, and we would not be truly saved.[65] With the same vehemence he rejects the idea of a "form of corporeity" to which his Augustinian opponents appeal in order to ensure the identity of the body of Christ: The body in the Holy Sepulchre remains the body of Christ in virtue of the action of the Word, who does not abandon his body or his soul; but the body of the dead Christ, deprived of its union with the soul, is no longer identical with his living

---

64 *ST* I, q. 29, a. 1, ad 5: "Ad quintum dicendum quod anima est pars humanae speciei, et ideo, licet sit separata, quia tamen retinet naturam unibilitatis, non potest dici substantia individua quae est hypostasis vel substantia prima; sicut nec manus, nec quaecumque alia partium hominis. Et sic non competit ei neque definitio personae, neque nomen." See ibid., q. 75, a. 4, ad 2; *De potentia*, q. 9, a. 2, ad 14.

65 *ST* III, q. 50, a. 4.

body. The faith itself is here at stake: Thomas considers the opposite position to be a manifestation of monophysitism and docetism.[66]

Here the existence of the separated soul must be conceived of in terms of a twofold relation: first, a relation to the earthly existence in which the soul was united to the body in the dignity of a person (the soul did not exist before this union with the body); and second, a relation to the resurrection, which is held by faith, since the general resurrection will restore to the dead the human completeness of the person.[67] The separated soul subsists in this twofold "tension."

A State Contrary to Nature

St. Thomas expresses this tension by explaining that when the soul is separated from the body by death, it is situated in a state "outside its nature" or "contrary to nature":

> For if it is natural to the soul to be united to the body, it is unnatural *(contra naturam)* to it to be without a body, and as long as it exists without a body it does not have the perfection of its nature.[68]
>
> To be separated from the body is not in accordance with its nature *(praeter rationem suae naturae)*.[69]

The expression "contrary to nature" here carries great weight, if one recalls the exceptional importance that St. Thomas accords to the integrity of nature in the creating and saving plan of God. Furthermore, the qualification "contrary to nature" does not specifically concern man or the body, but the *soul*. In fact, from the point of view of the body, death is natural, since the body is corruptible by nature; while the soul is both incorruptible and made for union with the body. Thus if St. Thomas teaches that the state of the separated soul is "contrary to nature," it is because the soul is a *subsistent form*.[70] The separated soul exists therefore

---

66 Specifically, it would be a manifestation of what is known as aphthartodocetism; see *ST* III, q. 50, a. 5: Christ would not truly be dead, and we would not be truly saved.

67 *ST* II–II, q. 83, a. 11, arg. 5 and ad 5.

68 *ST* I, q. 118, a. 3: "Si enim animae naturale est corpori uniri, esse sine corpore est sibi contra naturam, et sine corpore existens non habet suae naturae perfectionem."

69 Ibid., q. 89, a. 1: "Unde modus intelligendi per conversionem ad phantasmata est animae naturalis, sicut et corpori uniri, sed *esse separatum a corpore est praeter rationem suae naturae*, et similiter intelligere sine conversione ad phantasmata est ei praeter naturam."

70 *Compendium theologiae* I, ch. 152. Note that the gift of immortality that was conferred on Adam in the state of original justice did not derive from nature, but from a supernatural disposition (*ST* I, q. 97, a. 1).

in a state of imperfection, deprived as it is of that which its nature requires. The expression "contrary to nature" means that death is a profound evil *for the soul.* Death is repulsive to the deepest nature of man because of the dignity of his soul.

Taking on the condition of a pure form, which does not correspond to its nature but which is the consequence of the corruptibility of the human composite, the separated soul reflects man's unique complexity. Mortal, but endowed with an imperishable principle, man possesses a soul that situates him "on the horizon between eternity and time."[71] This complexity originates in the soul itself, endowed with independence of existence but not of essence. This provides us with an important clue for understanding the immortality of the soul properly. In fact, the state of the soul separated from the body after death is often included under the heading of the immortality of the soul. But this is inadequate. In a certain way, the immortality of the soul implies its union with the body, since a perpetual existence in a state "contrary to nature" is hardly thinkable. The immortality of the soul must be considered in terms of its relation to the resurrection.

The Immortality of the Soul in the Context of the Resurrection

Unlike many of today's authors, St. Thomas does not place the incorruptibility of the soul in opposition to the resurrection. These two truths are not alternatives; rather, they are mutually converging or cohering truths about man. On one side, as noted previously, the incorruptibility of the soul guarantees the identity between the person living on earth and the resurrected person; it also constitutes an argument in favor of the credibility of the resurrection. On the other side, the resurrection confirms and upholds the affirmation of the soul's incorruptibility.

> To establish that there will be a resurrection of the flesh there is an evident supporting argument which is based on the points made earlier. For we showed that the souls of men are immortal. They persist, then, after their bodies, released from their bodies. It is also clear from what was said that the soul is naturally united to the body, for in its essence it is the form of the body. It is, then, contrary to the nature of the soul to be without the body. But nothing which is contrary to nature can be perpetual. Perpetually, then, the soul will not be without the body. Since, then, it persists perpetually, it must once again be

[71] *SCG* II, ch. 81 (#1625); see the *Liber de causis*, prop. 2, and Aquinas's commentary: St. Thomas, *Super Librum de causis expositio*, ed. Henri-Dominique Saffrey (Paris: Vrin, 2002), 10–16. See footnote 41 above.

united to the body; and this is to rise again. Therefore, the immortality of souls seems to demand a future resurrection of bodies.[72]

If the resurrection of the body is denied, it is not easy, on the contrary it is difficult, to sustain the immortality of the soul. For it is clear that the soul is naturally united to the body and is departed from it, contrary to its nature and *per accidens.* Hence the soul devoid of its body is imperfect, as long as it is without the body. But it is impossible that what is natural and *per se* be finite and, as it were, nothing; and that which is against nature and *per accidens* be infinite, if the soul endures without the body.[73]

According to these texts, there are two aspects to the relationship between the soul's incorruptibility and the resurrection. On the one hand, faith in the resurrection is sustained by the truth of the incorruptibility of the soul, which, as a form, persists in the expectation of its reunion with the body. On the other hand, faith in the resurrection upholds the truth of the soul's incorruptibility, as Cajetan would later note, since it is difficult to conceive of a soul remaining forever in a state that is contrary to nature. At this point, philosophical reflection on the soul reaches its furthest limit. The soul cannot reunite itself to the body on its own:

> There is no active principle of resurrection in nature, neither regarding the reunion of the soul with the body, nor regarding the disposition which is necessary for such a reunion. [. . .] This is why the resurrection, absolutely speaking, is miraculous and not natural.[74]

---

72 *SCG* IV, ch. 79 (#4135): "Ad ostendendum etiam resurrectionem carnis futuram evidens ratio suffragatur, suppositis his quae in superioribus sunt ostensa. Ostensum est enim in secundo animas hominum immortales esse. Remanent igitur post corpora a corporibus absolutae. Manifestum est etiam ex his quae in secundo dicta sunt, quod anima corpori naturaliter unitur: est enim secundum suam essentiam corporis forma. Est igitur contra naturam animae absque corpore esse. Nihil autem quod est contra naturam, potest esse perpetuum. Non igitur perpetuo erit anima absque corpore. Cum igitur perpetuo maneat, oportet eam corpori iterato coniungi: quod est resurgere. Immortalitas igitur animarum exigere videtur resurrectionem corporum futuram." See Georges Cottier, "La résurrection des corps, un problème philosophique?" *Nova et Vetera* (French) 78/1–2 (2003): 9–27, especially 23–27.

73 *In 1 Cor* 15:19 (#924): "Quia si negetur resurrectio corporis, non de facili, imo difficile est sustinere immortalitatem animae. Constat enim quod anima naturaliter unitur corpori, separatur autem ab eo contra suam naturam, et per accidens. Unde anima exuta a corpore, quamdiu est sine corpore, est imperfecta. Impossibile autem est quod illud quod est naturale et per se, sit finitum et quasi nihil; et illud quod est contra naturam et per accidens, sit infinitum, si anima semper duret sine corpore."

74 IV *Sent.*, dist. 43, q. 1, a. 1, qla 3: "Nullum autem activum principium resurrectionis est in natura neque respectu conjunctionis animae ad corpus, neque respectu

Here we are touching the question of the supernatural. The resurrection does not derive from the order of nature but surpasses it; yet it answers a desire that God himself has inscribed in the nature of the incorruptible human soul. In any case, one principle must be upheld: The Christian theologian cannot consider the incorruptibility of the soul in isolation from faith in the resurrection. It is in context of the resurrection that St. Thomas considers the incorruptibility of the soul; within this same context, he is able to show that the doctrine of the immortality of the soul and the doctrine of the resurrection mutually support each other in Christian thought.

Man's Perfect Beatitude Requires His Integrity as a Composite of Body and Soul

Without the body, the soul exists in a state of imperfection and incompleteness. In conformity with Catholic faith, St. Thomas explains that the saints experience the supreme happiness of the vision of God immediately after death if they do not need to be purified of anything. Nevertheless, in the same way that grace presupposes nature, glory likewise presupposes nature: "Perfection of beatitude cannot exist if perfection of nature is lacking. [. . .] This is why the separated soul cannot attain the ultimate perfection of beatitude."[75] The object of beatitude is not a good of the body but the glorified human vision of God *per essentiam*; in this respect, it must be said that man's happiness consists formally and essentially in the soul's vision of God. Nevertheless, the attainment of full happiness requires the participation of the body, since the substantial union between soul and body belongs to man's very nature.[76]

Without the resurrection, man could never be perfectly happy, since the soul's desire would never be totally satisfied.[77] When souls behold God before the resurrection,

> the separation from the body is said to hold the soul back from tending with all its might to the vision of the divine essence. For the soul desires to enjoy God in such a way that the enjoyment also may overflow into

---

dispositionis quae est necessitas ad talem conjunctionem; quia talis dispositio non potest a natura induci nisi determinato modo per viam generationis ex semine. Unde etsi ponatur esse aliqua potentia passiva ex parte corporis, seu etiam inclinatio quaecumque ad animae conjunctionem, non est talis quod sufficiat ad rationem motus naturalis; unde resurrectio, simpliciter loquendo, est miraculosa, non naturalis, nisi secundum quid, ut ex dictis patet."

75 *De potentia*, q. 5, a. 10. Since the union of soul and body is natural and substantial, the soul cannot experience the perfection of happiness if it is not united to the body, since it is lacking the perfection of its nature.

76 *ST* I–II, q. 4, a. 7.

77 *SCG* IV, ch. 79 (#4136).

> the body, as far as possible. And therefore, as long as it enjoys God without the fellowship of the body, its appetite is at rest in that which it has, in such a way that it would still wish the body to attain to its share.[78]

Thus the body enters into the fulfillment of beatitude by participating in the glory of the soul, which overflows into it in such a way that the whole person experiences the happiness that God has prepared for his saints.[79] St. Thomas's *Commentary on the Sentences* beautifully expresses this supernatural vocation of the human body:

> On the one hand, the corporeal sight will consider God's great glory in the bodies, and especially in the glorified bodies, and most of all in the body of Christ; on the other hand, the intellect will see God so clearly that God will be corporeally perceived in things, just as life is perceived in speech. Although, in fact, our intellect will not see God from *(ex)* the creatures, but it will see him in *(in)* the creatures corporeally seen. [. . .] Man's beatitude principally consists in an act of the soul from which it overflows onto the body. Nevertheless there will be a certain beatitude of our body insofar as it will see God in creatures that can be sensed, and especially in the body of Christ.[80]

According to this line of thought, the bodily senses of the resurrected saints thus operate with a true bodily activity. The senses, as St. Thomas explains, cannot directly perceive God's essence, since this activity belongs to the human spirit assisted by the light of glory. But the senses will perceive God through the glorified world that will shine with divine glory. Here St. Thomas's anthropology reaches its culminating conclusions.

---

78 *ST* I–II, q. 4, a. 5, ad 4: "Et sic separatio a corpore dicitur animam retardare, ne tota intentione tendat in visionem divinae essentiae. Appetit enim anima sic frui Deo, quod etiam ipsa fruitio derivetur ad corpus per redundantiam, sicut est possibile. Et ideo quandiu ipsa fruitur Deo sine corpore, appetitus eius sic quiescit in eo quod habet, quod tamen adhuc ad participationem eius vellet suum corpus pertingere."

79 Ibid., q. 4, a. 7.

80 IV *Sent.*, dist. 49, q. 2, a. 2, corp. and ad 6: "Cum ergo visus et sensus sit futurus idem specie in corpore glorioso, non poterit esse quod divinam essentiam videat sicut visibile per se; videbit autem eam sicut visibile per accidens, dum *ex una parte visus corporalis tantam gloriam Dei inspiciet in corporibus, et praecipue gloriosis, et maxime in corpore Christi, et ex parte alia intellectus tam clare videbit Deum, quod in rebus corporaliter visis Deus percipietur, sicut in locutione percipitur vita: quamvis enim tunc intellectus noster non videat Deum ex creaturis, tamen videbit eum in creaturis corporaliter visis. [. . .] Ideo beatitudo hominis non consistit principaliter nisi in actu animae, et ex ea derivatur ad corpus per quamdam redundantiam,* sicut patet ex his quae dicta sunt 44 dist. q. 2, a. 4, in corp. *Quaedam tamen beatitudo corporis nostri erit, inquantum Deum videbit in sensibilibus creaturis, et praecipue in corpore Christi.*"

In conclusion, St. Thomas's thought is able to defend two fundamental truths: (1) the unity of man, taking the requirements of strict hylomorphism to their most stringent conclusion against every form of dualism; and (2) the primacy of the soul, that is, the privileges of the soul and man's spiritual dignity, against every form of materialism. St. Thomas also demonstrates that it is possible to uphold the subsistence and incorruptibility of the soul without making any concessions to dualism. Moreover, the existence of the separated soul makes it possible to discuss the resurrection coherently. Throughout its development, this anthropology is constantly guided by the notion of the soul as the sole and subsistent substantial form. St. Thomas thus demonstrates that far from prejudicing man's unity, this appeal to the notion of the soul is indispensable to a true consideration of man's corporeal condition. His doctrine of the soul makes it definitively possible to account for the truth of the body and the dignity of man's corporeal condition.

CHAPTER 9

The Question of Evil and the Mystery of God in Charles Journet

THE QUESTION of evil is present throughout the works of Charles Journet.[1] Journet not only wrote a book on evil,[2] several parts of which appeared as articles in the journal *Nova et Vetera*,[3] but also published various short works,[4] as well as numerous studies[5]

---

1 Translation by Robert E. Williams, SSI, and Paul Gondreau of "La question du mal et le mystère de Dieu chez Charles Journet," in *Charles Journet: Un témoin du XXe siècle*, Actes de la Semaine théologique de l'Université de Fribourg, Faculté de théologie, 8–12 avril 2002 (Paris: Parole et Silence, 2003), 301–25.

2 Charles Journet, *The Meaning of Evil*, trans. Michael Barry (New York: P. J. Kennedy, 1963); French: *Le mal: Essai théologique* (Paris: Desclée de Brouwer, 1961).

3 C. Journet, "La question du mal," *Nova et Vetera* (French) 32 (1957): 190–201; idem, "Les formes du mal," *Nova et Vetera* (French) 34 (1959): 26–31; idem, "Le mal de la nature," *Nova et Vetera* (French) 34 (1959): 100–17; idem, "Dieu est-il responsable du péché?" *Nova et Vetera* (French) 34 (1959): 206–36; idem, "Le mystère de l'enfer," *Nova et Vetera* (French) 34 (1959): 264–87.

4 C. Journet, *Le purgatoire* (Liège-Paris: La Pensée Catholique, 1932); idem, *Notre-Dame des sept Douleurs* (Juvisy: Cerf, 1934); idem, *Frère Jérôme Savonarole: Dernière méditation sur le Psaume "Miserere" et sur le début du Psaume "In te Domine speravi"* (Fribourg: Librairie de l'Université, 1943 [Paris: Desclée de Brouwer, 1947, 1961, 1968]); idem, *Les sept Paroles du Christ en Croix* (Paris: Seuil, 1952); cf. idem, "La quatrième parole du Christ en Croix," *Nova et Vetera* (French) 27 (1952): 47–69; idem, *La Volonté divine salvifique sur les petits enfants* (Paris: Desclée de Brouwer, 1958); idem, *Sur le pardon du péché et la part laissée aux indulgences* (Saint-Maurice: Éditions Saint-Augustin, 1968); C. Journet, J. Maritain, and Philippe de la Trinité, *Le péché de l'ange* (Paris: Beauchesne,1961).

5 C. Journet, "Les maladies des sens internes," *Revue Thomiste* 29 (1924): 35–50; idem, "La peine temporelle du péché," *Revue Thomiste* 32 (1927): 20–39, and

touching on several aspects of evil (suffering, sin) or related questions ("tragedy," man's condition before sin, hope, redemption, and so on).[6] Under Charles Journet's editorship, the journal *Nova et Vetera* devoted much space to a number of reflections on the question of evil in the events that struck the world in the twentieth century (the events in Poland, in Russia, the occupation and resistance, deportations, anti-Semitism, reprisals, war and peace, atomic weapons, and so on).[7] Journet also preached spiritual retreats on the mystery of evil.[8] A brief glance at Charles Journet's publications shows us right away the exceptional place of evil at the heart of his theological thought from his first writings to the last.

On a great number of essential points, Charles Journet's doctrine on evil goes back to and develops the "classic" Thomistic doctrine: Evil is defined as "the privation of a good that should be present" (evil is a "negativity of privation"); it is divided into three forms (evil of nature, of fault, and of punishment); in man, after the original fall, it takes on only the forms of the evil of punishment and the evil of fault, and so on.[9] But the

---

89–103; idem, "Le péché comme faute et comme offense," in *Trouble et Lumière*, Études Carmélitaines (Paris: Desclée de Brouwer 1949), 21–29; idem, "Pour une théologie du martyre," in *Limites de l'humain*, Études Carmélitaines (Paris: Desclée de Brouwer 1953), 215–24; idem, "Dieu et le mal: Aspects métaphysiques du problème," *Revue Thomiste* 59 (1959): 213–69; idem, "Un affrontement de Hegel et de la sagesse chrétienne," *Nova et Vetera* (French) 38 (1963): 102–28; "La peine du péché actuel," in *Le Christ devant nous: Études sur l'eschatologie chrétienne* (Paris: Desclée, 1968), 71–126.

6 C. Journet, "Notes sur le tragique," *Nova et Vetera* (French) 18 (1943):185–97; idem, "L'univers de création ou l'univers antérieur à l'Église," part 1, *Revue Thomiste* 53 (1953): 439–87, and part 2, *Revue Thomiste* 54 (1954): 5–54; idem, "De la condition initiale privilégiée de l'homme," *Nova et Vetera* (French) 29 (1954): 208–29; idem, "De l'espérance," *Nova et Vetera* (French) 45 (1970): 161–222; idem, "La Rédemption, drame de l'amour de Dieu," part 1, *Nova et Vetera* (French) 48 (1973): 46–75, and part 2, *Nova et Vetera* (French) 48 (1973): 81–103.

7 See, for example, C. Journet, "Représailles," *Nova et Vetera* (French) 18 (1943): 113–23; idem, "Résistance," *Nova et Vetera* (French) 18 (1943): 209–21; idem, "Au nom du droit chrétien," *Nova et Vetera* (French) 18 (1943): 321–38; and so on. Concerning these contributions, see Guy Boissard, *Quelle neutralité face à l'horreur? Le courage de Charles Journet* (Saint-Maurice: Éditions Saint-Augustin, 2000).

8 C. Journet, *Le mal*, retreat preached at Ecogia, August 17–30, 1953, typewritten notes. A retreat on *God*, preached several times with some changes, also testifies to the presence of the question of evil in Charles Journet's meditation on the mystery of God; the same preoccupation appears again in the retreat on *Les paradoxes des Noms divins* (preached in 1971 at Notre-Dame d'Argentan Abbey). I should mention still other meditations of Journet, notably the last part of his retreat on the Our Father, *Notre Père qui es aux cieux* (Saint-Maurice: Éditions Saint-Augustin, 1997), with the text of a radio address in the appendix.

9 See, in particular, C. Journet, *Meaning of Evil*, 27–57.

thought of Journet is not limited to the rehearsal of a common doctrine. It has its own characteristics that express the theologian's fundamental preoccupation: evil in its relation to the mystery of God. For it is this relation, which Journet pondered and delved into ever more deeply in the course of his work, that forms the core of his study of evil. This is what I would like to outline here, without dealing with all the aspects that caught Journet's attention (the redemptive suffering of Christ, the Virgin's compassion, and human suffering), but rather limiting ourselves to some fundamental characteristics dealing with the mystery of God and evil.

1. Evil: A Question Put to Us . . . by God

In all his writings, Charles Journet lays particular stress upon the interdependence of the knowledge of God and the knowledge of evil. "The rule of both fields of knowledge is not to destroy each other but to enrich each other by advancing together": These two fields of knowledge either "extinguish one another" or "deepen one another." Hence, to answer the question of evil means "to clear up a mystery with a mystery."[10] Journet's thought, insisting on mystery, resolutely parts company with a rationalistic kind of approach that aims at integrating evil into a purely rational grasp of the universe. With just as much vigor, his thought rejects a dialectical approach in which evil and good would be engaged in a process that tends toward unity.[11] Since good and evil cannot be placed on the same level, it is in the mystery of God that light can be brought to bear on the mystery of evil. It is from this height that we must look at the presence of evil in history.[12] For this reason Journet's approach is rigorously *theological*, because for pure philosophy, evil remains an *enigma.* Faced with the evil undergone by the innocent, faced with the suffering of little children, Journet suggests the state of mind a Christian philosophy must adopt: "At this point, philosophy cannot be integrally constructed without borrowing higher data from theology."[13]

On this high level, according to Journet, evil must be looked at through the "eyes of God," that is, with the vision of God himself: "We should turn to God to see evil through his eyes, with the penetrating sight that theologians call the vision of wisdom. Then we can get to the bottom

---

10 Ibid., 21–23.

11 See, in particular, his critique of Leibniz, in C. Journet, *Meaning of Evil,* 119–24; and of Hegel, "Un affrontement de Hegel et de la sagesse chrétienne," 102–28. In this regard we should keep in mind the dedication of his work *The Meaning of Evil*: "To those who know how to hate the absurd and worship mystery."

12 Ibid., 21–23 and 275.

13 C. Journet, "La quatrième parole du Christ en Croix," 58; idem, *Le mal: Essai théologique,* 266.

of things."[14] Hence, an authentically Christian look at evil is one of "faith illuminated by the gift of wisdom," which is "the only light which allows the mind to plumb the depths of evil without foundering."[15] With St. Thomas, we must understand the "gift of wisdom" as the gift of the Holy Spirit that, linked to charity, enables us to judge things by using as our guideline the highest cause, which is God himself.[16] Journet gives as examples the Blessed Virgin Mary, St. Thomas Aquinas, St. Catherine of Sienna, and St. Angela of Foligno.[17]

This "point of view" profoundly modifies the question of evil as commonly posed. It reverses it. Journet invites us here to take "question" in its primitive meaning of "torture," of scandal, and to put it on the high level of God himself. From this perspective, it is not so much man who puts the question of evil to God, like a cry rising to heaven, but rather it is God who "puts before each one of us, in ever more harrowing ways, the question of evil, not in order to shake our faith and trust but to make them truer and more intense."[18] The question of evil invites us consequently to look closely at the divine design, at God's permission and knowledge of evil.

2. God's Permission of Evil

Following Maritain, Journet reproaches Hegelian rationalism for positing evil's dialectical or metaphysical necessity.[19] A similar criticism is leveled against Leibniz's theodicy.[20] Their mistake consists in failing to recognize the essential place that belongs to the divine "permission" of evil: "The idea of the permission of evil is misunderstood."[21] This is what can help us grasp correctly the place of evil in God's design: While God wills the

14 C. Journet, *Le Mal,* retreat (1953), 8th conference, according to typewritten notes unrevised by the author; cf. idem, *Meaning of Evil,* 247–49, which invites us to look at what evil becomes "in the eyes of God."

15 C. Journet, *Meaning of Evil,* 281.

16 St. Thomas, *ST* II–II, q. 45, a. 1.

17 C. Journet, *Meaning of Evil,* 280–81; idem, *Le Mal,* retreat (1953), 8th conference.

18 C. Journet, *Meaning of Evil,* 285; cf. 289: "The question of evil can never be sidestepped, for God sets it before every man from the time he first comes into the world"; idem, *Le Mal,* retreat (1953), 8th conference: "The problem of evil, the question of evil—I stress this word, understanding it in its primitive sense of torture: put to the question—the question of evil is addressed by God to each one among us several times in our life. He asks you to answer this direct question that is put to you without losing faith or love, but instead to seize the opportunity of this question, this scandal, to grow in your faith and your love."

19 C. Journet, "Un affrontement de Hegel et de la sagesse chrétienne," 124–25 (texts of J. Maritain).

20 C. Journet, *Meaning of Evil,* 119–24.

21 Ibid., 83.

good directly and per se, he does not will evil directly but *permits* it *per accidens.* With St. Thomas, Journet explains: "It is not true to say that *God wills evils to be* [. . .]. Nor is it any more true to say that *God wills evils not to be* [. . .]. The only thing left to say is that *God wills to permit evil.*"[22] Journet stands here, with St. Thomas, on the dividing line that affirms the universal scope of divine providence as well as the efficacy of the divine will without sacrificing the rights of reason (irrationalism).

On this basis, Journet, again with St. Thomas, carefully distinguishes the three forms of evil. The evil of nature (for example, the suffering of the animal killed by another animal that makes it its meal)[23] is willed in the sense that in and of itself it is linked inseparably to a good intended by God: "It is tolerated and accepted by God but not intended [. . .], it is willed indirectly and *per accidens.*"[24] As for the evil of punishment (the punishment incurred through sin: human illnesses, the infirmities of old age, death), in an analogous way it is *permitted* by God, willed in indirect fashion; in itself it is not intended by God, but "willed" inasmuch as he intends a good to which this evil is connected by virtue of divine justice.[25] But the evil of fault (sin) is absolutely *not* willed by God: There can be no question of God willing it, not even accidentally or indirectly. The evil of sin is "*permitted*, tolerated and suffered in a completely different sense from the evil of nature; it is permitted as a rebellion, an offense, *which God cannot will in any way,* which he cannot acquiesce in or *consent* to without denying his own being." So, when we say that the evil of sin is permitted, "this cannot be taken to mean that it is accepted, consented to and tolerated, in other words indirectly willed, as the reverse side of some good looked for by God."[26] Among the diverse forms of evil, then, it is the evil of fault that presents the greatest theological difficulty. For if we look at evil from man's point of view, in the light of creatures, the evils of nature and punishment, especially suffering, will seem to be the most "revolting." But if we look at evil in God's light, "from God's point of view," then it is the evil of sin, the refusal of the love offered by God, that stands out as the evil most "unacceptable" to God, as the most radical form of evil.

Following St. Thomas Aquinas to the letter, Journet is extremely firm and reminds us constantly of this fundamental truth: In no way *(nullo modo)*

---

22 Ibid., 82.

23 The evil of nature, insofar as it assails man, is an evil of punishment; every evil of man comes down to the evil of punishment or the evil of fault. On this point, Charles Journet clearly adopts the teaching of St. Thomas.

24 C. Journet, *Meaning of Evil,* 147; cf. idem, "Dieu est-il responsable du péché?" 207.

25 C. Journet, *Meaning of Evil,* 186; cf. St. Thomas, *ST* I, q. 19, a. 9.

26 C. Journet, *Meaning of Evil,* 147; cf. idem, "Dieu est-il responsable du péché?" 207–8; idem, "Dieu et le mal: Aspects métaphysiques du problème," 213–69.

does God will the evil of fault.[27] When we speak of the allowance of sin, it is more a question of God's respect for the creature, even to the point of the created will's resistance that God may allow "to happen and bear fruit indirectly in other things."[28] Up to now, Journet's thought is in agreement with the common teaching of Thomists,[29] but it departs from the common tradition in its explanation of the divine knowledge of sin and the permissive decree. We need to point out that the main difference between Journet and other Thomists is not about the evil of nature or the evil of punishment, but about the evil of fault, as well as the divine decree by which sin is permitted.

3. How Does God Know Sin?

God, who does not possess the idea of evil, knows evil by knowing the good of which the evil is a privation: Evil is known through the good.[30] God does not draw this knowledge from creatures, for the divine knowledge cannot be specified immediately by a created object as such; divine knowledge cannot be passive in regard to a creature that would determine it. It is in himself, through his essence, that God knows the good of creatures and hence the evil that is its privation. As regards the evil of nature and of punishment, Journet, with Jacques Maritain, explains that God knows it "by the science of vision, *by a creative knowledge giving form and not receiving it, by seeing it in his essence alone.*"[31] This is the way God knows everything of which he is the cause.[32] This thesis fits in with the common teaching of Thomists.

But how does God know sin, the free act of the creature who separates himself from God? Réginald Garrigou-Lagrange may serve as an example of the teaching of Thomists: God knows when a sin exists in some soul "inasmuch as He permits this moral defect in which He cannot concur, and

---

27 St. Thomas, *ST* I, q. 19, a. 9: "Malum culpae, quod privat ordinem ad bonum divinum, Deus nullo modo vult."

28 C. Journet, *Meaning of Evil,* 147.

29 See, for example, Réginald Garrigou-Lagrange, *God, His Existence and His Nature: A Thomistic Solution of Certain Agnostic Antinomies,* vol. 2, trans. Bede Rose (London: B. Herder, 1936), 380. With Journet we must stress the broad and *analogical* use of the term "permission."

30 St. Thomas, *ST* I, q. 14, a. 10; q. 15, a. 3, ad 1.

31 C. Journet, "De la condition initiale privilégiée de l'homme," 217–18; idem, *L'Église du Verbe Incarné,* vol. 3 (Paris: Desclée de Brouwer, 1969), 273–74.

32 What we call "science of vision" *(scientia visionis)* is the knowledge of what was, what is, or what will be in reality, that is, knowledge joined to will in the exercise of causality. This "science of vision" is not the same as the "science of simple understanding" *(scientia simplicis intelligentiae),* which has to do with the knowledge of possible things and does not involve any act of the will; cf. St. Thomas, *ST* I, q. 14, a. 9.

inasmuch as He concurs as first cause in the physical entity of the sin."[33] God knows the sin insofar as he is the first cause of the creature's act (he enables the creature to act); as for the failing, God is not its cause but he knows it insofar as he permits it, although this permission is not the cause of the sin.

This allows Garrigou-Lagrange to maintain a twofold affirmation: the universal scope of divine Providence (nothing escapes divine Providence, not even sin), and the guiltlessness of God (God is not responsible for sin). "Therefore evil is known by God in his decree permitting through condemning it. He also envisages it in His sublime motives for permitting it."[34] According to this teaching, God knows the creature's free acts "in the divine decree by which they are made present to Him from all eternity."[35] By *decree* we mean the act of knowing joined to the will: The "permissive decree" is thus the act whereby God knows sin and allows it.[36] This decree is therefore the *medium* by which God knows the wicked human act. If we take into account God's causality as it relates to the human act (the creature could not act, even for evil, without the efficacious concurrence of the first cause that gives the necessary impulse to the act as such), Garrigou-Lagrange's position may be summed up this way: "God knows future sins in a twofold decree, namely, permissive and effective."[37] In a similar vein, Jean-Hervé Nicolas specifies that first, God knows the subject of sin; second, God knows the failing in his permissive decree; and third, God knows the sinful act in the causal idea of this act (determining decree).[38]

Journet parts company with this teaching on certain points and qualifies it on others. With Maritain, Journet stresses the *eternity* of divine knowledge: God does not know sin *beforehand*, but knows it in his "eternal now,"

---

33 R. Garrigou-Lagrange, *God, His Existence and His Nature,* 70.

34 Ibid., 70–71.

35 Ibid., 73; idem, *The One God: A Commentary on the First Part of St. Thomas' Theological Summa,* trans. Bede Rose (London: B. Herder, 1946), 444–46.

36 R. Garrigou-Lagrange, *God, His Existence and His Nature,* 66–67. The expression "divine decree," corresponds to what St. Thomas calls "determinatio voluntatis et intellectus Dei" (idem, *The One God,* 521). In the case of the permissive decree, the knowledge in question is the "science of vision" *(scientia visionis).*

37 R. Garrigou-Lagrange, *The One God,* 587: "God knows future sins in a *twofold decree,* namely, *permissive and effective*; for there is a *positive element* in sin, that is, the act or effect, which can be produced only with the concurrence of the First Cause; and there is the *privative element,* and this comes, however, solely from a defectible and deficient cause."

38 Jean-Hervé Nicolas, "La permission du péché," *Revue Thomiste* 60 (1960): 516; there is a priority of the "permissive decree" over the "determining decree," just as in sin there is the natural priority of the failing over the positive determination. In no case does God determine the failing itself (see below).

wherein all the moments of time are indivisibly present.[39] This teaching does not differ from that of Garrigou-Lagrange, except for the stress Journet lays on this point by reprising a famous page from Maritain's *Existence and the Existent*, repeated several times in the writings of the theologian: "The divine plan is not a scenario prepared in advance."[40] Journet's position, like Maritain's, is clear: It is a matter of avoiding all determinism and thus preserving the divine guiltlessness.

As for the divine knowledge of sin by means of the permissive decree, it seems unacceptable to Journet (as well as to Maritain). It is not enough to say that God knows sins in his essence alone, but we must also say that he knows them "in his essence insofar as created existents are seen in it, and in them this privation which their freedom is the first cause of."[41] In other words, through his science of vision, God sees the sin *in the will* of the man who refuses grace, and he sees it *in the instant* when this will refuses the divine impulse of love.[42] Here Journet takes up again and at length Maritain's position in his *Existence and the Existent* and in *La clé des chants*, explaining that "evil can only be known in the instant when it wounds existence" and that the science of vision attains it eternally, in its presentness, in that very instant when it happens.[43] God sees sin, of which he is not the cause, in the will of the man who brings to nothing ("nihilates") the divine motion to the good; he knows sin "in the creature's freely nihilating will."[44] With Maritain, then, Journet denies the place that Garrigou-Lagrange's Thomism assigns to the permissive decree as a means of knowing sin: "Unlike several theologians that we usually follow, we do not conceive of this permissive decree as the 'medium' by which God knows the deficiency of his creatures."[45]

What is at stake in this thesis is obvious: Journet will not accept the view that the permissive decree *precedes* man's sin in any way whatever

39 C. Journet, "De la condition initiale privilégiée de l'homme," 217–19; idem, *L'Église du Verbe Incarné,* vol. 3, 274.

40 C. Journet, "De la condition initiale privilégiée de l'homme," 218; idem, *L'Église du Verbe Incarné,* vol. 3, 274; cf. Jacques Maritain, *Existence and the Existent* (Garden City, NY: Doubleday, Image Books, 1956), 122.

41 C. Journet, "De la condition initiale privilégiée de l'homme," 218; idem, *L'Église du Verbe Incarné,* vol. 3, 274.

42 C. Journet, "De la condition initiale privilégiée de l'homme," 216–22; *L'Église du Verbe Incarné,* vol. 3, 273–78; *Meaning of Evil,* 180–82.

43 C. Journet, "De la condition initiale privilégiée de l'homme," 216–22; *L'Église du Verbe Incarné,* vol. 3, 273–78; *Meaning of Evil,* 180–82; J. Maritain, *Existence and the Existent,* 112–22; idem, *"La clé des chants,"* in *Œuvres complètes,* vol. 5: *1932–35* (Fribourg: Éditions Universitaires; Paris: Éditions Saint-Paul, 1982), 790–92.

44 C. Journet, *L'Église du Verbe Incarné,* vol. 3, 278.

45 Ibid.; Journet refers to J. Maritain, *Existence and the Existent,* 122–25. See C. Journet, "De la condition initiale privilégiée de l'homme," 221–22.

(hence the insistence on the eternal *presentness* of divine knowledge), for man has the entire initiative in sinning (hence the statement that God knows sin *in man's failing will*). With Maritain, he endeavors to exclude every divine initiative in connection with moral evil, even the permissive decree, and recognizes the divine initiative only in connection with the good. Thus, in the case of sin, every determining knowledge on the part of God must be put aside since God is absolutely not the author of sin. Therefore God knows sin only *in the culpable will* that has refused the divine motion to the good and not in the intervention of a divine decree. In a similar vein, Journet explains that "God knows the creature's refusal—certainly not by causing it, for he does not cause what nihilates—in the positive motion to the good that the creature nihilates."[46] These explanations rest upon the understanding of sin as a "nihilation" (in French, *néantement*) and upon the position of the permissive decree as a consequence (Maritain).[47]

4. In What Way Does God Permit Sin? The Consequent Permissive Decree

According to the usual thesis of Thomists, sin "only takes place following a purely permissive decree of God."[48] With this statement the Thomists do not intend to attribute causality to God with respect to the sinful failing: God "only concurs in the physical act of the sin, not in any way in the disorder inherent in it."[49] As Garrigou-Lagrange explains, the creature's free will needs a divine *motion* to be determined to something. God and man must be considered as two "total causes," one of which (the creature as second cause) is subordinated to the other (God, the first cause). If the human will could be determined by itself alone, our freedom would have the dignity of God's primary freedom, or resemble it univocally.[50] Far from suppressing our freedom, the motion by which God moves our will to

---

46 C. Journet, "Dieu est-il responsable du péché?" 232.

47 As regards the critique that Journet makes of knowledge by permissive decree, we should point out that Réginald Garrigou-Lagrange, while professing the teaching that Charles Journet rejects, nevertheless does not make of the permissive decree a cause of moral evil. Rather, what is proper to Maritain and Journet's position is the exclusion of all divine activity that would precede the wicked human action, in order to exclude any divine intervention in the realm of evil: God has all the initiative in the realm of the good, the creature has all the initiative in the realm of the bad. For a balanced overview of this debate, if yet close to Journet's explanation concerning the knowledge of sin, see Georges Bavaud, "Comment Dieu permet-il et connaît-il le péché?" *Revue Thomiste* 61 (1961): 226–40.

48 R. Garrigou-Lagrange, *Les perfections divines* (Paris: Beauchesne, 1936), 115.

49 Ibid., 116.

50 R. Garrigou-Lagrange, *God, His Existence and His Nature,* 356–57.

determine itself is the source of our freedom: In us and with us, the divine will causes the free mode of our act. This does not mean that God is the cause of moral failing: If in the acts that precede the definitive choice, there comes into play a bad movement that inclines us to a sinful choice, God is in no way the cause of this failing, as it belongs entirely to the defectible nature of the creature.[51] When we say then that God permits sin, we mean that God allows sin to happen. This doctrine tries to account for the guiltlessness of God without lessening his universal causality (God's causality in human action, even wicked, considered as action and as free).

Pushing further the reflection on the relationship between God's permission and man's sin, the usual teaching of Thomists insists that human failing does indeed precede God's refusal of actual grace, but this failing presupposes the divine allowance of sin and would not happen without it.[52] In other words, if sin happens, it is because God permits it, but this permission in no way is the cause of sin. Such, in its broad outlines, is the solution of the "antecedent permissive decree."[53]

Like all Thomists, Journet agrees that sin must be explained in virtue of a divine permission, but he denies the antecedent permissive decree. Firstly, Journet takes up from Maritain the idea of "nihilation." While every initiative comes from God as it relates to the good, man alone takes the initiative for sin: Sin "is produced *without* God."[54] Journet subscribes wholly to Maritain's observations on the dissymmetry between the realm of the good and that of evil.[55] He reproaches certain Thomists (such as Bañez and the school that follows him) for trying to explain evil in the same way as we explain good, despite the total dissymmetry between the two realms. By sinning, man on his own initiative, "sprung from his nothingness," eludes the flow of divine causality. "For a free creature, insofar as it has come out of nothing, has this fearful privilege of being able to nullify within itself the influence of God."[56]

51 Ibid., 380–4; idem, *Les perfections divines,* 211–24.

52 R. Garrigou-Lagrange, *God, His Existence and His Nature,* vol. 2, 372–73. Here the divine allowance of sin is linked to the absence of "efficacious grace." What we call "efficacious grace" is the grace that effectively moves to action, as distinct from "sufficient grace," which gives the proximate power to act but not the acting itself.

53 See J.-H. Nicolas, "La permission du péché," 509–46; see footnote 38 above.

54 C. Journet, *Meaning of Evil,* 178.

55 Ibid., 179: "In the line of evil-doing, the creature is first cause. [. . .] The first initiative towards good acts comes always from God [. . .] but [. . .] the first initiative to evil-doing always comes from the creature." Cf. idem, "Dieu est-il responsable du péché?" 222 and 230–32. On this dissymmetry between the realm of the good and that of evil, Journet follows Maritain expressly: see J. Maritain, *Existence and the Existent,* 94–99. See Journet, "De la condition initiale privilégiée de l'homme," 217.

56 C. Journet, *Meaning of Evil,* 178; idem, "Dieu est-il responsable du péché?" 231–32.

This nihilation must not be understood as an act of annihilation, like a reduction of a being to nothingness, for that would take us back to the positive line that Journet precisely wants to avoid in explaining sin. Rather, we are dealing with a privation, a negation. More exactly, Journet—like Maritain—calls *nihilation* the non-consideration of the rule, the first principle of sin, the free will's initiative of nothingness. Thus the first moment of sin, which is a privation, consists in the creature's "nihilation" of the divine motion to the good. Here Journet is quite close to Maritain's thinking on the "shatterable motion," that is, the divine motion to considering the right rule of action, which the creature can put in check. Based on this, Journet takes up one of Maritain's central theses: The permissive decree is not antecedent but *follows upon* the evil will's nihilation of the shatterable motion.[57]

According to Charles Journet, as we have already noted, God knows sin by knowing the nihilating initiative in man's free will. When we say then that God "permits sin," this means that God "abstains from supplying a remedy to the first failing of man and lets the act, deviated at its source, play itself out according to its own rules. [. . .] God permits the sin simply by not intervening to prevent it: Here we have 'the permissive decree of sin.' "[58] For those Thomists whom Journet wishes to part company with, "the permissive divine will precedes the nihilating initiative of the free creature." Instead, Journet holds that "God forsakes the creature only after having been forsaken by the creature," in such a way that "the withdrawal of the creature precedes the withdrawal of God."[59] Subsequently, as we have seen, the withdrawal of the creature is not known to God by an antecedent permissive decree.

More precisely, Journet distinguishes two moments in the resistance to divine motion: A first moment when God may intervene to stave off the sin, and a second moment when the sin occurs if God has not come to counter the nihilating will.[60] No sin occurs, therefore, without a permissive decree of

57 J. Maritain, *Existence and the Existent,* 99–112.

58 C. Journet, "De la condition initiale privilégiée de l'homme," 220.

59 Ibid., 221, note 2. This affirmation is not lacking in traditional Thomistic teaching (see R. Garrigou-Lagrange, *Les perfections divines,* 233). The debate arises rather from the usage of the sufficient grace/efficacious grace distinction (R. Garrigou-Lagrange, J.-H. Nicolas), or shatterable motion/unshatterable motion (J. Maritain, C. Journet), and therefore from the relationship between the permissive decree and the withdrawal of God, as well as from the notion of "nihilation."

60 Following J. Maritain, C. Journet explains that in the first moment the human will can, "by nihilating it, interrupt the shatterable motion whereby God directs it to consider the rule before acting"; in the second moment, "the will proceeds to the election that will be disordered"; when the shatterable motion is not shattered, it then gives way to an unshatterable motion under which the good act is produced (C. Journet, "De la condition initiale privilégiée de l'homme," 221, note 1). Thus there are "two divine permissions": in the first instance, there is a

God, but far from coming before the nihilation of the divine will, this decree is by nature subsequent to it. "For us, the permissive decree is God's decision not to use extraordinary means to intervene and prevent the evil act from unfolding."[61] The permissive decree looks, then, like a divine non-intervention in face of a human initiative (the non-consideration of the rule that the shatterable divine motion would lead us to consider; this is not yet a moral evil, but it gets the creature's process toward it underway). These explanations are based on the distinction between shatterable motion, which the human will can put in check, and unshatterable motion, a divine motion that intervenes in every morally good act by determining it. They can give rise to questions about Maritain's position, questions raised some time ago by Marie-Joseph Nicolas and Jean-Hervé Nicolas.[62]

By and large, these explanations of Journet give Jacques Maritain great credit for untying the knotty problem of the relationship between divine grace and human freedom. Maritain's contribution, underlined and adopted by Journet, consists in the two following affirmations: first, the dissymmetry between the order of the good and the order of evil (man has all the initiative in the realm of evil, while God has all the initiative in the realm of the good); and second, the denial of a "scenario played out in advance" (eternity of divine knowledge, the creature's nihilation of the divine motion, denial of the antecedent permissive decree, the divine knowledge of sin in the nihilating human will). According to Journet, it is in this way that Maritain enabled theology to strictly affirm the *guiltlessness of God*, who wills sin neither directly nor indirectly.[63]

---

conditional permission implied in the possibility of thwarting the motion that directs us to considering the rule of acting; in the second instance, there is the permission, pure and simple, of letting the free action continue with its own dynamism (C. Journet, *L'Église du Verbe Incarné,* vol. 3, 166–67). Journet refers expressly to Maritain, *Existence and the Existent,* 176–90.

61 C. Journet, "De la condition initiale privilégiée de l'homme," 222.

62 Marie-Joseph Nicolas, "La liberté humaine et le problème du mal," *Revue Thomiste* 48 (1948): 191–217; Jean-Hervé Nicolas, "La permission du péché," 5–37 and 185–206. The criticism deals not only with Maritain's position as it relates to the universality of providence (God's causality only in the realm of the good), but also with the distinction between shatterable motion and unshatterable motion, as well as the notion of "nihilation," which J.-H. Nicolas deems ambiguous (nihilation, a pure negation that is not yet a fault, would still already be resistance to God). As we shall see further on, it also deals with the motive for permitting evil. Maritain responded to J.-H. Nicolas's criticism: J. Maritain, *Dieu et la permission du mal* (Paris: Desclée de Brouwer, 1963). For a critical appreciation favorable to Maritain's position, see Michel-Louis Guérard des Lauriers, "Le péché et la causalité," *Bulletin Thomiste* 11 (1960–62): 553–637.

63 C. Journet, "Jacques Maritain Theologian," *The New Scholasticism* 46/1 (1972): 33–35. For Maritain, the absolute guiltlessness of God is "the fundamental certitude,

5. Why Does God Permit Sin?

When Journet speculates about the motive for the divine permission of evil, he comes up with a clear and unchanging answer: Evil is permitted *for a greater good.* He grounds this response on his reading of St. Augustine and St. Thomas. He stresses its mysterious character by making clear that this kind of answer does not flow from an a priori metaphysical necessity, but rather from an investigation that takes into account three statements of fact: an infinitely good and powerful God, a world where evil is rife, and the necessary triumph of good over evil (the good's superabundant compensation for evil).[64] The particular characteristic of Journet's thinking is his insistence on the *analogical value* he sees in this response, as it applies to all forms of evil: the evil of nature, the evil of punishment, "and even the evil of fault." God permits each form of evil "for some greater good."[65] Of these three forms, Journet pays most attention to the evil of fault (sin),[66] while professing a basic Chistocentrism.

What is this "greater good" for the sake of which God permits sin? Journet gives his clear answer in his very first writings, and particularly in his study of the original fall: Adam's transgression is "preordained to Christ," not, to be sure, as a means, but insofar as sin, once allowed, will be repaired by Christ. In the single design of God, "all things are ordered to the glory of Christ the Redeemer."[67] For Journet, the glory of Christ is thus God's *first aim*, the *very reason for the universe* and its *crowning*, the *highest cause* for which everything has been arranged.[68] Here Journet is expressly following the Christocentrism of the *Salmaticenses*, for whom all things, including the grace of the angels and the primordial grace of man in the state of innocence, existed for Christ, *propter Christum.* This priority of Christ must be understood in the order of values and of the end "in view of which" *(finis cujus gratia).*[69] This does not mean that in the order of conditionality Christ was willed independently of certain events (according to the Thomistic thesis, the incarnation of Christ was decreed as a remedy for sin).[70] Journet

---

the rock to which we must cling in this question of moral evil" (J. Maritain, *Dieu et la permission du mal,* 11).

64 C. Journet, *Meaning of Evil,* 85–86.

65 Ibid., 85; cf. idem, "Dieu et le mal: Aspect métaphysique du problème," 234–36.

66 Concerning the evil of nature and the evil of suffering, Journet's thinking repeats the common teaching of Thomists.

67 C. Journet, "De la condition initiale privilégiée de l'homme," 213–16.

68 Ibid.

69 The end "cujus gratia" is the reason for which other things are willed, the end for which everything has been arranged; see idem, *L'Église du Verbe Incarné,* vol. 3, 270, note 2.

70 C. Journet, "De la condition initiale privilégiée de l'homme," 213–16; idem, *L'Église du Verbe Incarné,* vol. 3, 270–72.

knows that on this point, St. Thomas's interpretation is delicate. Thomists agree in principle on one affirmation: If Adam had not sinned, the Son of God might have not become flesh. But a difference arises concerning the relationship between the permission of sin and the good willed by God. Certain masters of the Thomistic school (Cajetan, John of St. Thomas) refuse to appeal to Christ immediately in answering the question, "Why did God permit Adam's sin or original sin?" More precisely, Cajetan explains that God allows sin because he is exercising his providence in respecting the conditions of created beings, that is, by acting in conformity with the nature of creatures. Respecting man's freedom, God allows sin and then seizes the *occasion* of the sin to bring about the redeeming incarnation of the Son of God.[71] Pursuing this line of thought, Jean-Hervé Nicolas, in his debate with Maritain, explains that sin is the occasion of this good, with God turning the evil that happens to the best advantage, but evil is not allowed only for the good things that God can draw from it: The permission of evil is not of itself ordered to the obtaining of this good as its raison d'être.[72] For his part, Journet prefers the solution of the Carmelites of Salamanca, who answer that God permitted the sin of Adam *for the sake of the redeeming incarnation*, in anticipation of the glory of Christ, since God allows sin only for the sake of a greater good.[73] Such is the "simple and grandiose" solution that Journet rallies to (without giving up the thesis that finds the reason for the permission of sin in the freedom that God has willed for his spiritual creatures).[74] All things, including Adam's grace and the permission of sin, are ordered to the glory of Christ the Redeemer, albeit in different ways: Sin cannot be a means to the glory of Christ, but it is a precondition for its possibility. This thesis can be associated with Journet's teaching on the grace of the angels.

---

71 Cajetan, *In Tertiam,* q. 1, a. 3 (Leonine edition, vol. 11, 16). What is at stake in the debate has to do with the unity of the divine plan and the "contrariness" that sin sets against God's design. Must we posit one single divine decree whereby Christ is willed as Redeemer (the Carmelites of Salamanca, Journet), or one plan in which Christ would not have been foreseen, then another plan whereby Christ is willed, this last alone being willed with an efficacious will (John of St. Thomas continuing Cajetan)? Cf. M.-J. Nicolas, "La liberté humaine et le problème du mal," 205, note 1.

72 J.-H. Nicolas, "La permission du péché," 538–44; idem, *Synthèse dogmatique, Complément: De l'univers à la Trinité* (Fribourg: Éditions Universitaires; Paris: Beauchesne, 1993), 386–90. According to J.-H. Nicolas, we cannot say that sin is permitted for the sake of a greater good, but we have to say: God wills this good because sin has taken place. On evil as an "ocassion" *(occasio)* for some good, see St. Thomas, I *Sent.*, dist. 46, q. 1, a. 2; *In Rom* 6:1 (#469).

73 C. Journet, "De la condition initiale privilégiée de l'homme," 215, note 2; idem, *Meaning of Evil,* 256–59.

74 C. Journet, *Meaning of Evil,* 256–57.

From their first moment, the grace and substantial glory of the angels are ordered to Christ as to their final cause. The primordial grace of the angels, at the dawn of the world, is finalized by the influx of Christ.[75] In this way, Journet upholds the primacy of Christ even to its utmost consequences: *The glory of Christ the Redeemer is the end that, in and of themselves, all things willed or permitted by God are ordered to.*[76]

A final thesis comes into play to complete these explanations: The world of the redemption, the world of Christ's grace, is all in all *better* than the world of Adam's innocence.[77] Therefore, the "greater good" that the permission of Adam's sin anticipates is not only Christ himself (the hypostatic union of God and man in Christ),[78] or his Mother, but the order of Christ's grace in its full scope. The world of the Redemption, that is, participation in Christ's grace and glory, involves us in a higher destiny than the one Adam had before his fall. To lay out this Christological thesis, Journet calls upon St. Bonaventure, St. Thomas, the Carmelites of Salamanca, and in particular St. Francis de Sales, whom "[t]his view was exceptionally dear to."[79]

Such is the understanding of the *Exultet's* "Felix Culpa" that Charles Journet presents:[80] the Church is gathered around the Word made flesh, and a new universe is reshaped bit by bit, the universe of the Redemption, which all in all is incomparably better than what went before.[81] This understanding goes beyond the letter of St. Thomas and looks rather like a *Christocentric interpretation* of St. Thomas Aquinas (insertion of some elements of Duns Scotus's Christocentrism into the heart of a Thomistic theology).[82] As for Journet's thought itself, we can observe the convergence of his doctrine with that of Maritain.[83]

---

75 As regards Adam's state of innocence, Journet states: "If the humanity of the redemption is first in the order of intention, the humanity of innocence is first in the order of execution." C. Journet, *L'Église du Verbe incarné,* vol. 3, 279.

76 C. Journet, *L'Église du Verbe incarné,* vol. 3, 207–15 and 269–73.

77 C. Journet, "Dieu et le mal: Aspect métaphysique du problème," 268; idem, *Meaning of Evil,* 86 and 256–59.

78 As St. Thomas says, God loves Christ more than the whole human race and more than the whole universe. *ST* I, q. 20, a. 4, ad 1.

79 C. Journet, *Meaning of Evil,* 258; idem, "La Rédemption, drame de l'amour de Dieu," part 2, 82.

80 C. Journet, *Meaning of Evil,* 86 and 259; idem, "La Rédemption, drame de l'amour de Dieu," part 2, 82. Cf. Aquinas, *ST* III, q. 1, a. 3, ad 3.

81 C. Journet, "La Rédemption, drame de l'amour de Dieu," part 2, 82.

82 On this question of Scotist Christocentrism and Thomism, see Marie-Joseph Nicolas, "Le Christ et la création d'après saint Thomas d'Aquin," in *Studia mediaevalia et mariologica P. Carolo Balic, OFM septuagesimum explenti annum dicata* (Rome: Ed. Antonianum, 1971), 79–100.

83 J. Maritain, *God and the Permission of Evil,* trans. Joseph Evans (Milwaukee: Bruce Publishing Co., 1966), 62–63. Without going into the Christological question,

6. God Wounded by Sin

Sin does not destroy God's design since in this design sin is ordered to a greater good. Moreover, Journet is very firm on the singleness of the divine plan, as we have just recalled. This does not mean that God is "indifferent" to sin, as if sin did not touch God, did not bring him any vexation, any frustration. Journet does not merely invoke the infinite majesty of God, which sin strikes at by defrauding it of what is justly due to it: "More concretely, it [sin] hurts God *Himself*, admittedly not *in* Himself, but where He is vulnerable, that is to say, in the love by which He strives to save us,"[84] for "it was impossible for God to love us *without at the same time needing our love*."[85]

This consideration of God's vulnerability and the wound sin inflicts on him, which Journet reminds us of repeatedly, picks up on Maritain's explanation in his *An Introduction to the Basic Problems of Moral Philosophy*:

> Sin *deprives* the divine will of something it really desired [. . .]. If I sin, something which God desired and loved will not be for all. This is through my first initiative. I am therefore the cause—the nihilating cause—of a privation with respect to God, a privation as to the terminus or desired effect (in no way as to the good of God Himself). [. . .] Sin deprives God Himself of something which He conditionally but really desired. [. . .] Moral defect affects the Uncreated, in no way in Himself, since He is absolutely invulnerable, but in the things and the effects He desires and loves. Here, one can say that God is the most vulnerable of beings.[86]

Journet continues: "God indeed is afraid of sin, *He is afraid on my account of the evil I can do to Him*."[87] In Journet as in Maritain, this explanation of God's vulnerability and the deprivation of love that sin inflicts on God shows a very vivid perception of a real divine wounding, the depth of

---

Jacques Maritain (in answer to the criticism J.-H. Nicolas had leveled against him) maintains here that "God permits evil only *in view* of a greater good, that is to say, by referring or ordaining this evil to a greater good"; God allows sin "because God is certain that He will draw a greater good from the evil which the creature will be able to commit."

84 C. Journet, *Meaning of Evil,* 182. Journet repeats and develops the same explanation in the passages indicated in the following footnotes.

85 C. Journet, "De l'espérance," 211.

86 Jacques Maritain, *An Introduction to the Basic Problems of Moral Philosophy,* trans. Cornelia Borgerhoff (Albany, NY: Magi Books, 1990), 196–97, quoted in C. Journet, *Meaning of Evil,* 183; idem, "Dieu est-il responsable du péché?" 235–36; idem, "De l'espérance," 204–5; idem, "La Rédemption, drame de l'amour de Dieu," part 1, 53–54.

87 C. Journet, *Meaning of Evil,* 183.

moral evil in the eyes of God, "this thing, *unacceptable to God,* that sin is":[88] Sin cannot destroy God in himself, but it is truly *God himself* that sin wounds. In their basic elements, these explanations that distinguish the being of God from his effects, God's conditional will from his absolute will, or God's antecedent will from his consequent will, remain right in line with the doctrine of St. Thomas Aquinas.

When St. Thomas analyzes the distress that is tied to mercy, he explains, as a matter of fact, that the merciful person is the one who is affected by the distress of another, who feels sorrow for the misery of another "as if it were his own misery."[89] Compassion lies in this: "He who loves looks upon his friend as another self, and counts his friend's hurt as his own."[90] This is why the merciful man acts: He provides a remedy for another's misery out of love, "as if for his own misery." As regards God, St. Thomas explains, he does not experience mercy inasmuch as it is a passion tied to the sensible appetite (because of the immateriality and immutability of God): God is not afflicted *in himself,* but he is merciful *in his effects,* in the activity of his love for the creatures he loves.[91] It is in the effects of God's love that his compassion, distress, or sorrow find their reality: "Mercy is especially *(maxime)* to be attributed to God, as seen in its effect *(secundum effectum),* but not as an affection of passion *(non secundum passionis affectum).*"[92] This is the teaching that Journet repeats while stressing the reality of the love that God has for his creatures and that sin wounds. In his last writings, however, Journet goes a step further by posing the question of a real suffering *in God.*

7. The "Mysterious Suffering" of God

A work by Jacques Maritain gave Charles Journet the opportunity to delve more deeply into his reflection on God's vulnerability. In the course of an article on theological knowledge, which was published in the *Revue Thomiste* in 1969, the philosopher included several pages titled "A Great Problem."[93] Maritain's reflection starts with the Thomistic teaching on the divine names. Analogy implies that the names we use to speak of God have a twofold aspect: (1) the perfections themselves that the names signify and

---

88 C. Journet, "De l'espérance," 205.

89 St. Thomas, *ST* I, q. 21, a. 3.

90 St. Thomas, *ST* II–II, q. 30, a. 2.

91 St. Thomas, *ST* I, q. 21, a. 3.

92 Ibid.

93 Jacques Maritain, "Quelques réflexions sur le savoir théologique," *Revue Thomiste* 69 (1969): 5–27, cf. 14–27. This article presents the fruits of a seminar that Maritain held with some superiors of the Little Brothers of Jesus at Kolbsheim in the summer of 1968.

that exist properly in God, and even more properly in him than in creatures wherein they exist by participation in the divine plenitude; and (2) the manner of signification ("mode of signifying") of these names, a manner by which no name is properly attributed to God since in our language names retain the mode of signifying that befits creatures.

Maritain pushes this doctrine of St. Thomas higher and to its furthest point when reflecting on God's mercy. As we cited above, according to St. Thomas, "mercy is especially to be attributed to God, as seen in its effect, but not as an affection of passion." While recognizing the perfect truth of this doctrine, Maritain nonetheless adds, "Yet that leaves the mind unsatisfied"; must we not recognize in God's mercy a reality as we concede to his love? "Should we not say of mercy, then, that it exists in God according to what it is, and not only according to what it *does*?"[94]

In answer, Maritain asserts that mercy exists in God as a perfection of his being, "though in a state of perfection *for which there is no name*: a glory or splendor unnamed, implying no imperfection, unlike what we call suffering or sorrow, and for which we have no idea, no concept, and no name that would be applicable to God."[95] Here Maritain evokes divine perfections that are "nameless," "unnamable" *(innominabiles).* In this way, the affection of passion, the suffering linked to the human experience of mercy, although embedded in our imperfection, would be a participation in this "nameless and unnamable" perfection of God, a perfection that affects neither his plenitude of being, nor his immutability, nor his happiness.

These observations, inspired by Scripture and theology, make an appeal to considerations of an anthropological nature as well. In our human experience, the suffering of love is not a wholly negative reality; it is not merely a deprivation but also carries a positive and noble element, fertile and precious, in short—a perfection. The "mysterious exemplar" of such nobility would be the analogate in God. Such an exemplar of merciful suffering in God, in whom all is perfection, would then be a part of God's happiness and beyond what is humanly conceivable.[96] Two references to the thought of Raïssa Maritain suggest her influence on the position worked out by Jacques Maritain, as well as the influence of Léon Bloy.[97] Journet paid great attention to these pages, and he cites them several times

---

94 Ibid., 16–17.

95 Ibid., 17.

96 Ibid.

97 Quoting Maritain, Journet explicitly repeats the mentioning of Raïssa Maritain and Léon Bloy, C. Journet, "De l'espérance," 206. For a short survey of Maritain's teaching and how it is confronted with that of St. Thomas, see Gilles Emery, "L'immutabilité du Dieu d'amour et les problèmes du discours sur la 'souffrance de Dieu,'" *Nova et Vetera* (French) 74/1 (1999): 5–37, cf. 17–20 and 27–37.

in his last writings.[98] The French journal *Nova et Vetera* has published extracts from them.[99]

Along with Maritain, Journet gives Marie-Dominique Molinié credit for having stressed the "quasi-suffering" of God, a deep mystery of the unspeakable sorrow that our sin causes God, which, instead of disintegrating the Godhead, "reveals the existence in It of an unsuspected grandeur." "It is important that we take very seriously the biblical expressions that show God as 'moved to his depths.'"[100] If it is indeed with Maritain that Journet's speculation delves more deeply into the mystery of God's suffering, his references to Molinié make clear the biblical and spiritual inspiration of this reflection. Journet shows a great appreciation for Molinié: In the French journal *Nova et Vetera,* he presents his papers under the title "A Theology of Great Style"[101] (there is nothing humdrum about such praise from the pen of Charles Journet).

Molinié's paper dealing with the *Mystery of the Redemption* (1970) contains an important reflection on the "suffering" of God in a chapter on the divine mercy that arrives at Maritain's conclusions, albeit by a different path.[102] Journet retains Molinié's affirmation of God's "quasi-suffering" as it relates to the refusal of the creature to whom he wishes to give himself.[103] As in Maritain, so in Molinié, Journet finds the expression of a sound grasp of the divine immutability, as well as the recognition of the mysterious and exemplary reality of suffering in the Triune God:

> In God, impassibility is not an *absence* of emotion, it is not indifference, it is an excess of love and of joy [. . .]. Hence, we must be careful before we say that God does not suffer . . . , because his love for us is no joke. Those who have not sounded the depths of this mercy infallibly imagine that God does not suffer by virtue of a kind of indifference . . . , and this mistake is much more catastrophic than the anthropomorphism that pictures God as suffering [. . .]. The sufferings of

98 C. Journet, "De l'espérance," 205–6; idem, "Jacques Maritain Theologian," 35–36; idem, "La Rédemption, drame de l'amour de Dieu," part 1, 57–60.

99 C. Journet, "La souffrance de la créature," *Nova et Vetera* (French) 44 (1969): 226–28.

100 C. Journet, "La Rédemption, drame de l'amour de Dieu," part 1, 55–56.

101 C. Journet, "Une théologie de grand style. Les cahiers de M.-D. Molinié, OP, sur la vie spirituelle," *Nova et Vetera* (French) 48 (1973): 299–310.

102 Marie-Dominique (André) Molinié, *Le mystère de la Rédemption,* mimeographed paper (1970), 37–45. This paper has recently been published in book form: Marie-Dominique Molinié, *Un feu sur la terre,* vol. 6: *Le mystère de la Rédemption* (Paris: Téqui, 2001), cf. 54–64.

103 See, for example, Journet, "La Rédemption, drame de l'amour de Dieu," part 1, 56.

> Christ merely reflect in a human way the absolutely divine mystery of the Trinitarian love wounded by our refusal.[104]

This being the case, the thought of St. Thomas cited above (God is merciful in respect to the *effectus* of mercy but not in respect to the *passionis affectus*) seems insufficient. We must "go a step further on the road opened by St. Thomas,"[105] for St. Thomas has left this question open: It has remained "incompletely resolved by St. Thomas."[106] There is, to be sure, a certain suffering that is incompatible with God's absolute perfection. But there exists an unutterable compassion affecting God in his relation to our wretchedness (our sin) that does not entail any imperfection. It has to do with a "pure perfection" that we must acknowledge in God, for which we have no concept, and which is the "hurt of God."[107] The created analogate of this perfection is *magnanimity*, the nobility that sorrow carries with it when it is overcome by greatness of soul. In this manner, Journet, with Maritain, holds that mercy exists in God not merely with respect to its effects, but *according to what it is*, taken however to a degree of completion above every name, an "unnamed" perfection, the exemplar of what it is in us when it is lived with nobility and magnanimity.[108]

This meditation on "the troubling mystery"[109] of the "mysterious suffering" or "quasi-suffering"[110] of God stays very close to Maritain's reflections. Journet contents himself with brief comments on these reflections without developing at length their epistemological (divine names) and metaphysical aspects. At the same time, Journet does not give up his conviction that sin reaches unto God himself, though *not in himself* (following the previous explanations of Maritain),[111] thereby suggesting the great caution this mystery imposes on our human reflections:

> It will be difficult for theology to go further than the great meditation we have just summarized, albeit quite rashly. It remains satisfied in showing that there is no metaphysical impossibility in saying that God, absolutely invulnerable in himself, is unutterably vulnerable in

---

104 M.-D. (A.) Molinié, *Le mystère de la Rédemption,* 40–42; quoted in C. Journet, "La Rédemption, drame de l'amour de Dieu," part 1, 56.

105 C. Journet, "De l'espérance," 206, quoting Maritain.

106 C. Journet, "La Rédemption, drame de l'amour de Dieu," part 1, 52 and 57.

107 Ibid., 57.

108 C. Journet, "De l'espérance," 203–8; idem, "La Rédemption, drame de l'amour de Dieu," part 1, 57–60.

109 C. Journet, "La Rédemption, drame de l'amour de Dieu," part 1, 57.

110 Ibid., 55–56.

111 Ibid., 53–54.

the love he bears for us and which is the arena of his mercies. It does not betray the truth since it leads us to a divine perfection that for us remains nameless and unnamable.[112]

We can easily recognize an important pastoral motive at the heart of Journet's and Maritain's theological reflections on the mysterious suffering of God. Care for those to whom Christian preaching is directed does not dictate to theology what is true and what is not, but it makes it attentive to the way the faith is expressed. Certainly God is not wounded in himself; he knows no deficiency:

> On this we are clear. But if we preach to men that God cannot be hurt by the sight of their disorders and the sufferings that ensue, will they not picture some impassible God, indifferent to pity, too far above them to worry about their lot? Are they not going to turn away from the true God and even end up getting angry at him? So what will the Christian do?[113]

Preaching in univocal fashion on the divine impassibility runs the risk of presenting God as a stranger to man, as man's *competitor.* Preaching thus on the divine immutability, not well clarified, may then beget indifference or rebellion. With Molinié, Journet agrees that the concept of an immutability of indifference is a graver error than the anthropomorphism that endows God with passions, for *nothing* that concerns creatures can be indifferent to God.[114] Recognition of a nameless perfection, the eternal exemplar in God of what in us is distress with nobility (magnanimity), permits us to "banish from the mind of men the abominable idea of an impassible God who abandons the creature to itself and who takes pleasure at the sight of an unfolding human history where evil abounds."[115]

In these reflections, Journet made every effort to avoid a contradiction. If mystery can be adored, contradiction is hateful. The affirmation of God's "quasi-suffering" must not be understood in dialectical fashion, as though God had within himself an element of negativity and thus underwent a process on account of his differences.[116] With the utmost firmness, Journet rejects the idea of a becoming in God in the manner of Böhme's gnosis, of Hegel's panlogism, of Berdyaev's tragic sense, or of the theories

---

112 Ibid., 58.

113 C. Journet, "De l'espérance," 204.

114 C. Journet, "La Rédemption, drame de l'amour de Dieu," part 1, 54–56.

115 J. Maritain, quoted in C. Journet, "La souffrance de la créature," 227.

116 C. Journet, "Un affrontement de Hegel et de la sagesse chrétienne," 123–25.

of divine kenosis.[117] The divine immutability and impassibility remain absolutely inviolate.

Here we touch upon the perception of the *divine paradoxes* that animates Charles Journet's theology: the paradoxes of a wealthy God who begs, of a good and mighty God who allows evil, of God's peace that troubles, and of an impassible God who yet conceals within himself the mysterious exemplar of magnanimous suffering. "To respect better the mystery of the Divine Essence," Journet tells us,

> it is good and helpful to designate it by using words together that seem incompatible, that seem contradictory. I do not say: they *are* in fact incompatible and contradictory. That would be to make of God a focal point of inconsistencies, that would be to destroy God in our understanding, that would be to sweep him forever from our thinking.[118]

But these seemingly contradictory words "cease to be so if we go beyond, if we strip them of their covering and only keep their clearest, purest, and most sublime content": "All the names we utter foreshadow the unique *unutterable* Name into which they vanish."[119] For Journet, the affirmation, paradoxical but neither absurd nor contradictory, of the mysterious suffering of God remains in the clarity-obscurity of what we know and do not know about God.

8. Some Questions

It was my intention to present Charles Journet's thought, not to subject it to a critique. However, we have to recognize that for the Thomist, Journet's doctrine may raise some problems. These difficulties have to do in particular with the evil of fault, that is, sin, in its relation to God. I would like to point out these problems, at least as questions addressed to Journet's doctrine.

1. The main difficulty has to do with the action of God and with his knowledge. We have seen that when Journet says that God "permits"

---

117 C. Journet, *Meaning of Evil,* 97–102. Journet refuses to speak of a "kenosis" in God himself; he explains this in the sixth conference of his retreat "The Paradoxes of the Divine Names" (preached in 1971) about the humility of God. Those who say that the Father is humble because he gives his divinity to the Son strip the word "humility" of its meaning. Divinity cannot be lost, but in the human attitude of humility there is something that answers to the divine nature, namely, the magnanimity that exists in the eternal Godhead.

118 Charles Journet, "Dieu. I. Paradoxes divins," *Nova et Vetera* (French) 34 (1959): 134.

119 Ibid.

moral evil, he denies the classical Thomistic thesis of the "antecedent permissive decree." According to Journet, this thesis involves God himself too deeply in the scandal of evil. He replaces it therefore with Jacques Maritain's explanation of the "shatterable" and "unshatterable" divine motion while asserting the notion of "nihilation" by the human will. But Maritain's explanation itself raises a problem. The notion of "nihilation" and of "shatterable motion" is problematic, for if nihilation is something "positive," it must be caused by God; but if nihilation is purely negative, this means that God has not given something positive to the human person: In either case, it is not easy to see how the explanation can avoid the intervention of an antecedent decree.[120] According to Journet, the denial of the "antecedent permissive decree" and of the "determining decree" does not weaken God's action in the world. But a question remains: Can the theory of the "consequent permissive decree" preserve the universal scope of God's providence and, above all, God's *independence*?[121]

In a famous article published in 1992, Fr. Jean-Hervé Nicolas (whom Maritain strongly opposed on this topic) surrendered to Maritain's objections and acknowledged that the modern Thomistic doctrine on God's knowledge of sin and on God's permission of sin (antecedent permissive decree) should be abandoned.[122] The main reason given by Fr. Nicolas for rejecting the antecedent permissive decree was God's absolute innocence: God is not responsible for sin.[123] But although he accepted Maritain's objections, Fr. Nicolas was still not fully satisfied with Maritain's answer to the problem. The doctrine of "nihilation" and of the "consequent permissive decree" may not be the decisive answer for the Thomist.

2. The second difficulty has to do with the motive for which God allows sin. Journet constantly repeats that evil is permitted for the sake of some good, and more specifically, for the sake of some *greater* good. No

120 For these criticisms, see Stephen A. Long, "Providence, liberté et loi naturelle," *Revue Thomiste* 102 (2002): 355–406, esp. 376–98.

121 Classical Thomism answered the question with the doctrine of "physical premotion." For this theory and how it applies to evil moral actions, see Réginald Garrigou-Lagrange, "Prémotion physique," in *Dictionnaire de Théologie Catholique*, vol. 13 (Paris: Letouzey et Ané, 1936), col. 31–77, esp. 71–77 ("La causalité divine et l'acte physique du péché").

122 Jean-Hervé Nicolas, "La volonté salvifique de Dieu contrariée par le péché," *Revue Thomiste* 92 (1992): 177–96.

123 Ibid., 185–86: the antecedent permissive decree would imply that the failing of the free will ("la défaillance de la liberté") must follow infallibly from God's permission, to such an extent that it is difficult to avoid making God responsible for evil.

doubt this Augustinian type of response is fundamental, but Journet goes further. On the one hand, Journet makes clear that this "greater good" is the glory of the incarnate Word. In the final analysis, this means that moral evil (sin) is permitted *propter Christum.* This explanation puts Christ at the heart of God's initial plan, that is, at the starting point of the divine economy. Following the *Salmaticenses,* Journet here professes an absolute Christocentrism that strays from the thought of St. Thomas. On the other hand, Journet considers the state of the redemption "all in all" better than the world of Adam's innocence (the world or the state of man "before" the fault of Adam). This explanation likewise goes beyond the thought of Thomas Aquinas. For St. Thomas, the incarnation procures this "greater good," which is the union of man with God in the Person of the incarnate Word; it also allows certain persons (for instance the Blessed Virgin Mary) to attain a higher grace. But Journet generalizes this affirmation by applying it *universally* to the state of redemption in itself.

To sum up, Journet is not satisfied with saying that God can draw good from a permitted evil, but maintains that God allows the evil *for* the good that he draws from it. He adds that this good is *greater* than the one lost by the original evil, and he puts Christ at the heart of the initial plan of God.[124] Paradoxically, this explanation seems to integrate evil into God's design. Does God permit moral evil (sin) *propter Christum*?

3. The last difficulty concerns the affirmation of the "mysterious suffering of God," which Journet takes over from Maritain. For Journet, this suffering or "quasi-suffering" of God is the perfect exemplar of the wound of love, that is, a pure perfection, a nobility for which we have no human word. As we have seen, we are dealing with a "nameless and unnamable" perfection. On this point too, Journet's reflection (like Maritain's) shows the profound humility the theologian must dwell in when he contemplates the mystery of God. Undeniably, this doctrine is of exceptional profundity. We find in it the penetrating expression of a thought seeking to uncover in God not suffering strictly speaking, but the transcendent exemplar of the suffering of Christ and of the saints.

   Still we must ask the following question: The noble element in mercy, the fruitful and precious aspect of the suffering of love, is it not *charity*? Is not the perfection Journet calls "quasi-suffering" instead

---

124 For St. Thomas's teaching and the difficulties of Journet's solution, see François Daguet, *Théologie du dessein divin chez Thomas d'Aquin: Finis omnium Ecclesia* (Paris: Vrin, 2003), 252–59.

God's incomprehensible *love* in his fruitful activity, which we signify by the word "mercy?" In other words, if we exclude privation and evil from God, as Journet certainly does, what is the gem that the notion of "mercy" contains, what is the pure perfection that is contained in love suffering to overcome suffering? Here we are faced with a dilemma that Journet solves only by appealing to the obscurity of a "nameless" mystery:

> a. either God *suffers* in the strict meaning of the word, and then would know pain in his very being and would be subject to becoming and change; or
>
> b. God in his merciful activity knows neither pain nor suffering—certainly not because of a lack or a defect, but because of his eminent perfection—and then it is his *Love* that we are naming, Divine Love working to heal human beings and their misery. Scripture gives us a name, a word to signify this perfection: God is *Agape* (1 John 4:8). Is the perfection and the nobility of compassion a *suffering* or a *quasi-suffering*? Is it not rather the *unchanging love of God*?[125]

After reading the pages that Charles Journet devoted to the mystery of evil, we cannot but be struck by the continual progress in his thinking, a non-stop development whereby the theologian deepens his meditation on the path "opened by St. Thomas." This deepening owes much to Jacques Maritain, whose original theses Journet followed from the beginning (God's knowledge of evil, nihilation of the divine motion, rejection of the antecedent divine decree) and whom he followed right up to his final meditations (the mystery of quasi-suffering in God).[126]

Journet's theological meditation sought understanding while avoiding the absurd. Without taking anything away from the worth and necessity of rigorous metaphysical thinking, Journet wanted to shed light on such thinking by a higher outlook, that of an evangelical *vision of wisdom*, like the saints, for

> if [the most orthodox doctrine is] repeated without being plunged back into the flame where it was wrought or vivified by some secret power of the Gospel, [it] will mislead and may turn

125 For the teaching of St. Thomas and the criticism of it by Maritain and Journet, see G. Emery, "L'immutabilité du Dieu d'amour," 5–37.

126 For the early stages of the discussion between Journet and Maritain, see Michael Torre, "Francisco Marín-Sola, OP, and the Origin of Jacques Maritain's Doctrine on God's Permission of Evil," *Nova et Vetera* (English) 4 (2006): 55–94.

> to poison. How then are we to avoid trembling at causing scandal where it was hoped to bring light?[127]

The spiritual and theological journey of Charles Journet shows an ever more vivid awareness of the scandal of evil, an ever deepening wound, given the *excess of evil* in the world. We are not dealing here merely with what is usually called "post-Auschwitz theology," but with the profound misery that strikes all the world's forsaken people: not only those in Europe who died lingering deaths in the prisons and camps, perishing under torture because they had resolved to resist their conquerors, but also

> so many poor souls who had been doing nothing but their normal, humble jobs and upon whom, like a beast, sudden death fell [. . .], millions of the poor throughout the centuries, crushed by the huge machine of pride and plunder as old as mankind [. . .], the slaves of all times [. . .], the proletarians of the industrial age, all those that destitution has deprived of their status as men, all the damned of society here below.[128]

Such an awareness of the excess of evil, whereby the question of evil can become a "torture,"[129] draws its profundity from a lively faith in God. The most terrible evil, sin that wounds God, cannot be grasped "so long as we have not glimpsed how serious is his love for us."[130] It is in the divine gift of redeeming love that the evil of sin is seen as absolutely "unacceptable" to God. Likewise, it is Christ who reveals to us the nobility of suffering undergone with magnanimity and lets us catch sight of the eternal exemplar, in God, of such grief.[131] Journet has only unfolded here the "point of view" or outlook that he himself had invited us to adopt when faced with the mystery of evil: "We must try to go to God in order to grasp evil from his viewpoint."

---

127 C. Journet, *Meaning of Evil,* 20. This is very well illustrated by Journet's theses on God's knowledge and permission of evil, or by his presentation of the divine impassibility.

128 C. Journet, "La Rédemption, drame de l'amour de Dieu," part 1, 74. Here, as is often the case, Journet borrows his words from Maritain.

129 C. Journet, *Meaning of Evil,* 15–16.

130 C. Journet, "La Rédemption, drame de l'amour de Dieu," part 1, 54.

131 Ibid., 59.

CHAPTER 10

Thomas Aquinas, Postliberal? George Lindbeck's Reading of St. Thomas

THE PLACE of Thomas Aquinas in the cultural-linguistic model promoted by George Lindbeck may surprise.[1] Lindbeck's proposition touches on specifically contemporary issues: ecumenism, theory of religion, the debate with modernity, the contribution of the study of language, and so on. On first glance, one could suppose that the name of Thomas Aquinas would appear as a foreign body, superimposed rather than really present in the reflection. In fact it is quite otherwise. George Lindbeck elaborated his cultural-linguistic proposition in constant dialogue with his two favorite authors: Thomas Aquinas and Martin Luther.[2] Lindbeck's references to Thomas Aquinas are not merely conventional asides, but an original reading of Thomas's *corpus*, in critical discussion with diverse Thomist currents. In order to understand George Lindbeck, it is necessary to be able to understand the purposes of Luther, Wittgenstein, and Aquinas.[3]

---

1 Translation by Matthew Levering of "Thomas d'Aquin postlibéral ? La lecture de saint Thomas par George Lindbeck," in *Postlibéralisme? La théologie de George Lindbeck et sa réception,* ed. Marc Boss, Gilles Emery, and Pierre Gisel (Geneva: Labor et Fides, 2004), 85–111.

2 George A. Lindbeck, "Foreword to the German Edition of *The Nature of Doctrine*" (1994), in *The Church in a Postliberal Age,* ed. James J. Buckley (London: SCM Press, 2002), 196–200 (and endnotes 282), at 199: "The two theologians with whom I have been most in conversation over the years, Thomas Aquinas and Martin Luther."

3 Cf. James J. Buckley, "Introduction: Radical Traditions: Evangelical, Catholic and Postliberal," in *The Church in a Postliberal Age,* vii–xviii (and endnotes 253–56), at xiv.

1. A Constant Interest in Thomas Aquinas

Lindbeck himself describes his debt with respect to Aquinas. In a response to Bruce Marshall concerning the interpretation of *The Nature of Doctrine*, he explains that his cultural-linguistic interpretation of religious beliefs is in part the expression, in the framework of modern philosophy and sociology, of what Thomas Aquinas had taught him:

> I mean this quite literally. It is not simply that some of the contemporary intellectual developments on which I have drawn happen to converge with some Thomistic ideas, but rather that my utilization of the contemporary developments has been heavily influenced by the reading and teaching of St. Thomas that I have done since my undergraduate days four decades ago. Aquinas was a constant, even if background, presence while I wrote *Nature of Doctrine*.[4]

In fact, the index of authors in *The Nature of Doctrine* shows that Thomas Aquinas is one of the most cited.[5] If one held to the material references, Thomas appears in third place, after Bernard Lonergan and Karl Rahner (two Catholic authors who, in a different manner, also wrote in part in the tradition of interpretation of Thomas Aquinas). The references to Thomas Aquinas are more numerous than the mentions of Luther or of Wittgenstein. It would be necessary, certainly, to judge these references as regards their content and their signification in Lindbeck's project, but their material importance is worthy of remark. These references do not present a detailed analysis of the thought of Thomas Aquinas. In *The Nature of Doctrine*, Lindbeck is limited to mentioning, without truly deploying, the sources by which he is inspired (Aquinas, the Reformers, and Karl Barth, in particular).[6]

Let us specify at once that Lindbeck has always presented a "non-Thomistic" reading of Thomas Aquinas, that is, not influenced by the sub-

---

[4] G. Lindbeck, "Response to Bruce Marshall," *The Thomist* 53 (1989): 403–6, at 405. Lindbeck explains at the beginning of this article: "If I had referred more to the Thomistic ideas he [Bruce Marshall] elucidates when I was writing *Nature of Doctrine*, it would have been a better book" (403). Further on, he adds: "I intended what I wrote to be read in a way congruent with the interpretation of him [St. Thomas Aquinas] which Marshall here presents" (405–6). See Bruce Marshall, "Aquinas as Postliberal Theologian," *The Thomist* 53 (1989): 353–402.

[5] George A. Lindbeck, *The Nature of Doctrine: Religion and Theology in a Postliberal Age* (Philadelphia: Westminster Press, 1984): 139–42. One can also see the index of the French translation: *La nature des doctrines: Religion et théologie à l'âge du postlibéralisme* (Paris: Van Dieren, 2003), 185–88.

[6] G. Lindbeck, *The Nature of Doctrine,* 135.

mission to a determined type of Thomism.[7] He does not consider Aquinas as the representative of a "particular party" within Western Christendom, "but as one who belongs to us all."[8] In this approach, Thomas Aquinas is resolutely envisaged as an author open to the thought of others.[9] This reading therefore takes up, on the one hand, a *historical* approach to Aquinas, and, on the other hand, a *confrontation* with other currents of modern and contemporary thought: These are the two constant traits of the reading proposed by Lindbeck. This reading is distinguished not only from neo-Thomism, but equally from the interpretation habitually practiced in continental Europe (even in the most recent currents of Aquinas research). It is connected instead to the kind of Aristotelianism and Thomism of Anglo-Saxon authors such as Alasdair MacIntyre, Victor Preller, David Burrell, Fergus Kerr, and Bruce Marshall.[10] This aspect is of the first importance for understanding well Lindbeck's use of Aquinas. This use is not inscribed in the European continental Thomist tradition. It is rather attached to a current that one can associate with "analytic Thomism," a Thomism after Wittgenstein.[11] We will see this characteristic approach notably in the non-foundationalist interpretation of Aquinas.

In return, Thomists have shown great interest in *The Nature of Doctrine* since its publication in 1984. One finds a good example of this interest in the discussions that have appeared in *The Thomist* (the journal of the Dominicans of the Eastern Province in the United States), in which many articles have debated the postliberal theology of Lindbeck. One finds here, since 1985, a dozen articles, of which many are quite extensive.[12] Few journals inscribed in a particular theological current have given such place to the postliberal proposition of *The Nature of Doctrine*. And, among

---

7 George A. Lindbeck, "Participation and Existence in the Interpretation of St. Thomas Aquinas," *Franciscan Studies* 17 (1957): 1–22 and 107–25, cf. 1–2.

8 George A. Lindbeck, "Discovering Thomas (4). Hope and the *Sola Fide*," *Una Sancta* 25/1 (1968): 66–73, at 66.

9 See, for example, George A. Lindbeck, "Discovering Thomas (2). Tentative Language about the Trinity," *Una Sancta* 24/3 (1967): 44–48, at 47.

10 Lindbeck himself indicates his affinities with these authors. See G. Lindbeck, "Scripture, Consensus and Community," in *The Church in a Postliberal Age*, 201–22 (and endnotes 282–85), at 283, note 8.

11 In French, see notably Roger Pouivet, *Après Wittgenstein, saint Thomas* (Paris: PUF, 1997).

12 See especially *The Thomist* 49/3 (1985); 53/3 (1989); 56/3 (1992). Fr. Augustine Di Noia, OP, then editor-in-chief of *The Thomist*, played an important role in the reception given to the thought of Lindbeck, with whom Di Noia had studied at Yale. For an overview of the interest raised by *The Nature of Doctrine* among Catholic theologians, and its reception, see Gilles Emery, "L'intérêt de théologiens catholiques pour la proposition postlibérale de George Lindbeck," in *Postlibéralisme?* 39–57.

Thomists, even the most critical as regards Lindbeck agree that "anyone who shares the metaphysical epistemology of Aquinas is likely to be open to the cultural-linguistic approach."[13] Other interpreters of Thomas Aquinas (Bruce Marshall in particular) attempt to show that the thought of Lindbeck converges strictly with the teaching of Aquinas himself, or at least that Lindbeck presents a coherent reading that is just as plausible as any other.[14]

If one observes more precisely Lindbeck's reading of Aquinas, one finds that it possesses three aspects, or three levels. First, on a general level, Lindbeck attempts to recover, in a contemporary formulation, the heritage of the ancient Christian tradition, with the intention of avoiding the difficulties of modernity that he criticizes in the "experiential-expressive" model (illustrated notably by Karl Rahner and Bernard Lonergan, and more broadly by liberal theology stemming from Schleiermacher), and also in the "cognitive-propositional" and "informative" model of the fundamentalist type, depending also upon modernity.[15] The properly ecumenical value of Aquinas is clearly underscored: Aquinas is anterior to the divisions of the sixteenth century. In this context, Lindbeck considers St. Thomas as a theologian who "magisterially summed up the first twelve hundred years of the tradition."[16] The theology of St. Thomas offers in this regard a double advantage: "Less polemical" than the theologies after the Reformation, it is also "less systematic" than the theologies developed since Schleiermacher. Aquinas "was a rigorous, comprehensive and orderly thinker, but he had no 'system' in the Schleiermacherian, Rahnerian or even Barthian sense."[17] Aquinas offers therefore a source for peaceable ecumenical reflection, by offering also an open framework capable of stimulating or of integrating other approaches. The framework of interpretation proposed by Lindbeck is particularly interesting. It suggests clearly that the reduction of Aquinas to a "system" belongs to his modern interpretation and not to his original thought.

---

13 Colman E. O'Neill, OP, "The Rule Theory of Doctrine and Propositional Truth," *The Thomist* 49 (1985): 417–42, at 428.

14 See Bruce Marshall, "Aquinas as Postliberal Theologian," 353–402; idem, "Thomas, Thomisms, and Truth," *The Thomist* 56 (1992): 499–524.

15 Cf. G. Lindbeck, *The Nature of Doctrine,* 16–18, 31–32, and so on.

16 G. Lindbeck, "Hope and the *Sola Fide*," 66.

17 George A. Lindbeck, "Article IV and Lutheran/Roman Catholic Dialogue: The Limits of Diversity in the Understanding of Justification" (1981), in *The Church in a Postliberal Age*, 38–52 (and endnotes 264–65), at 45. Lindbeck gives here, as an example, the Thomist teaching on hope: Aquinas associated to *hope* what Luther attached instead to *faith.* In Lindbeck's interpretation, the absence of "system" enables one also to show that the Thomist use of metaphysical categories (substance, for example) remains compatible with the Lutheran *sola fide.*

The reading of Aquinas is thus inscribed in the theological project of avoiding certain impasses of modernity, by retrieving the ancient tradition of the Church, anterior to the Western rupture of the Reformation (and anterior to modernity). The integration of Aquinas into the postliberal view holds precisely to his "premodern" character. At this same general level, but with a more philosophical focus, Lindbeck considers that the Anglo-American linguistic and empirical approach possesses certain affinities with premodern Aristotelianism and Thomism, whereas it is distinguished from the Platonist and Augustinian traditions and above all from the continental tradition of idealism, romanticism, and phenomenological existentialism.[18] We find again here the connection of Lindbeck with the Anglo-Saxon "analytical Thomism."

In the second place, Lindbeck has direct recourse to many precise themes of the thought of Aquinas. It is on this second level of reading that we will focus our attention. At a third level, finally, Lindbeck contrasts his reading with the interpretation given by other currents of interpretation of Aquinas (in particular Karl Rahner, but also Étienne Gilson); we will limit ourselves to indicating some aspects in this regard. But, before undertaking these tasks, it will be useful to set forth briefly the extent and range of Lindbeck's Thomist writings.

2. An Overview of the Thomist Writings of George Lindbeck

Lindbeck's interest in Aquinas and in Scholastic thought does not date from *The Nature of Doctrine*: One finds it since his first works. This interest accompanies all Lindbeck's research. There is not a "Thomist stage" displaced by another approach, but one discovers rather a Thomist interest that is constantly deepened.

Existence and Participation

At the frontier of philosophy and theology, the doctoral thesis of George Lindbeck was devoted to Duns Scotus, under the title "Is Duns Scotus an Essentialist?"[19] This first study revealed a properly historical interest, not only for the thought of Scotus and of Aquinas, but also for their repercussions in the later history of doctrine during the late Middle Ages and still today. Concerning St. Thomas, Lindbeck shows in particular that the "existential" interpretation of his doctrine of *esse* (act of existence) as it was promoted by Étienne Gilson (systematic primacy of existence) and widely received among contemporary Thomists, lacks foundations in the texts.

---

[18] G. Lindbeck, *The Nature of Doctrine,* 63.

[19] Dissertation presented in 1955 to Yale University.

Lindbeck shows here a rare knowledge of the different currents that traverse contemporary Thomism.[20] He keeps his distance not only from the positions of Étienne Gilson and Jacques Maritain, but also from other forms of Thomism, notably those of Joseph Maréchal that Rahner extends (cognitive existentialism, transcendental deduction). For our purpose, it is necessary to observe that, since these first studies, Lindbeck has shown himself to be critical as regards "cognitive existentialism," for which the affirmation of the infinite is set as a preliminary condition of all apprehension of finite objects and is explained by a dialectical return to experience.[21] The critique is formulated not only on philosophical and theological grounds, as in *The Nature of Doctrine*, but also on grounds properly historical: This cognitive existentialism lacks decisive supports in the original Thomism, that of Thomas Aquinas.[22] Besides transcendental Thomism (deduction of a transcendental idea of being), Lindbeck shows himself also very reserved regarding the theory of the intuition of being (Maritain) or regarding the thesis of a priority of existence grounded on the nonconceptual knowledge of the act of existence by judgment (Gilson).[23]

From the beginning of his work, Lindbeck manifests important reservations with regard to a priori and intuitionist systems, reservations that we find in his non-foundationalist reading of Thomas Aquinas. Positively, he proposes an interpretation that gives primacy to the doctrine of participation (and to that of analogy, which participation implies): One recognizes here another major theme of Lindbeck's thought. Participation, in St. Thomas, is not solely the historical source of the doctrine of the *actus essendi*, but also the systematic origin. The Thomist doctrine of *esse* is the necessary consequence of the fact that all the relations of unity and plurality must be explained in terms of ontological participation. Priority is given, therefore, not to "existence" ("existentialist" interpretations), but to participation.[24]

The Theory of Knowledge

The judgment taken regarding the transcendental deduction of being is nuanced in a later study that treats the *a priori* in St. Thomas's theory of knowledge. The problem resides essentially in the confrontation of the

---

20 G. Lindbeck, "Participation and Existence in the Interpretation of St. Thomas Aquinas." This study constitutes an adaptation of part of Lindbeck's doctoral thesis. See especially the distinction of four groups of interpreters of Aquinas (6–7), who will be discussed in the remainder of the essay: All the greatest names of contemporary Thomism are reviewed in a critical fashion.

21 Ibid., 18–20.

22 Ibid., 19.

23 Ibid., 20–21.

24 Ibid., 107–25.

"ancient" thought of St. Thomas with his modern interpretation, more precisely Kantian and transcendental. Here again, Lindbeck envisages the problem not only from a philosophical and theological point of view, but also from a historical point of view. It is on the basis of texts of Aquinas that he tries to evaluate the plausibility of a post-Kantian reconstruction of the Thomist theory of knowledge, with mitigated results. On the one hand, Lindbeck shows that the theory of a transcendental, pre-reflexive opening on absolute Being (conducing to associate "natural theology" with a non-objective pre-apprehension of infinite being as the horizon of thought), if one seeks to find it explicitly in St. Thomas, lacks decisive textual grounds.[25] On the other hand, he tries to establish that the thought of Aquinas is open to a transcendental interpretation, and that some such interpretations, Rahner's in particular, are plausible, although the arguments of historical exegesis of texts do not settle the question.[26]

This examination of the theory of knowledge reveals a double trait that one will find also in *The Nature of Doctrine*. It is a matter, on one side, of the attention paid to the "experiential-expressive" model, here in its transcendental form. Lindbeck analyzes this model in direct reference to the texts of St. Thomas. He does not separate himself from this model by reason of an incompatibility with the thought of Aquinas, nor solely because of its internal difficulties, but rather by opposing it with another interpretation of Aquinas, that is to say, a positive alternative. On the other side, Lindbeck affirms the validity of a "projectionist" interpretation of Aquinas: "Aquinas does not reject the view that intelligibility is 'projected' into the sensible content of our knowledge rather than 'extracted' from it."[27] In order to show this, he relies especially on an interpretation of the role of the agent intellect, whose "light" is included in the known object, of such kind that, in making the known object actually intelligible, human understanding gives it its "visibility." This exegesis appeals also to the Thomist theory of the first principles of the intellect, which are naturally known and which "constitute the general formal structures exemplified in objects of knowledge." The first principles, in this interpretation, are "the general rules in terms of which sense experience is organized."[28] This theory supports the "projectionist" understanding of the activity of the mind. The reading of Aquinas leads therefore to recognizing that the

---

25 George A. Lindbeck, "The *A Priori* in St. Thomas' Theory of Knowledge," in *The Heritage of Christian Thought: Essays in Honor of Robert Lowry Calhoun*, ed. Robert E. Cushman and Egil Grislis (New York: Harper and Row, 1965), 41–63; cf. 45, 47, and 53.

26 Ibid., 44, 46, 52, 61, and 63.

27 Ibid., 47; see 48–49, 56, and 63.

28 Ibid., 55; cf. 53–54.

human mind "constructs" the world out of the unformed material supplied by sensible experience.[29] This thesis will be reprised in *The Nature of Doctrine*.[30] It explains in part how Lindbeck could invoke St. Thomas as a moderate realist whose doctrine of knowledge is open to the intratextuality of a cultural-linguistic model.

In the same sense, Lindbeck has recourse to the Thomistic distinction of the *modus significandi* and the *res significata.* In his interpretation, this distinction means that the metaphysician "can indicate what he is talking about only by denying that the concepts he uses are adequate to his referents,"[31] to the degree that, for St. Thomas, "there is only non-objective knowledge of nonsensible realities."[32] This thesis, to which we will return in more detail, will occupy a significant place in *The Nature of Doctrine.* At every step, Lindbeck's epistemology rests, in an important part, on a reading of Aquinas placed in critical debate with classical Thomism as well as with transcendental Thomism.

A Panorama of Great Thomist Themes

Two encyclopedia articles enable us to specify the themes that, more broadly, Lindbeck emphasizes. The first article, appearing in 1958, is devoted to Thomism.[33] The presentation of St. Thomas here is at the same time critical and very positive. Thomism is characterized by the following traits: its Aristotelian empiricism (rejection of Platonism and of Augustinian illuminationism), its moderate intellectualism, the doctrine of the hylomorphic unity of man, analogy and participation (creatures exist only by participating in God's being), the equilibrium of the relationships of nature and grace (and of faith and reason), and the central place of faith. Aquinas is here depicted as a critical adversary of liberal theology. Lindbeck underscores in particular the *integrative* value of the thought of St. Thomas, who seeks to give a comprehensive description of reality and experience. One finds here, both as regards the critique of liberalism and as regards the integrative vision of Aquinas, a constant trait that *The Nature of Doctrine* will take up: St. Thomas appears as one of the authors having "absorbed" the world in a Christian religious understanding.

---

29 Ibid., 50.

30 G. Lindbeck, *The Nature of Doctrine,* 39.

31 G. Lindbeck, "The *A Priori* in St. Thomas' Theory of Knowledge," 59.

32 Ibid., 60.

33 George A. Lindbeck, "Thomism," in *A Handbook of Christian Theology: Definition Essays on Concepts and Movements of Thought in Contemporary Protestantism,* ed. Marvin Halverson and Arthur A. Cohen (New York: World Publishing Company, 1958), 361–63.

More developed, an article titled "Medieval Theology" inscribes St. Thomas in the larger movement of Scholastic thought.[34] This presentation of Scholastic method, in a Lutheran encyclopedia, is remarkably positive. Concerning St. Thomas, Lindbeck notes in the first place his Augustinianism as regards the doctrines of predestination and of grace ("Aquinas is perhaps the most Augustinian theologian of the century").[35] From the start, the aspects that are emphasized are those that connect Aquinas and the Lutheran Reform (primacy of grace and of faith). As regards the theory of knowledge, Aquinas is again presented as a "moderate realist." More striking, undoubtedly, is the presentation of Duns Scotus and William of Ockham, in which the account rendered is typically "Thomist," if one may speak so, because it directs attention to the major points of rupture with Thomism: rejection of the *Ipsum esse* in Scotus, an extrinsic conception of law, a sharp reinforcement of the distinction of faith and reason (to the point that Ockham attains "a practical Pelagian system, ordained by God, in which man really saves himself").[36] The progress of medieval studies in recent decades would lead no doubt to some nuances. It is nevertheless noteworthy, for our purpose, that St. Thomas emerges from this overview as the master of a balanced synthesis of Christian thought, not by reason of the credit that Catholic ecclesiastical authorities have accorded to Thomism, but indeed "because of its intrinsic characteristics."[37]

Discovering Thomas

It is necessary also to draw attention, in Lindbeck's theological work, to a small series of articles titled "Discovering Thomas." These articles are engaged in presenting many volumes of the English translation of the *Summa theologiae*: the treatise on the essential attributes of God, the treatise on the Trinity, the treatise on the creation of man, and finally the treatise

---

34 George A. Lindbeck, "Medieval Theology," in *The Encyclopedia of the Lutheran Church*, ed. Julius Bodensieck, vol. 2 (Minneapolis, MN: Augsburg, 1965), 1510–16 (for Aquinas: 1513–14).

35 Ibid., 1513.

36 Ibid., 1514–15. The rupture emphasized by Lindbeck, under this aspect, anticipates certain traits of the historical-speculative reading developed later by another Anglo-Saxon movement (however, completely different from the postliberal theology of Lindbeck), that of Radical Orthodoxy. In French, see Olivier-Thomas Venard, OP, "Radical Orthodoxy," *Revue Thomiste* 101 (2001): 409–44; Adrian Pabst, "De la chrétienté à la modernité? Lecture critique des thèses de *Radical Orthodoxy* sur la rupture scotiste et ockhamienne et sur le renouveau de la théologie de saint Thomas d'Aquin," *Revue des Sciences Philosophiques et Théologiques* 86 (2002): 561–99.

37 G. Lindbeck, "Medieval Theology," 1512.

on hope.[38] These articles give not only a critique of the translation and of its annotation, but above all a glimpse of the thought of St. Thomas that Lindbeck seeks to retrieve for a new day. The discussion of the creation of man and of hope shows the limits of Aquinas but also his openness to other currents of reflection: his convergence with the Lutheran doctrine on the theme of nature and grace, on the image of God, on salvation by faith and on the certitude of salvation (which Lindbeck finds in the Thomist doctrine of hope as *certa expectatio futurae beatitudinis*, that is, as a reliance on God that involves certitude).

The discussion of the treatise on God is particularly interesting for our purpose, because we already find there, clearly affirmed, many theses of *The Nature of Doctrine.* On the one hand, Lindbeck shows that the thought of Aquinas presents nothing comparable to the foundationalism of modern "natural theology." The five "ways" to the existence of God, according to Lindbeck, do not constitute a strict proof or demonstration of the existence of God in the sense of later natural theology, but rather are "extrinsic and probable" arguments to which no salvific value is connected, and on whose validity "nothing of decisive importance depends," so that "there is perhaps no fundamental conflict between St. Thomas and the reformation tradition on the relation of faith and reason, of philosophy and theology."[39] One can see that this interpretation corresponds, in a fashion, to that which Karl Barth gave of St. Anselm.[40] There is not, in Thomas Aquinas, a foundational enterprise independent of faith and of a strictly theological purpose: The ways to the existence of God are inscribed in a discourse regarding the God who has revealed himself, the Father of Jesus Christ.[41] On the other hand, Lindbeck proposes a linguistic and "agnostic" reading (the word is borrowed from the French Dominican A. D. Sertillanges) of Aquinas's teaching on the words by which we name God: We do not know the meaning that these names have when they are applied to God, "but only that they are rightly said of him."[42] In consequence, "the treatise *De Deo Uno* is not designed to supply us with information about God."[43] In this "agnostic" reading, the essential attributes of God only indicate the context within which "the creedal descriptions of

---

38 George A. Lindbeck, "Discovering Thomas (1). The Classical Statement of Christian Theism," *Una Sancta* 24/1 (1967): 45–52; idem, "Discovering Thomas (2). Tentative Language about the Trinity," *Una Sancta* 24/3 (1967): 44–48; idem, "Discovering Thomas (3). The Origin of Man," *Una Sancta* 24/4 (1967): 67–75; idem, "Discovering Thomas (4). Hope and the *Sola Fide*," *Una Sancta* 25/1 (1968): 66–73.

39 G. Lindbeck, "The Classical Statement of Christian Theism," 46–47.

40 Karl Barth, *Anselm: Fides Quarens Intellectum,* trans. Ian W. Robertson (Richmond: John Knox Press, 1960).

41 G. Lindbeck, "The Classical Statement of Christian Theism," 52.

42 Ibid., 49.

43 Ibid.

who God is" can be given a specifiable referent.[44] We find here, directly drawn from the reading of Aquinas, two theses absolutely central to *The Nature of Doctrine*, which we will examine in more detail in the next section.

Let us summarize the interest of this brief journey through Lindbeck's work before *The Nature of Doctrine.* On the one hand, Aquinas receives a privileged place among the sources of theological reflection. His teaching on God, for example, is considered as "*the* classical systematic presentation of traditional Christian theism. It magisterially organizes and sums up twelve hundred years of Greek and Latin fathers."[45] The attention that one pays to Aquinas will not therefore be marginal. On the other hand, this place is resolutely envisaged through a historical approach,[46] but also through the openness of Aquinas to new contemporary interpretations: It is precisely in such a "reinterpretation" that the rediscovery of St. Thomas consists.[47] Each treatise of Aquinas opens onto the possibility of a new interpretation, by reason of characteristics proper to Thomistic thought.[48] In short, Lindbeck's interpretation is characterized by a linguistic approach, of the "agnostic" type, in which Aquinas furnishes the "rules of language" rather than an objective cognitive content. Many theses absolutely central to *The Nature of Doctrine* are thus grounded in the reading of Thomas Aquinas. Lindbeck's early work shows that he is developing a consistent line of interpretation.

3. The Appeals to Thomas Aquinas in *The Nature of Doctrine*

Our brief overview of Thomist themes has already suggested the general framework of the references to Aquinas in *The Nature of Doctrine.* The principal themes are those that we have indicated. Without entering into

44 Ibid., 50. Lindbeck holds a "minimalist" interpretation of Aquinas's doctrine on our human knowledge of God's attributes. However, my intention here is not to criticize Lindbeck. For a deeper and integral view, see the superb book of Thierry-Dominique Humbrecht, *Théologie négative et noms divins chez saint Thomas d'Aquin* (Paris: Vrin, 2005).

45 G. Lindbeck, "The Classical Statement of Christian Theism," 48.

46 G. Lindbeck, "Tentative Language about the Trinity," 46: "St. Thomas needs to be read in historical context, just as much, for example, as the New Testament. Once this is done, there is no more need to be scandalized by the Aristotelian complexities of his trinitarian speculation than at the Melchizedekian features of the christology of *Hebrews*."

47 G. Lindbeck, "The Origin of Man," 74–75: "We must ask not simply what an author says, but what he intends, and then try to determine how these intentions might be expressed in a different historical and intellectual context in the face of new problems."

48 Ibid. See G. Lindbeck, "Hope and the *Sola Fide*," 72–73; "Tentative Language about the Trinity," 47–48.

all the details, and without making mention of all the references (we have limited ourselves here to the more important for the fundamental purpose of *The Nature of Doctrine*), one can group them into three kinds: religion and experience, the rejection of foundationalism, and the "agnosticism" of Aquinas and the question of truth.

Religion and Experience

Knowledge by Connaturality

In his proposal of "a cultural-linguistic alternative," Lindbeck explains that he wishes to reverse, above all, the relation often posited between the internal and external dimensions of religion. Religion is not the expression of an interior experience, but, quite the reverse, it is rather religion that shapes religious experience and renders it possible. To become religious is not first to adopt an ensemble of beliefs regarding what is true or false (cognitivist perspective), nor to find symbolism expressing a fundamental attitude (experiential-expressive model), but instead it is to enter into a cultural and linguistic framework that determines and shapes the ensemble of life and thought, that is, to interiorize a way of knowing by practice and usage (skill): to learn to perceive, to act, to think in conformity with a religious tradition in its interior structure.[49] The most apt to offer a judgment in religious matters will therefore be those persons whose practices and usages are in conformity with the spirit of the religion (with "the interior rule of faith"), that is, those persons "who have effectively interiorized a religion."[50] It is in this context, in order to underscore the *non-discursive* dimension of religious knowledge, that one finds a first appeal to St. Thomas, in regard to his explanations concerning "connatural knowledge" or "knowledge by connaturality."[51]

In the order of grace, for St. Thomas, knowledge by connaturality flows from the gift of wisdom (a gift at the same time speculative and practical) attached to charity. The theological virtue of charity, given gratuitously by God, enables one to judge among things and to direct human action in conformity with God, according to an "instinct" of the Holy Spirit.[52] Aquinas

---

49 G. Lindbeck, *The Nature of Doctrine,* 32–41.

50 Ibid., 79.

51 Ibid., 36 and 79 (with endnotes 43 and 89). The references are to Aquinas, *ST* I, q. 1, a. 6, ad 3; and *ST* II–II, q. 45, a. 2. Note that, in this last passage on the gift of wisdom, St. Thomas speaks of the rectitude of judgment on account of a "certain" connaturality *(propter connaturalitatem quandam)* with the matter about which one has to judge. This connaturality belongs to the affective order and comes from the inclination given by virtues, either moral (the example given here is chastity) or theological (charity).

52 For a more complete exposition, see Ulrich Horst, OP, *Die Gaben des Heiligen Geistes nach Thomas von Aquin* (Berlin: Akademie Verlag, 2001), 130–45.

thus distinguishes several kinds of knowledge of the truth: "one which comes of nature, and one which comes of grace; the knowledge which comes of grace is likewise twofold: The first is purely speculative [. . .]; the other is affective, and produces love for God; which knowledge properly belongs to the gift of wisdom."[53] This leads to distinguish not only between natural knowledge and knowledge by grace, but also, within the knowledge that comes of grace, between a speculative wisdom acquired by theological effort *(studium)* and an infused wisdom (speculative and practical) that is a pure gift of sanctifying grace, poured out by the Holy Spirit.[54] This last kind of knowledge is described by Aquinas, with some nuances, as "judgment by inclination," "judgment by a certain connaturality," and "affective knowledge." In any case, it expresses a special *mode of knowing* that implies the affective side of the soul.[55]

Lindbeck does not limit himself to repeating this doctrine, but he interprets it. On the one hand, he expresses connatural knowledge in terms of "skill." On the other hand, by identifying the instinct of faith *(sensus fidelium)* with knowledge by connaturality,[56] he strongly emphasizes the difference between a knowledge of the dogmatic kind and the instinct of wisdom that procures a connatural knowledge, in specifying that those who benefit from this knowledge by connaturality "do not need the clumsy directives of official dogma."[57] (This last precision brings a Protestant flavor to the interpretation of Thomas Aquinas: It is not identical to the Catholic understanding of the *sensus fidei.*)[58] If to become religious is to obtain a knowledge by connaturality, then to become religious, for a Christian, is to live in grace. In this sense, by placing great emphasis on the difference between dogmatic knowledge and connatural knowledge, Lindbeck's interpretation displaces somewhat the question of intelligibility: In this reading of Aquinas, the question of intelligibility is formulated in terms of skills

---

53 St. Thomas, *ST* I, q. 64, a. 1: "Duplex est cognitio veritatis, una quidem quae habetur per gratiam; alia vero quae habetur per naturam. Et ista quae habetur per gratiam, est duplex, una quae est speculativa tantum, sicut cum alicui aliqua secreta divinorum revelantur; alia vero quae est affectiva, producens amorem Dei; et haec proprie pertinet ad donum sapientiae."

54 Note that judgment by connaturality can also apply to natural knowledge, cf. *ST* I, q. 1, a. 6, ad 3.

55 On Aquinas's doctrine, see Pierre-Antoine Belley, *Connaître par le coeur: La connaissance par connaturalité dans les oeuvres de Jacques Maritain* (Paris: Téqui, 2005), 44–79.

56 For this identification (not uncommon among interpreters of Aquinas) see G. Lindbeck, "Scripture, Consensus and Community," 221.

57 G. Lindbeck, *The Nature of Doctrine,* 79.

58 For the Catholic notion of the *sensus fidei,* see in particular Vatican II, *Lumen Gentium,* #12 (the *sensus fidei* is exercised "under the guidance of the sacred Magisterium").

and of the person's practical configuration to God.[59] The displacement of propositional truth by a conception of truth as correspondence with God is inscribed in a comparable movement.

The "First Intentions" and the "Second Intentions"

In a related context, Lindbeck applies to the cultural-linguistic model the Scholastic distinction between first intentions and second intentions, regarding which Aquinas is invoked again.[60] Let us explain briefly this Scholastic distinction. The word "intention" *(intentio)* in St. Thomas's theory of knowledge designates the conception that our mind forms about a known reality. Its being is not the "natural being" that this reality possesses in itself, but it is an "intentional being" (the term comes from Arabic philosophy), that is, the being it possesses in the mind that knows. On this basis, "first intentions" designate our concepts considered in their immediate relation with reality, or in their aptitude to express this reality; they correspond to the direct look of our mind on things themselves: The concept of *man*, for example, considered as a first intention, expresses the extramental reality of human nature in human beings. As regards "second intentions," they designate our concepts in the objective relations that they receive insofar as these concepts are themselves thought and involved in the human way of knowing: The concept of man, under the rubric of second intention, designates human nature in the state of a universal idea that it has in the mind, in relation with other things involved in our way of knowing. First intentions are the domain of the philosophy of the real, and second intentions constitute the object of logic.[61] Lindbeck presents this classification in designating first intention as the act by which we grasp objects, and second intention as the reflex act of grasping or reflecting upon first intentions. Concerning second intentions, Lindbeck's interpretation involves a certain displacement of the Thomist perspective, it seems to us, away from logic and toward psychology.[62]

However this may be, Lindbeck wishes to underscore by his position that we are not completely aware of our activities of "first intention" while we are engaged in them (we are only "unthematically" or "tacitly" aware of them): "Our attention is focused on 'objects', not on the subjective experience involved in knowing them."[63] It is only in the second intention that

---

59 Cf. G. Lindbeck, *The Nature of Doctrine,* 128–34: "Intelligibility as skill."

60 Ibid., 38–39.

61 For a classic overview, see Henri-Dominique Gardeil, *Initiation à la philosophie de saint Thomas d'Aquin,* vol. 1: *Introduction, Logique* (Paris: Cerf, 1952), 50–52.

62 Cf. C. E. O'Neill, "The Rule Theory of Doctrine and Propositional Truth," 424. It is necessary nevertheless to state that, in Aquinas, the distinction between logic and psychology was not as hardened as it is today.

63 G. Lindbeck, *The Nature of Doctrine,* 38.

we pay attention, in a reflexive way, to this experience. However, our activities of first intention are not "preverbal": They are "linguistically or conceptually structured."[64] The same point applies to religious experiences. Religious experience can be construed as a product of linguistically structured activities of which we are not directly conscious. Consequently, drawing upon Aquinas and other Aristotelian medievals, Lindbeck considers that our affective experiences "always depend on prior cognition of objects, and the objects available to us in this life are all in some fashion constructed out of (or, in medieval terminology, 'abstracted from') conceptually or linguistically structured sense experience."[65] The Scholastic theory of first intentions and second intentions furnishes a general category for supporting the linguistic theory of religion.

For Aquinas, knowledge and the affective life have their source in sensible experience. Thomists and, in a more general manner, all those who adhere to the broad lines of the Aristotelian structure of knowledge may feel here a fundamental sympathy with respect to the cultural-linguistic theory. But they would perhaps be much more reserved when called upon to grant that the objects of knowledge are "constructs" starting from sensible experience. We here encounter again a related aspect of the "projectionism" of cognitive activity that we have evoked above, and regarding which Lindbeck has admitted the Thomist plausibility. Certain readers of Aquinas think that the Thomism of Lindbeck stops here.[66] In any case, this interpretation manifests clearly enough precisely the intention to reinterpret the thought of St. Thomas in the context of contemporary thought.

Thomas Aquinas as "Non-Foundationalist"

Lindbeck above all invokes St. Thomas against the modern foundational enterprises, of the post-Cartesian or post-Kantian kind, that seek to ground religion in a common prior knowledge or experience. The name of Thomas Aquinas appears here side-by-side with that of Luther.

> Aquinas' use of reason does not lead to foundational or natural theology of the modern type. Even when he is most the apologist, as in demonstrating the existence of God, his proofs are, by his own account, "probable arguments" in support of faith rather than parts of an independent foundational enterprise.[67]

---

64 Ibid.

65 Ibid., 39. See above, our brief presentation of the theory of knowledge espoused by Lindbeck in his study "The *A Priori* in St. Thomas' Theory of Knowledge."

66 C. E. O'Neill, "The Rule Theory of Doctrine and Propositional Truth," 425–26.

67 G. Lindbeck, *The Nature of Doctrine,* 131, with reference to *ST* I, q. 1, a. 8, ad 2 (138).

Correlatively, referring to Aquinas, Lindbeck adds that "reasoning in support of the faith is not meritorious before faith, but only afterward."[68] In Lindbeck's exegesis, St. Thomas appears (along with Luther) as the example of a theologian for whom

> Revelation dominates all aspects of the theological enterprise, but without excluding a subsidiary use of philosophical and experiential considerations in the explication and defense of the faith.[69]
>
> The famous "five ways," for example, are not proofs or demonstrations in any strict sense. For the theologian, they function only as probable and extraneous arguments, because *sacra doctrina*'s proper authorities are those of canonical scripture.[70]

These "five ways" are equally deprived of all importance for salvation.[71] Aquinas thus possesses an affinity with postliberal theology, which does not exclude all apologetics, but only that which would be systematically prior and determining, in the manner of post-Cartesian natural theology and of liberalism.

Lindbeck associates, therefore, the project of Aquinas with that of postliberal theology, to the degree that, in Aquinas, the biblical and Christian world of Scripture is shown to be capable of "absorbing the universe." The reception of Aristotle in Aquinas furnishes an example: Extra-scriptural realities and experience are received into the biblical categories that mold them into the interior of a Christian conception. Even more, Lindbeck finds in Aquinas a certain "methodological legitimation" of this procedure. He points to the theory of the senses of Scripture, regarding which Thomas has given one of the "classic descriptions": Scripture "creates" its own domain of meaning, and "the task of interpretation is to extend this over the whole of reality."[72] The failure of modern hermeneutics, even before the introduction of critical methods, comes in part from the abandonment of patristic hermeneutics and medieval hermeneutics, such as found in Aquinas, who practiced the interpretation of Scripture within the universal community of faith casting light upon the whole of reality.[73] Postliberal theology invokes

[68] Ibid., 132; cf. G. Lindbeck, "The Classical Statement of Christian Theism," 46–47.

[69] G. Lindbeck, *The Nature of Doctrine,* 131.

[70] G. Lindbeck, "The Classical Statement of Christian Theism," 47. This regards the ways for establishing the existence of God (*ST* I, q. 2, a. 3) that Lindbeck interprets in the light of the explanations of *ST* I, q. 1, a. 8, ad 2.

[71] Ibid. Lindbeck states that there is no fundamental conflict between Aquinas and the Reformation on the relationships of faith and reason.

[72] G. Lindbeck, *The Nature of Doctrine,* 117. He indicates as a reference *ST* I, q. 1, a. 10 (on the plurality of the scriptural senses).

[73] G. Lindbeck, "The Reformation Heritage and Christian Unity" (1988), in *The Church in a Postliberal Age*, 53–76, at 72.

Aquinas therefore as representative of a premodern tradition for which to interpret the Bible is to employ the Bible for interpreting other things (including all search for God), not the reverse.[74] Against every foundational enterprise, Aquinas upholds the project of intratextuality.

In order to understand Lindbeck's interpretation, it is necessary to take account of the Anglo-Saxon currents of Thomist reading. On the one hand, until a very recent date, Anglo-Saxon thought (in contrast to the continental European tradition, especially the French) has principally retained from St. Thomas his philosophical theism. By simplifying, one can say that it is above all Thomas Aquinas the philosopher, rather than Thomas Aquinas the theologian, that one signified in speaking of "Thomism," to such a point that the properly *theological* nature of the enterprise of St. Thomas appears today as a veritable discovery to many American authors.[75] On the other hand, the critique of foundationalism does not mean the rejection of the search for intelligibility. By simplifying again, from an analytic point of view, one can distinguish two criteria of rationality. According to the first criterion, beliefs are justified when they are not stopped by a manifest proof and when one can show their coherence (internal and external). According to a second criterion, beliefs are justified only when they are established by a manifest proof, that is to say, when we have some foundational motives for holding such belief.[76] It is the second criterion, and not the first, that Lindbeck rejects.

One ought to accept without difficulty the resolutely theological purpose of Aquinas set forth by Lindbeck. The demonstration of the existence of God or of the preambles of faith does not constitute an enterprise independent of the *intellectus fidei* of believers, but rather it is inscribed in its core. This purpose is particularly clear in the *Summa theologiae*, in which the subject is the revealed God.[77] It is equally manifest, as Lindbeck explains elsewhere, that one cannot think in the categories of Aquinas without being familiar with Scripture, because Scripture furnishes Aquinas with his fundamental conceptual framework.[78] But the reduction of the

---

74 See George A. Lindbeck, "Atonement and the Hermeneutics of Intratextual Social Embodiment," in *The Nature of Confession: Evangelicals and Postliberals in Conversation*, ed. Timothy R. Philips and Dennis L. Ockholm (Downers Grove, IL: InterVarsity Press, 1996), 221–40 (and endnotes 294–96), at 227.

75 See on this subject Thomas F. O'Meara, OP, *Thomas Aquinas Theologian* (Notre Dame, IN: University of Notre Dame Press, 1997); *The Theology of Thomas Aquinas*, ed. Rik Van Nieuwenhove and Joseph Wawrykow (Notre Dame, IN: University of Notre Dame Press, 2005).

76 See on this subject the reflections of Roger Pouivet, "Religious Imagination and Virtue Epistemology," *Ars Disputandi* 2 (2002) (www.ArsDisputandi.org).

77 St. Thomas, *ST* I, q. 1, a. 1.

78 G. Lindbeck, "Scripture, Consensus and Community," 212–13.

arguments showing the existence of God to mere "probable arguments" is truly problematic. It can be well understood in the context that we have depicted, but it makes difficulty for the exegesis of the texts of St. Thomas himself. Lindbeck invokes in this regard *Summa theologiae* I, q. 1, a. 8, ad 2. But Aquinas does not here speak of his own arguments in favor of the existence of God, but of "authorities," that is to say, certain *texts of philosophical authors* of which "sacred doctrine" makes use "in those questions in which they were able to know the truth by natural reason."[79] These philosophical authorities (for example, a text of Plato or Aristotle) constitute "external" and "probable" arguments. The qualification of "probable arguments" does not apply in a general way to the reasons that St. Thomas himself brings forth in his theology (and of which certain are expressly declared necessary and demonstrative, and not only probable), but to *texts* of recognized authors, that is to say, to the documentary sources, outside the Bible, of theological reflection.[80] Furthermore, Lindbeck omits the distinction that St. Thomas posits between, on the one hand, what belongs purely to faith, and, on the other hand, the preambles of faith accessible to a rigorous demonstration. Among numerous texts of St. Thomas, we recall this one:

> We can use philosophy in sacred doctrine in three ways. First, in order to demonstrate the preambles of faith, which we must necessarily know in [the act of] faith. Such are the truths about God that are proved by natural reason, for example, that God exists, that he is one, and other truths of this sort about God or creatures proved in philosophy and presupposed by faith. Second, by throwing light on the contents of faith by analogies, as Augustine uses many analogies drawn from philosophical doctrines in order to manifest the Trinity. Third, in order to refute assertions contrary to the faith, either by showing them to be false or lacking in necessity.[81]

---

79 On this technical sense of the vocabulary of authority *(auctoritas)*, see Marie-Dominique Chenu, OP, *Toward Understanding St. Thomas,* trans. with authorized corrections by A.-M. Landry, OP and D. Hughes, OP (Chicago: Henry Regnery, 1964), 126–39.

80 For Aquinas, "sacred doctrine" makes use of the authorities of philosophers as "*extrinsic* and *probable* arguments," whereas the authority of the doctors of the Church is qualified as "*proper,* yet merely *probable.*" Only the authority of the canonical Scriptures provides the theologian with "*proper* and *necessary*" arguments (*ST* I, q. 1, a. 8, ad 2).

81 St. Thomas, *Faith, Reason and Theology: Questions I–IV of his Commentary on the* De Trinitate *of Boethius,* trans. Armand Maurer (Toronto: Pontifical Institute of Medieval Studies, 1987): q. 2, a. 3 (p. 49). See above, in "The Purpose of Trinitarian Theology," the section on "Truth and Error."

Thomas Aquinas thus presents a differentiated conception of the use of philosophy in theology. In certain cases (existence, unity, goodness of God), one can achieve strict demonstrations. The consistent vocabulary of St. Thomas (*demonstrare, probare, necesse est,* and so on) does not leave room for doubt. In other cases, one can only manifest the probability or the plausibility of the faith to human reason, by means of non-necessary arguments (arguments that are not necessary from a philosophical standpoint), in order to contemplate what one believes or in order to remove arguments raised against the faith (here again, in a diversified manner). By placing all knowledge of God in the second type of reflection, Lindbeck highlights a part of the thought of St. Thomas so as to apply it to *the whole of his project.* This looks like a reinterpretation.

One can formulate a similar observation with respect to the knowledge of God that a philosophical reflection can attain. According to Lindbeck, many Christians who used the word "God" in reference to biblical narratives have maintained that philosophers and others who do not advert to these narratives "mean something else" by this word "God." In support of this thesis, Lindbeck invokes not only the "God of Abraham, Isaac, and Jacob" of Blaise Pascal, but also Thomas Aquinas (*Summa theologiae* II–II, q. 2, a. 2, ad 3).[82] Lindbeck explains that, according to Aquinas, "Unbelievers" (that is, in the context of Aquinas's cited text, non-Christians holding that God exists)[83] "do not believe that God exists under the conditions which faith defines. Hence they do not really believe that there is a God."[84] For non-Christians, therefore, the word "God" does not mean the same thing as it does for Christians. The God of Christian faith and the God of non-Christians are thus different ("something else"), to such a degree that Bruce Marshall, in an interpretation that Lindbeck has himself accredited, affirms that when the coherence of the specifically Christian faith is lacking, there is a total lack of correspondence between the human mind and God, that is to say a *total lack of knowledge* of the Christian God.[85]

With Louis Roy, one can think that a Thomist would maintain rather that non-Christians "can very well mean the same thing" when they talk about God, "in so far as they restrict themselves to stating that there is an unknown first cause of the universe."[86] Under this aspect, as far as it is a

82 G. Lindbeck, *The Nature of Doctrine,* 48 and 70, note 3, that refers to the interpretation (in our view, debatable) of Victor Preller.

83 See St. Thomas, *ST* II–II, q. 2, a. 2, arg. 3.

84 G. Lindbeck, *The Nature of Doctrine,* 70, note 3.

85 B. Marshall, "Aquinas as Postliberal Theologian," esp. 380–87. For the agreement of Lindbeck with this interpretation, see G. Lindbeck, "Response to Bruce Marshall," 403–6.

86 Louis Roy, OP, "Bruce Marshall's Reading of Aquinas," *The Thomist* 56 (1992): 473–80, at 476.

matter of truth, St. Thomas recognizes without difficulty that philosophers, as philosophers, attain a *truth* concerning God.[87] Commenting on Romans 1:19, St. Thomas states that the "wise among the Gentiles" possessed the "truth of God" insofar as they had, in some respect, "true knowledge of God" by the natural light of reason.[88] The nuances of this teaching are perhaps insufficiently taken into account—if not by Lindbeck, whose thought remains remarkably open, then at least by Marshall.[89] St. Thomas shows that the knowledge of non-believers is not dependent on the assent of faith to the truth of God who reveals himself; consequently, the content of the Christian faith in God does not consist in the same aspects. The material object and the formal object of faith are connected. That does not necessarily mean that non-Christians envision another thing, or that they mean another God, but rather that they do not *believe* in God under the aspect by which Christian faith recognizes him.

In St. Thomas, the most clear example is perhaps that of creation. Aquinas explains that philosophers (we understand: non-Christian philosophers) have been able validly to demonstrate that creation implies the production of being by God, without any precondition in the things that are created. They have also been able to apprehend that the notion of creation involves the affirmation of an existence drawn from non-being and that, for this reason, creatures preserve a certain relationship to non-being. These two aspects constitute the idea of creation *ex nihilo*: Under these two aspects, for St. Thomas, "creation can be demonstrated and it is thus that philosophers have affirmed the creation." But the integral notion of creation possesses a third aspect: God has not created the world from all eternity, and the duration of the world has therefore a beginning. This third aspect is posited by faith (and faith alone).[90] This is why, continues

---

87 See especially *ST* II–II, q. 167, a. 1, ad 3: "The study of philosophy as such is lawful and laudable because of the truth that philosophers perceived *(propter veritatem quam philosophi perceperunt).*" Aquinas refers here to Rom 1:19. Cf. also *ST* I, q. 1, a. 8, ad 2: "Sacred doctrine uses the authority of philosophers where they have been able to perceive the truth by natural reasoning *(ubi per rationem naturalem veritatem cognoscere potuerunt)*."

88 *In Rom* 1:19 (#113–14): "Consentit quod sapientes gentilium *de Deo cognoverunt veritatem*. [. . .] Recte dico quod *veritatem Dei detinuerunt*, fuit enim in eis, quantum ad aliquid, *vera Dei cognitio*" (emphasis mine). Ibid. (#115) : "Huiusmodi autem cognitionem habuerunt per lumen rationis inditum." Cf. ibid. 1:28 (#153): "Lumine rationis per creaturas visibiles *veram Dei cognitionem habere potuerunt*" (emphasis mine).

89 The exegesis of Lindbeck by Marshall seems to me to lead to a sort of double truth and a dualism between nature and grace. See Bruce Marshall, *Trinity and Truth* (Cambridge: Cambridge University Press, 2000); cf. my review in *Revue Thomiste* 101 (2001): 620–23. I mean this with great esteem for Marshall's work.

90 St. Thomas, II *Sent.*, dist. 1, q. 1, a. 2.

St. Thomas, the philosophers have not known God the creator "as faith affirms him," but "they have apprehended creation according to another mode."[91] These philosophers do not thereby mean simply "something else." They have well understood, by a rigorous demonstration, two constitutive aspects of creation: They have attained a truth that faith recognizes. But they have not known creation in its integral content, in all its truth, because they have not received the knowledge in the light of faith. They have a partial knowledge (material aspect), by reason of the very mode of their knowledge (they have not "believed" in God the creator).

The interpretation proposed by Marshall is oriented in another direction. Still it is necessary, undoubtedly, to avoid projecting too completely Marshall's explication on the more brief and more nuanced purpose of Lindbeck, despite the accord expressed by the latter.[92] Furthermore, Lindbeck's thought presupposes a distinction between the philosophers of the past (those to whom Aquinas refers) and the foundational use of philosophy in theology today, in the sense in which Lindbeck understands the enterprise of foundationalism. The difference between Aquinas and Lindbeck resides perhaps in the characteristic accent that the latter places on *meaning*. But in any case, as much for Aquinas as for Lindbeck, biblical faith in God does not depend on foundational considerations *foreign* to the very movement of faith. Lindbeck's project appears, once again, as a reinterpretation of Aquinas in a contemporary problematic (the question of foundational theism and analysis of language).

4. The "Agnosticism" of Thomas Aquinas and Truth

Lindbeck refers equally to St. Thomas in order to set forth the very nature of religious doctrines. He employs in this regard the distinction that St. Thomas, following St. Albert the Great, establishes between the "mode of signifying" and the "signified." The use of this distinction appears already in the studies prior to *The Nature of Doctrine*. It plays a central role for

---

91 St. Thomas, III *Sent.*, dist. 25, q. 1, a. 2, ad 2: "Deum esse creatorem non cognoverunt philosophi sicut fides ponit, ut scilicet postquam non fuerunt, in esse producta sunt, sed secundum alium modum accipiunt creationem." Thomas speaks, in the same place, of the knowledge of God as defined by faith: "sicut fides supponit. . . sic determinat." The vocabulary is close to that of *ST* II–II, q. 2, a. 2, ad 3 (this latter text is the one invoked by Lindbeck).

92 Marshall reviewed the French version of the present essay, and dismissed my criticisms: see Bruce Marshall, "Lindbeck Abroad," *Pro Ecclesia* 15 (2006) 223–41, cf. 235–38. Although I remain unpersuaded by some aspects of Marshall's reading of Aquinas, I can agree with his conclusion: "But there is perhaps no more fruitful way of seeking out the coherence of our knowledge with God's transcendence than in dialogue with St. Thomas and his many interpreters" (ibid., 238).

understanding the regulative, rather than positively cognitive, function that Lindbeck assigns to doctrines. More precisely, it appears in the discussion of truth and of the conformity of the mind with God. Lindbeck, in this context, does not reject the cognitive aspect of religion, but he places it at a secondary level, even in the case of religions for which the claim to truth is of the greatest importance: "The cognitive aspect, while often important, is not primary." The cultural-linguistic model insists on the "code" rather than on what is "encoded" under the form of propositions.[93] Nevertheless, the cultural-linguistic model wishes to account for the claim of religions to truth. It tries therefore to integrate, at a secondary level, the epistemological truth of the conformity of intellect with reality,[94] while attributing to doctrines a principally regulative function. And it is here that Aquinas comes in. Lindbeck explains that a performative conformity of the person to God can be epistemologically realist (it can imply a correspondence of the mind to the divine reality). Certainly, the cultural-linguistic theory does not necessarily imply propositional truth, but neither does it exclude "the modest cognitivism or propositionalism represented by at least some classical theorists, of whom Aquinas is a good example."[95] Here is the heart of what Lindbeck draws from his reading of Aquinas:

> Aquinas holds that although in statements about God the human mode of signifying *(modus significandi)* does not correspond to anything in the divine being, the signified *(significatum)* does. Thus, for example, when we say that God is good, we do not affirm that any of our concepts of goodness *(modi significandi)* apply to him, but rather that there is a concept of goodness unavailable to us, viz., God's understanding of his own goodness, which does apply. What we assert, in other words, is that " 'God is good' is meaningful and true," but without knowing the meaning of "God is good."[96]

Before discussing Lindbeck's interpretation, let us first see how Aquinas presents it. In the context of divine names, where the doctrine of analogy occupies a central place, Aquinas explains that the words that we use to name God (including the words of the Bible) comprise two aspects. They possess, first, a "mode of signifying," that is, a manner of signifying a perfection. The mode of signifying of our language corresponds to the "mode of understand-

---

[93] G. Lindbeck, *The Nature of Doctrine,* 35.

[94] Lindbeck speaks of "truth" in three different ways: categorial (meaning), intrasystematic (warrant), and ontological ("truth" in the classic sense). We are dealing here with the third type of truth.

[95] G. Lindbeck, *The Nature of Doctrine,* 66.

[96] Ibid.

ing" of our mind, this latter itself corresponding to the "mode of existence" of the realities that compose the material world of our experience (one signifies the realities as one knows them, and one knows them according to the mode of being that they possess in the objects proportionate to our understanding). When I say "wise," for example, I conceive and signify wisdom like a quality, the habit that a subject *has*, and that is not identical to the subject itself, which is acquired or received and can be lost (and so on). *Under this aspect* of the "mode of signifying," our words are not at all fitting for God. God is wise and good in an entirely different way from the wisdom and goodness of creatures, for he is identical with his own wisdom and goodness, is good through himself; his goodness is simply his substance. It is the same when I say "love," "power," and so on. Under this first aspect, our words remain attached to the mode of existence that the perfections possess in our world; they are not therefore attributed properly to God, because their mode of signification corresponds to creatures. But the words by which we name God comprise equally a second aspect, namely the "perfection signified": God is truly wise, good, and so on. *Under this second aspect,* our names properly apply to God; as regards what is signified by these names, they belong properly to God, and even more properly to God than to creatures (the doctrine of participation and of analogy). Put otherwise, the "perfections" signified belong primarily to God and then, by participation, to creatures.[97]

Lindbeck's interpretation connects these two aspects by insisting upon the negative aspect (and upon the meaning of our statements): None of our concepts apply to God, so that there is an absolute non-adequation of our concepts and of our statements as such. In a certain way, it seems that, in Lindbeck, the inadequation of the "mode of signifying" has blocked all the meaning of our concepts and of our language, so that the affirmation "God is good" is characterized by what Lindbeck calls an "informational vacuity."[98] This understanding of analogy tends toward equivocity: We are in reality nearer to equivocal statements than to a properly analogical language.[99] On the propositional level, statements about God constitute,

---

97 St. Thomas, *ST* I, q. 13, a. 3, a. 5, and a. 6. These explanations are reprised in numerous places in the work of Aquinas. For an exposition, see John F. Wippel, *The Metaphysical Thought of Thomas Aquinas: From Finite Being to Uncreated Being* (Washington, DC: Catholic University of America Press, 2000), 543–72.

98 G. Lindbeck, *The Nature of Doctrine,* 67. In my opinion, if the affirmation "God is good" is "informationally vacuous," and if we do not know the meaning of "God is good," it will be hard to understand how, for example, the appropriation of divine goodness to the Holy Spirit can make the person of the Holy Spirit more manifest to our minds.

99 Cf. G. Lindbeck, "Infallibility" (1972), in *The Church in a Postliberal Age*, 120–42 (and endnotes 269–73), at 126. Lindbeck finds in Aquinas the affirmation of the "logically equivocal" character of religiously significant terms (see 269, note 12).

moreover, a kind of tautology. In addition, Lindbeck extends this theory to other statements of faith, the resurrection of Christ for example, or creation, and the final consummation.[100]

This interpretation appears already clearly in the small early study presenting the Thomist treatise on God. Lindbeck there describes the difference between the mode of signifying and the signified, by explaining it thus:

> In other words, we do not know the meaning that these names have when they are applied to God (for their meaning is radically different than when used of creatures), *but only that they are rightly said of him.*[101]

Consequently, according to Lindbeck, the treatise on God in Aquinas "is not designed to supply us with information about God, but to perform some other function."[102] What is this function? It consists of referring our creedal "descriptions of God" as agent in history, revealer, and savior, to something distinguishable from ourselves and from our world.

> If one interprets St. Thomas's discussion of the "metaphysical" attributes of God as "agnostically" as we have done, then it is really this referential problem to which they are addressed. They do not describe God, they do not tell us who he is, but rather indicate the context within which scriptural and creedal descriptions of who God is (e.g., the Trinity, the Father of Jesus Christ, and so on) can be given a specifiable referent.[103]

The referent appears on the level of intratextuality. The tautology evoked by *The Nature of Doctrine* is thus explained: "The essence of Aquinas' proposal is that the 'x' which the Christian believes has revealed himself as the self-explanatory explanation of absolutely everything."[104] It follows,

> If there is a self-explanatory explanation of absolutely everything, then, given the meanings which words have in Aquinas' modified Aristotelianism, it is logically necessary to say exactly the things he does about it. But the whole enterprise is entirely formal, purely vacuous and non-informative. The God which results is compatible with any state of affairs whatsoever. We do not know what this self-

[100] G. Lindbeck, *The Nature of Doctrine,* 67. Lindbeck takes care to specify that his extension of the distinction between *significatum* and *modus significandi* to the resurrection "goes beyond anything Aquinas says."

[101] G. Lindbeck, "The Classical Statement of Christian Theism," 49 (emphasis mine).

[102] Ibid.

[103] Ibid., 50.

[104] Ibid.

> explanatory explanation is. We have no insight into its being, and consequently no insight into how it explains the world.[105]

In brief, there is such an explanation, but we know nothing of its character. In consequence, according to this reading of Aquinas, theological study of religious language shows how we ought to speak of God, in order to illumine the prayer, the feelings, the action of believers. "Those who learn to speak of God rightly may not know what they are saying in any cognitively significant sense, but yet their very beings may be transformed into conformity with him who alone is the high and mighty One."[106] In this sense again, Lindbeck finds in Aquinas the conception of an exclusively "non-objective" metaphysical knowledge of nonsensible realities.[107] The conclusion is clear.

> When propositionalism becomes as modest as in this "agnostic" reading of Thomas Aquinas, it is no longer incompatible with the kind of "performative-propositional" theological theory of religious truth that fits a cultural-linguistic approach.[108]

Aquinas thus enables Lindbeck to render account of the place of truth in the cultural-linguistic theory. It is also on this basis that doctrinal statements can be understood as "rules of language" and that the propositional content can be placed on a secondary level, although Lindbeck recognizes its importance. This is likewise the reason why, by means of his Thomist reading, Lindbeck can interpret the changing of human expressions about God or about the divine act that are socially or culturally determined: The *"significatum"* can remain the same, although the *"mode of signifying"* changes.[109] And this is, lastly, the reason why Lindbeck can invoke St. Thomas in order to emphasize "intrasystematic" truth (coherence) and practical correspondence with God. For Lindbeck, Aquinas is an "apparent propositionalist" who, in his practice, is revealed to be much more "intratextual" than his theory would seem to allow.[110] Consequently, Aquinas is not only associated with the cultural-linguistic theory, but indeed he constitutes one of its main theological sources: the question of truth, the insistence on the regulative function of doctrines rather than their propositional content (recognized nevertheless in a "reduced" sense), intratextuality—all this can be supported by Thomas Aquinas.

---

105 Ibid.

106 Ibid., 51.

107 G. Lindbeck, "The *A Priori* in St. Thomas' Theory of Knowledge," 60.

108 G. Lindbeck, *The Nature of Doctrine,* 67.

109 Ibid., 82.

110 Ibid., 123.

This interpretation of Aquinas poses important problems. Rather than an interpretation, it is a reinterpretation starting from epistemological presuppositions (partly) different from those of Thomas Aquinas. Only with difficulty might this reading be reconciled with a historical study of St. Thomas.[111] This is not the place to develop another Thomist reading, but one can emphasize, with more probability, that for Aquinas our language about God in fact involves a positive cognitive content ("propositional," if one wishes, so long as one attaches the "proposition" to our intellect as well as to the reality that our understanding attains), although our language cannot join in God's mode of being and of understanding (God remains "uncircumscribable"). Lindbeck's interpretation is, as regards the exegesis of St. Thomas, subject to discussion. It seems to me difficult to find in St. Thomas the conception of doctrine, considered as ecclesial teaching (for example, the Nicene doctrine of the Trinity), as *solely* rules,[112] or as second-order propositions that "affirm nothing about extra-linguistic or extra-human reality."[113] The regulative function of doctrines, as regards both language and practice, is undeniable. It is the primacy or the exclusivity of the regulative or "corrective" function[114] that must be questioned and contested. Thomists will emphasize that, for Aquinas, a doctrine of faith and a theological teaching have a regulative function *because* they have a cognitive propositional content, and that it is this content, the object of knowledge, that confers on the doctrines their regulative function. In any case, the majority of Thomists, and certainly those who read Aquinas in another philosophical and theological context than Lindbeck, will experience the greatest difficulty adhering to his interpretation.

5. Conclusion

The appeals to Aquinas, in *The Nature of Doctrine*, are far from being marginal. It is the very project of a cultural-linguistic approach that Lindbeck elaborates by reference to Aquinas, as well as many elements occupying a central place: intratextuality, religious experience, the rejection of founda-

---

111 See C. E. O'Neill, "The Rule Theory of Doctrine and Propositional Truth," 433–34.

112 G. Lindbeck, *The Nature of Doctrine,* 18–19. Thomists would accept without difficulty "that at least part of the task of doctrines is to recommend and exclude certain ranges of—among other things—propositional utterances or symbolizing activities." But the cultural-linguistic proposition goes much farther: "What is innovative about the present proposal is that this becomes *the only job* that doctrines do in their role as church teachings" (our emphasis).

113 Ibid., 80.

114 G. Lindbeck, "Atonement and the Hermeneutics of Intratextual Social Embodiment," 224: The primary task of academic theology is "corrective rather than constructive."

tionalism, the theory of knowledge, the truth of our knowledge of God in particular. In the majority of these domains, however, Lindbeck proposes an reinterpretation of St. Thomas (following a rule that he himself formulated: It is necessary to reinterpret Aquinas in order to rediscover him), and sometimes a reinterpretation that is separated from the more evident interpretations of Aquinas.

Our purpose does not consist in calling into question Lindbeck's reading of Aquinas, nor in challenging it by opposing to it another reading. The time for this critique (which touches also other domains of Lindbeck's reflection) is, it seems, today passed. We have instead sought to show the originality of Lindbeck's interpretation, its characteristics and its perspective, by indicating its divergences in relationship to the reading of Aquinas habitually practiced by Thomist studies and by historical studies. This leads to a twofold conclusion. On the one hand, one should affirm that the reading of Aquinas is consistently present in the background of *The Nature of Doctrine*, in such a way that it is a profound source of inspiration for the cultural-linguistic model. On the other hand, the reading of Aquinas proposed by Lindbeck is only truly understood starting from a pre-understanding whose concrete form is partly different from Aquinas's epistemology.

One of the fundamental questions resides perhaps in the "formal" character of the cultural-linguistic alternative proposed by Lindbeck.[115] From one angle, Lindbeck avoids such a formalism, because he wishes to furnish a framework of analysis and of dialogue without determining religious experience by a prior structure of interpretation. From another angle, the result appears less clear. One sees this in particular when Lindbeck examines in chapter 5 of *The Nature of Doctrine* Christological and Mariological doctrines and infallibility. A constant theme is that of "different doctrinal formulations" that the cultural-linguistic theory not only permits, but posits or requires for its very validity. Here the model proposed is, methodologically, sufficiently formal or abstract to render account of numerous possibilities, including some mutually contradictory possibilities. This method rests necessarily on a reductive ("agnostic") conception of the cognitive contents of doctrinal propositions.

In this regard, the "premodern" method of Aquinas could constitute a challenge for the cultural-linguistic model. On the question of God, for example, Aquinas introduces his reflections on method and on epistemology in only the course of his treatise, after having specified in a sufficiently precise manner the reality studied, that is to say, *after* a certain determination of the object. It is the object, concretely, that governs the method. One sees this clearly, for example, in the case of the knowledge of divine

115 See the remarks of C. E. O'Neill, "The Rule Theory of Doctrine and Propositional Truth," 421–22.

attributes or in the case of our knowledge of the Trinity: In the *Summa theologiae*, it is in the context of these treatises that the methodological and epistemological considerations appear, concretely determined by the nature and the properties of the reality studied. One could perhaps find there a suggestion for continuing the reflection inaugurated by George Lindbeck in his dialogue with Thomas Aquinas.

Bibliography of Primary Sources

This bibliography includes only ancient and medieval sources in the original editions and in the translations employed in this book. The works of ancient and medieval authors that are edited in the Patrologia Latina (PL) or in the Patrologia Graeca (PG) are not included in this list.

Albert the Great. *Commentarium in I Sententiarum.* In *Opera Omnia.* Vols. 25–26. Edited by Auguste Borgnet. Paris: Louis Vivès, 1893.

———. *Commentarium in IV Sententiarum.* In *Opera Omnia.* Vols. 29–30. Edited by Auguste Borgnet. Paris: Louis Vivès, 1894–95.

———. *De homine.* Edited by Henryk Anzulewicz and Joachim R. Söder. Hamburg: Meiner, 2004.

———. *Summa de creaturis. Secunda Pars: De homine.* In *Opera Omnia.* Vol. 35. Edited by Auguste Borgnet. Paris: Louis Vivès, 1896.

———. *Summa theologiae sive De mirabili scientia Dei Libri I Pars I.* In *Opera Omnia.* Vol. 34/1. Edited by Wilhelm Kübel. Münster: Aschendorff, 1978.

Alexander of Hales. *Summa theologica seu Summa fratris Alexandri.* Vol. 1. Quarrachi: Editiones Collegii S. Bonaventurae, 1924. Vol. 2. Quaracchi: Editiones Collegii S. Bonaventurae, 1928.

Ambrose of Milan. *De sacramentis.* Edited by Bernard Botte. *Sources Chrétiennes.* Vol. 25 bis. Paris: Cerf, 1994.

Aristotle. *Categoriae et Liber de interpretatione.* Edited by L. Minio-Paluello. Oxford: Oxford University Press, 1966.

———. *Topica et Sophistici elenchi.* Edited by W. D. Ross. Oxford: Oxford University Press, 1970.

Athanasius. *On the Incarnation.* Translated by a Religious of CSMV. Crestwood, NY: St. Vladimir's Orthodox Theological Seminary, 1993.

———. *Werke.* Vol. 3/1: *Urkunden zur Geschichte des arianischen Streites 318–328.* Edited by Hans-Georg Opitz. Berlin/Leipzig: De Gruyter, 1935.

Augustine. *Confessionum libri XIII.* Edited by Lucas Verheijen. Corpus Christianorum, Series Latina. Vol. 27. Turnhout: Brepols, 1983.

———. *Contra sermonem Arrianorum praecedit Sermo Arrianorum.* Edited by Max Josef Suda. Corpus Scriptorum Ecclesiasticorum Latinorum. Vol. 92. Vienna: Verlag der Österreichischen Akademie der Wissenschaften, 2000.

———. *De doctrina christiana. De vera religione.* Edited by Joseph Martin. Corpus Christianorum, Series Latina. Vol. 32. Turnhout: Brepols, 1962.

———. *De Genesi ad litteram libri duodecim.* Edited by Joseph Zycha. Corpus Scriptorum Ecclesiasticorum Latinorum. Vol. 28/1. Prague/Vienna: Bibliotheca Academiae Litterarum Caesareae Vindobonensis, 1894.

———. *De moribus Ecclesiae Catholicae.* In *Œuvres de saint Augustin.* Vol. 1. Edited by Bernard Roland-Gosselin. Paris: Desclée de Brouwer, 1936, 29–122.

———. *De quantitate animae.* In *Œuvres de saint Augustin.* Vol. 5. Edited by Pierre de Labriolle. Paris: Desclée de Brouwer, 1939, 225–396.

———. *De Trinitate libri XV.* 2 vols. Edited by W. J. Mountain. Corpus Christianorum, Series Latina. Vols. 50–50A. Turnhout: Brepols, 1968.

———. *In Iohannis Evangelium Tractatus CXXIV.* Edited by Radbodus Willems. Corpus Christianorum, Series Latina. Vol. 36. Turnhout: Brepols, 1954.

———. *Soliloquia.* In *Œuvres de saint Augustin.* Vol. 5. Edited by Pierre de Labriolle. Paris: Desclée de Brouwer, 1939, 24–162.

———. *The Trinity.* Introduction, translation, and notes by Edmund Hill, OP. Edited by John E. Rotelle. New York: New City Press, 1996.

Basil of Caesarea. *Against Eunomius.* 2 vols. In Basile de Césarée: Contre Eunome, edited by Bernard Sesboüé. *Sources chrétiennes.* Vols. 299 and 305. Paris: Cerf, 1982–83.

———. *Letters.* In *Saint Basile: Lettres.* Edited by Yves Courtonne. Vol. 3. Paris: Belles Lettres, 1966.

———. *On the Holy Spirit.* In *Basile de Césarée: Sur le Saint-Esprit.* Edited by Benoît Pruche. *Sources Chrétiennes.* Vol. 17 bis. Paris: Cerf, 1968.

Bonaventure. *Opera Omnia.* Vol. 1: *Commentarium in Primum Librum Sententiarum.* Quaracchi: Editiones Collegii S. Bonaventurae, 1882.

———. *Opera Omnia.* Vol. 2: *Commentarium in Secundum Librum Sententiarum.* Quaracchi: Editiones Collegii S. Bonaventurae, 1885.

———. *Opera Omnia.* Vol. 4: *Commentarium in Quartum Librum Sententiarum.* Quaracchi: Editiones Collegii S. Bonaventurae, 1989.

———. *Opera Omnia.* Vol. 5: *Opuscula Varia Theologica.* Quaracchi: Editiones Collegii S. Bonaventurae, 1892.

Cajetan (Thomas de Vio). *Commentaria in Summam theologiae sancti Thomae de Aquino.* In *Sancti Thomae Aquinatis Opera omnia iussu Leonis XIII P.M. edita.* Tomus 4–12. Rome: Ex typographia polyglotta S.C. de Propaganda Fide, 1888–1906.

Cyprianus. *Epistularium.* Vol. III/2. Edited by G. F. Diercks. Corpus Christianorum, Series Latina. Vol. 3 C. Turnhout: Brepols, 1996.

Decrees of the Ecumenical Councils. 2 vols. Edited by Norman P. Tanner. Washington, DC: Georgetown University Press, 1990.

Didache. Edited by Willy Rordorf and André Tuilier. *Sources Chrétiennes.* Vol. 248. Paris: Cerf, 1978.

Enchiridion symbolorum definitionum et declarationum de rebus fidei et morum. Edited by Henricus Denzinger and Adolfus Schönmetzer. Editio XXXVI emendata. Freiburg im Breisgau: Herder, 1971.

Gregory of Nazianzus, *Orations 27–31.* In *Grégoire de Nazianze: Discours 27–31,* edited by Paul Gallay. *Sources Chrétiennes.* Vol. 250. Paris: Cerf, 1978.

———. *Oration* 39. In *Grégoire de Nazianze: Discours 38–41.* Edited by Claudio Moreschini. *Sources Chrétiennes.* Vol. 358. Paris: Cerf, 1990.

Hilary of Poitiers. *De Trinitate.* Edited by Pieter Smulders. Corpus Christianorum, Series Latina. Vols. 62 and 62 A. Turnhout: Brepols, 1979–84.

Humbert of Romans. *Opus Tripartitum.* In *Fasciculus Rerum Expetendarum et Fugiendarum Prout ab Orthuino Gratio Presbytero editus est.* Edited by Edward Brown. London: Chiswell, 1690, 185–228.

John Damascene. *De fide orthodoxa: Versions of Burgundio and Cerbanus.* Edited by Eligius M. Buytaert. Louvain: E. Nauwelaerts; Paderborn: Schöningh, 1955.

Nemesius of Emesa. *De natura hominis: Version of Burgundio of Pisa.* Edited by G. Verbeke and J. R. Moncho. Leiden: Brill, 1975.

Origen. *On Principles.* In *Origène, Traité des principes.* Vol. 1. Edited by Henri Crouzel and Manlio Simonetti. *Sources Chrétiennes.* Vol. 252. Paris: Cerf, 1978.

Peter Lombard. *Sententiae in IV Libris distinctae.* Edited by Ignatius Brady. 2 vols. Grottaferrata/Rome: Editiones Collegii S. Bonaventurae ad Claras Aquas, 1971 and 1981.

Praepositinus of Cremona. *Summa "Qui producit ventos."* Liber primus: *De divinis nominibus.* In *L'ortodossia e la grammatica: Analisi di struttura e deduzione storica della Teologia Trinitaria de Prepositino.* Edited by Giuseppe Angelini. Rome: Gregorian University Press, 1972, 191–303.

Thomas Aquinas. *Catena aurea in quatuor Evangelia.* 2 vols. Edited by Angelico Guarienti. Turin/Rome: Marietti, 1953.

———. *Commentary on the Gospel of John.* Part I. Translated by James A. Weisheipl and Fabian R. Larcher. Albany, NY: Magi Books, 1980. Part II. Translated by James A. Weisheipl and Fabian R. Larcher. Petersham, MA: St. Bede's Publications, 1999.

———. *Commentum in librum IV. Sententiarum: Dist. 23–50.* In *Opera omnia.* Vol. 11. Edited by Stanislas E. Fretté. Paris: Louis Vivès, 1882.

———. *Compendium Theologiae.* In *Opera omnia iussu Leonis XIII P.M. edita.* Tomus 42. Edited by Gilles de Grandpré. Rome: Editori di San Tommaso, 1979, 83–205.

———. *Contra doctrinam retrahentium a religione.* In *Opera omnia iussu Leonis XIII P.M. edita.* Tomus 41 C. Rome: Ad Sanctae Sabinae, 1970.

———. *Contra errores Graecorum.* In *Opera omnia iussu Leonis XIII P.M. edita.* Tomus 40 A. Edited by Hyacinthe F. Dondaine. Rome: Ad Sanctae Sabinae, 1967.

———. *Contra Impugnantes Dei cultum et religionem.* In *Opera omnia iussu Leonis XIII P.M. edita.* Tomus 41 A. Edited by Hyacinthe F. Dondaine. Rome: Ad Sanctae Sabinae, 1970.

———. *De articulis fidei et Ecclesiae sacramentis.* In *Opera omnia iussu Leonis XIII P.M. edita.* Tomus 42. Edited by Hyacinthe F. Dondaine. Rome: Editori di San Tommaso, 1979, 245–57.

———. *De forma absolutionis.* In *Opera omnia iussu Leonis XIII P.M. edita.* Tomus 40 C. Edited by Hyacinthe F. Dondaine. Rome: Ad Sanctae Sabinae, 1968.

———. *De rationibus fidei.* In *Opera omnia iussu Leonis XIII P.M. edita.* Tomus 40 B. Edited by Hyacinthe F. Dondaine. Rome: Ad Sanctae Sabinae, 1968.

———. *Expositio super Isaiam ad litteram.* In *Opera omnia iussu Leonis XIII P.M. edita.* Tomus 28. Edited by Hyacinthe F. Dondaine and L. Reid. Rome: Editori di San Tommaso, 1974.

———. *Expositio super primam et secundam Decretalem.* In *Opera omnia iussu Leonis XIII P.M. edita.* Tomus 40 E. Edited by Hyacinthe F. Dondaine. Rome: Ad Sanctae Sabinae, 1968.

———. *Faith, Reason and Theology: Questions I–IV of His Commentary on the* De Trinitate *of Boethius.* Translated by Armand Maurer. Toronto: Pontifical Institute of Medieval Studies, 1987.

———. *In duodecim libros metaphysicorum Aristotelis expositio.* Edited by Raimondo Spiazzi. Turin/Rome: Marietti, 1950.

———. *In librum Beati Dionysii de divinis nominibus expositio.* Edited by Ceslas Pera. Turin/Rome: Marietti, 1950.

———. *In symbolum Apostolorum expositio.* In *Opuscula Theologica.* Vol. 2. Edited by Raimondo Spiazzi. Turin/Rome: Marietti, 1954, 193–217.

———. *Liber de Veritate Catholicae Fidei contra errores Infidelium qui dicitur Summa contra Gentiles.* Edited by Petrus Marc, et al. 3 vols. Turin: Marietti; Paris: Lethielleux, 1961–67.

———. *Officium de festo Corporis Christi.* In *Opera omnia.* Vol. 29. Edited by Stanislas E. Fretté and Paul Maré. Paris: Louis Vivès, 1889, 335–43.

———. *Officium de festo Corporis Christi.* In *Opuscula Theologica.* Vol. 2. Edited by Raimondo Spiazzi. Turin/Rome: Marietti, 1954, 275–81.

———. *Officium de festo Corporis Christi.* In Ronald J. Zawilla, *The Historiae Corporis Christi attributed to Thomas Aquinas: A Theological Study of Their Biblical Sources.* Diss., University of Toronto, 1985.

———. *On the Power of God.* Literally translated by the English Dominican Fathers. 3 vols. London: Burns Oates and Washbourne, 1934.

———. *Opera omnia ut sunt in indice thomistico.* Edited by Roberto Busa. 7 Vols. Stuttgart: Frommann, 1980.

———. *Quaestio disputata de spiritualibus creaturis.* In *Opera omnia iussu Leonis XIII P.M. edita.* Tomus 24/2. Edited by J. Cos. Rome: Commissio Leonina; Paris: Cerf, 2000.

———. *Quaestio disputata de unione Verbi incarnati.* In *Quaestiones disputatae.* Vol. 2. Edited by Pio Bazzi et al. Turin/Rome: Marietti, 1965, 421–35.

———. *Quaestiones disputatae de anima.* In *Opera omnia iussu Leonis XIII P.M. edita.* Tomus 24/1. Edited by Bernardo C. Bazán. Rome: Commissio Leonina; Paris: Cerf, 1996.

———. *Quaestiones disputatae de potentia.* In *Quaestiones disputatae.* Vol. 2. Edited by Pio Bazzi et al. Turin/Rome: Marietti, 1965, 7–276.

———. *Quaestiones disputatae de veritate.* In *Opera omnia iussu Leonis XIII P.M. edita.* Tomus 22 (3 vols.). Edited by Antoine Dondaine. Rome: Editori di San Tommaso, 1975–76.

———. *Quaestiones de Quolibet.* In *Opera omnia iussu Leonis XIII P.M. edita.* Tomus 25. 2 vols. Edited by René-Antoine Gauthier. Rome: Commissio Leonina; Paris: Cerf, 1996.

———. *Reasons for the Faith.* Translated by Joseph Kenny. *Islamochristiana* 22 (1996): 31–52.

———. *Scriptum super Libros Sententiarum.* Vols. 1–2. Edited by Pierre Mandonnet. Paris: Lethielleux, 1929. Vols. 3–4. Edited by Maria F. Moos. Paris: Lethielleux, 1933 and 1947.

———. *Sentencia libri de anima.* In *Opera omnia iussu Leonis XIII P.M. edita.* Tomus 45/1. Edited by René-Antoine Gauthier. Rome: Commissio Leonina; Paris: Vrin, 1984.

———. Sermon *Homo quidam fecit cenam magnam.* Edited by Louis J. Bataillon. *Revue des Sciences Philosophiques et Théologiques* 67 (1983): 353–69.

———. *Summa contra Gentiles.* In *Opera omnia iussu Leonis XIII P.M. edita.* Tomus 13–15. Rome: Typis Riccardi Garroni, 1918–30.

———. *Summa contra Gentiles: On the Truth of the Catholic Faih.* 5 vols. Translated by Anton C. Pegis et al. Notre Dame, IN: University of Notre Dame Press, 1975.

———. *Summa theologiae.* In *Opera omnia iussu Leonis XIII P.M. edita.* Tomus 4–12. Rome: Ex typographia polyglotta S.C. de Propaganda Fide, 1888–1906.

———. *Summa theologiae.* Cura et studio Instituti Studiorum Medievalium Ottaviensis. Editio altera emendata. 5 vols. Ottawa: Harpell, 1941–45.

———. *Summa theologiae.* Latin text and English translation, Introductions, Notes, Appendices, and Glossaries. Edited by Thomas Gilby and T. C. O'Brien. Blackfriars. 60 vols. London: Eyre and Spottiswoode; New York: McGraw-Hill, 1964–73.

———. *Super Boetium de Trinitate.* In *Opera omnia iussu Leonis XIII P.M. edita.* Tomus 50. Edited by Pierre-M. J. Gils. Rome: Commissio Leonina; Paris: Cerf, 1992, 75–171.

———. *Super Epistolas S. Pauli lectura.* Editio VIII. 2 vols. Edited by Raffaele Cai. Turin/Rome: Marietti, 1953.

———. *Super Evangelium S. Ioannis lectura.* Edited by Raffaele Cai. Turin/Rome: Marietti, 1952.

———. *Super Evangelium S. Matthaei lectura.* Edited by Raffaele Cai. Turin/Rome: Marietti, 1951.

———. *Super Librum de causis expositio.* Edited by Henri-Dominique Saffrey. Paris: Vrin, 2002.

———. *Traités: Les raisons de la foi, Les articles de la foi et les sacrements de l'Eglise.* Introduction, traduction du Latin, et annotation par Gilles Emery. Paris: Cerf, 1999.

———. *Truth.* Vol. 1. Translated by Robert W. Mulligan. Chicago: Henry Regnery Company, 1952.

William of Auxerre. *Summa aurea.* Vol. 1: *Liber primus.* Edited by Jean Ribaillier. Paris: Vrin; Grottaferrata: Editiones Collegii S. Bonaventurae, 1980.

William of Sherwood. *Introductiones in Logicam.* Edited by Hartmut Brands and Christoph Kann. Hamburg: Felix Meiner, 1995.

Index of Names

This index lists the names of persons and authors mentioned in this book. However, Thomas Aquinas, referred to throughout this work, and biblical figures are not included here. This book does not have an index of subjects, see the table of contents at the front of this volume.